AN INTRODUCTION TO MARITAL THEORY AND THERAPY

AN INTRODUCTION TO MARITAL THEORY AND THERAPY

Leroy G. Baruth • **Charles H. Huber**
Appalachian State University   *New Mexico State University*

WAVELAND

PRESS, INC.

Prospect Heights, Illinois

For information about this book, write or call:

Waveland Press, Inc.
P.O. Box 400
Prospect Heights, Illinois 60070
(847) 634-0081

PREFACE

There are many current books on that unique interpersonal human relationship known as marriage. A great number of these are written directly to couples for their use as self-help resources. The couple experiencing marital distress may benefit from these books; both clinical reports and psychological research have indicated that bibliotherapeutic resources are often quite effective in facilitating better adjustment. However, most troubled couples do not avail themselves of these resources, or they need additional processing and rehearsal of the written material in constructive therapy with a trained clinician.

Ironically the same books are commonly used to supplement the basic textbooks offered to therapists-in-training. The vast majority of introductory textbooks available to the instructor and students of a course in marital theory and therapy are simply inadequate in themselves. A review of these textbooks shows that most have obvious deficiencies in their applicability to the therapeutic process; hence the need to supplement with practical, technique- and procedure-oriented self-help literature. The deficiencies include an overly sociological bent; too narrow a focus, making the books more useful as supplementary (rather than primary) resources; in compilations, disjointedness of related readings; and finally, in books that are combinations of textbooks and guides to the therapeutic process, a primary focus on family therapy, not specifically marriage and marital therapy.

A major concern for the instructor and students of a course in marital theory and therapy is that of integrating theory and research (forming a knowledge base) with practice and procedure (forming a specific skill repertoire). Field experiences soon follow classroom coursework for the graduate-level therapist-in-training. Yet without both an understanding of theory, research, and practice, and an ability to apply them, these field placements become an anxiety-producing and less-than-hoped-for learning endeavor, wherein they may even do their clients more harm than good. Students are too often heard to remark that their theory and techniques course was all too much theory and too little technique to effectively implement the approaches presented in an actual setting.

We recall our own initial confusion as beginning clinicians in combining research, theory, and cognitive classroom practice. Therapist-client/couple interchanges were not always as they were presented in our former textbooks. The fuzzy predicaments put forth by couples just didn't follow the theoretical ideal. Our actual and most valuable training came through clinical supervision. Supervisors, knowledgeable and skilled by virtue of numerous hours of first-hand contact with couples in therapy, gave us a wealth of techniques, practices, and procedures with which to augment and make practical sense of our theoretical learnings and thereby to facilitate effective interventions with our clients.

Being both practicing clinicians as well as therapist/mental health educators, we have written this book in response to a perceived need by ourselves, our students, and our colleagues for an introductory textbook codifying many of the oral supervisory teachings (which form the basis of the self-help literature), while simultaneously integrating them within a theoretical and research base, in a usefully outlined, concrete, and structured manner.

It is our goal that this book provide you with options relating to theory, technique, and research data so as to best organize your therapeutic observations. We have found that beginning marital therapists must identify and clearly comprehend some general assumptions about marital relationships and working with couples before considering the specific approach the beginning therapists themselves might take in conducting marital therapy efforts. When they have achieved comprehension of these general assumptions we encourage them to look at the major theoretical orientations available, select one, and gain expertise in that approach.

It is our belief that beginning therapists should initially identify with one basic theoretical approach that has been tested in practice and about which material has been published. However, we realize that a therapist concentrating on one approach can develop theoretical tunnel vision and not use the aspects of other approaches that may prove to be more efficient and effective with particular couples. To avoid that tunnel vision, we recommend attaining clear comprehension of the major theoretical approaches, which allows you to select the approach most compatible with your own values and beliefs and still to be knowledgeable enough to integrate the parts of other approaches that at times are more appropriate. We have found that this comprehension is best accomplished when therapists acquire a process understanding of marital therapy—an outline of how marital therapy begins, is carried on, and ends.

Finally, we find that the most effective marital therapists are clinically accountable. That is, they are well aware of their legal and ethical responsibilities as well as their professional duty to upgrade themselves and to advance the profession through conducting and supporting research efforts. Therefore we have organized our presentation into four major sections.

Section One presents fundamental assumptions that have been found necessary for therapists to comprehend in order to conceptualize marital theory and therapy. In this section, Chapter 1 contains an analysis of those aspects that make the marital relationship a unique form of interpersonal functioning. Chapter 2 explores general introductory issues to consider when involved with couples in a therapeutic effort.

Section Two offers an extensive presentation of the major theoretical approaches to marital therapy that to date have provided the most substantial models for the understanding and treatment of married couples experiencing discord in their relationships. Chapter 3 investigates psychoanalytic theory by emphasizing the fundamental concepts of object relations as related to marriage and marital therapy. Chapter 4 provides a social-learning conceptualization of marriage with a corresponding treatment model for conducting behavioral interventions with couples. Chapter 5 reviews two major systems-theory approaches for understanding marriage and conducting marital therapy. Chapter 6 presents a case illustration that is designed to further clarify the various ways that therapists with each of these theoretical orientations might approach the same couple, in order to highlight similarities and differences.

Section Three focuses on the pragmatic procedural aspects of conducting marital therapy. The chapters in this section are particularly process oriented, pulling together clinical practice and research-proven techniques and applying them to marital therapy. We believe that therapists are specialists in their own particular setting who can and will successfully select those therapeutic interventions likely to be most effective with individual partners and couples, and will integrate the interventions with a primary theoretical orientation, if they have the proper framework to do so. Chapter 7 presents an atheoretical five-stage sequential conception of the marital therapy process—the framework for the integration that is the subject of this section. Chapter 8 discusses general therapeutic strategies with suggestions for their implementation and also examines some areas of more contemporary concern. Chapter 9 addresses special problems that may arise during the therapeutic effort. In this chapter we advocate procedures to facilitate solutions to these problems. Chapter 10 takes a look at family theory and therapy, involving significant family members in the therapeutic process, as a means of understanding and treating marital distress and related family concerns.

Section Four considers the critical issue of clinical accountability.

Chapter 11 examines a variety of professional and ethical issues of importance to marital therapists. Chapter 12 reviews important considerations relating to the current state of research in marriage and marital therapy.

The authors would like to thank a number of reviewers for their constructive suggestions during manuscript development. They include: Ben Ard, San Francisco State University; Jeanette Coufal, University of Wisconsin-Stout; Edwin Cox, California Family Study Center; Richard Dracha, Shippensburg State College; Diane Henschel, California State University, Dominguez Hills; Victoria McGillin, Clark University; and James Trotzer, University of Wisconsin.

We are expecially grateful to Dr. Dominic F. DiMattia at the University of Bridgeport and also to the associates at the Institute for Rational-Emotive Therapy for their support and encouragement during the writing of this book (C.H.H.); and to Robert N. Crowe for his tireless research and work on some of the preliminary drafts, and to Martha Lucky and Lela Anastasion for their willingness to work on details such as double checking bibliographic citations (L.G.B.). We are particularly indebted to Claire Verduin for her belief in us, Candy Cameron for making sure the deadlines were met, Carey Charlesworth for editing our manuscript, and Katherine Minerva and Debbie Wunsch for their design work.

Leroy G. Baruth
Charles H. Huber

CONTENTS

An Introduction to Marital Theory and Therapy

Marital Theory and Therapy: Basic Assumptions

Current trends in the study of family relations are focused primarily on the family aspects of the relations to the relative exclusion of the marital aspect. Yet, to point out the obvious, there are three sets of relationships within the nuclear family: marital, intergenerational, and sibling. The most basic of these three is the relationship between husband and wife. It is from the marital relationship that the family evolves. Given the fundamental importance of the marital relationship, certain questions naturally arise. How can we best understand and conceptualize marital relationships? And, how can we work with them intelligently and effectively when therapeutic efforts are called for?

In this section, we propose to answer these questions. Chapter 1 depicts the marital relationship as a unique form of interpersonal functioning. In this chapter, we introduce the factors that engender this uniqueness, as well as other properties essential to understanding and conceptualizing marriage.

Chapter 2 explores the major issues therapists encounter in their work with couples. After briefly tracing the development of current marital theory and therapy, we look at specific couple, therapist, and couple-therapist relationship factors to consider when initiating therapeutic work.

CHAPTER ONE

The Marital Relationship

The interactions between a married couple are in many ways like those between any two people. Almost all interpersonal encounters involve attempts to communicate ideas and information, thoughts and feelings, needs and desires; to replay some past situation or forecast a future one. Yet the marital relationship is a particular kind of relationship. While marriage does bear many of the properties of other forms of relating, it also has particular aspects of its own.

We begin this chapter by stressing the uniqueness of the marital relationship. This uniqueness is viewed as emanating from the expectations of society, of one's family of origin, and of the individuals themselves regarding the roles partners should play in their marital relationship. We then look at the potential effects that individual and marital developmental life cycles and their related adjustment tasks may have upon a couple. This is followed by discussion of the systems-functioning properties of the marital relationship. The chapter concludes with a clinical conceptualization of the marital relationship as a process of interaction involving these role expectations, developmental challenges, and systems functions.

Role Expectations

We have often observed that a male and female can live together in an intense relationship which appears to have all of the properties of a marriage but is not the same, socially or psychologically, as being married. Couples who have lived together without major problems frequently encounter difficulties when they do marry. For example, Nichols (1978) reported cases in which couples lived together rather satisfactorily for varying periods of time. Upon marrying, they began to encounter difficulties that either were not present before they married, or, if they were present, were not a significant source of conflict or concern. He particularly noted that a number of couples described their sexual relationships before marriage as "good" or "very good," with problems arising immediately or soon after they wed.

What creates change in an intimate relationship once it becomes a "marital" relationship? One factor commonly accepted as contributing to marital conflict concerns the expectations spouses each have of their own role performance and the role performance of their partners. It is important that partners meet one another's expectations if they are to have a satisfying relationship. If expectations cannot be met, adjustments must be made. Without these adjustments, confusion, concern, and conflict are bound to occur.

A review of the literature reveals three commonly agreed upon sources of marital role expectations: (1) society's view of the roles of husband and wife, (2) the perception of roles derived from one's family of origin, and (3) prior interactions between partners. We now look at each of these three sources.

Marriage as a Societal Institution

Society's views of "living together" and legitimate marriage are very different, even in today's relatively liberal cultural atmosphere. Marriage is seen as an institution basic to our cultural functioning. Perceiving marriage as a societal institution can have a powerful effect upon spouses' perceptions of and reactions to themselves, their behaviors, and their partners. There is little doubt that our society is oriented toward marriage. Traditionally in our culture, for men especially, marriage frequently has been seen as a necessary framework for conducting a full life. That is, apart from providing domestic comfort and a ready companion for social and sexual activities, being married may enhance individuals' attractiveness to employers, who perceive married people as settled and reliable. For either sex, marriage may also increase the ability to move upward in a career through contacts made by entertaining employers and associates. And, it is a common belief that being married enhances the political profile of candidates for public office.

The marital relationship can function as a springboard to many activities. However, a closer look at these benefits gained through marriage suggests that they result primarily from the value society places on the institution of marriage as opposed to anything in the relationship of the marriage partners. That is, marriage facilitates access to many social, economic, and political advantages only because it is commonly acknowledged that to be married is good (Abernathy, 1976). Society seems to award privileges to married people because their needs are seen as greater, and because people have indirectly been taught that family people are somehow better than single ones (Murstein, 1976).

Expectations about the marital relationship, generally held by society, do provide distinct advantages to married couples. Yet accompanying these advantages are responsibilities, which can exert strong pressures on couples. Consider, for example, the responsibility that has the greatest cultural consensus and that carries the greatest pressure: the marital function of legitimizing offspring and of guaranteeing to society the responsible raising of its members. While relevant only to couples desiring children, the role of parent and the role of marital partner must often conflict. Simple limitations on time and energy force couples to make painful choices. Having an intimate, heart-to-heart conversation with your partner when a diaper needs to be changed or a child is crying can be an impossible situation. Yet partners are expected by society to raise children free of psychological problems, well liked by all, moral and hardworking, and at the same time to function as good providers, housekeepers, and loving partners (Grunebaum & Christ, 1976).

In recent years, societal expectations have become focused even more on nontraditional roles than on the traditional roles of parent, provider, and partner. More and more, couples are expected to excel also as intimate companions, completely satisfying sexual matches, and sources of mutual support in solving personal dilemmas that arise. Ironically, as these role expectations increase and become better defined, the criteria for succeeding, particularly in the roles emphasized recently, are decreasing and becoming less well-defined. Earning a living, raising children, and caring for each other in times of illness are specific, identifiable responsibilities. However, the ability to provide such things as psychological assistance in time of emotional distress, sexual fulfillment, and intimate companionship is not so clear-cut, and it requires behavior that varies complexly. At one time, fulfilling such nontraditional responsibilities may call for assertively pointing out destructive behaviors and suggesting alternative actions, whereas at another time it requires partners to quietly comfort and support each other no matter what the problem behavior. As has been suggested by Grunebaum and Christ (1976), "To be a best friend, a favored bed companion, and a 'therapist' are difficult tasks, especially 'through sickness and health, for richer and poorer, for better and worse'" (p. 4).

Paradoxically, many problems that occur within marriages seem to result from those societal expectations that encourage and support marriage as an institution. Too many and too great expectations, when not put into an adaptive perspective and when the expectations are not realized, often lay the groundwork for couples' future discouragement and distress.

Relationship Models

Less obvious than societal expectations, but equally influential in defining a marital relationship as a unique relationship, are the expectations that partners have internalized from their families of origin. Partners' perceptions of their own parents or surrogate parents interacting vitally influence the kind of marriage the partners themselves will have. All people, at times without even realizing it, have expectations of improving upon the family they came from. They attempt to incorporate what they perceive as having been positive and eliminate what they saw as negative. Much of what happens between partners in a marital relationship, much of what they aspire to, and much of what they believe in, depends upon how they perceive their parents' functioning.

If your parents' relationship was a healthy, adjusted one and you model their positive behaviors in your own marriage expecting a similarly healthy relationship, chances are good that, assuming your partner's expectations are compatible, your expectations will be realized. However, should your partner's expectations not be compatible and adjustments not negotiated, conflict becomes inevitable. Consider the following example:

> *John and Mary faced what for them had become a severe crisis because of differing expectations regarding how to spend their vacation time. John's family had spent its vacations at a mountain lake each summer. Mary's family, on the other hand, traveled all over the country. John's resultant expectations concerning vacations were to relax and do as little as possible, while Mary's were to get out and do new and exciting things. In the first two years of their marriage John and Mary compromised; they went to the mountains their first year and took a cross-country trip the second. Mary complained of acute boredom in the mountains and John argued that being on the go his whole time off from work was no vacation at all.*

It is difficult for partners to disown their upbringing. Their parents' habits, principles, and problems are part of them. Partners are who they are to a great extent because of what they learned from their parents. Fogarty (1976) described the amazing frequency with which words such as "should," "ought to," "fairness," "right," "wrong," "fault," and "blame" appear when conflict in a marital relationship arises. It was his opinion that these shoulds and ought tos have to be traced back to their origins in partners' extended families and be reevaluated if marital harmony is to be achieved.

Marital Rules

The development of a mutually satisfying marital relationship can be viewed as a process of working out shared agreements, or marital rules, between two people. These rules involve individual partners' expectations for the relationship and develop largely undiscussed, evolving from prior interactions and perceived understandings. Consider the amount of time and energy expended by prospective partners before marriage to determine whether they are sufficiently similar in values, attitudes, and interests, and sufficiently complementary in needs and role conceptions, to get married. Yet in actually living together there are numerous additional areas about which partners must agree. For example, who is to do the cooking, food shopping, cleaning of the house, and other similarly necessary tasks? How often and when are in-laws and others to be invited to visit? Do the partners make love in the evening or in the morning? Will one partner take the dominant role in the relationship, or will the responsibilities be divided equally?

Partners in a newly formed marital relationship establish explicit or implicit rules in order to deal with each situation they encounter and the expectation is that these rules will be followed in the future. Haley (1963) described marital rules as being of three sorts: (1) rules that partners would announce, such as an agreement that each partner can have a night out with his or her friends each week, (2) rules that partners would not mention but would agree to if they were pointed out, such as a rule that each partner will speak with the other before making any major decisions, and (3) rules that an observer would identify but partners would likely deny, such as a rule that one partner is always to be on the defensive and the other accusatory, and never the reverse. Haley further noted the importance of understanding that partners cannot avoid establishing rules; whenever they interact, a rule is being established, followed, or adjusted. Even if they set out to behave spontaneously, they are either establishing a new rule or adhering to an expectation that they are to behave in that way.

If all expectations partners hold concerning their future marital interactions could be easily worked out by applying a simple decision-making process, marriage would be a relatively logical, deliberate affair. Clearly, it isn't. Many partners frequently find themselves struggling intensely over minor matters and doing so in a most illogical way. If the cook chooses not to cook, the compliant partner becomes assertive, or if the decision-maker refuses to make decisions, that partner is rejecting the "expected" manner of interaction. Problems can arise quickly when one partner begins to change and the other refuses to renegotiate or adjust his or her rule expectations.

Sager (1976) postulated that in every marital relationship there are *contracts,* the dynamics of which determine partners' behaviors within the relationship, as well as the quality of the relationship. Sager defines the individual marital contract as "a person's expressed and unexpressed, conscious and beyond awareness concepts of his obligations within the marital relationship, and the benefits he expects to derive from marriage in general and from his spouse in particular" (p. 4). We have often found Sager's notion of marital contracts to be an enlightening concept for couples to understand. Using this view of the effects of their individual role expectations most partners can readily see how contractual disappointments are a major source of any marital conflict they experience.

Types of Marriages

Occasionally, the partners in a marital relationship hold different expectations of the form that the relationship should take. As therapists, we have frequently been called upon to assist people in finding or creating a marital lifestyle tailored to their unique personalities and abilities. Partners' ability and willingness to come to some agreement about the qualitative characteristics of their relationship have important implications for that relationship. If partners are to relate successfully to each other, they must generally agree on the form of their relationship.

James (1979) outlined six types of marriage that provide useful insights for couples seeking a better understanding of their relationship. Although each of these six types of marital relationships involves different role expectations, all include similar social, sexual, emotional, and functional needs.

1. *Traditional Marriage.* This type of marital relationship is firmly grounded in the past, its tradition coming from patterns of understanding developed through partners' families of origin or society at large. Traditional marriages are described in terms of, "This is the way our relationship should be, and other alternatives are not as good." In a typical traditional marital relationship, the wife assumes responsibility for household chores, the couple's social life, and for most of the child care. The husband functions as the family provider, makes all major decisions, and administers discipline to the children.

2. *Marriage for Personal Interest.* The reasons for this form of marital relationship include opportunities to have a sexual partner, financial gain, social status, and other advantages. These are trade-off relationships, in which each partner simply fulfills the desired needs of the other. James (1979) suggested that many people consider age-discrepant, so-called May-September marriages, in which one partner is much older than the other, to be relationships of personal interest. The younger partner may be seeking a substitute parent's support while the older partner is looking for the physical and emotional excitement youth can bring.

3. *Nondirected Marriage.* This type of marriage is a product of the "do your own thing" attitudes prevalent in today's culture. This form includes the "open marriage," a concept formalized by O'Neill and O'Neill (1972). The essence of the openness is that each partner is an individual and should be free to function as such. How each partner interacts with people outside the relationship is based on his or her own activities, not on the other partner's activities or the designation of being someone's spouse. Separate social appearances and sexual associations outside the marital relationship are permitted if desired, although they are not a necessary part of a nondirected marriage. Each couple develops its own expectations.

4. *Marriage Influenced by Institutions.* This type of marital relationship can be seen best in the planned marriages frequently encountered in such countries as the Soviet Union, China, and India. In the United States, tax laws, welfare regulations, and social security regulations often influence individuals' decisions whether to marry. Also, some religious organizations strongly influence their members' marital relationships.

5. *Group Marriage.* In this form of marriage, several adults live together and share the marital and parental responsibilities and role functions. Many group marriages are formed for a collateral purpose, such as for religious study, or for the members to support each other professionally. Members are often monogamous with another member of the group and desire to stay that way, so sexual promiscuity need not be an issue. Another objective of this type of marital relationship is to provide a strong and supportive milieu in which to raise children.

6. *Holistic Marriage.* In this form of marital relationship, partners maintain their individuality but interact effectively together. Partners come together and then remain together because they want to be, not because either is afraid not to be. Individuals function as equal partners in holistic marital relationships. For example, whether or not the wife works, she and her husband share marital responsibilities and do so by choice, not by stereotype. The husband may participate in the household chores while the wife may do yard work or various repairs. Child care is shared equally.

A Transitional View of Marriage

Perhaps the most obvious and yet remarkable element of life is change and development. Infants and young children must depend upon their parents in order to exist. Then, arriving at adolescence, these former children strive for a sense of identity, tending to reject the advice and direction of their parents and others they formerly depended upon. They rebel against feeling dependent. The next step for most young people is to move away from home, become self-supporting, and make decisions for themselves, thereby becoming independent. At a later point in life, the offspring and parents frequently develop a new relationship with each other characterized by mutual respect, caring, and love. They become "interdependent by choice" (James, 1979).

Most couples go through life stages, similar to those of an individual, in their marital relationship. Like role expectations, the identifiable developmental stages contribute to the marital relationship's uniqueness—its difference from other forms of relating. Although exceptions to the development that typifies many marriages could be pointed out, the fact remains that people do have to make adjustments when they marry. Many couples then have children and must make the further adjustments from being spouses to being spouses and parents. A number of other, similar transitions become evident as a marital relationship evolves. The sequence of these events forms the developmental life cycle of a marital relationship. These stages and the accommodations they require a couple to make in their relationship may be viewed as transition points in the ongoing evolution of a marital relationship.

Studies of developmental stages and transitional turning points have shown them to involve considerable stress and disequilibrium (Caplan, 1967; Levinson, Darrow, Klein, Levinson, & McKee, 1979; Neugarten, 1977; Sheehy, 1976). Life changes associated with biological development, such as pregnancy, childbirth, or old age; changes involving social transitions, such as becoming parents, moving to a new locale, or changing jobs; and changes connected with loss, such as the death of a loved one, all create situations of concern within a marriage. Marital partners may question thoughts and feelings they have about themselves and about their relationship. During the change and for some time thereafter, partners alone, or together as a couple, face tasks that are unfamiliar and are not simply and readily solved during the couple's usual coping processes. Periods of confusion and frustration are to be expected. Consider the following example:

Ken and Sue found themselves having more and more disagreements soon after their first child was born. These disagreements eventually evolved into a severe crisis. Ken felt totally ignored and neglected while Sue saw herself as being trapped and tied down to doing little else but caring for the baby. Ken and Sue alternately complained to each other and depressed themselves over their seemingly hopeless circumstances. Eventually they sought professional assistance in coping with their difficulties.

In therapy, Ken and Sue were aided in examining their thoughts and feelings about themselves, each other, their child, and their marital relationship. They soon came to see their problems as a reaction to a stage in the marital developmental cycle when critical accommodations are necessary: they were now parents as well as individual spouses.

The stages of marital development compose one of the fundamental frameworks for marriage presented in this chapter. However, as background for discussion of marital relationship development, we first examine the life stages of the individual—of the basic unit of marriage. When the individual development of one partner does not synchronize with that of the other partner, conflicts may arise in the marriage relationship. It might also occur that the developmental issues of one or both partners conflict with the development of their marital relationship. Therefore, understanding individual development can be as important as understanding marital development in order to fully comprehend the dynamics of a marital relationship.

Individual Development

Studies of childhood, of adolescence, and of young, middle-aged, and aging adults have sought to record and outline the process of human development throughout the life span. These professional observations, combined with statistical analyses, provide a remarkably consistent profile of human development from birth until death (Duvall, 1977). Individuals apparently pass through a number of sequential stages of life. Each stage builds upon the previous stages. Within each stage, the individual faces characteristic concerns which can be anticipated and encountered either successfully or unsuccessfully. Recognizing an individual's life stage can help predict the personal crisis he or she may face, both in the present stage and in the transition to the stage that is next.

The theory of individual development that is most comprehensive and most often referred to is that put forth by Erik Erikson. Erikson (1963) proposed eight stages of individual development. Each stage represents a critical transition point in the course of a lifetime. Involved at each transition point are certain learning tasks that must be accomplished and that are crucial to further development. Erikson identified these learning tasks as "crises." His stages can be described as "either-or" propositions. Either individuals successfully accomplish the relevant learning task or their forward movement is distorted. For each of eight stages, Erikson specifies the nature of the learning tasks and the result of either success or failure in accomplishing it.

Stage 1: Infancy, Birth–1 Year.   The crisis to be resolved in this stage is of *trust versus mistrust.* Trust involves the growth of infants' confidence in themselves and their environment. This development of trust seems to depend primarily on the mother-child relationship. Children learn to put up with frustration because of the feeling of purpose and meaning given them by their mothers. Should the crisis of trust not be resolved, children are likely to develop a sense of being deprived or abandoned.

Stage 2: Early Childhood, 1–3 Years.   The basic crisis at this time is one of *autonomy versus shame and doubt.* This is a period of muscular development, when children need reassurance and support. If encouraged, children will develop a sense of autonomy. If shamed for their failures, they experience self-doubt. This stage is decisive in children's development of a ratio of love to hate, compromise to willfulness, and freedom of self-expression to its suppression. Children's success in accomplishing learning tasks at this time determines whether they will be able to adjust to others' demands or, instead, stubbornly insist on having their own way, as well as whether they will be able to offer their own opinions or be afraid to speak. It is during this period of the life span that children begin to learn the value of self-control without the loss of pride and goodwill.

Stage 3: Childhood, 3–6 Years.   Between the ages of 3 and 6 children face their next crisis, *initiative versus guilt.* In this stage, children's imaginations expand greatly because of their increased ability to move around freely and to communicate. It is an age of activity, curiosity, and fantasy and a stage that can engender feelings of guilt and anxiety over what is right and wrong. This is the stage wherein children begin to establish a conscience. Children whose tendencies to feel guilty are nurtured by the adults around them may develop the conviction that they themselves are essentially bad, with a resultant stifling of initiative.

Stage 4: School Age, 6–12 Years.   This is the stage when children learn *industry versus inferiority.* Their imaginations are tamed, and they become ready to apply themselves to skills and tasks. By learning how to use utensils and tools they can develop a sense of industry and a sense of the technology in their world. If these learning tasks are not accomplished successfully, there is the danger that children will feel inadequate and inferior.

Stage 5: Adolescence, 12–18 Years.   The crisis at the age of adolescence involves the growth of a sense of *identity versus role confusion.* Adolescents not only face the physiological changes of puberty but must also engage in a process of personal identification. They become concerned with what they are in the eyes of others compared to what they feel they are. And at this time, youths have to connect their skills and prior learnings with occupational roles. They must develop a sense of their own identity—a summary of all they have experienced—and use this sense in the search for a career. The dangers to be experienced are role confusion, not knowing how to be individuals in their own right, and not knowing what career to focus on.

Stage 6: Young Adulthood, 18–35 Years.   Having successfully established their identity during adolescence, young adults face another crisis—*intimacy versus isolation.* During this stage, people seek fusion of their identity with others' in friendships and in love-based sexual relationships with members of the opposite sex. In doing so, young adults must learn to deal with the sacrifices and compromises that sharing calls for. People who are unable to enter intimate relationships because of fears of losing their own identity may develop a sense of isolation.

Stage 7: Adulthood, 35–50 Years.   Mature people, having established themselves in their social group, face a new crisis. This is the crisis of *generativity versus stagnation.* These are the years when adults produce their life's work. Generativity refers to the contributions that outlive the contributor and to an interest in establishing and guiding the next generation. People must pass on the culture and institutions of their society to their offspring. Erikson believes that this is a basic necessity and that an older generation needs this relationship with a younger one. If it is not obtained, stagnation occurs, and individuals become concerned primarily with their own physical well-being and begin to indulge themselves.

Stage 8: Senescence, 50 Years–Death.   The last crisis is *integrity versus despair.* In old age people are ready to accept the integrity of their lifestyle. Those who have achieved satisfying intimacy with others and who have adapted to the triumphs and disappointments of their generative activities reach the later years of life with an acceptance of their own responsibility for what their lives are and what they have been, and an acceptance of their place in the flow of time. They accept the thought of death. Those who fail to develop this sense of integrity develop a sharp fear of death; there is a sense that life has been wasted, and despair sets in.

Erikson's ideas have been greatly complemented in recent years by a number of researchers who have concentrated specifically on adulthood and aging (Gould, 1972; Kimmel, 1974; Levinson, et al., 1979; Lowenthal, Turner, & Chiriboga, 1975; Neugarten, 1977). The work of these researchers has fostered enhanced recognition of one commonly neglected assumption. That is, although childhood and adolescence are past, an individual does not simply and finally become an adult. Adulthood is a continuing developmental process in itself.

Many adult concerns are longstanding, with a history of antecedents extending back to unaccomplished childhood and adolescent learning tasks. Other concerns are of more recent occurrence, a function of adult developmental learning tasks wherein the "crises" are the difficulties adults experience trying to cope with the tasks to be encountered and mastered. Bocknek (1977) identified several of these potential adult developmental crises:

Fear of an Impending Life Stage.   Forthcoming life changes may be viewed as threatening, frightening, or damaging. Examples include having children, fearing the demands parenting will bring, and entering late adulthood, fearing death.

Reluctance to Leave a Gratifying Stage.   Birthdays, anniversaries, and some holidays tend to put people in touch with the passage of time. Anxiety, depression, or feelings of loss are often precipitated by the awareness that life can no longer continue as it has, that a period that brought satisfaction or security has been outgrown.

Trauma of Unexpected Developmental Demands.   For some, the arrival of an anticipated developmental period brings unexpected and unpleasant side effects. A parent's liberation from the demands of parenting when the children leave home can be darkened by loneliness and the silence of an empty house.

Unresolved Earlier Issues.   It is possible to conceal, even from oneself, psychological challenges inherent in developmental growth. For example, attaining sexual competence can present the appearance but lack the substance of a capacity for intimacy, love, and sharing. One's commitment to a relationship as challenging as marriage may provide one's first real confrontation with critical developmental issues heretofore avoided.

Cumulative Erosion of Energies.   At times, the sheer energy needed to meet a developmental demand may cause increased concern. One more bill to be paid, another pregnancy, additional work responsibilities—any further strain on someone already extended to his or her psychic limit can precipitate serious difficulties.

Positive Growth Experiences.   Beside the extremely satisfying life experiences that some adults enjoy, characteristics or conditions that inhibit further self-growth may stand in stark contrast. The inhibitive factor may be an environmental condition (such as a poor job or marriage) or a personal characteristic (such as a lack of assertiveness or social skills). Either way, the satisfying experiences serve to highlight by contrast the areas of dissatisfaction.

Whether pertaining to adulthood, adolescence, or childhood, it is essential to keep in mind that not all people pass through all developmental stages. Not all people encounter all developmental tasks in the same manner, nor do all people pass through them at the same speed. Individuals, like marital relationships, resemble each other in numerous ways yet are also unique entities. Let us now explore developmental principles and their applicability for understanding and conceptualizing marriage.

Marital Development

Milton Erickson was one theorist and therapist who approached working with couples from primarily a developmental viewpoint. Erickson regarded the life cycle as the broad frame of reference for determining strategies of marital intervention. It was Erickson's belief that marital problems occur when couples have difficulty mastering specific learning tasks required in each stage of the life cycle. Basically, his main goal was to help couples with the resolution of developmental-stage-related problems in order to get their life-cycle process moving again.

Haley (1973), in presenting Erickson's conceptualization of the marital life cycle, emphasized the transition points in marital relationships. These are the points at which developmental processes tend to facilitate crises. In the following list of Erickson's six phases of marital development, the issues characteristic of each phase are outlined.

Phase 1: The Courtship Period.   This phase has two critical tasks for individuals to master. The first is learning to deal with the opposite sex, utilizing socially appropriate behaviors. The second task is a weaning process for potential partners. This process involves individuals becoming sufficiently detached from their families of origin to go through the necessary stages of selecting a partner and establishing their own intimate bonds outside their original families.

Phase 2: Marriage and Its Consequences.   The challenges of this phase are many. Whatever a couple's relationship before marriage, the commitment they have now made can shift the nature of that relationship in unpredictable ways. By the act of marrying, partners often feel relieved of the need to hold back from each other; this greater openness may be welcome, but it can also create stress in the relationship. This openness, combined with the realization that many of the partners' marital expectations may be exaggerated, frequently results in disappointment, confusion, and conflict.

In learning to live together satisfactorily as a couple, partners must work out a number of agreements. Relationships with in-laws, relationships with friends and career associates, leisure activities, household chores, and many more segments of the lives couples assume constitute an arena for issues that were likely not worked out or even anticipated before marriage. Also, as the individual issues are worked out, partners must devise ways to deal with disagreements. A great amount of effort, compromise, and negotiation are necessary during this time.

Phase 3: Childbirth and Dealing with the Young.   Although partners may have worked out an acceptable manner of living together during their early marriage, many find that childbirth raises new issues and unsettles old ones. Couples who considered their marriage a trial arrangement now find separation a less acceptable option. Others, who thought they were committed to each other, find themselves feeling different with the arrival of a child.

With the birth of a child the couple automatically forms a triangle. Partners must learn to share with each other and with their child as well, otherwise one partner may feel the other is more attached to the child than to him or her. When problems are present or suddenly arise, it is crucial that partners not use the child as a scapegoat—an excuse for any difficulties they experience. When a child is scapegoated, ultimately he or she is likely to be blocked in development, and the actual partner-to-partner issues are likely never to be resolved.

The birth of a child also represents the coming together of two families and creates grandparents, aunts, uncles, and other degrees of relationship on both sides. Naming children, deciding how they are to be disciplined, determining which family will have more influence on their development, and other child-rearing issues all constitute potential crises unless couples are able not only to adequately agree but to do so under strong pressures from two sets of kin.

A second potential period of crisis during this phase occurs when the child starts school. Conflicts between partners about child rearing become most manifest when their product is put on display. In addition, sending children to school represents for partners the first experience of the fact that their children will ultimately leave home and the parents will be faced with only each other as immediate family.

Phase 4: Middle Marriage Difficulties. Couples who have been married for 10 or 15 years must make transitions that can be viewed in terms of the individual, marital pair, or whole family. Individually, partners are by now reaching the middle years of their life cycles. Accommodating themselves to successful or unsuccessful career and personal ambitions can be a crucial task for both partners.

Maritally, the couple has experienced much conflict as well as comfort in the middle years, and the partners have worked out relatively stable patterns of interacting with each other. By this middle phase, the patterns are likely set and habitual. As the children develop and the structure of the home scene changes, these previously effective interaction patterns can prove inadequate, and crises can arise. Adjustments must be made or new means of coping devised.

The middle years can also be a time when partners look more closely at whether to stay together or go their separate ways. The children are home less often, and partners realize that soon the children will be gone altogether. If partners have depended upon the children's presence for motivation to stay together, as they see the time approaching for the children to leave, problems arise.

In the family as a whole, the children, now adolescents, are experiencing their own turmoil and identity crises. Struggles for power and

control can escalate between adolescents and their parents. And as partners attempt to maintain the previous family hierarchical structure and
find that they can't do so successfully, the struggles between adolescents
and parents can spill over into the marital relationship.

Phase 5: Weaning Parents from Children. At the outset, this
phase is often a time of intense marital turmoil, which subsides as the
children leave and partners work out new ways of relating as a pair. In
some families the turmoil between partners comes when the oldest child
leaves home, in others it becomes worse as each child successively leaves,
and, in still others, it occurs only when the youngest is about to depart. In
most cases where extreme difficulties in the marital relationship arise it is
because a child or the children have been of special importance in the
marriage. Partners may have been able to communicate with each other
only through or about their children. Or, a couple's relationship may have
been held together only by common concern and care for their offspring.
If so, new ways of relating must be arrived at.

A second major transition of this phase involves the shift partners
must make in becoming grandparents. They must learn to be what they
feel are good grandparents, work out agreeable rules for participating in
their now adult children's lives with or without the grandchildren, and
still remember that, when home alone, they must function once more as a
dyad. Often, a third major transition in this phase involves partners dealing with the loss of their own parents and the resultant grief.

Phase 6: Retirement and Old Age. When a couple has successfully
negotiated the tasks of the weaning phase, they often experience a period
of relative harmony until the time that they retire. Now that partners are
faced with each other 24 hours a day, retirement often contributes to
problematic situations. Resolving issues related to the frequency of time
together as well as what to do with that time constitutes the major challenge for the marital relationship during this phase. Also during this
phase the variables in aging concerned with physical, psychological, and
economic well-being must be faced and resolved.

Eventually, one partner dies and the relationship physically ceases to
be. The issues involved with mourning and working through any unfinished business regarding the deceased partner are important tasks for the
widow or widower, as is, later, establishing a new lifestyle and manner of
existence.

Additional Marital Models

We have presented the preceding models of individual and marital
development to provide you with an understanding of how a marital relationship can be viewed developmentally as a series of stages through

which partners as individuals and as a couple progress. Although these conceptualizations tie in with and parallel each other in specific areas, lending credence to their validity, a number of other developmental schemes have been postulated. These other models can be just as valued as those we have discussed and in fact can add further substance to what has been presented. For this reason, we briefly describe two additional models of marital development that have been put forth.

The first additional model is a product of Taylor and Taylor (1978), who suggest a four-stage conceptualization of marital development they call the couple life cycle. Each stage of the couple life cycle has special characteristics that affect a couple:

1. *Commitment.* This initial stage begins with partners' agreement to function as a twosome. In this stage, contracts denoting the needs of each partner, to be met by the other and by the relationship, are formed.

2. *Accommodation.* The accommodation stage constitutes a period of adjustment wherein the couple bond weakens somewhat as frequent differences arise. Each partner must learn to adapt to new needs, stresses, and unmet expectations emanating from the commitment stage.

3. *Assessment.* This stage involves a close scrutiny of the relationship, each partner carefully examining its worth. "Dreams of the Commitment Stage have faded and during the Accommodation Stage most of the partner's annoying habits, traits, and demands have been discovered" (Taylor & Taylor, 1978, p. 80). Decisions are made regarding whether the relationship's benefits outweigh its disadvantages, with partners deciding to continue together or separate.

4. *Recommitment.* This period is one of stability for couples who have survived the stage of assessment and made the decision to continue together. Partners have responded to one another's unacceptable behaviors, passed judgment on the relationship, and found that it meets their needs. When couples emerge from the assessment stage with a "no" verdict and decide to separate, the couple life cycle is broken and assessment is followed by termination.

Taylor and Taylor support a view that all couples pass through the same stages, although some move slowly and some more rapidly. In addition, Taylor and Taylor propose that partners can and do pass through their couple life cycle more than once. Each time recommitment is reached, a new contract is agreed to. This new contract will be followed by accommodation, assessment, and, again, another decision to continue or end the relationship.

A second and rather unique additional conceptualization of marital development is that proposed by Tamashiro (1978). He presented the idea of a marital relationship as a mental "concept" defined by what partners see as its benefits and costs and by the criteria they consider for determining whether it is a successful union. "Marriage concepts are not necessarily the same as actual marital status or relationship; they are people's mental idea of marriage" (Tamashiro, 1978, p. 237).

This mental concept model, like Taylor and Taylor's, also contains four stages that are ordered in an unchangeable developmental sequence because each stems from the previous one and is the foundation for the next. Partners can progress through the stages at varying speeds; however, the sequence always remains the same. The stages represent a continuum of increased mental complexity, each requiring a deeper emotional awareness and greater interpersonal sensitivity. Table 1-1 identifies the four stages and the characteristic themes and concerns involved in each stage.

The themes and concerns of each stage represent cognitive issues for partners to grapple with in the development of their marital relationship. For example, in the magical stage, major issues revolve around what is externally obvious and observable: material objects, other people, sex, money. At the later individualistic stage, however, major issues have evolved to less observable, self-evaluated standards and criteria: beliefs, freedom of choice, self-chosen goals.

Compared to Erikson's model of individual development and Erickson's model of marital relationship development, the models of Taylor and Taylor and of Tamashiro present a view of life-cycle development that is different, in being less related to such variables as the presence of

TABLE 1-1   Characteristics of Marriage Concepts Stages

Stage	Dominant Thought Orientation	Common Themes Mentioned in Describing "Marriage"
Magical	Linking simple ideas to observable actions and things.	Overt behaviors; money; sex; house; personal appearance; specific individuals.
Idealized Conventional	Following social rules and conventions.	*Add:* Financial opportunity; jobs; "getting along" with spouse, friends; related interests and ideas; reputation; rules; being "better" or "good"; romance; home and family; community acceptance.[a]
Individualistic	Living according to personally defined values and emotions.	*Add:* Personal rights; ideals; personal satisfactions; emotions; beliefs; free choice; self-chosen goals; self-improvement; mutual companionship; achievements.[a]
Affirmational	Finding significance in self and others without relying on social conventions or personal standards.	*Add:* Conflicting emotions; inner distresses; uncertainty; human commonality; life's meaningfulness; ambiguity; qualified emotions; unconditional respect of self and others.[a]

[a] *"Add"* means in addition to, or superseding, the themes in the previous stage(s).
Note: From "Developmental Stages in the Conceptualization of Marriage," by R. T. Tamashiro, Family Coordinator, 1978, 27, 237–244. Copyright © 1978 by the National Council on Family Relations. Reprinted by permission.

children or the chronological age of the partners. We offer the additional models to provide further understanding of the whys and wherefores in the development of a marital relationship. We also present them to suggest the utility of synthesizing from a number of informative sources rather than sticking strictly to one model. There is something to gain from each, and each model supports the importance of viewing marital relationships from a developmental viewpoint.

The Marital Relationship as a System

A system may be defined as a set of interacting units with relationships among them (Miller, 1978) or as sets of elements standing in interaction (Bertalanffy, 1968). The concept of *system* thus treats people and events in terms of their interactions rather than their intrinsic characteristics. The most basic principle underlying the systems viewpoint has been understood for some time. An ancient astronomer once said, "Heaven is more than the stars alone. It is the stars and their movements."

Systems Theory

The conceptualization of a marital relationship as a system has its basis in general systems theory, which was pioneered by Ludwig von Bertalanffy (1934, 1968). Miller (1965), in applying general systems theory to living systems, proposed that like the rest of the universe, from galaxies to subatomic particles, living organisms can be viewed as part of a sequence of larger systems—such as family, community, and nation—and as composed of a series of ever smaller subsystems—such as organs, tissues, and cells. Each system has a measure of independence from the larger system, or *suprasystem*, of which it is a part. (For example, the individual is somewhat independent of the family, and the family, of the community.) But each system is independent only within certain limits, beyond which it must comply with the strictures of the larger wholes. The individuality of each system is maintained by its *boundary*, defined as a region that contains and protects the parts of the system and where the transfer of information and matter/energy is restricted to those regions internally and externally related to it. The communication across this boundary, as well as the coordination of the subsystems within it, is controlled by the *decider subsystem* (such as parents in a family or an individual's conscience). Boundaries maintain a degree of autonomy for the system apart from the control exerted upon it by the suprasystem of which it is a part. Similarly, *feedback mechanisms* adjust the functioning of a system according to its performance (like a thermostat in a heating and cooling system), maintain a general continuity of structure, and yet still function flexibly enough to permit change and growth within permissible limits.

By these mechanisms, individuals and elements of their environment, although separate entities, interact with one another so that each influences, and in turn is influenced by, the other. Taken together, this produces a *whole*—a system—that is larger than the sum of its individual parts. This system exists as part of a hierarchical order of systems; each higher or more advanced level is made up of systems of lower levels. Marriage qualifies as such a system. To fully understand a marital relationship, therefore, one must be aware of the component parts that make up the marriage, as well as the place of that marriage within the various larger systems of which it is a part.

General systems theory encompasses a number of other core concepts which are formulated around the notions of (1) organization, (2) control, (3) energy, and (4) time and space. All of these conceptualizations have applicability for understanding marital functioning; however, each is emphasized to a differing degree by the various systems approaches to marital therapy (Steinglass, 1978). We now consider some systems concepts commonly applied to couples.

Systems Properties in Marriage

The marital relationship is a complex unity made up of at least three different but interdependent parts: (1) the male element, comprising his total being; (2) the female element, comprising her total being; and (3) the marital system that develops from the interaction of the male and female elements being joined together (Lederer & Jackson, 1968). The marital system comes into being automatically upon the joining of the male and female elements. It provides an excellent example of how the whole can be viewed as being more than the sum of its parts: one plus one equals three. This process can be seen in Figure 1–1.

A change in one part of a system has a definite effect on all parts of a system. This idea relates to a major organizational aspect of viewing a marital relationship as a system—the concept of *wholeness*. Wholeness is

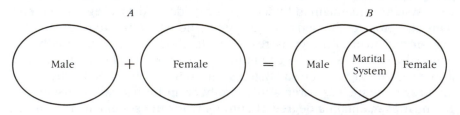

FIGURE 1-1.   The Origination of a Marital System. (A) Before their marital relationship has begun, the male and female function as separate elements. (B) After their marital relationship has begun, the male and female still function partially as separate elements; however, their now mutual interactions form a third element, the marital system.

perhaps the most revolutionary of all the concepts introduced by general systems theory (Steinglass, 1978).

Marital partners frequently react quite differently when they are together as opposed to when they are apart. The marital relationship as a system seems at times to have its own essence—a wholeness—independent of the two partners who comprise it.

> *Sam Cates was very much liked and admired by all his coworkers. He was noted for his usually positive comments and patient demeanor. Yet at home, Sam's wife, Cathy, felt intimidated by his constant demands and generally "bossy" attitude.*

The implications of wholeness are manifested in the preceding example. Any attempt to understand one partner's behavior alone would likely be futile; both partners need to be considered for an accurate understanding to take place. Partners' behavior cannot be isolated but must be seen as evolving in a larger context. Further, the wholeness concept suggests the importance of assessing environmental influences that may affect how the marital system functions. Such suprasystemic influences could include a couple's extended family, the community they live in, and other systems of which their marital system is a part.

A second important systems principle, *circular causality*, is based in the notion that interactions between partners are not necessarily related in a simple cause-and-effect manner. Rather, events take place in a circular manner; the behavior of one person influences that of a second which influences that of a third, which may return to have an impact on either the first or second person, triggering a new cycle of similarly related events. Thus, the behavior of each person involved can affect and is affected by each other person's behavior (Watzlawick, Beavin, & Jackson, 1967).

As follows from the principle of circular causality, it becomes meaningless to speak in terms of, in effect, A leads to B, as though a problem resides in one partner and is unilaterally imposed on the other. Instead, partners' individual behaviors are viewed as both effects and causes. There is a circularity in partners affecting each other, but no real beginning or end to the circle. Each partner's behavior is simultaneously caused by and causative of behaviors exhibited by his or her mate.

Take the example of Sam and Cathy Cates. Sam initially may have yelled and shouted defensively at home because he felt threatened by some behavior of Cathy's. Cathy yelled back in response; however, her reaction to Sam's initial shouting made him feel further threatened and intensified both his defensive behavior of the moment and the likelihood of more defensive behavior in the future. Where marital difficulties that are chronic, pathological patterns of behavior are of a longstanding nature, the principle of circular causality often explains their maintenance.

A third systems principle, *homeostasis,* describes the tendency of the control aspects of a system to maintain the system in a steady state. The principle of homeostasis is especially relevant to stress in a marital relationship. For most marital relationships there are fairly well-defined limits on how much stress will be tolerated within the system. If a change in the system raises the level of stress beyond those defined tolerable limits, the partners will seek to lower the stress to or below its original level. Often, the changes in one partner of a marital relationship brought about by therapy raise the level of stress in the system to an intolerable level. Homeostatic mechanisms then are frequently employed; for example, the couple may decide that therapy is too expensive, too time-consuming, or not effective (Woodburn & Barnhill, 1977).

While homeostasis explains a great number of phenomena within a marital relationship, by itself it is insufficient to explain a relationship's dynamics. After all, a couple undergoes many changes and transitions throughout the life cycle of their relationship. Change is inevitable if the system is to adapt and survive, so homeostasis can't solve every problem. For the system to be viable, it must also have the dynamic of a fourth systems principle—a means to elaborate and restructure itself. This means, which is the ability to be sensitive to a deviation from the usual interactions among the component parts of the system and to amplify that deviation, is referred to as *morphostasis.* This change-inducing mechanism provides a balance to the stability assured by homeostasis. When combined, homeostatic stability and morphostatic flexibility appear to account for a healthy range of marital functioning. The levels of homeostasis and morphostasis optimal for a particular couple vary according to the needs of the couple and the environment in which they function. It is important, however, that both mechanisms be considered in order to fully understand couples' behaviors.

The fifth and final systems property we consider in application to marital therapy is the principle of *equifinality.* Equifinality refers to the similarity of results of the interaction between the parts of the system. Specifically, this principle suggests that no matter what information is put into the system, the outcome will be the same. Sam and Cathy Cates tended, in times of conflict, to yell and shout defensively and then to isolate themselves from each other instead of sharing their real thoughts and feelings. One result of this lack of emotional closeness was that Cathy had very little desire to engage in sexual relations. She sought individual therapy for "her problem" and came to understand that her lack of sexual desire was a passive expression of her anger towards Sam. She shared this insight with Sam, who found it threatening and so responded in his usual defensive manner in such interactions, shouting "What do you want me to do!" and then withdrawing. Cathy yelled back but, as usual, knew she wasn't being listened to.

Even though the therapeutic insight Cathy had gained was accurate, it was ineffective in changing the relationship because it was processed like any of her input to the system. No matter what the input, the same outcome is likely to be obtained. One implication of equifinality is that, in marital concerns, it may be necessary to change the system's usual information-processing rules before any change can take place. These rules must be blocked or altered for communications to have new results.

A Clinical Conceptualization of Marriage

When two people marry, they assume that they will fulfill their own and their partner's expectations. They may or may not fulfill them, depending upon how realistic the expectations. Even if the partners do meet many of their own and the other's needs as they conceive of them, there is no guarantee that they will continue to do so. In a marital relationship, partners' expectations just do not remain constant. They evolve as the relationship evolves and develops. The way we might conceptualize a marital relationship when a couple is first married will be quite different from the way we will view it 5, 10, and 20 years later. Thus, when marital discord arises and a couple seeks marital therapy, examination of the present and potential effects of role expectations and of transitional issues on partners' perceptions of themselves and their relationship is critical.

As clinicians, our first introduction to therapy was through traditional individual and group models of counseling and psychotherapy. Additional professional training and clinical experiences, especially with couples and families, further emphasized these individual and group approaches and, at the same time, allowed us to see the need for understanding and utilizing various systems concepts in our work. These systems concepts have come to tie together the package of our therapeutic approaches. Consider the following situation:

> *Juan and Jane finally sought marital therapy after having had much turmoil in their relationship since their 6-year-old son began his first year of elementary school. Jane had left her career in nursing when the child was born and, now that he was in school full time, wanted to return to work. Juan, raised in a traditional Cuban home environment, felt that Jane should stay home and not work, as he was the breadwinner. He saw it as a poor reflection on himself if he was unable to be the sole support of his family. Juan did not want to come to therapy and did so only at Jane's and the therapist's insistence.*

Juan and Jane's situation illustrates the need to consider a number of different yet interwoven variables when looking at relationship concerns. Specifically:

1. *Role Expectations.* Juan grew up in a family where his mother didn't work outside of the home. His father was the sole supporter of the family. From his parents Juan adopted the role expectation that Jane would not work. From his Cuban cultural upbringing, he also adopted societal role expectations concerning his being able to support his family. Finally, he had his own expectations regarding Jane's role in their relationship. As she hadn't worked since their son was born, there was no need to begin to do so now. Jane, on the other hand, had a mother who worked outside the home, saw that most of her friends who were also mothers were working, and had herself expected that she would return to work when her son went to school full time.

2. *Transitional/Developmental Issues.* Jane and Juan's level of marital satisfaction was at a low ebb during the period of their marriage when they sought therapy. They had allowed their parenting responsibilities to overshadow their relationship responsibilities. In addition, Jane realized in this period that eventually their son would leave home not just to go to school for the major part of the day but completely. She wanted to have more goals to work for in her life and saw her former career in nursing as a means of establishing and achieving a greater purpose for herself.

3. *Systems Concepts.* Applying the concept of wholeness, the therapist realized the importance of Juan's presence in therapy, so with Jane's assistance, this was pursued strongly. Another systems-theory consideration was to block existing homeostatic mechanisms until therapeutic inroads could be established, as it was evident that the stress in the relationship was already much above this couple's normative level. Further, an understanding of the partners' morphostatic mechanisms was sought and the means by which the couple processed information were assessed, so as to better understand how positive changes in their relationship might be facilitated.

A knowledge of the potential effects of role expectations, transitional issues, and systems concepts provides a therapist with a comprehensive view of any marital concerns a couple is experiencing. This comprehensive conceptualization of a marital relationship also allows the therapist (and the couple as well) to discount the probable effects of some variables and to address others more pointedly. For example, when a newly married couple consulted Erickson for an emerging sexual difficulty, he suggested (Haley, 1973) to them that their problem was not uncommon and that in time it would likely resolve itself. In doing so, he framed their concern as a normal transitional issue in the current development of their relationship. Of course, even framed in this way, the problem still required their attention and cooperation to be resolved. However, by identifying the problem as the developmental learning task it was, he divested the couple of their concern that it was pathological, which could have snowballed into even more problems and loss of self-esteem. Similar examples and experiences exist with regard to all those aspects of a marital relationship addressed within this chapter.

Summary

We have devoted this chapter to presenting variables that are key to clinically conceptualizing the unique interpersonal encounter that is a marital relationship. Our comprehensive conceptualization has involved three areas of specific concern. The first area includes the expectations of society, of one's family of origin, and of the individuals themselves regarding the roles partners should take in marital relationships. The second area concerns a transitional view of marriage and the potential evolutionary effects that individual and marital life-cycle development may have upon partners and their relationship. Finally, we have addressed the importance of understanding basic systems-theory concepts, notably wholeness, circular causality, homeostasis, morphostasis, and equifinality.

The ability to tie together as well as to differentiate the importance of these key variables with couples with whom therapists work provides a strong knowledge base. This ability therefore also provides the means to choose the most appropriate, efficient, and effective intervention strategies. In Chapter 2, we focus on basic issues involved in working directly with couples. In addition, we examine some of the background issues, looking at the origins and current development of the marital therapy field.

References

Abernathy, V. D. American marriage in a cross-cultural perspective. In H. Grunebaum & J. Christ (Eds.), *Contemporary marriage: Structure, dynamics, and therapy.* Boston: Little, Brown, 1976.

Bertalanffy, L. von. *Modern theories of development: An introduction to theoretical biology.* London: Oxford University Press, 1934.

Bertalanffy, L. von. *General systems theory.* New York: Braziller, 1968.

Bocknek, G. A developmental approach to counseling adults. In N. K. Schlossberg & A. D. Entine (Eds.), *Counseling adults.* Monterey, Calif.: Brooks/Cole, 1977.

Caplan, G. *A chance to grow.* Boston: WGBH Educational Foundation, 1967.

Duvall, E. M. *Marriage and family development* (5th ed.). Philadelphia: Lippincott, 1977.

Erikson, E. H. *Childhood and society.* New York: Norton, 1963.

Fogarty, T. F. Marital crisis. In P. J. Guerin, Jr. (Ed.), *Family therapy: Theory and practice.* New York: Gardner Press, 1976.

Gould, R. The phases of adult life: A study in developmental psychology. *American Journal of Psychiatry,* 1972, *129,* 521–531.

Grunebaum, H., & Christ, J. (Eds.), *Contemporary marriage: Structure, dynamics, and therapy.* Boston: Little, Brown, 1976.

Haley, J. Marriage therapy. *Archives of General Psychiatry,* 1963, *8,* 213–234.

Haley, J. *Uncommon therapy.* New York: Norton, 1973.

James, M. *Marriage is for loving.* Reading, Mass.: Addison-Wesley, 1979.

Kimmel, D. *Adulthood and aging.* New York: Wiley, 1974.

Lederer, W. J., & Jackson, D. D. *The mirages of marriage.* New York: Norton, 1968.

Levinson, D. J., Darrow, C. N., Klein, E. B., Levinson, M. H., & McKee, B. *The seasons of a man's life.* New York: Knopf, 1979.

Lowenthal, M. F., Turner, M., & Chiriboga, D. *Four stages of life.* San Francisco: Jossey-Bass, 1975.

Miller, J. G. Living systems: Basic concepts. *Behavioral Science,* 1965, *10,* 193–245.

Miller, J. G. *Living systems.* New York: McGraw-Hill, 1978.

Murstein, B. I. The stimulus-value-role theory of marital choice. In H. Grunebaum & J. Christ (Eds.), *Contemporary marriage: Structure, dynamics, and therapy.* Boston: Little, Brown, 1976.

Neugarten, B. L. Adaptation and the life cycle. In N. K. Schlossberg & A. D. Entine (Eds.), *Counseling adults.* Monterey, Calif.: Brooks/Cole, 1977.

Nichols, W. C. The marriage relationship. *Family Coordinator,* 1978, *27,* 185–191.

O'Neill, N., & O'Neill, G. *Open marriage: A new life style for couples.* New York: M. Evans, 1972.

Sager, C. J. *Marriage contracts and couples therapy.* New York: Brunner-Mazel, 1976.

Sheehy, G. *Passages: The predictable crises of adult life.* New York: Dutton, 1976.

Steinglass, P. The conceptualization of marriage from a systems theory perspective. In T. J. Paolino, Jr., & B. S. McCrady (Eds.), *Marriage and marital therapy.* New York: Brunner-Mazel, 1978.

Tamashiro, R. T. Developmental stages in the conceptualization of marriage. *Family Coordinator,* 1978, *27,* 237–244.

Taylor, A., & Taylor, R. *Couples: The art of staying together.* Washington, D.C.: Acropolis, 1978.

Watzlawick, P., Beavin, J. H., & Jackson, D. D. *Pragmatics of human communication.* New York: Norton, 1967.

Woodburn, L. T., & Barnhill, L. N. Applying family systems therapy principles to couples counseling. *Personnel and Guidance Journal,* 1977, *55,* 510–514.

CHAPTER TWO

Working with Couples

Working with married couples can be an extremely complicated process. Marital therapists have to develop not only a firm understanding of marital and family relationships and relevant treatment techniques but also a treatment style and philosophy that is appropriate to themselves. Correspondingly, working effectively with couples requires therapists to seek insight into the feelings, behaviors, and roles not only within the therapeutic relationship but within their own marital and family relationships. Working with couples means working with a system, and that system can exert personal pressures. If therapists unwittingly become part of the dysfunctional marital system, therapeutic effectiveness can be severely hampered. It is vital that therapists be able to recognize and respond to these issues.

In this chapter we explore the major issues relevant to working with couples in a therapeutic relationship. We begin by tracing the development of current marital theory and therapy. This discussion is followed by a look at specific treatment factors to consider when initiating marital therapy. We then examine the therapeutic issues related to therapists themselves, both as professionals and simply as people. Finally, the chapter focuses on the synthesis of couple and therapist factors resulting in a therapeutic relationship.

The Development of Current Marital Theory and Therapy

Simply stated, marital therapists are therapists who work with people presenting marital problems. Until recently, such a casual description would have been not only the simplest but, because of its simplicity, the only possible one; beyond this description, the similarity between many marital therapists was minimal. Not only did marital therapists come from many disciplines, even those from the same discipline often had notable differences in their approach to similar presenting problems. Recent years, however, have seen a refinement of therapeutic approaches. And, concurrently, steps have been taken to examine and codify the presuppositions of various theories and therapists (Olson, Russell, & Sprenkle, 1980b).

There is no agreed upon date when marital therapy had its origin as a profession, but the major currents in which it originated and evolved to the present can be noted. In 1929, Abraham and Hannah Stone founded the Marriage Consultation Center in New York. This pioneer venture was followed by the founding of the American Institute of Family Relations in 1930 and the Marriage Council of Philadelphia in 1932. In 1942, the American Association of Marriage Counselors was founded.

Following these initial developments, because of the post–World War II dissolution of a dramatic number of young marriages, the field of marital therapy began a tremendous upsurge. A key year was 1948 (Prochaska & Prochaska, 1978). That year Mittleman (1948) published his definitive paper on concurrent analysis of married couples; Mace (1948), in England, published the first book on marriage counseling; and a few months later there appeared the first American book on marriage counseling, by John Cuber (1948).

These early writings generally supported "concurrent marital therapy," in which the therapist saw each partner separately. In 1948 psychoanalysis was the dominant approach to therapy, and its focus was on the pathology within individuals, not marriages. The transference relationship between client and therapist was seen as central to therapeutic progress; and inevitably the presence of both marital partners during sessions presented conflicts that disrupted the classical transference relationship. By instead analyzing the partners separately the therapist was better able to discuss which marital interaction concerns were determined realistically and which were determined neurotically. Also, when information from both was available, the therapist could gain a clearer awareness of the neurotic trends in each partner (Mittleman, 1948). Concurrent analysis had as its primary goal each partner developing insight into the particular needs that he or she brought into the marriage. With this insight, partners could begin to change the way they saw each other and to relate on a more mature level.

Psychoanalytic theory and practice and, correspondingly, concurrent marital therapy remained the most widely utilized approach for working with couples throughout the 1950s. During the decade of the 1960s the dominance of psychoanalytic approaches lessened, and an increasing importance came to be placed upon working not only with the individuals in a relationship but with the marital relationship itself as the treatment focus. With this focus on the relationship came a dramatic increase in the development and advocacy of new styles and practices in marital therapy. However, most of the new styles had the common bond of holding that in order for the therapist to understand most completely and intervene most directly the partners would need to be seen together, in joint therapy sessions. The practice of seeing the spouses together during all therapeutic sessions came to be known as "conjoint marital therapy" (Brody, 1961; Haley, 1963; Satir, 1965). Marital therapists came to be differentiated, as a group, by their emphasis on the marital relationship and their preference for the practice of conjoint therapy (Olson, 1970).

Although in the 1960s the major focus of treatment efforts was the marital relationship, predominantly with conjoint therapy, many new theories and practices were experimented with, in a search for the single best theory and approach to marital therapy (Manus, 1966). Social-learning, systems, and various "client-centered" theories as marital therapy modalities began to come to the fore, and along with them came an increase in new and varied practices. Olson, Russell, and Sprenkle (1980b) characterized the main feature of clinical marital practice during this period as therapists "doing their own thing" (p. 974). The mixing of conjoint and concurrent sessions became known as "combined marital therapy" (Greer & Solomon, 1963). The use of two therapists, each seeing one marital partner and then consulting together, was identified as "collaborative therapy" (Martin & Bird, 1963). "Collaborative combined therapy" involved the use of separate therapists for each marital partner with all four meeting together at regular intervals for joint sessions (Royce & Hagan, 1960). In addition, the use of varied forms of group marital therapy underwent simultaneous experimentation.

By 1970, all possible combinations and variations of concurrent, conjoint, collaborative, and combined formats, each with different theoretical bases, had been practiced with groups or with individual couples. Yet surprisingly little was known about the effectiveness of each of these modalities. There simply was no adequate research that tested the therapeutic efficacy of the various approaches (Prochaska & Prochaska, 1978).

Thus, in spite of the abundance of innovative practices, the development of marital therapy lacked the adequate theory and research data to provide a systematic rationale and assessment.

In 1970, Olson proposed that "the search for *the* theory of marital therapy is slowly changing to a realization that there needs to be considerably more exploration of various theoretical approaches before a more integrated and comprehensive approach can be developed" (p. 516). This exploration marked the development of marital therapy during the 1970s.

Characterizing the decade of the 1970s was the examination and refinement of existing ideas rather than the introduction of dramatically new approaches. Olson, Russell, and Sprenkle (1980b) proposed that three significant advances occurred during this decade. These were: (1) the integration and refinement of previous models; (2) simplified descriptions of previous work; and (3) extension of existent theoretical models to specific marital problems, such as chemical addiction (Steinglass, 1979) and aging (Herr & Weakland, 1979).

Thus, the charge that marital therapy was a set of practices in search of a single theory (Manus, 1966) became no longer applicable. In addition to refining particular theoretical approaches, steps were also taken to examine the presuppositions of the various theories and therapists. Empirical research improved in both quantity and quality. This progress was clearly documented by a number of comprehensive reviews (Beck, 1976; Gurman, 1973; Gurman & Kniskern, 1978).

Olson, Russell, and Sprenkle (1980b) summarized the recent evolution of marital therapy as a mental health profession most aptly: "Viewed from a developmental perspective, the field of marital therapy has emerged from its infancy in the 1950s, achieved childhood in the early 1960s, adolescence in the late 1960s, and has reached young adulthood in the 1970s" (p. 974).

The Couple

Working with couples requires that therapists pay close attention to a number of factors. One class of factors relates to each of the partners individually. To each case, each individual marital pattern brings personal, familial, and societal expectations, which may or may not be quite different from the other partner's expectations. One or both partners may be experiencing developmental or other concerns unrelated to the relationship but with serious impact upon the partners' behaviors. Further, the coming together of these two individuals creates a unique marital relationship, which is characterized by another class of factors.

The marital relationship can be described by itself as a system and viewed with a separate focus apart from the two individuals that form it. Inherent in the relationship are those developmental concerns and systems-functioning properties discussed in Chapter 1. The multiplicity of these potential factors suggests the need for therapists initiating therapy with couples to give thought to some categories of considerations that are basic. These include general treatment issues, treatment units, and treatment approaches.

Treatment Issues

Advocates of the different theoretical approaches to conducting marital therapy with couples all have made proposals as to where the true focus of therapeutic intervention should be, or what really needs to be changed in order to effectively treat marital disorders. Olson, Russell, and Sprenkle (1980a) classified this considerable variety of proposed treatment issues into three major dimensions, each of which can be viewed as lying on a continuum of functioning. The three dimensions are cohesion, adaptability, and communication.

Cohesion.   Cohesion is defined as the emotional bonding that marital partners have with one another and the degree of individual autonomy they experience (Olson, Russell, and Sprenkle, 1980a). In an optimally functioning marital relationship, a clear boundary exists between the partners. Each partner has an individual sense of "I-ness" along with a relationship sense of "us." Thus, each partner maintains his or her individuality but not at the expense of a feeling of relationship belongingness.

The therapeutic relevance of cohesion has been primarily developed through the work of Minuchin (1974). Minuchin identified relationships as falling along a continuum of cohesion between the extremes of *enmeshment* and *disengagement.*

Enmeshment refers to an extreme form of proximity and intensity in marital interactions in which partners are overconcerned and overinvolved in each other's lives. Boundaries are unclear, and there is an overidentification between partners so that loyalty to the marital system and consensus with it limits the autonomy of individual partners. Being married dominates all experiences, at the expense of each partner having a separate sense of self. In enmeshed relationships, excessive togetherness and sharing often lead to a lack of privacy, as partners constantly intrude on each other's thoughts and feelings. Further, in their overemphasis of relationship belongingness, partners in an enmeshed marital system are unwilling or unable to respond to problems in an individual, autonomous manner, which is often necessary in order to react appropriately.

Disengagement, at the opposite extreme of the cohesion continuum, refers to a marital relationship in which partners are able to function separately and autonomously but with little loyalty to their mates. In a disengaged relationship, partners lack interdependence. Boundaries in a disengaged relationship are so inappropriately rigid that only a very high level of stress disposes one partner to request support from the other, or for either partner to perceive the other's need for support. Even in extreme circumstances, however, the mate whose help is needed may seem hardly to respond at all. In a disengaged relationship, partners tend not to respond when a response is called for because each feels isolated from the other.

Extreme degrees of enmeshment and disengagement are seen as problematic, and most couples who come for therapy exhibit one of these extremes (Olson, Russell, & Sprenkle, 1980a). It is the central area of the continuum where partners are able to experience the balanced state of being independent from as well as connected to each other. This is illustrated in Figure 2-1.

Adaptability.   Adaptability is defined as the ability of a marital system to change its power structure, role relationships, and relationship rules in response to situational and developmental stress (Olson, Russell, & Sprenkle, 1980a). The most effectively functioning marital relationship is one in which partners are open and willing to change when it is in their best interest to do so. As with cohesion, marital relationships are seen as falling along a continuum of adaptability between two extremes, *rigidity* and *chaos.* Rigidity refers to exaggerated and excessive resistance to change. Couples at the low end of the adaptability continuum, which is characterized by rigidity, are unable or unwilling to change even when it clearly appears necessary to do so. At the other extreme, couples at the high end of the adaptability continuum, characterized by chaos, have too little stability and are constantly changing; their chaotic life prevents the partners from establishing even the minimum set of common meanings, values, and expectations that are essential for communication and the survival of an intimate relationship (Wertheim, 1973). Accordingly, chaotic couples, like rigid couples, have difficulty dealing with situational stresses and developmental concerns.

Minuchin (1974), mentioned previously in relation to cohesion, also devoted considerable attention to the therapeutic importance of adaptation. He stressed the significance of being able to change in the face of external or internal pressures—for example, pressures related to develop-

Low Level of Cohesion	Moderate Level of Cohesion	High Level of Cohesion
Disengaged System	Functional System	Enmeshed System
Isolation	Independence + Connection	Overidentification
Maladaptive Separateness	Adaptive Balance	Maladaptive Closeness

FIGURE 2-1.   The cohesion-dimension continuum of marital functioning.

Low Level of Adaptability	Moderate Level of Adaptability	High Level of Adaptability
Rigid System	Functional System	Chaotic System
Excessive Resistance to Change	Structure + Flexibility	Little Stability/ Constant Change
Maladaptive Rigidity	Adaptive Balance	Maladaptive Chaos

FIGURE 2-2. The adaptability-dimension continuum of marital functioning.

mental issues, such as a change in a life-cycle stage or the addition or loss of a family member. Minuchin suggested that many couples in treatment are simply going through transitions and are in need of assistance in adapting to them. In this regard, he stated: "The label of pathology would be preserved for families [couples] who, in the face of stress . . . avoid or resist any exploration of alternatives" (Minuchin, 1974, p. 60).

As with cohesion, levels of adaptability that are balanced are seen as optimal for marital functioning. Moderate levels of adaptability (structure and flexibility) are conducive to effective relationship functioning, while the extremes (rigid and chaotic) tend to result in problems and dysfunction. Thus, it is the central positions on the adaptability continuum where balance is found, with problematic couples functioning at either the extreme of continual change, leading to chaos, or that of no change, resulting in rigidity. This is illustrated in Figure 2-2.

Communication. The communication dimension differs from the cohesion and adaptability dimensions in that, although it too falls along a continuum, the continuum midpoint is not prescribed as the most adaptive focus for marital partners. The clearest consensus among practitioners of the various approaches to marital therapy regarding communication within a marital relationship is on this point: the more positive the communications between marital partners, the better their relationship functions. Communicating positively includes sending clear and congruent messages, expressing empathy, making supportive statements, and utilizing effective problem-solving skills. By contrast, negative communications involve sending incongruent and disqualifying messages, showing lack of empathy, making nonsupportive (negative) statements, using poor problem-solving skills, and sending paradoxical and double-bind messages (Olson, 1972). The communication dimension is illustrated in Figure 2-3.

These three dimensions offer general parameters for therapists to assess; the resulting judgments help determine the best course of therapy. From this general assessment process, specific therapeutic objectives can be naturally derived. However, it is important to remember that treatment

Low Level of Communication	Moderate Level of Communication	High Level of Communication
Poorly Functioning System	Moderately Functioning System	Effectively Functioning System
Negative Communications	Moderately Positive Communications	Positive Communications

FIGURE 2-3. The communication-dimension continuum of marital functioning.

issues are not an either-or consideration; the impaired functioning of any couple is usually best viewed in terms of a hierarchy of focus. For instance, a couple's cohesion and adaptability might be at extreme—and thus maladaptive—levels. Yet communication concerns might be perceived by the therapist to be the most crucial and immediate treatment issue. The other parameters are not ignored but, rather, approached secondarily. Consider the following example of a couple in therapy and the assessments made of their cohesion, adaptability, and communication.

> *Barry and Cindy were quite happy in their marriage until Barry decided to leave his present job and return full time to graduate school to pursue an advanced degree. Cindy initially accepted Barry's decision, agreeing that they could survive on her salary and their savings during the time it would take Barry to complete the degree. Soon after Barry began his studies, they began to constantly argue and at times to react quite viciously toward each other. They wisely decided to seek assistance and entered therapy. Therapeutic discussion suggested that Cindy felt her role as breadwinner was inappropriate. This feeling was closely related to the fact that her expectation had been to have children sooner in the marriage, although this had never really been discussed or agreed upon between the two. Now, exaggerating what was only a temporary situation, she thought they would never have children. She also saw herself as being forced to support Barry. Barry expressed similar feelings of resentment, his being related to the economic dependence on Cindy. He too saw this as inappropriate, in accordance with his adopted societal expectation that the man should be the breadwinner.*

Cohesion: Barry and Cindy's marital system seemed to be functioning toward the high end of the cohesion dimension—the end indicating an enmeshed system. Due to their economic overidentification in their present circumstances, neither Barry nor Cindy could experience the more balanced feeling of being independent from as well as connected to the other.

Adaptability: Unlike the couple's functioning at the high end of the cohesion dimension, the marital system seemed to be functioning at the low end of the adaptability dimension—the end indicating a rigid system. There was surely a need to consider possible changes or alterations in expectations at that point in their lives, and, as concerned future plans, an even greater need. Yet both partners perceived themselves as locked into their circumstances and responded poorly to situational stresses as a result. Their circumstances themselves were also open to change. For example, Barry could have returned to work part-time and completed his education part-time. But again neither partner could or would consider an alternate course of action.

Communication: It is obvious from the short situational summary given that communication patterns were dysfunctional between Barry and Cindy. Cindy apparently accepted Barry's decision to leave his job to pursue a degree, but she never agreed to it; nor did she take an active part in the decision-making process, expressing her own desires. It would also appear that there was never a direct, clearly understood discussion of parenting plans between the couple.

With any couple in therapy, which treatment issue becomes the primary focus for initial therapeutic goal-setting is a matter of the discretion of the therapist and couple in consultation with each other. This decision is affected by the couple's most pressing concern and area of major commitment, their circumstances at present, the therapist's theoretical orientation, or any one or combination of these. Furthermore, different issues can emerge as therapy progresses, so that the hierarchy set may need to be adjusted. Continuing evaluation of therapeutic progress is a major component of the ongoing assessment process.

Treatment Units

Although both marital partners may present themselves for treatment, the most appropriate unit of treatment may or may not be both partners together as a couple. Two specific considerations need to be made in order to determine the best course of therapy. The first consideration is whether the partners' difficulties are indeed marital or are more individual in nature. The second consideration concerns the motivation, accessibility, and ability of each partner to work on either individual or marital problems. In the following discussion the units of treatment most frequently used in marital therapy are identified and explained.

Individual Therapy for Each Partner with Separate Therapists. With such an arrangement, the therapists may or may not confer with each other. This form of treatment is usually most appropriate in cases where individual concerns, rather than relationship problems, are of most pressing importance. It may also be the method of choice when the focus on the marital relationship is not established at the onset of treatment and becomes an important issue only as therapy progresses. One partner entering a therapeutic setting wherein his or her mate has previously established him- or herself often perceives the situation as an already biased one, and this problem can be avoided with individual therapy. Finally, this method is frequently preferred by therapists who choose to focus on individuals rather than on relationships per se as a function of therapeutic orientation.

Concurrent Therapy.   Each partner is seen individually by the same therapist. Occasionally, there may be sessions when both partners meet with the therapist at one time. Concurrent therapy is usually called for when there are other major issues to be dealt with at the same time as the marital issues. For example, one partner may be particularly immature or exhibit some type of neurotic or psychotic behavior that is better treated individually. Also, for therapists who are relatively inexperienced or are insecure in working with both partners always together, concurrent therapy can be a more comfortable and facilitative mode.

Conjoint Therapy.   Both partners are seen together by one therapist. This treatment form is most appropriate when the difficulties presented by a couple are especially relevant to the relationship itself, when there is at least minimal communication between partners, and when they are reasonably motivated to work on their marital problems. Conjoint marital therapy is most successful when both partners recognize their need for assistance, as opposed to when one comes to therapy in response to an ultimatum, looking for permission to get out of the relationship, attempting to avoid any personal responsibility for their marital problems, or simply seeking validation that one and only one of the partners is the cause of all of their difficulties.

Co-therapy.   Both partners are seen together by two therapists. This treatment form often provides a great degree of therapeutic flexibility. For example, as one co-therapist confronts, the other can play a more supportive role, or vice versa. This allows therapeutic efforts to focus on two or more treatment issues simultaneously. Male-female co-therapy teams can provide role models for couples, both individually and as an effectively working pair. And, for the therapists themselves, the mutual support and reinforcement as well as constructive criticism may be useful in facilitating therapeutic efforts. One area where the use of co-therapists has been especially recommended is the treatment of couples with sexual concerns (Masters & Johnson, 1970).

Couples Group Therapy.   Several couples are seen together by one or more therapists. This form of treatment is often utilized as a means of defusing intensely emotional relationships; partners tend to behave more rationally in a group with other people than when alone together. The group setting provides the partners a better opportunity to clearly observe and listen to each other in an appropriate manner. Especially when there are desirable role models in the form of other couples who are adaptively coping with their marital concerns, the group setting offers a valuable social context—one in which trust can develop and from which support can be drawn. The varied models for relating and the additional sources of feedback in a group can provide couples clearer perspectives on their own marital concerns. Couples group therapy is also the treatment of choice when economic worries are a primary factor in a couple's marital distress; group therapy may not offer the individual attention of other forms, but the cost can be much more reasonable.

Treatment Approaches

As noted earlier in this chapter, the 1960s spawned a flood of new approaches to treating couples experiencing marital distress. Yet little if any empirical evidence exists even today as to the actual effectiveness of the majority of these approaches. Additionally, most offer only very weak theoretical substance.

We have chosen to focus our analysis of major approaches to marital therapy on those that provide the most substantial models for the understanding and treatment of married couples in a therapeutic setting. These are psychoanalytically oriented (object-relations) theory, social-learning theory, and systems theory (Gurman, 1978; Gurman & Kniskern, 1980; Paolino & McCrady, 1978). In this chapter we offer some brief assumptions to consider regarding the utilization of these theoretical orientations; in Section Two (Chapters 3, 4, 5, and 6) we provide more in-depth presentations and critiques of the approaches.

Psychoanalytic Theory.   The theory conceptualizing marital interactions in terms of *object relations* is the theory discussed here. Object-relations theory, although it is psychoanalytical, differs somewhat from classical psychoanalytic theory in suggesting that mental disturbance originates through a disruption in the normal course of human emotional development.

Object-relations theory concerns the manner in which individuals seek out and become emotionally attached to people and things outside themselves—"objects." When two partners enter into a marital relationship, each brings the psychological heritage that has characterized his or her own emotional development. The resulting interactions between partners depend upon the elements of each partner's psychological heritage.

Meissner (1978) suggests that marital partners' experiences, and the manner in which they approach and accomplish developmental tasks, are determined to a large extent by the "residues" of their internalized objects and by the way in which they organize aspects of their parents that have been introjected as part of their own views of themselves. These factors form the core of the sense of self and contribute significantly to the integration of the partners' respective identities. The extent to which marital partners are able to successfully merge their individual identities in a constructive and productive shared marital experience depends heavily upon the adaptiveness of the introjections each brings, as well as on how successful they have been in differentiating senses of self and identity for themselves from their families of origin.

The marital relationship is considered to be intricately bound to partners' parent-child relationships in their families of origin; the capacity to successfully function as a marital partner is seen as principally a consequence of each partner's childhood relationships with his or her own parents. Therefore, issues regarding marital interactions cannot avoid the discussion of partners' parent-child interactions. If the marital system is conceptualized from the psychoanalytic perspective of object relations, then the logical assumption is that the same strengths and weaknesses are involved in both marital and parent-child relationships. So therapists utilizing this approach not only deal with the partners' marital relationship but also look critically at their past mother-child and father-child relationships as well as the two-parents-and-child triad configurations as the partners each experienced them. Through therapist interpretation and the development of insight, partners can begin to change the way they see themselves and each other and relate on a mature rather than infantile or childhood level.

Social-Learning Theory.   Social-learning or behavioral theory posits several assumptions regarding what leads to satisfaction and dissatisfaction in marriage. Establishing and then maintaining marital satisfaction most basically requires effort and commitment from both partners, as well as the development of certain skills to ensure open and constructive communications.

Each partner in a marital relationship has needs for affection, sex, recreation, companionship, status, approval, and more. In addition, each partner must contribute to the needs of the marital and family unit in such areas as finances, household tasks, social activities, and child rearing.

Satisfaction is the result of reciprocity in providing for each of these individual and family needs. Research has indicated that the amount of pleasure and range of pleasurable actions a partner receives are proportional to the amount and range that he or she gives (Liberman, Wheeler, deVisser, Kuehnel, & Kuehnel, 1980). This is the principle of reciprocity: partners get what they give and give what they get.

According to social-learning theory, when each partner is receiving pleasurable words and actions adequate to meet his or her needs, the marriage will be experienced as satisfying to both of the partners. Dissatisfaction occurs when too few pleasurable behaviors are exchanged or when there is an imbalance, with pleasurable interactions limited to one area (for example, sexual relations) or with one partner giving much more than he or she receives.

A second major assumption of the social-learning approach to marital therapy is that marital satisfaction is increased when partners' ability to communicate both the positive and the negative aspects of their marriage is improved. Therapists must often teach couples communications skills that facilitate their mutual exchange of pleasurable behaviors, improve their ability to solve problems that arise, and assist them in expressing both their positive and negative feelings in a constructive manner.

The social-learning focus is on skill building. While insight as to the "why" of partners' marital difficulties may occur during therapy, it is considered secondary to their efforts to learn and use new skills to improve the relationship. The focus is on the present and working toward the future, rather than interpreting the past.

Systems Theory.   Systems theory presents what many professional clinicians consider to be, when compared to the psychoanalytic and social-learning approaches, a whole new way of conceptualizing marital distress, understanding partners' behaviors, and viewing the development of symptoms and their resolution. The basic conceptual framework that characterizes the systems-theory approach to marital therapy concerns its major focus: the transactions between partners rather than the characteristics of each individual partner. Even when, for one reason or another, attention is zeroed in on one partner, his or her behavior is analyzed in terms of its power to affect and shape the behavior of the other partner of the marital system and in terms of the variables of the marital system itself (Sluzki, 1978).

When observing partners' interactions, systems-oriented therapists take into consideration effects, rather than intentions. The effects of behaviors upon behaviors and the way interpersonal sequences are organized are carefully noted, while little attention is directed to the motivation of the partners. In fact, issues about motivation or intentions are often considered irrelevant to the understanding of the interactional processes occurring. This focus on processes is not a denial that motivations and intentions exist; it stems from the belief that they offer little relevant information for purposes of conceptualizing and treating marital distress.

The Therapist

The second major component in a therapeutic relationship with a couple in marital therapy, apart from the couple itself, is the significance of the therapist. Since therapists enter into a relationship with a couple and ask them to take an honest look at themselves and to make decisions as to how they will change, it is critical for therapists to hold open their own lives to this same kind of scrutiny.

Marital therapists as professionals acquire an extensive theoretical and practical knowledge base and utilize this knowledge in their work assisting couples. But to every session they also bring themselves as persons. Therapists' values, beliefs, personal attributes, life experiences, and ways of living are all intrinsically related to the way they function in a therapeutic setting. If effective therapeutic intervention is to occur, concentrated effort to be aware of these potential influences is vital.

The Therapist as a Person

The personal characteristics and behaviors marital therapists display are intrinsically related to the formation of working relationships that will stimulate couples to move forward in their therapeutic endeavors. It is crucial that therapists be aware of and strive to attain and exhibit those characteristics that will most likely facilitate successful therapeutic outcomes.

The research of Rogers, Gendlin, Kiesler, and Truax (1969) and that of Truax and Carkhuff (1967) presented evidence suggesting that therapists' ability to function in three "core" emotional and interpersonal dimensions has a significant influence on their therapeutic effectiveness. These core characteristics, with descriptions of how each can be communicated to couples, are:

Empathy.   Empathy is a therapist's ability to accurately perceive what partners are experiencing and to communicate that perception to them. An empathic therapist is attuned not only to the verbal expressions of partners but also to the nonverbal aspects of their behavior. By "return communication," an empathic therapist lets a couple know that he or she is aware of positive experiencing as well as their negative distress. This return communication includes acknowledging both what partners are apparently feeling and what they seem to be thinking. For example:

Therapist: It sounds as if you're very angry and you're thinking about how you might get revenge.

When both emotion and thought are reflected, the partner or couple has the option to begin dealing with either; reflecting emotion or thought alone, however, precludes this option. Often couples are impressed by such dual reflections and respond "Yes, that's exactly it."

Respect.   Respect is evident when the therapist indicates a deep and honest acceptance of the worth of a couple in therapy, apart from the partners' behaviors. The mere fact of the partners' existence justifies this respect. The respectful therapist recognizes the rights of a partner or partners to make their own decisions. Even if the therapist is relatively sure that a decision made is an unwise one, much can be learned from the experience of its consequences.

It is especially important that respect be stressed throughout therapy. Egan (1975) identified one critical variable in a therapist's manifesting respect toward a client as "cultivating the resources of the client." This cultivation of a couple's resources follows from a therapist's recognition of the worth and value of that couple. A respectful therapist searches for resources a couple has and helps them identify these assets. That therapist does not act in the couple's stead unless it is absolutely necessary, and then only as a step toward assisting the partners to act on their own. Consider the following example:

Marital Partner: There are a number of things I'm finding very hard to discuss. I'd rather have you just ask me questions and I'll answer them.

Therapist: If I ask you a lot of questions I'm sure I'll get information that I might think is important, but I'm not so sure how valuable that would be for you. Having to discuss specific aspects of their marriage with me is new and difficult for most people, and you're finding it even more so for you.

The therapist assumes that the marital partner does have the personal resources necessary to discuss difficult issues. The therapist expresses this to the partner and tries to understand the partner's reluctance. The therapist communicates respect with willingness to help the marital partner work through any reluctance and to facilitate the utilization of those personal resources potentially available to deal with the issues. Thus, a respectful therapist is neither judging nor overprotective. Instead he or she works to foster a couple's independence, self-confidence, and self-reliance.

Genuineness.   Genuineness is a therapist's ability to be honest with him or herself and with a couple. It has both positive and negative implications; it means doing some things and not doing others (Egan, 1975). A genuine therapist does not take refuge in a professional role. The therapist's basic manner of behavioral expression in therapy is not dramatically different from that outside of therapy. A genuine therapist is also nondefensive. Should a couple express negative attitudes toward the therapist, he or she attempts to understand what the couple is thinking and feeling and continues to work with them, simultaneously seeking to resolve their criticisms. Finally, a genuine therapist is spontaneous, although tactful. This therapist is able to call upon a wide variety of responses, without having to constantly weigh what to say. Carkhuff and Berenson (1977) offer one caution, however: negative therapist genuineness is nonfacilitative. Genuineness should not be confused with a license to say or do what one feels at any moment. A therapist must be guided by what is effective for a couple and, in doing so, may withhold some genuine responses. As Carkhuff and Berenson have stated, a therapist displaying the highest possible level of genuineness is freely and deeply him or herself in the therapeutic relationship; the therapist is completely spontaneous but makes responses that may be hurtful to a couple in a constructive manner, so as to open additional areas of inquiry for both the therapist and the couple.

Although no therapist is likely to possess empathy, respect, and genuineness to the highest possible level, this is not a barrier to success. Effectiveness, and thus success, is not synonymous with perfection. Empathy, respect, and genuineness are best viewed as lying along a continuum. The more they are attained and exhibited the more likely the therapist's effectiveness and experience of therapeutic success. Figure 2-4 pictures this continuum.

Although life and continuing clinical experiences offer the main means of increasing empathy, respect, and genuineness, we as therapist trainers and practicing clinicians always stress the value of personal therapy for therapists. This may be on a continuing or intermittent basis, as called for. All therapists are likely to have some blind spots and unfinished business that can potentially interfere with their effectiveness in working with others. Some have areas in their lives that are not as fully developed as they might be for optimal therapeutic effort. Personal therapy, whether individual, group, or as part of clinical supervision, is one way of coming to grips with these and other issues. In addition, the best way of learning therapeutic empathy is to experience what being a client is really like.

The Therapist as a Professional

In this discussion, we take a somewhat arbitrary focus in considering the therapist "as a professional" without directly taking into account the personal qualities that influence simultaneously the kind of professional he or she is. As was noted earlier, personal characteristics are intrinsically

Poor Therapist Characteristics	Moderately Beneficial Therapist Characteristics	Highly Beneficial Therapist Characteristics
Low Degree of Therapeutic Effectiveness	Moderate Therapeutic Effectiveness	High Degree of Therapeutic Effectiveness
Infrequent Awareness		Constant Awareness
Display of Core Characteristics Inconsistent		Display of Core Characteristics Consistent

FIGURE 2-4.   Therapist's personal-characteristics continuum of therapeutic effectiveness.

related to the manner in which therapists function as professionals. Nevertheless, therapists do have professional identities, and some issues in working with couples are specifically related to therapist professionalism.

A major factor in this regard—one that is frequently overlooked—is the psychotherapeutic community in which therapists function. The psychotherapeutic community is composed both of the immediate arena in which therapists conduct their activities and the broader professional community with which they come in contact. Given the degree of controversy in the field of marital therapy over therapeutic approaches, this community may offer therapists more or less support for their views of marital distress. Depending upon the situation, this can either help or deter therapists—especially beginning therapists—in their struggles to learn their own most effective and efficient manner of therapeutic intervention.

On a more subtle level, the psychotherapeutic community can also promulgate various expectations (at times, unrealistic expectations) that may affect therapists to the degree that the community is an important reference point. Wahle (1976, p. 460), in working with a group of mental health professionals, identified a number of unrealistic expectations they had experienced:

- The therapist should make everything better.
- Confrontation is not nice.
- Being human is bad—we must be strong.
- There is a right way to do it.
- The answer is outside of me.
- I have to have the answer.
- Spontaneity is unprofessional.
- It's wrong to try something unless you know it works.
- I have to be liked.
- Negative feedback means that you don't like me.
- Being perfect is good.
- Craziness is bad.

The major professional associations to which most marital therapists belong (the American Psychological Association, American Personnel and Guidance Association, American Psychiatric Association, American Academy of Psychotherapists, American Association for Marriage and Family Therapy, and National Association of Social Workers) have established codes of ethics that provide guidelines for therapists. Although therapists should be familiar with the ethical standards of the profession, they will still be constantly challenged to develop their own personal professional codes of ethics to govern their practice. The general guidelines offered by professional organizations do not make specific choices for therapists; these guidelines represent only minimal standards of practice. Therapists must strive to develop their own ethical awareness, reflecting on those issues that aren't clear cut. They can then interpret and translate general guidelines into day-to-day choices as professionals in the therapeutic setting.

The Therapeutic Relationship

It is important for a marital therapist to be accurately aware of that process by which a therapeutic relationship between the therapist and a couple with whom he or she works is established and maintained. As this relationship is originated and evolves, the couple and therapist variables previously described in this chapter become especially relevant. One particularly relevant issue in the therapeutic relationship that has not previously been discussed is the manner in which responsibility is divided between the therapist and the couple.

The manner in which the therapeutic relationship is established sets the stage for the therapy process. For this reason, it is of critical importance to consider how responsibility is initially divided between the couple and the therapist. This allocation of responsibility is an active issue, one directly affecting how growth and change occur, and it needs to be examined throughout the therapy process. For example, when therapy reaches a stalemate and is not progressing, it is frequently because the allocation of therapeutic responsibility was mismanaged or had not been successfully completed (Wahle, 1976). Reviewing this responsibility issue can provide a valuable way for therapists to identify why it happened and how to correct it.

One of the most common mistakes beginning therapists make in working with couples is to start dealing with the content of what is distressing the partners without having established a *contract* defining the division of responsibility in the therapeutic relationship. This contract, whether explicit or implicit, is based on negotiations between the therapist and couple about how to define the problem, what the couple expects from therapy, what the therapist feels that he or she is realistically able to do, the therapist's expectations from the couple, and what the partners are willing to commit themselves to do. The contract need not be static; it represents the agreement between the therapist and couple about the context of the entire therapy process, and it may be important to renegotiate or change it at times.

Wahle (1976) suggested that therapeutic responsibility is divided appropriately between the therapist and couple if the therapist is in charge of the treatment and each partner is actively engaged in doing the work necessary to grow and change. A therapist who sets appropriate limits on his or her responsibility is seen as being in charge of treatment. This means functioning with integrity, having a sense of one's own identity apart from the couple, and being able to move freely in and out of the marital system. When in charge, therapists feel comfortable with themselves and what they are doing, not as if they're compromising themselves out of deference to one of the partners or the marital system. This doesn't mean that therapists must remove themselves from the marital system but that they instead constantly examine and be aware of how the system may impinge on them and they on the system.

Establishing an effective therapeutic relationship with a couple can be quite demanding; to avoid judging or taking sides is often difficult. Patience and stamina are needed to stick with many couples, especially when progress appears to be at a standstill. Yet therapists' confidence in their therapeutic abilities and in their skills in providing appropriate direction, combined with a couple's commitment to work on the relationship and individual concerns, will usually lead to successful therapeutic outcomes.

Summary

In this chapter we present some of the basic issues relevant to conducting marital therapy with couples. To provide a background for relating the importance of these primary issues to current practice, we offer a brief presentation of the historical development of current marital theory and therapy. With this as a context, we explore some fundamental assumptions to consider when initiating therapeutic work with couples. These assumptions take three forms.

The first set of assumptions pertains to the couple in marital therapy. We suggest that therapists take into account some general treatment issues, determine the most appropriate unit of treatment, and select a primary theoretical approach in initiating work. The second set of assumptions concerns therapists themselves and their potential impact upon the therapeutic process from both a personal and professional perspective. Third, we address the importance of the appropriate allocation of responsibility as crucial to the success of the therapeutic relationship between therapist and couple.

Our viewpoint in presenting these assumptions for consideration is that accurate comprehension of relevant concepts is critical to achieving successful therapeutic outcomes. There are obviously no clear-cut guidelines. However, from an awareness and understanding of basic couple, therapist, and relationship factors, information essential for fully comprehending and implementing intervention strategies to assist couples experiencing marital distress can be derived.

References

Beck, D. F. Research findings on the outcomes of marital counseling. In D. H. Olson (Ed.), *Treating relationships*. Lake Mills, Iowa: Graphic Publishing, 1976.

Brody, S. Simultaneous psychotherapy of married couples. In J. Masserman (Ed.), *Current psychiatric therapies.* New York: Grune & Stratton, 1961.

Carkhuff, R. R., & Berenson, B. G. *Beyond counseling and therapy* (2nd ed.). New York: Holt, Rinehart & Winston, 1977.

Cuber, J. *Marriage counseling practice.* New York: Appleton-Century-Crofts, 1948.

Egan, G. *The skilled helper: A model for systematic helping and interpersonal relating.* Monterey, Calif.: Brooks/Cole, 1975.

Greer, B., & Solomon, A. Marital disharmony: Concurrent psychotherapy of husband and wife by the psychiatrist. *American Journal of Psychiatry,* 1963, *17,* 443–450.

Gurman, A. S. The effects and effectiveness of marital therapy: A review of outcome research. *Family Process,* 1973, *12,* 145–170.

Gurman, A. S. Contemporary marital therapies: A critique and comparative analysis of psychoanalytic, behavioral and systems theory approaches. In T. J. Paolino, Jr., & B. S. McCrady (Eds.), *Marriage and marital therapy.* New York: Brunner-Mazel, 1978.

Gurman, A. S., & Kniskern, D. F. Research on marital and family therapy: Progress, perspective, and prospect. In S. L. Garfield & A. E. Bergin (Eds.), *Handbook of psychotherapy and behavior change.* New York: Wiley, 1978.

Gurman, A. S., & Kniskern, D. F. (Eds.). *Handbook of family therapy.* New York: Brunner-Mazel, 1980.

Haley, J. Marriage therapy. *Archives of General Psychiatry,* 1963, *8,* 213–234.

Herr, J. J., & Weakland, J. H. *Counseling elders and their families.* New York: Springer, 1979.

Liberman, R. P., Wheeler, E. G., deVisser, L., Kuehnel, J., & Kuehnel, T. *Handbook of marital therapy: A positive approach to helping troubled relationships.* New York: Plenum Press, 1980.

Mace, D. *Marriage counseling.* London: Churchill, 1948.

Manus, G. I. Marriage counseling: A technique in search of a theory. *Journal of Marriage and the Family,* 1966, *28,* 449–453.

Martin, P., & Bird, W. An approach to the psychotherapy of marriage partners: The stereoscopic technique. *Psychiatry,* 1963, *16,* 123–127.

Masters, W. H., & Johnson, V. E. *Human sexual inadequacy.* Boston: Little, Brown, 1970.

Meissner, W. W. The conceptualization of marriage and family dynamics from a psychoanalytic perspective. In T. J. Paolino, Jr., & B. S. McCrady (Eds.), *Marriage and marital therapy.* New York: Brunner-Mazel, 1978.

Minuchin, S. *Families and family therapy.* Cambridge, Mass.: Harvard University Press, 1974.

Mittleman, B. The concurrent analysis of marital couples. *Psychoanalytic Quarterly,* 1948, *17,* 182–197.

Olson, D. Marital and family therapy: Integrative review and critique. *Journal of Marriage and the Family,* 1970, *32,* 501–538.

Olson, D. Empirically unbinding the double bind: Review of research and conceptual reformulations. *Family Process,* 1972, *11,* 69–94.

Olson, D. H., Russell, C., & Sprenkle, D. H. Circumplex model of marital and family systems II: Empirical studies and clinical intervention. In J. P. Vincent (Ed.), *Advances in family intervention, assessment and theory* (Vol. 1). Greenwich, Conn.: JAI Press, 1980a.

Olson, D. H., Russell, C. S., & Sprenkle, D. H. Marital and family therapy: A decade review. *Journal of Marriage and the Family,* 1980b, *42,* 973–993.

Paolino, T. J., Jr., & McCrady, B. S. (Eds.) *Marriage and marital therapy.* New York: Brunner-Mazel, 1978.

Prochaska, J., & Prochaska, J. Twentieth century trends in marriage and marital therapy. In T. J. Paolino, Jr., & B. S. McCrady (Eds.), *Marriage and marital therapy.* New York: Brunner-Mazel, 1978.

Rogers, C., Gendlin, E. T., Kiesler, D. J., & Truax, C. B. *The therapeutic relationship and its impact.* Madison, Wisc.: University of Wisconsin Press, 1969.

Royce, J., & Hagan, P. *Co-therapy in a special situation.* Paper delivered at the meeting of the American Group Psychotherapy Association, 1960.

Satir, V. Conjoint marital therapy. In B. C. Greene (Ed.), *The psychotherapy of marital disharmony.* New York: Free Press, 1965.

Sluzki, C. E. Marital therapy from a systems theory perspective. In T. J. Paolino, Jr., & B. S. McCrady (Eds.), *Marriage and marital therapy.* New York: Brunner-Mazel, 1978.

Steinglass, P. An experimental treatment program for alcoholic couples. *Journal of Studies on Alcohol,* 1979, *40,* 159–182.

Truax, C. B., & Carkhuff, R. R. *Toward effective counseling and psychotherapy: Training and practice.* Chicago: Aldine, 1967.

Wahle, L. P. Learning to work with couples. In H. Grunebaum & J. Christ (Eds.), *Contemporary marriage: Structure, dynamics, and therapy.* Boston: Little, Brown, 1976.

Wertheim, E. Family unit therapy and the science and typology of family systems. *Family Process,* 1973, *12,* 361–376.

Dynamics of Marital Adjustment and Discord

Theoretical models serve a number of important purposes. Conceptually they serve as catalysts for the generation of hypotheses to be tested, thereby refining current ideas and facilitating further theory development. As concerns the therapeutic process, they serve three additional functions essential to the success of any intervention efforts.

First, theoretical models allow therapists to organize the immense amount of information they are confronted with. This information must be prioritized in such a manner that therapists are able to propose potential hypotheses to guide the course of therapy.

Second, theoretical models offer therapists an understanding of adaptive and maladaptive behavior. Although appropriate behaviors are identified primarily as a result of societal values and norms, theory serves to underscore and explain the etiology of behavior, thus forming a basis for the third function.

Third, theoretical models provide a conceptual foundation for developing intervention strategies and determining their appropriateness. In doing so, models propose a role for therapists to pursue in facilitating behavior change.

With Chapter 3 we begin our presentation of the major theoretical approaches to marriage and marital therapy that to date have provided the most substantial models for the understanding and treatment of couples experiencing distress in their relationships. Our presentation of approaches is selective; we base our selection on an in-depth review of the professional literature relating to marital theory and therapy, as well as on questioning discussions with our colleagues concerning their predominant approaches for working with couples.

In Chapter 3 we investigate psychoanalytic theory by focusing on the fundamental concepts of object relations as applied to marriage and marital therapy. Chapter 4 explores the social-learning or behavioral approach for working with couples. Chapter 5 reviews two representative systems-theory approaches and provides conceptualizations of the therapeutic process along with selected treatment techniques derived from each approach. Chapter 6 offers a case illustration designed to show how each of the theoretical orientations discussed might proceed therapeutically with the same couple.

CHAPTER THREE

Psychoanalytic Theory

There can be little argument that psychoanalytic theory has had a greater impact on the conceptualization of human behavior than has any other psychological school of thought. Sigmund Freud, in creating a psychodynamic approach to understanding the human condition, gave psychology a new look and discovered vast new horizons. Freud's work stimulated tremendous controversy and in doing so also encouraged exploration and research and laid the foundation upon which many later psychological systems rest.

In a therapeutic context, as with theory, psychoanalytically oriented therapists did the advance work, examining the nature of marriage and marital dysfunction long before applications to this area by systems theory or social-learning theory even existed (Ackerman, 1958; Mittleman, 1948; Oberndorf, 1938). Orthodox psychoanalytic treatment practices, however, concentrated primarily on the intrapsychic components of marital dysfunction—those within the individual—to the relative exclusion of the interactional aspects of marital relationships—those between individuals. As a result, there is relatively little psychoanalytic theory that directly addresses the treatment of the marital relationship as the primary therapeutic focus. Therefore, while many current marital therapists are significantly influenced by psychoanalytic thought, few interactional treatment strategies have emanated from this approach (Gurman, 1978).

With these circumstances in mind, we approach this chapter with the view that most psychoanalytically oriented marital therapists today are, although psychoanalytic in their understanding of marital dynamics, necessarily eclectic to a great degree in their actual treatment interventions. The work of Ables and Brandsma (1977), Martin (1976), Nadelson (1978), Sager (1976), and Skynner (1976) all support this contention. It is therefore important to separate the theoretical framework and terminology used to conceptualize individual and relationship dynamics from the treatment process itself. (This will be especially evident in the section later in this chapter on the structure of therapy.) The understanding obtained from the psychoanalytic perspective does provide the basis for therapy; however, this basis is relatively independent from the therapist's choice of techniques.

Our main focus in this chapter is object-relations thinking, which is within psychoanalytic theory. Reducing object-relations thought to its central thesis, this phase of psychoanalytic theory asserts that early childhood relationships, especially those with one's parents, shape adult relationships with respect to desires, fears, and expectations. For example, as contrasted with classical psychoanalytic theory, object-relations theory pays far more attention to an infant's seeking a relationship with the mother than does the classical approach, which focuses on the infant's seeking instinctual gratification. By replacing the concept of id, ego, and superego with the concept of internalized "objects" representing early real or fantasized relationships between the child and his or her parents, psychoanalytic theory gains a much clearer application to the study of how adult relationships are influenced by early parental relationships.

Meissner's (1978) description of object-relations thought relating to marital interactions aptly summarizes its application:

> The capacity to successfully function as a spouse is largely a consequence of the spouse's childhood relationships to his own parents. Furthermore, if the family system is conceptualized from a psychoanalytic perspective of object relations, then a logical assumption is that the same strengths and weaknesses are involved in both marital and parent-child relationships [p. 26-27].

Major Concepts

Psychoanalytic theory assumes that intrapsychic factors, those that are conscious and especially those that are unconscious, exert a significant influence on the choice of a marital partner, the nature of partners' subsequent interactions, the kinds of concerns and conflicts partners experience, and the possible resolutions they reach. Intrapsychic factors therefore affect the quality of the entire marital relationship. The psychoanalytic therapist views individual marital partners as functioning according to basic intrapsychic principles.

Psychoanalytic Axioms

Paolino (1978) proposed that in order to fully grasp the therapeutic concepts from which the psychoanalytic approach to marital therapy has evolved it is necessary to understand some basic axioms, which are summarized below:

1. *Unconscious intrapsychic conflicts are the direct cause of marital symptoms.* A dysfunctional marital relationship often results from a collection of psychic "symptoms" belonging to one or both partners. These symptoms emerge from partners' attempts to adjust to unconscious intrapsychic conflicts and to the anxiety that is generated from these conflicts. These intrapsychic conflicts are seen as mental occurrences wherein different psychic parts of the same partner oppose each other. In the traditional Freudian conceptualization, for instance, the primary conflict creating any symptom is the reaction of the ego to the instinctual demands of the id or the moralistic demands of the superego.

Mental symptoms and neurotic anxiety in an objective-relations sense result from some force drawing a partner's mind away from an object, while other influences are attracting him or her toward the object. For example, a husband would like his wife to share decision-making power with him in their relationship but also unconsciously fears that she would then dominate the relationship, as his mother dominated his father. He wants to share power but fears domination; hence, he develops anxiety, stress, and tension, which are manifested in the marital relationship.

Unconscious intrapsychic conflicts within the individual also activate processes called defense mechanisms to deal with anxiety and potential symptom formation. Defense mechanisms can be a major part of partners' transactions as well as being what each partner reacts to in the other's behavior. It is important to understand that defense mechanisms are not necessarily pathological, and that they can have adaptive value if they don't become permanent means of avoiding reality. Because defense mechanisms facilitate stress and anxiety reduction they can be effective in helping partners to achieve their goals. However, if partners' use of defense mechanisms causes distancing or is threatening and excluding it can lead to dissension and hostility in a marriage (Sager, 1976).

The defense utilized depends upon a particular partner's level of personal development and degree of anxiety. All defense mechanisms can be identified on two counts: they operate on an unconscious level, and they either distort or deny reality. The following are brief descriptions of some defense mechanisms commonly exhibited in marital relationships:

Denial. This defense works against anxiety by not allowing recognition of a threatening reality. The partner refuses to accept some aspect of reality that provokes anxiety. For example, a husband won't allow himself to see that his wife is overly critical of him. He instead sees her comments as constructive criticism and tries to change his behavior, failing to see her hostility toward him. To accurately perceive her hostility would mean he would have to challenge what she is doing, and that would be too anxiety provoking.

Displacement. When a problematic person is inaccessible, strong feelings may be displaced—directed toward another person. For example, the husband who comes home from work angry toward his wife instead of the boss who unfairly reprimanded him earlier in the day has displaced his feelings.

Reaction Formation. This is behavior that is directly opposite to that unconsciously wished; when deeper feelings are threatening, a partner may use the cover-up of opposite behavior to deny them. For example, a wife who actually desires a close, loving relationship will not allow herself to feel her husband's attempt to fulfill these desires for fear that she may someday be rejected by him.

Regression. This defense used in a marriage means relating to one's partner from an earlier phase of one's life, when demands were not so great. For example, partners often are seen relating to each other from parent-child roles rather than from adult-to-adult roles, even though the couple may respond to people other than their mates in a perfectly mature and appropriate manner.

Repression. When experiences and the feelings associated with them are traumatic or anxiety provoking they may be forgotten—actually, repressed. Repression is described as pushing unacceptable reality into the unconscious or never becoming conscious of painful thoughts. It is a common defense used in marriage to cope with past anxiety-provoking experiences.

Sublimation. This is using a higher or more socially acceptable outlet for meeting basic desires. It is a defense that often goes along with one or both partners' acceptance of a limitation within a marital relationship. For example, a couple unable to have children of their own became house parents at a home for abandoned children.

2. *Conflict resolution results from making the unconscious conscious.* One of Freud's earliest therapeutic principles was that cures are effected by making the unconscious conscious. As he used the word, *unconscious* refers not only to forgotten memories but also to current psychic processes of which an individual is unaware. Freud later discovered this to be an oversimplified assumption, and then added to this basic principle the tenet that some kind of emotional experience must be associated with intellectual insight in order for any change to result. That is, the individ-

ual must not only know the forgotten desire or idea but must also feel the emotions associated with it, as well as experience more appropriate emotions. Therefore, no matter how painful self-discovery may be, increased awareness of the unconscious combined with a more appropriate emotional experience is ultimately the therapeutic combination necessary to effect resolutions or adaptations to the problems of intrapsychic and external life.

3. *Serial associations are consciously or unconsciously connected.* It is presupposed that verbalizations following one another have some conscious or unconscious connection. And, although a therapist cannot learn the meaning of every verbalization made in therapy, it is assumed that all communication during a therapy session has one or more unconscious meanings. Therefore, any, and likely all, of partners' inhibited and freely expressed communication could and probably will eventually lead to an understanding of the primary intrapsychic conflicts causing the symptoms of marital dysfunction. The therapist's task is to determine which associations are the most clinically significant.

4. *Verbal and emotional expression of thoughts and feelings is superior to the therapeutic influence of deeds.* Emotional insight must come before behavioral change. It is more effective to verbalize and "feel" thoughts and feelings than to act them out. In fact, it may even be destructive to partners' well-being to employ behavioral solutions to intrapsychic conflicts and anxiety if emotional insight has not been experienced. Behavioral attempts at symptom reduction are often seen as ways to avoid the pain of dealing with the intrapsychic conflict. However, initial verbal and emotional insights are viewed as stimulants for additional and similar insights, which eventually lead to more adaptive and constructive actions. Thus, permanent resolution is possible only when there is some modification of the underlying intrapsychic conflicts that are present.

5. *Neurosis is duplicated within the therapeutic setting.* Past and present unconscious intrapsychic infantile and childhood conflicts are gradually and progressively encouraged, mobilized, and reexperienced during the course of therapy; neurosis is duplicated within therapy itself. This is called the *transference neurosis.*

The transference neurosis constitutes the central factor in psychoanalytic theory and clinical practice. It is a process wherein intrapsychic conflicts are purposefully encouraged and manifested in the interaction between the therapist and client. The client is urged to project onto the therapist his or her unconscious wishes and expectations, and to reexperience any projected conflicts with intense affect and fantasy within the therapy setting.

The development of the transference provides a present psychical reality for the exploration of unconscious content and function. It offers a set of currently occurring circumstances upon which to base therapeutic interpretation and insight. The establishment, the nature, the interpretation, and the eventual resolution of transference issues are what ultimately determine psychoanalytic therapeutic success (Elkun, 1980).

Transferences can be formed with all persons, at all places, and at all times and can occur with consistency in marital relationships, with profound effects. Interpretation of the transference relationship that exists between partners also constitutes a major aspect of psychoanalytic marital therapy.

How do these axioms relate to the psychoanalytic approach to marriage and marital therapy? This can be best understood by expounding upon certain core concepts or events in partners' past and present experiences, which we now address.

Family of Origin

Psychoanalytic object-relations theory conceptualizes all interpersonal interactions in terms of the manner in which individuals seek out and become emotionally attached to people and things outside themselves. When two partners enter into a marital relationship, each brings the psychological heritage that has characterized his or her own uniquely personal emotional development. This development is directly related to the parent-child relationships in the partners' families of origin.

In conceptualizing a marital relationship from the psychoanalytic perspective of object relations, one important determination to be made involves identifying the strengths and weaknesses of the parent-child relationships in the partners' families of origin. This includes not only the father-child and mother-child dyadic relationships but also the two-parents-and-child triadic relationships.

The early attachment between mother and child has been shown to be a critical experience (Bowlby, 1968). If there is not "good enough mothering" to provide an attachment experience, subsequent personality development will be impaired (Winnicott, 1965). Therefore that first object relationship, between mother and child, is of crucial importance; it affects the pattern of later interpersonal relationships, one of which may be marriage. The process of forming original object ties is precarious and unpredictable, resulting from the realities and actual requirements of mothering such as nurturing, disciplining, loving, and meeting physical needs. Somewhat similar dynamics apply to the father-child and two-parents-and-child object relationships and their development. Inevitably, for many people, suspicion and even rejection of object relationships in later life derive from early difficulties. All people have some degree of mistrust and reluctance to give love because of past attempts that were not always successful or consistently reciprocated (Fairbairn, 1954).

When individuals reach adolescence new desires relating to dependence and independence emerge, creating conflict between the wish to regress to earlier objects and the want to move toward new ones. At this time, there may be not only a defense against the pressure to form new object ties but also feelings of inability to love, resulting in the adolescent and, later, the adult driving away new and potential love objects in anticipation of disappointment. Thus, in addition to the impact of early family life experiences that were unsatisfactory, anticipation of object loss or of disappointment by the object can play an important part in the development of adult object ties (Nadelson, 1978). Consider the following couple's situation:

> *Bill and Julie came to therapy explaining that Julie wanted children and Bill was unwilling to make that commitment. A historical assessment showed that Bill, the only boy in his family, was adored and pampered by his mother and sisters. He was always their center of attention. Bill's father was threatened by this and competed strongly for his wife's and daughters' attention, ultimately becoming sullen and dissatisfied. As an adult in his own marriage, Bill related well to Julie, but he feared parenthood because of potential identification with his father's circumstances.*

Ambivalence is thus a part of early object relations, with an individual's ego developing through the experiencing of a succession of ambivalent positions toward objects. The development begins with the objects of early infancy in the family of origin, characterized as either good or bad, and evolves toward an integration of ambivalence that can be tolerated in the self and others without having to split the contrasting components into opposing parts (Dicks, 1963). This provides a basis for an internalized object consistency wherein perceived negative responses can be tolerated and mastered.

Since marriage is the nearest adult equivalent to the original parent-child relationships, an important condition for marital satisfaction is to be allowed by one's partner—as well as to allow one's partner—the freedom to bring out infantile or regressive issues without loss of dignity or security. This is made possible through a knowledge that one's partner accepts the needs of his or her mate, because he or she can projectively identify or tolerate these needs as a good parent. The reasons for which marital partners are chosen are therefore of crucial importance in understanding the dynamics of any marital relationship.

Choice of a Marital Partner

The early psychoanalytic view of partner selection was based in the concept of complementarity of needs (Mittleman, 1948; Winch, 1958). This view postulated that an individual with strong needs to be dominant, for example, would seek a mate who has strong needs to be submissive. In psychoanalytic terms, this need-complementarity process represents a form of idealization in which "the object becomes a substitute for some unattained ego ideal of the subject" (Meissner, 1978, p. 41). It has been suggested, however, that this classical model of need complementarity has a major deficiency; because of its nearly exclusive focus on individual mate selection it is a relatively static construct. That is, this psychoanalytic conceptualization attempts to explain how partner A chooses partner B and vice versa but does not clearly account for how or why A and B choose each other as a joint venture (Gurman, 1978).

This deficiency appears to have been clarified, if not resolved, in the work of a number of psychoanalytic practitioners who adhere to a need-complementarity framework of marital choice but do so in a different way. For example, Dicks (1967) refers to the process whereby partners A and B choose each other as a joint venture termed "collusion." This process of collusion involves the "active, yet unconscious, collaboration of the two partners, wherein each partner does not merely 'choose' the other, but enters into an implicit agreement to both choose the other on the basis of one's own unfulfilled needs *and* to form an implicit 'contract' (Sager, 1976; Sager, Gundlach, Kremer, Lenz, & Royce, 1971) to meet the unfulfilled needs of the one chosen" (Gurman, 1978, p. 452). Further, implicit in this contract is a clause that each partner will join his or her mate to protect one another from those aspects of intra- and interpersonal experience wherein anxiety and conflict are present (Dicks, 1967). Therefore, the contract is focused on maintaining each partner's consistent self-perception, and, as a consequence, the unconscious agreement is for each partner to regard the other as that partner needs to regard him- or herself. Stated in this way, need complementarity involves not merely two simultaneously occurring sets of events but rather one shared exchange process, in the definition of self.

Marital Functioning

The marital relationship has been described as one of the most significant human experiences, wherein individual development can be fostered in a number of important ways (Blanck & Blanck, 1968). The establishment of a close and sexual union provides marital partners the unique opportunity to work through and resolve the prohibitions and inhibitions of childhood in the context of a new, adult level of object relations. However, achieving marital satisfaction involves the ability of partners to relate to each other on a reciprocal basis. It assumes that individual development has proceeded beyond the stage of infantile need gratification and that separation from early objects (termed *differentiation*) has occurred. Marriages in which the greatest satisfaction is experienced are those in which both partners entering this phase of life-cycle development have reached a level of maturity with sufficient resources to cope with the future developmental tasks, now both individual and marital, to be mastered. The successfully functioning marital relationship therefore consists of two fully differentiated individuals, both with clear sex roles, who work together to satisfy each other, themselves, and their responsibilities to society (Erikson, 1968).

Unlike the individuals described, many people bring into their marital relationships unresolved developmental conflicts, thereby contributing to potential marital discord and dysfunction. For some, the developmental impetus and the marital relationship's mobilization of potential resources allow further individual developmental work to be done. In others, however, in whom the organization of maladaptive object internalizations blocks the accomplishment of developmental tasks, growth may be impeded, or intrapsychic needs may lead to a search for gratification in marriage for which marriage is an inappropriate vehicle (Meissner, 1978). In such cases, partners' unconscious expectations are simply unrealistic. The frustration resulting from inappropriate needs combined with the inability to cope with the disappointment and disillusionment that result tends to create an environment of continual hostility and antagonism, resulting in a state of severe marital dysfunction.

Obviously, despite growth-oriented purposefulness of marital choice and the growth possibilities inherent in the marital relationship, marital dysfunction is quite common. Besides resulting from the scenario described, marital dysfunction can also arise when the honeymoon is over; that is, when partners begin to sense the reality of who their mates actually are, rather than seeing their mates through the distorted perception of a state of need (Gurman, 1978). Psychoanalytic theory suggests that a major factor in the choice of a marital partner is unconscious idealization—the ego's repression of ambivalent feelings toward a love object—with the resulting conscious perception of only the partner's positive aspects. Paradoxically, the characteristics that initially attracted one partner to another often become the focus if not the cause of marital dysfunction. With the return of previously repressed negative feelings toward the love object (one's partner), the emotions that initially were nonambivalent, as seen through the filter of need complementarity, now become ambivalent, and also become part of one's intrapsychic conflict. What becomes problematic is not a mate's inability to meet his or her partner's needs but the contradictions inherent in the ambivalence within that partner's intrapsychic structure. The contradictions make the partner's needs impossible to fulfill. Consider the following couple's experience:

> *Kathy and Wayne, a couple in their late twenties, came to therapy with Kathy complaining of Wayne's "changing." Kathy was an assertive, controlling, and strong-willed individual. Wayne was successful, efficient, and ambitious at work, but when at home he tended to be lax and often procrastinated in necessary maintenance tasks. The house, for instance, needed numerous minor repairs, which had remained in need of correction for some*

time. Early on it became evident that Kathy had chosen in Wayne a husband whom she perceived as a powerful person in every respect and against whom she was now rebelling, after seeing the reality of his total functioning. Her idealized image of him had eventually become a realistic one—one to which she was unable to adaptively respond.

Another basis for marital dysfunction in a relationship is the advent of a change in one or both partners' needs or role demands at critical developmental life-cycle transition points, such as the birth of the first child or the return to work of a nonworking partner (Gurman, 1978). No such event is sufficient in itself to cause dysfunction in a marital relationship. Rather, it is the combination of the transition-point experience with one or both partners' object relations systems, when the systems are rigid and undifferentiated yet must accommodate the transitional change. The successfully functioning relationship—one in which conflict and concerns can be dealt with appropriately—requires each partner to be able to adapt and change his or her role behaviors in response to his or her mate's needs being expressed. This calls for an emotional flexibility that "betokens a secure sense of identity—adequate ego—strength. It means that the self is sufficiently at ease in varied aspects of itself . . . a person with this degree of ego-strength can bear to see the partner as different, and the self as distinct from the partner without feeling threatened . . . by contrast" (Dicks, 1967, p. 31).

We have presented some of the major concepts relating to psychoanalytic marital therapy. With these basic premises forming a conceptual foundation, we now examine specific aspects of the therapeutic process as seen from a psychoanalytic perspective.

The Therapeutic Process

The classical psychoanalytic position does not offer a distinct approach for the treatment of marital dysfunction, because its goals are exactly the same for marital therapy as for individual therapy. Orthodox psychoanalytic therapists adhere to the view and practice that the marital relationship per se, the interactive variables in marital dysfunction, need not be dealt with. Accordingly, the primary treatment variables to address are instead the intrapsychic ones; and no matter what the presenting problem, individual therapy is the treatment modality of choice.

We agree that individual therapy is appropriate when (1) marital dysfunction is not the primary problem, (2) a couple appears uncommitted to working out their difficulties together, or (3) the therapist is inexperienced or untrained in a conjoint approach. However, when initially one partner or a couple present themselves for therapy, expressing marital difficulties as their primary concern, and when they are motivated to work together with the therapist on alleviating these difficulties, we see a primarily conjoint format as the modality to utilize. And, we have successfully used the conjoint format from a psychoanalytic perspective, focusing on intrapsychic concerns first and foremost. Depending upon the related circumstances, co-therapy, concurrent, or group formats may also be appropriate, as may individual sessions as an adjunct to conjoint sessions. For purposes of this discussion, however, we focus primarily on presenting the therapeutic process in a conjoint setting.

Goals of Therapy

As noted, marital dysfunction is seen by the psychoanalytic therapist as a breakdown in the mutual gratification of the conscious and especially the unconscious needs of both partners. Hence, the primary goal of therapy involves restructuring of both partners' internally based perceptions of, expectations of, and reactions to themselves and each other. That is, the primary goal is to deal with the aspects of personality functioning that are of specific importance to the marital relationship (Gurman, 1978). Although the goals of therapy are primarily oriented toward improving the quality of partners' marital interaction, intrapsychic growth and awareness are seen as the means to this end. Therefore, both individual personality change and, as a consequence, dyadic change are the primary goals of treatment.

Role of the Therapist

The therapist utilizing an object-relations approach to working with a couple focuses on diagnosing and explaining the partners' interactions in terms of the discrepancies between the relationship that is being sought after and that partners intend, and the relationship that exists. The therapist attempts to note, in the partners' dysfunctional interactions, elements of dependency or coercion that point to childhood origins. In doing so, he or she hopes to provoke exploration of these origins and of the consequences resulting from current conscious and unconscious internalizations of them. Often the therapist seeks patterns of mutual dependency and care, as well as agreed-to role performances and expectations that are threatened or disrupted by forces emanating from the childhood remnants. Such patterns, which are unconscious or only partially accessible and recognized, often have played a part in the process of mate selection; now, by paradoxically emerging in a way opposite that initially sought and desired, the patterns lead to marital distress and dysfunction. The identification of these maladaptive internalizations and patterns both reduces the force of behaviors based on them and opens the way for their abandonment.

Therapeutic Relationship

The initial role of the therapist with a couple in marital therapy is to bring that which is out of partners' immediate awareness into their conscious awareness. This includes helping them recognize conflicts, their associated affects and memories, the connections between similar present and past conflict situations, and the means to effectively resolve the conflicts. It is the responsibility of the therapist to help create an atmosphere in which partners can comfortably and with feelings of support allow themselves to experience the effects of their maladaptive intrapsychic conflicts and work to achieve constructive change.

It is best if partners come to therapy with a sense of basic trust. That is, they need enough positive, enriching past experiences of such significant "helping" people as parents, teachers, doctors, and clergy to allow confidence in therapy. Such experiences facilitate partners' allowing themselves to become committed to an in-depth involvement in the "helping" therapeutic relationship, with firm expectations that the relationship will be of assistance to them. Also, the therapist should have the capacity to offer a sense of trust, being empathic with the struggles of the couple and exhibiting a willingness to participate with them in a nonjudgmental, consistent, and supportive manner, as they attempt to resolve their individual and marital concerns. Thus, the couple and the therapist both must contribute to the establishment and maintenance of a workable therapeutic relationship.

The therapist exercises his or her major role through attempts to interrupt established dysfunctional psychical patterns of operation. The actual techniques of pattern interruption include repeated clarification, elaboration, and interpretation of the factors leading to and maintaining current conflict and concern. Even more basic, however, is allowing the dysfunctional patterns to be manifested in therapy; this is accomplished in a large part through the therapist providing a *transference object,* around whom conflicts are reenacted, reexperienced, and eventually resolved. Partners also provide transference objects for each other, and the therapist must interpret these occurrences as he or she would interpret those directed at him- or herself.

If therapeutic efforts are to be successful, transference issues must be *worked through.* That is, partners must explore the parallels between past and present object-relations experiences. It is assumed that unconscious material from early childhood experiences with significant adults causes partners to distort the present and to react to each other or the therapist as they did to their mothers, fathers, or other notable people from their early years. The partners are inappropriately using their reactions to these early relationship experiences as a framework for current living. Consider the experiences of the following couple:

John and Wendy had been married only one year. John's mother had been a dominant, demanding woman, and his father had been passive and subservient to her. John himself had always felt unable to please his mother. Wendy was an only child whose emotionally distant mother and father had never been very encouraging and were, in fact, frequently quite open in their disappointment that they had not had a son. John saw Wendy as competitive and controlling, while Wendy constantly sought John's approval and attention. When he spoke of his concern about satisfying her desires, she only reinforced his anxiety by complaining that he never did a good job at anything.

Gradually, with the therapist's assistance, each partner worked through the transference identification with the other. For instance, where conflict had occurred about having a baby, both partners could understand their respective points of view. Wendy saw her wish for a child as fulfilling her desire for unambivalent love; John saw himself as the baby. He was conflicted about the helplessness he experienced in response to his wife's demands. He recognized that he projected onto Wendy his conflict about being a baby—about being controlled and wanting to be nurtured by his mother. Wendy noted her view of John as the sibling she had not actually had but with whom she had to compete, and always unsuccessfully.

As a result of the therapeutic relationship, partners acquire insights about the unconscious psychodynamics of their marital dysfunction and affectively experience them. As therapy progresses, the clarification/elaboration/interpretation function of the therapist is increasingly taken over by the partners themselves. This results in the establishment of a self-observing and self-analyzing capacity that ensures a couple's ongoing ability to confront new marital stresses, as well as to continue to deal with past stresses, should they reemerge.

Structure of Therapy

In presenting a structural conceptualization of the psychoanalytic therapy process, we emphasize that the various stages are presented as separate and distinct entities for the purpose of clarity. In reality, the stages and the variables particular to each often overlap considerably, or they are repeated or even purposefully overlooked. The structure presented is merely intended as a guide or cognitive map for better understanding how the therapy process might ideally proceed.

Nadelson (1978) identified a four-stage conceptualization of the marital therapy process from a psychoanalytic perspective. As we review each of these four stages, we highlight the therapeutic concerns that accompany each stage. As we do, remember our earlier cautions that many psychoanalytic marital therapists are eclectic in their selection of treatment interventions. Nadelson's approach to the therapeutic process exemplifies the use of psychoanalytic theory for background along with more recently developed techniques. While psychoanalytic theory obviously provides the basic understanding for her overall treatment strategy, and intrapsychic factors provide her primary therapeutic focus, she also includes teaching couples communication and problem-solving procedures as additional means of improving their marital interactions.

Stage 1. Contract Negotiation.   During this initial stage of therapy a therapeutic contract is negotiated. This includes the administrative aspects of therapy, such as fees, vacations, and appointment times. The contract negotiation also involves an assessment and affirmation of a couple's goals and motivation for therapy. Once a basic diagnosis has been arrived at, the form of therapy is another area to discuss. For example, are marital issues the primary concern, and are both partners motivated to work on them? If so, then a conjoint format is indicated.

Problems with these initial therapeutic aspects may foreshadow future resistances between the partners, individual partners and the therapist, or both partners and the therapist. It is in this stage that the basis for the therapeutic alliance is formed. If feelings of mistrust or suspicions of collusion develop, or if therapy becomes focused on a struggle for power or control between one or both partners and the therapist, rather than on a commitment to work together, the necessary therapeutic alliance cannot begin to evolve.

Stage 2. Initial Phase of Treatment.   This stage of therapy involves the clarification of communication patterns between partners, the development of tools for effective problem solving, and the establishment of the therapeutic alliance. Couples in this stage are facilitated in becoming aware of the nature of their interaction as two separate individuals with different past experiences, needs, and perceptions who have entered into a mutual relationship. The primary focus of therapeutic efforts in this initial phase is on the symptoms presented by the couple. While underlying intrapsychic issues are identified, interpretations made by the therapist are focused more often on the partners' interaction and the psychic elements that relate to it than on either partner's separate functioning. The emphasis is on communication and role patterns. In addition, the presenting symptoms are explored, and partners are assisted in attempting to deal with them. Concrete and specific concerns are the focus—for example, children, finances, and in-laws.

Stage 3. Middle Stage of Therapy.   In this stage of the therapeutic process, the therapist assists partners to strengthen their alliances with each other by encouraging them to share past experiences and crisis perceptions and events. This facilitates partners in being more empathetic and supportive of each other and can lead to a renewal of their original marital commitment to each other. The understanding of unconscious material becomes an integral part of the therapy during this middle stage. The interpretation of unconscious material is more in-depth in this stage, with the therapist more often including him or herself as a participant in the interaction. The form and content of the therapeutic alliance also provides significant interpretive material. The therapist can use the alliance to interpret and clarify pathological defensive maneuvers that partners may employ in therapy as well as in their marital relationship. Several levels of transference of one partner to the other and to the therapist are also addressed. In this middle stage of therapy, simple motivation may be insufficient for successful therapeutic work. Partners need the abilities to develop a working therapeutic alliance and to tolerate an amount of delay and anxiety. They also need to develop an observing ego, which enables them to understand, affectively experience, and integrate what occurs in therapy, in order to produce insight and change.

Stage 4. Termination Phase.   Termination is often a time when many conflicts and defenses reemerge. During this time, the therapist assists the couple in identifying and working through the anxiety they are likely to experience regarding this separation, and also reviews and further defines the therapeutic gains achieved. Individual and couple dynamics dealing with separation are clarified and interpreted. The primary therapeutic objective during termination is to decrease partners' ambivalent feelings about separation from the therapist, to reinforce gains that have been made, and to develop techniques for continued psychic growth. The end point of therapy is usually the acceptance and understanding of the integrity of each partner by the other and the development of mechanisms of conflict resolution that evolve from this mutual respect and commitment.

The treatment of marital dysfunctions with a psychoanalytic approach can often be a complicated process. The therapist not only must understand major theoretical concepts and be able to conceptualize their application to varying dysfunctions but must also have developed a repertoire of techniques and procedures to effectively intervene therapeutically with couples. Having addressed theoretical issues of the therapeutic process generally, we turn to a presentation of relevant techniques and procedures for the psychoanalytic marital therapist to employ.

Therapeutic Techniques and Procedures

The techniques and procedures employed during psychoanalytic marital therapy are geared to gaining intellectual insights into partners' behaviors, and to understanding the meaning of the symptoms the behaviors present. The therapeutic progression is from diagnosis of partners' individual and marital dysfunction, to working through unconscious intrapsychic material toward the therapeutic objectives of intellectual and affective understanding, and finally to experiencing and reconceptualization, which, it is hoped, will lead to individual and dyadic change.

Assessment of Marital Dysfunction

Accurate and appropriate assessment of marital dysfunction is perhaps the most critical component of a psychoanalytic therapist's skill repertoire. In marital therapy, the diagnosis itself can effect a dynamic understanding of each partner and his or her contribution to the marital dysfunction. The diagnosis allows the therapist to determine what problems must be addressed and which intervention strategies are most likely to achieve the desired results. Of equal concern is assessment of partners' commitment and motivation to change and the type of change sought.

Although a presenting problem of marital distress requires the participation of both partners for any therapeutic plan to be developed, it has been suggested that partners be evaluated individually and then be seen as a couple (Nadelson, 1978). The therapist should emphasize the confidentiality of the individual session so that the partner present feels free to share with the therapist what may not be readily expressed with both mates present. (Another reason to see partners separately for evaluation purposes.) For example, a partner may actually be seeking to end the marital relationship and coming to therapy only as a way of minimizing future guilt feelings, with the thought that "I did all I could to make the marriage work." If such a circumstance is not identified early, it will arise early during therapy as resistance that the therapist will be at a loss to understand and that will thus block therapeutic progress entirely.

Gurman (1978) has proposed that a distinction be made between the painstaking rigid diagnostic procedures and techniques that occur in individual psychoanalysis and the relative lack of agreement as to what constitutes necessary assessment dimensions in psychoanalytic marital therapy. It is his belief that psychoanalytic marital assessment largely reflects the interests of the individual therapist. With this in mind, we present the psychoanalytic diagnostic procedure found by Martin (1976) to provide succinct information to guide his therapeutic efforts in working with couples.

Martin outlined a psychoanalytic diagnostic procedure for therapists to follow when gathering information for the purpose of better understanding who these individuals are that entered into this relationship with each other; how the relationship promotes, impedes, or prevents the continuing growth and development of these two people; what specific areas need treatment; and the best means of treatment. The three-point outline of Martin's diagnostic procedure first encompasses an opening presentation, then an individual history of each partner, and finally a history of the marital relationship. From the information gathered, therapeutic objectives and plans are formulated.

Opening Presentation.   The data the therapist gathers during this aspect of the assessment concerns the major complaints of each partner about the marriage, their mates, children, and other areas of perceived distress. Information about positive factors in each of these areas is also requested. "What needs to be increased and what needs to be decreased?" is the primary question for the therapist and partners to consider. The positive forces that brought the partners together originally and the manner in which individual needs were curtailed to make the relationship initially satisfying are identified, as are the forces presently promoting dysfunctional interactions. This opening information is used to begin determining what has to be changed and what, if anything, is available to replace that which may be removed in the changes.

Individual History of Each Partner.   After gathering the opening information, the therapist assesses the individual life history of each partner in five specific areas of inquiry.

1. *Earliest Memories.* People's memories evoke questions that provide leads for determining images that partners hold of both themselves and the family figures either present in the memories or conspicuous by their absence. The emotions accompanying these memories provide additional understanding, about the partners' perceptions of themselves and of people significant early in their lives.

2. *Later Childhood and Adolescent Memories.* Using earliest memories as a beginning point, remembrances of any childhood difficulties are assessed. These might include toilet training, thumb sucking, bed-wetting, illnesses, and fearful incidents, with their accompanying emotions. Family history and the history of parents' marriages are also assessed, since they can provide understanding of partners' identifications and of repetitions being carried into their own marriage. Information about school, such as scholastic and academic abilities and peer-group relations provide pictures of partners' early lives outside their families. Taking this history through adolescence provides data concerning dating and sexual experiences prior to the couple's meeting, all of which sheds light on the dynamics that may operate in the partners' current marital relationship.

3. *Dreams.* Questions about dreams, especially recurrent dreams during childhood and adolescence, often add to an understanding of partners' development during that time of their lives. Current dreams often provide a clearer conceptualization of the dynamics of present marital dysfunction. Martin (1976) offered the following case example of this:

A man with depression and onset of obsessive thoughts of suicide has a current dream of his wife and two children who have fallen overboard from their sailboat. He is frantically but unsuccessfully trying to reach them before they drown. A case history showed that his symptoms developed two months before, and that he was married four months before to a widow with two children [p. 72].

4. *Fantasies.* Conscious fantasies and daydreams about one's partner or the marriage, as well as past, present, and long-standing fantasies, provide information similar to that offered by dream analysis. The nature of the relationship between participants in a fantasy can be enlightening.

5. *Medical History.* A medical history is important to a complete diagnostic picture. It is necessary to differentiate psychic problems that lead to physical symptoms from physical conditions that cause psychological symptoms.

History of the Marital Relationship.   Using the partners' individual histories as a basis for understanding, in the last segment of the assessment process the history of the marital relationship is examined. Why partners chose each other and their original marriage contract provides the first focus of attention. Developmental stages relating to the marital life cycle are then investigated as they relate to the onset and course of complaints and symptoms leading to the current dysfunction in the relationship. A sexual history and considerations regarding the therapeutic contract conclude the diagnostic procedure.

1. *The Marriage Contract.* The accompanying box presents a schematic model of the "marriage contract," a clinical tool for the clarification and treatment of marital dysfunction developed by Sager, Gundlach, Kremer, Lenz, and Royce (1971).

Their conceptualization involves a couple's expressed and unexpressed, conscious and unconscious beliefs about the partners' obligation within the relationship as well as the benefits they expect to derive from the relationship and, individually, their mates. Much of the material previously assessed will have already revealed many of the conscious and unconscious aspects of the marriage contract. Further questioning will clarify these areas and also provide additional data for mapping areas of agreement and disagreement on which to base treatment intervention procedures. Specific questions for this purpose suggested by Martin (1976) include:

• What qualities and characteristics of your partner were most important to you when you married, and why?
• Are they still important to you?
• Are there other aspects of your partner that have become important to you since you married?

THE MARRIAGE CONTRACT

Terms of Agreement
that are Conscious

- **Verbalized**. What each partner expresses to a mate in clearly understandable language concerning his or her expectations. Although partners may express themselves understandably, this does not necessarily mean that the messages have been heard, or, if so, that they have been clearly comprehended and accepted. Also, many expectations expressed in too general a manner, as a desire or loosely defined plan rather than in such straight forward terms as "This is what I expect."

- **Not Verbalized**. Each partner's expectations, plans, beliefs, and fantasies that differ from the verbalized terms only in not being said aloud, usually because of possible embarrassment or fear of rejection. Difficulties potentially traceable to unverbalized conscious terms include uncertainties about the marital relationship, behaviors causing irritation and conflict, and a variety of disappointments. At times, willful deceptions for purposes of self-gain are effected through conscious but unverbalized terms of agreement.

Terms of Agreement
that are Unconscious

- **Beyond Awareness**. The desires or needs of a partner who has no immediate awareness of them. Often these are unrealistic and contradictory. They may be similar to or in conflict with the needs and expectations understood in conscious terms, both verbalized and not verbalized. Some terms may be preconscious—close to the surface. Others may be further from awareness. Potential difficulties with unconscious terms of agreement include unrecognized needs for intrapsychic power, control, or dependency, and parent-child conflicts emanating from partners' families of origin.

- What parts of your life experience influenced your desiring certain qualities and characteristics in a marital partner? Have your life experiences since then changed your desires?
- How reasonable did your desires and expectations seem to you before marriage? Do they seem as reasonable to you now?
- Do you want to change any expectations you have for your partner? Do you want to change his or her expectations of you? Of him- or herself?

Responses to questions regarding the marriage contract provide especially valuable diagnostic information in formulating a direction for the therapy to follow.

2. *The Marital Life Cycle.* Questioning concerning marital life-cycle development is to determine whether marital adjustment tasks for specific stages of development have been successfully achieved and, if they have not, what conflicts have resulted as a consequence. (See Chapter 1 for a more complete discussion and outline of this concept.)

3. *Sexual History.* Many aspects of the couple's history will have already been revealed without in-depth questioning specifically about it. However, this area is one that is especially likely to be avoided or disguised by many couples. Sexual problems, because they often mask underlying individual and relationship problems, must be adequately assessed in order to determine their relevance to other aspects of the marital dysfunction as well as to the dysfunction as a whole.

4. *The Therapeutic Contract.* The marriage contract has both conscious and unconscious aspects. A similar type of contract exists within the therapeutic relationship. An assessment of how partners formulated their marriage contract often indicates how they will react in establishing and maintaining a therapeutic contract. What are their beliefs and expectations about their obligations within the therapeutic relationship, and what benefits do they expect to derive from that relationship and from the therapist in particular? An understanding by the therapist of these conscious and unconscious areas of agreement and disagreement allows for the interpretation of ineffective contracts and the development of more workable contracts. In addition, in the therapist's continual assessing and clarifying the therapeutic contract as therapy proceeds and facilitating its utility with a couple, the couple gains a model to follow in establishing and maintaining their own workable marriage contract.

Intervention Strategies

Five basic therapeutic techniques—intervention strategies—are fundamental to conducting marital therapy from a psychoanalytic perspective. These are: (1) development of the therapeutic alliance, (2) interpretation, (3) dream work, (4) analysis and interpretation of resistance, and

(5) analysis and interpretation of transference and countertransference. In addition to discussion of these five, we include a short discussion of intervention strategies emanating from other theoretical stances that are often employed by psychoanalytically oriented marital therapists.

Development of the Therapeutic Alliance.   The therapeutic alliance is defined as the working relationship between the partners and the therapist. The basis for developing this relationship lies in helping a couple to ally themselves with the "observing ego" of the therapist in order to better understand the conflicts and overall marital dysfunction they are experiencing. For progress in therapy to occur, it is vital that the couple be able to identify with the logic of the therapist. Even when seeing the therapist in a distorted manner as a consequence of a transference neurosis, partners must still be able to ally themselves with this logic, in order to appropriately analyze their situation. This requires a mature capacity on the part of partners to maintain object relationships—to have a sense of self and the therapist as separate.

Building a trusting relationship between partners and the therapist establishes the basis for the therapeutic alliance. The therapist and couple work together to reach agreement on goals and expectations for therapy. There also must be motivation to examine and deal with the determinants of any resistances that may arise. The agreement and the motivation are the key aspects of the therapeutic alliance, and weakness in either blocks therapeutic efforts. For example, both partners may outwardly state that they would like their relationship to succeed, when one partner is actually poorly motivated and would just as soon end the relationship as expend any real effort to continue.

Smith and Grunebaum (1976) identified a number of constellations of partners' lack of agreement or motivation, which are thus detrimental to the formation of the therapeutic alliance. These constellations, each characterized by a phrase encapsulating the primary dynamic, are summarized here:

Looking for an Exit. In this constellation characterized by the search for an exit, the request for therapeutic assistance is actually a covert communication of the desire of one or both partners to end the marriage with a minimum of guilt. "I did all I could to save the marriage, even therapy."

Looking for an Ally. This situation has one or both partners seeking to utilize the therapist to gain the strength to stand up to their mates. "I'm in the right, as you can obviously see, so let's convince my partner of his/her wrong behavior."

Looking for Reentry. This constellation is composed of partners who seek professional assistance for marital problems in the hope that the therapist will declare them in some sense sick and thereby enable them to get back into their marriage. "I'm an alcoholic and not fully responsible for my destructive actions."

Response to an Ultimatum. In this case, an ultimatum has instigated the request for the therapist's help. "Go to therapy or else!" The ultimatum can be issued to a partner by his or her mate or to both partners by an outside authority—for example, by the judicial system.

Avoidance of Self-Observation. This situation presents itself when one partner complains excessively about his or her mate and how he or she must change, in a concentrated effort to resist self-examination and change. This partner seeks no ally, being fully confident and unfortunately quite rigid in his or her beliefs. "It's all my partner's problem, not mine."

Being able to recognize and understand the dynamics involved in these constellations can facilitate their being dealt with appropriately. Blocking of the therapeutic alliance through agreement and motivation that are lacking or are inappropriately directed should be diagnosed by the therapist as resistance, and should be interpreted and worked through accordingly. For the work of therapy, recognition and eventual understanding of the dynamics of the therapeutic alliance are just as essential as recognition and understanding of therapeutic insights regarding marital interactions.

Interpretation.   Interpretation is the fundamental means utilized by the psychoanalytic therapist in analyzing dreams, resistances, transferences, and other intrapsychic therapeutic phenomena. Interpretation consists of the therapist's pointing out, explaining, and even teaching partners the meaning of behaviors that are manifested by these intrapsychic elements. The functions of interpretation are to allow partners to assimilate new material and to speed up the process of uncovering further unconscious material. The interpretations are aimed at providing insight and at unblocking unconscious material relating to partners' dysfunctional behaviors.

The main consideration in how to use the technique of interpretation is appropriate timing. Inappropriately timed interpretations will likely be rejected. Generally, the risk of rejection is lessened if the interpretation is presented at a point when the experience to be interpreted is close to partners' awareness. The interpretation is thus of material that partners have not yet seen for themselves but are capable of tolerating and incorporating as their own. A second important consideration in the use of interpretation is that its elaboration should proceed only as far as the partners are able to follow while experiencing the situation emotionally. The importance of this consideration is based in the fundamental psychoanalytic belief that emotional experience must accompany intellectual insight in order for any meaningful change to result from making the unconscious conscious.

A third and final consideration in utilizing interpretation is that it is best to point out the resistance or defense before interpreting the emotion or conflict that lies beneath it. This is simply for the sake of clearer conceptualization or association on the part of the partners whose experiences or behaviors are the focus of the interpretation.

Dream Work.   Dream analysis is an important procedure for bringing unconscious material to light and giving partners insight into areas of unresolved conflicts. Freud saw dreams as the "royal road to the unconscious," for he believed that in dreams unconscious desires, needs, and fears are expressed. Freud proposed that, during sleep, defenses are lowered and repressed feelings are able to surface. Some of these feelings are so unacceptable to the dreamer that even in sleep they are expressed only in disguised or symbolic form, rather than being revealed openly and directly.

Dreams are perceived as having two levels of content: latent and manifest. Latent content is the disguised, hidden, and symbolic unconscious aspects of dreams. Because these aspects are so painful and threatening, the latent content is transformed into the more acceptable manifest content, which is the dream as it appears to the dreamer. The therapist's task is to uncover the unconscious and disguised latent content by analyzing and interpreting the manifest content of a dream. This is often accomplished by analyzing the manifest content with regard to concerns, experiences, and communications being expressed by partners to the therapist or to each other during therapy. An illustration of the applicability of dream work in marital therapy is the case example offered by Martin (1976) that is included in the preceding section of this chapter on assessments.

Analysis and Interpretation of Resistance.   Resistance is anything that works against the progress of therapy, prevents partners from producing unconscious material, or both. It often arises as a defense against change and thereby blocks the giving up of maladaptive mechanisms of functioning that have been identified during therapy. Identification of resistance and intervention regarding it are especially relevant to marital therapy. Consider, for example, the resistance constellations identified by Smith and Grunebaum (1976) cited previously as potential threats to the formation of the therapeutic alliance. Other forms of resistance abound at all phases of the marital therapy process.

Freud viewed resistance as an unconscious dynamic that attempts to defend an individual against anxiety feared to be intolerable that would arise if he or she were to become aware of repressed feelings and impulses. Seen as a defense against anxiety, resistance operates in psychoanalytic marital therapy by preventing a couple and the therapist from succeeding in their efforts to gain what is often painful and anxiety-provoking insight into partners' unconscious thoughts. Since resistance keeps from awareness the material that, although threatening, can effect therapeutic insight and emotional experiencing, the therapist must point it out and partners must confront it.

The therapist's interpretation of resistance is aimed at assisting partners to gain insight into the reasons for the resistance so they can begin to deal with it. As with any interpretation, it is generally best to initially call partners' attention to the most obvious resistances in order to both lessen the possibility of their rejecting the interpretations and to increase the probability that they will begin to examine these resistances.

Resistances are not merely behaviors to be changed. Because they are representative of partners' usual defense approaches in their marriage and daily lives, resistances must be identified not only as devices that defend against anxiety but also as devices that interfere with partners' ability to experience general marital satisfaction and more gratifying experience of life. Similarly, resistance devices interfere with partners' progress in therapy. Working through them not only alleviates the maladaptive behaviors but increases satisfaction in life, as well as increasing progress in therapy.

Analysis and Interpretation of Transference and Countertransference. Transference, with the potential of accompanying countertransference, is likely the most fundamental treatment concept in the practice of psychoanalytic marital therapy. Transference is manifested in the therapeutic process and in the marital relationship as well. It occurs when partners project early objects that were internalized onto each other or onto the therapist, causing the partners to distort the present and to react to each other or the therapist as they did to significant others in their past. Countertransference is a reaction: the transference reaction of the individual at whom the projecting was directed.

When a couple enters marital therapy, there is already an ongoing transference interaction between the partners. Therefore the therapist will have to consider at least five potential transference manifestations: (1) husband to wife, (2) wife to husband, (3) husband to therapist, (4) wife to therapist, and (5) couple to therapist. And, corresponding to these potential transference manifestations, there are possible countertransference reactions (Nadelson, 1978).

Interpretation of transference and countertransference responses of partners is the primary technique of dealing with these manifestations. When negative images are projected onto one partner, he or she may respond through a distorted view emanating from his or her own early internalized objects. Thus an unconscious collusive interaction occurs, which can maintain a dysfunctional state in a marital relationship indefinitely. It is this process that the therapist must understand and interpret to partners if constructive change is to take place. The interpretation enables partners to achieve insight into the nature of their individual intrapsychic conflicts and provides an understanding of how internalized past objects are related to present functioning. Interpretation gives partners the information required to work through old maladaptive conflicts that presently keep them from achieving more satisfying relations. As another result of interpretation of transference/countertransference behaviors, symptoms that are present may be improved. The interpretation often can provide a rationale for what was seen as irrational behavior, thereby relieving guilt, confusion, or frustrations that had resulted from self-blame for a partner's responses (Sager, 1967).

Any transference and countertransference manifestations may be extremely significant. It should be emphasized, however, that it is not necessary to completely resolve all transference or countertransference issues. Transference and countertransference are addressed in therapy only insofar as they have a pathological effect on a couple's interaction. Accordingly, some defenses are analyzed; others, with adaptive value, are supported (Nadelson, 1978).

The therapist's own reactions and conflicts can often enter into the therapeutic setting in the form of a countertransference toward one or both partners and can thereby block his or her ability to assist the couple. Thus, it is critical that therapists be aware of how their own intrapsychic conflicts can be triggered by some clients. The therapist must guard against potential disturbing countertransference effects by developing some level of objectivity, and must not react irrationally and oversubjectively in the face of anger, love, criticism, admiration, or other intense feelings from his or her clients. If a therapist becomes aware of negative countertransference symptoms, such as an excessively strong attraction or aversion to certain types of clients or psychosomatic reactions at definable times in the therapeutic relationship, it behooves him or her to seek professional consultation or to enter therapy for a time, to work through any issues that block therapeutic effectiveness (Corey, 1982).

A caution: it is a mistake to assume that all intense feelings occurring within therapy are manifestations of transference or countertransference issues. Many reactions have a reality base and may simply be directed to the here-and-now of the present therapeutic setting. Transference and countertransference are recognizable when there is inappropriate affect, when individuals respond in unrealistic ways or from distorted perceptions, or when objectivity is lost due to the triggering of intense intrapsychic conflicts.

Based on the circumstances, the therapist must choose what to interpret or clarify and the level of interpretation and clarification most appropriate. Most important to consider, however, is the goal for that stage of the therapeutic process and the degree of probability that the intervention regarding the manifestation of transference and countertransference will lead toward that goal.

Associated Intervention.   Gurman (1978) proposed that the psychoanalytic approach to marital therapy requires a great deal of "technical flexibility" on the part of the therapist. In this regard, he stated: "The truth of the matter is that psychoanalytically oriented marriage therapy is largely 'analytic' in the way it organizes the complex material at hand and conceptualizes the nature of marital discord, but is, of necessity, quite pragmatic, if not eclectic, in its selection of actual therapeutic interventions" (p. 466).

In this vein, Berman and Lief (1975) endorse a "systems-behavioral approach as particularly helpful" (p. 584). Sager (1976) and Martin (1976), both psychoanalytically oriented by training and in current practice, often employ essentially the type of strategies involving contracts that were developed by behavioral marital therapists. Further, Nadelson, Bassuk, Hopps, and Boutelle (1977) include among their intervention strategies the development of tools for effective problem solving, of techniques for clarifying communication patterns, and of skills for negotiating concrete and specific issues, such as budgeting and doing housework.

In the upcoming chapters, these associated strategies and others are presented. As they are discussed in more detail, their potential for use within a primarily psychoanalytic perspective will become clearer.

Evaluation and Summary

This chapter has described the major aspects of the psychoanalytic approach to understanding marriage and marital therapy. Despite the fact that psychoanalytic object-relations theory has added greatly to the understanding of subtle and vague aspects of marriage, it has yet to foster the development of new techniques and procedures with which to therapeutically intervene. Therefore, while most psychoanalytically oriented marital therapists are psychoanalytic in their basic conceptualization of marital dynamics, they are also rather eclectic in their use of treatment interventions. The psychoanalytic interventions of interpretation, dream work, and analysis of resistance and transference are employed, but contributions from other approaches (some usually thought to be irreconcilable with individual psychoanalytic theory and treatment) are also incorporated into the therapeutic process.

Of special relevance to the treatment of marital dysfunction, the psychoanalytic approach does provide an understanding of both the function and the meaning of marital behaviors that on the surface may appear completely confusing. For example, consider a person deeply involved in a marriage yet coldly alienating his or her partner. Although expressing a desire for a close, loving relationship, this partner will not allow the other to meet the need, for fear of eventual rejection. The mechanism of reaction formation casts light on the contradictory behavior.

The object-relations explanation of marital choice, conflict, and interaction, by viewing marriage as a logical outgrowth of prior interpersonal experiences, also offers a rich perspective for understanding the interactive influences of individual development on marital relationships. A therapist who ignores the early histories of marital partners truly limits understanding of the bases for current mental dysfunction. We don't suggest that the past is all-important; however, to completely deemphasize early experiences as determinants of current behavior restricts the therapist's ability to assist couples in distress. Consider the partner described as fearful of forming a close relationship. Understanding the roots of this fear provides the therapist and marital partner with a framework for working through them.

The psychoanalytic approach is of particular treatment value in its focus on transference and countertransference issues. Viewing the therapeutic relationships themselves (both therapist-partner(s), and partner-partner) as vehicles for change offers marital therapists the opportunity to help couples experience and understand influences of the past in the here-and-now therapy. Old conflicts that retard emotional and interpersonal growth can be addressed directly. In essence, analysis of transference and countertransference allows the psychopathological effects of undesirable early relationships to be counteracted by being worked through in a similarly emotionally conflicted experience within the therapeutic setting.

Some additional applications to consider in reviewing this approach include the following:

- understanding how the overuse of defense mechanisms can keep partners from functioning effectively and recognizing the ways these defenses operate both in the therapeutic and marital relationships;
- recognizing that difficulty in forming early relationship ties can lead to faulty interpersonal relationship development later in life and why this occurs;
- acknowledging the effects of resistance (for example, missed appointments, premature termination of therapy, and partners' refusal to explore themselves, their relationship, or both) on therapeutic efforts.

Finally, we note that the psychoanalytic approach to marital therapy has become increasingly criticized for its lack of experimental validation. It is true that many of its concepts have not yet stood the test of the experimental method, but is experimentation the only approach to truth? Many of the major concepts have been quite adequately verified by clinical experience. Therapists, irrespective of their main theoretical orientations, accept aspects of the psychoanalytic perspective, incorporating in therapy much of the understanding and many of the methods of this approach.

References

Ables, B., & Brandsma, J. *Therapy for couples.* San Francisco: Jossey-Bass, 1977.

Ackerman, N. *The psychodynamics of family life.* New York: Basic Books, 1958.

Berman, E. M., & Lief, H. I. Marital therapy from a psychiatric perspective: An overview. *American Journal of Psychiatry,* 1975, *132,* 583–592.

Blanck, R., & Blanck, G. *Marriage and personal development.* New York: Columbia University Press, 1968.

Bowlby, J. *Attachment and loss: Attachment* (Vol. 1). London: Tavistock, 1968.

Corey, G. *Theory and practice of counseling and psychotherapy* (2nd ed.). Monterey, Calif.: Brooks/Cole, 1982.

Dicks, H. V. Object relations theory and marital studies. *British Journal of Medical Psychology,* 1963, *36,* 125.

Dicks, H. V. *Marital tensions.* New York: Basic Books, 1967.

Elkun, L. Family therapy and psychoanalysis. In W. M. Walsh (Ed.), *A primer in family therapy.* Springfield, Ill.: Charles C. Thomas, 1980.

Erikson, E. *Identity, youth and crisis.* New York: Norton, 1968.

Fairbairn, W. R. D. *An object relations theory of personality.* New York: Basic Books, 1954.

Gurman, A. S. Contemporary marital therapies: A critique and comparative analysis of psychoanalytic, behavioral, and systems theory approaches. In T. J. Paolino, Jr. & B. S. McCrady (Eds.), *Marriage and marital therapy.* New York: Brunner-Mazel, 1978.

Martin, P. A. *A marital therapy manual.* New York: Brunner-Mazel, 1976.

Meissner, W. W. The conceptualization of marriage and family dynamics from a psychoanalytic perspective. In T. J. Paolino, Jr. & B. S. McCrady (Eds.), *Marriage and marital therapy.* New York: Brunner-Mazel, 1978.

Mittleman, B. Concurrent analysis of marital couples. *Psychoanalytic Quarterly,* 1948, *17,* 182–197.

Nadelson, C. C. Marital therapy from a psychoanalytic perspective. In T. J. Paolino, Jr. & B. S. McCrady (Eds.), *Marriage and marital therapy.* New York: Brunner-Mazel, 1978.

Nadelson, C., Bassuk, E., Hopps, C., & Boutelle, W. Conjoint marital psychotherapy: Treatment techniques. *Psychiatric Quarterly,* 1977, *38,* 898–907.

Oberndorf, C. P. Psychoanalysis of married couples. *Psychoanalytic Review,* 1938, *25,* 453–475.

Paolino, T. J. Introduction: Some basic concepts of psychoanalytic psychotherapy. In T. J. Paolino, Jr. & B. S. McCrady (Eds.), *Marriage and marital therapy.* New York: Brunner-Mazel, 1978.

Sager, C. Transference in conjoint treatment of married couples. *Archives of General Psychiatry,* 1967, *16,* 185–193.

Sager, C. *Marriage contracts and couple therapy.* New York: Brunner-Mazel, 1976.

Sager, C., Gundlach, R., Kremer, M., Lenz, R., & Royce, J. R. The marriage contract. *Family Process,* 1971, *10,* 311–326.

Skynner, A. C. R. *Systems of family and marital psychotherapy.* New York: Brunner-Mazel, 1976.

Smith, J. W., & Grunebaum, H. The therapeutic alliance in marital therapy. In H.

Grunebaum & J. Christ (Eds.), *Contemporary marriage: Structure, dynamics, and therapy*. Boston: Little, Brown, 1976.

Winch, R. F. *Mate-selection: A study of complementary needs*. New York: Harper & Row, 1958.

Winnicott, D. W. *The maturational processes and the facilitating environment*. New York: International Universities Press, 1965.

CHAPTER FOUR

Social-Learning Theory

Social-learning theory has its basis in the general principles of learning theory or behaviorism. Most early learning occurs in the family environment; family members provide initial exposure to basic living skills and social behaviors. Children are learning behaviors from their parents beginning with their first moment of contact. As the infant is introduced to the home environment, brothers and sisters, grandparents, and all others who have significant contact with the child also become teachers. In turn, the child also teaches the others, through his or her own behaviors, how to behave with these behaviors. A mutual, reciprocal learning process occurs; all family members train one another. Many of the fundamental behaviors learned are skills for living in a society of people—hence the term *social learning* (Walsh, 1980).

The social-learning or behavioral approach[1] to marital therapy had its beginnings in and was most heavily influenced by the operant-conditioning model used to modify the behavior of children (Patterson, 1971; Pat-

[1]Although they vary subtly, the identifiers *social learning* and *behavioral* are used interchangeably in the literature and here as well.

terson & Gullion, 1968). As behavior modifiers were training parents to modify the behaviors of their children, they also collected data on the exchange of reinforcement and punishment among family members. Interest soon shifted from the behaviors of the individual family member identified as the problem (usually a child) to the interaction of the various family members. This, of course, included those interactions occurring between marital partners (Patterson & Hops, 1972). Initial attempts to change the dysfunctional behaviors of couples experiencing marital distress essentially transferred the operant principles used to modify children's behavior to work with adults.

This extrapolation of procedures from children to adults had certain limitations. The operant procedures used to modify children's behavior required that a behavioral change agent have control over the delivery of reinforcers and punishers. With children, this control was accomplished through consultation with significant adults in the child's immediate environment, usually his or her parents or teachers. With married couples, however, the therapist had no such control. Instead, the therapist had to persuade marital partners to collaborate to produce an environment supportive of desirable relationship behaviors. This required that the couple learn to negotiate with each other (Jacobson, 1981). As a result, it became necessary for therapists to augment their use of basic operant procedures with interventions designed to teach couples communication and problem-solving skills (Patterson & Hops, 1972; Jacobson & Weiss, 1978).

It is these augmented procedures that we primarily address in this chapter; they are what methodologically distinguish behavioral marital therapy from behavioral therapy in general. The procedures include behavior exchange, communication enhancement, problem solving, and marital contracting. Before exploring these aspects of the behavioral or social-learning perspective, we first examine the major concepts of the approach, forming an overview of the therapeutic process as a conceptual foundation.

Major Concepts

The social-learning or behavioral approach to therapy has come to represent the application of a diversity of techniques and procedures that are rooted in a variety of theories of learning. It involves the systematic application of principles of learning to change individuals' behavior in order to allow them to function in more adaptive ways.

The behavioral approach does not spell out any philosophical assumptions regarding human behavior. Individuals are simply seen as having an equal potential for functioning both in adaptive and maladaptive ways. All behavior is viewed as being learned—essentially through experiences within a sociocultural environment. Behavioral theorists, who believe that ultimately all behavior is the result of environmental forces and individuals' genetic endowment, include such cognitive "actions" as decision making as a type of behavior. Unfortunately, the behavioral view is often distorted by an oversimplified explanation of the individual as a helpless pawn of fate whose actions, solely determined by environmental and genetic influences, are reduced to those of a mere responding organism (Corey, 1977). In fact, contemporary behavior therapy is far from being a strictly deterministic and mechanistic approach that rules out any possibility of individuals' potential to make their own choices.

The primary concern of the contemporary behavioral marital therapists is behavior change. In working to achieve this change, emphasis is always placed on operationally defined, observable, and measurable behaviors. Behaviors themselves, not the objectively unmeasurable personality constructs utilized in most psychodynamic-based approaches, provide the focus for therapeutic efforts. This emphasis offers the behavioral marital therapist and those couples with whom he or she works an objective indicator of success or lack of success in achieving therapeutic objectives. Utilizing behavior change as the criterion of success also allows behavioral marital therapists to judge immediately and at any time the rate of progress being made toward the clearly specified objectives.

Jacobson and Margolin (1979) suggested a number of general considerations upon which the behavioral approach to marital therapy is based. These considerations—the utility of functional analysis, positive tracking, positive control, positive reciprocity, and relationship skills, are summarized here.

Functional Analysis. The critical component of a behavioral approach to marital therapy is what's termed a *functional analysis* of partners' presenting concerns. Prior to implementing any treatment interventions, assessment procedures are conducted to determine the environmental antecedents of current marital dysfunction, as well as the reinforcement contingencies that maintain the problem behaviors. From this analysis, hypotheses are generated as to the bases for current dysfunction. These hypotheses are then tested by formulating and implementing intervention strategies designed to produce more desirable relationship behaviors. The functional analysis does not end after the initial assessment. It continues into the treatment phase of therapy in order to evaluate the effects of the intervention strategies attempted. Should these interventions not be successful, hypotheses are reformulated, and the intervention strategies are adjusted accordingly or new ones applied. Thus, both the conceptualization of marital partners' initial concerns and the ongoing evaluation of therapeutic efforts form the functional analysis.

Positive Tracking. Throughout the social-learning therapeutic process, the primary focus is placed upon marital partners' strengths and assets—the desirable aspects of their relationship. This emphasis on the positive is purposefully designed to alter partners' tendencies to selectively track one another's negative behaviors and to emphasize the undesirable aspects of their relationship. Negative biases often exaggerate and worsen an already objectively distressed situation by preventing partners from viewing their concerns as simply part of a total picture that includes both positive and negative aspects and behaviors. If partners can learn to surrender their negative biases and to focus more on increasing the amount and quality of their reinforcing exchanges, their situation will likely improve significantly. Because the couple's circumstances are no longer perceived in a pessimistic manner, a mutually satisfying relationship seems easier to attain and maintain.

Positive Control.   Couples experiencing marital dysfunction often rely on punishment and other forms of aversive control to produce desirable behaviors in each other. Verbal threats and demands, the withholding of rewards, and other forms of coercion provide the couple's primary means of interacting.

These aversive methods are appealing because they are compelling and often very effective in producing short-term changes. Yet the accompanying negative consequences of utilizing predominantly aversive means of achieving gratification in the relationship eventually build up. Partners who are on the receiving end of attempts at aversive control by their mates come to see the benefits they are receiving as not worth the costs they must pay to maintain the relationship. Therefore, therapeutic efforts must focus on reversing the negative exchange pattern, and the means to this reversal is providing partners with more productive ways of effecting desirable behaviors in each other (more productive in both the short and long term). Positive control offers this means; it is the use of mutually rewarding exchanges to initiate and maintain positive relationship behaviors.

Positive Reciprocity.   Positive reciprocity is the providing of reinforcement for desirable behaviors. If each partner is to please his or her mate, it is necessary for each to reinforce the occurrence of pleasurable behaviors so that they continue to be exhibited. The more frequent and varied the reinforcement exchanged between partners over a wide range of behaviors, the greater the reciprocity in the relationship. Research has repeatedly demonstrated that successful relationships are characterized by a high degree of positive reciprocity between partners (Gottman, Markman, & Notarius, 1977; Gottman, Notarius, Markman, Bank, Yoppi, & Rubin, 1976; Wills, Weiss, & Patterson, 1974). In social-learning-oriented work with couples, therapeutic efforts are focused on persuading them that their difficulties reflect a mutual withholding of reinforcement, and also that these difficulties can be ameliorated only by each partner giving careful, systematic attention to increasing his or her delivery of reinforcement for pleasurable behaviors exhibited by the other partner.

Relationship Skills.   The behavioral marital therapist strongly emphasizes mastery of the skills necessary for successful enactment of relationship roles and functions. Primary among the skills identified as crucial to a functional relationship are behavior-exchange, communication, problem-solving, and contracting skills, with instrumental behaviors such as the handling of finances, household responsibilities, and personal-living habits of lesser but still important concern. This skill orientation lends itself to a preventative as well as remedial emphasis in therapy, since therapeutic objectives are not merely to remedy current deficiencies but also to teach partners skills that allow them to cope effectively with concerns arising after therapy has ended.

With these general considerations as a basis, let us now look at some concepts relating specifically to marital partners as a couple—how and why they come together and the means by which they create and maintain either a satisfying and functional relationship or one that is distressed and dysfunctional.

Choice of a Marital Partner

Behavioral marital therapists have said little about the process of marital choice. This is not accidental, since most behavioral marital therapists, like behavioral therapists in general, have little concern with the past. Rarely does a history taken in behavioral couple therapy extend in time beyond the history of the marriage itself (D'Zurilla, 1976). In fact, most therapists attempt no comprehensive or systematic assessment of the early development of the relationship at all, placing almost exclusive emphasis on present behaviors (O'Leary & Turkewitz, 1978).

While no behavioral marital therapists have yet researched or applied their work to explain marital choice, presumably the factors that influence current marital satisfaction involve the same determinants and processes as initial attraction and marital choice (Gurman, 1978). It might therefore be suggested that one is likely to enter into a relationship with a particular person because of a learning history as well as a constitution that predisposes him or her to find certain partner-initiated behaviors reinforcing. Thus, as noted by Jacobson (1981), writing from a social-learning standpoint:

> People marry because of both the actual and perceived potential for the provision of benefits and rewards. During courtship, partners experience one another in a limited but substantial number of situations, and they sample the other's ability to provide them with benefits. The commitment to cohabitation and/or marriage always involves both an appraisal of the adequacy of current outcomes and a forecast, albeit often implicit, regarding the continuance and expansion of such outcomes into new domains [p. 560-561].

Like Jacobson, we perceive the social-learning model of marital partner choice to be a useful one, remembering that the developmental model also suggests looking for the antecedents to current behavior in one's past learning history. Therefore, when utilizing a social-learning approach in our clinical practice with couples, we do place emphasis upon information relating to marital choice. Each partner brings into the relationship a set of role expectations that are the result of his or her accumulated previous experiences, including cultural background and norms and parental role models. Bringing these to light in the context of how partners chose each other can provide a better understanding of their present behavior and make for more valid assessment and treatment planning.

Marital Satisfaction

The social-learning approach views marital satisfaction from a quasi-economic perspective. Every marital relationship is seen as satisfying to the degree that partners provide one another with benefits relatively greater than the costs inherent in being in the relationship. Each partner has needs for affection, approval, status, sex, recreation, and more. In addition, each partner must contribute to the ends of the marital and family unit, in such areas as household management, finances, child rearing, and social activities. Satisfaction in marriage occurs as a result of positive reciprocity in providing for each of these individual and family needs. When each partner receives pleasing words and actions adequate to meet his or her needs, the relationship will be experienced as satisfying. Of course, it takes effort and commitment as well as specific skills on the part of both partners to be able to meet one another's needs. In addition, not every need can always be met, so disappointment, frustration, and anger are a part of every relationship. When the effort is seen as too great, or the exchange of negative feelings regularly exceeds the exchange of positive feelings, the result is discomfort, distress, and dissatisfaction with the relationship Simply stated, the costs become greater than the benefits. Thus the maintenance of a high benefit/cost ratio is the basic criterion for marital satisfaction. Individual couples, however, vary widely in their own standards of what constitutes a sufficiently high benefit/cost ratio.

Since satisfaction in marriage depends upon maintaining a high level of benefits relative to costs, a continuing perception of the relationship as pleasurable will result only if partners can respond successfully to the numerous obstacles to the maintenance of this ratio. Throughout their relationship partners are faced with factors that threaten either to diminish their currently acceptable rate of pleasurable exchanges or to increase the present costs. Marriage, especially in being the long-term relationship it is, can become more costly as it evolves over time. As partners spend more time together, and as they take on new roles, such as parenthood, that are more costly to the relationship, the initial attraction and novelty of courtship and early marriage often wane. More time devoted to providing a pleasurable environment for children means less time to devote to satisfying each other's needs. In addition, as interdependence grows, the costs of being committed to each other also grow. Commitment entails that each partner accommodate the other. Inevitably, when partners realize they have less independence to take individual action, conflicts arise. Therefore a critical component in maintaining marital satisfaction is partners' skill in conflict resolution (Jacobson & Margolin, 1979).

Lederer and Jackson, in *The Mirages of Marriage* (1968), suggest that one of the false assumptions held in our society is that effective relationship skills are a natural outgrowth of being in love. Many couples are unfortunately without the skills to negotiate mutually acceptable solutions to problems. Thus, many partners attempt to simply ignore their relationship problems, hoping that somehow their love will ultimately resolve them. Others do attempt to discuss their problems, but in a way that only heightens concern and conflict. Coercion, threats, and humiliation are poor substitutes for effective negotiation skills. Partners who talk and who also listen to each other about their problems, keeping the issues in perspective and seeking some mutual resolution through a positive interchange, are bound to see their relationship as satisfying. Therefore, it is not the presence of problems but rather the ability not to become excessively alarmed or surprised by their occurrence, along with the ability to speak openly and directly so as to negotiate their resolution, that promotes marital satisfaction.

In addition to highlighting conflict-resolution or negotiation skills, the social-learning view of marital satisfaction also places heavy emphasis on other skills necessary for the effective enactment of marital roles and functions. These include primarily communication skills but also the ability to engage in gratifying sexual interaction and, to a slightly lesser degree, competency in various instrumental behaviors, such as financial management, household and domestic responsibilities, and accommodation to one's partner's personal living habits (Jacobson, 1981).

Finally, in further considering the potential for partners' benefit/cost ratio to decrease as the length of marriage increases, it is important that couples continually expand upon their abilities to reinforce each other by seeking new and different areas for positive exchanges. When partners consistently depend upon the same quality and variety of reinforcers, eventually their interactions lose reinforcement value. Satisfied couples cope with this inevitable "reinforcement erosion" by varying their shared activities, seeking new common interests, expanding their sexual repertoires, and developing their communications to a point where each continues to find interest in what the other has to say (Jacobson, 1981).

Marital Dysfunction

The social-learning perspective regarding marital dysfunction suggests that there are some rather predictable, general distinctions between couples that are distressed and those that are nondistressed, or satisfied. Research on the exchange of pleasing and displeasing behaviors exhibited by married couples has demonstrated that distressed couples are more likely to reciprocate displeasing behavior than are nondistressed couples (Gottman, 1979). Jacobson, Waldron, and Moore (1980) proposed a behavioral profile for marital distress in which they attempted to pinpoint these distinctions. Their research found that, as compared to nondistressed couples, distressed couples:

- Engage in fewer reinforcing and more punishing behavior exchanges.
- Differ radically in the types of behaviors correlating with daily marital satisfaction. For nondistressed couples, the more pleasing the behaviors exhibited, the higher the level of satisfaction. For distressed couples, the less displeasing the behaviors exhibited, the greater the level of satisfaction.
- Are particularly reactive to negative behaviors. The partners react immediately and to the negative stimuli alone, rather than looking objectively at the overall picture.

Thus, couples experiencing marital distress and dysfunction can be characterized by a tendency to react strongly to punishing behavior and to respond in kind. Behavior change and compliance likewise appear to hinge almost exclusively upon negative and aversive control tactics.

The Therapeutic Process

The social-learning approach to marital therapy is characterized by (1) a primary focus on overt and specific behaviors, (2) a concrete analysis and identification of presenting concerns, (3) the formulation of a specific treatment program appropriate to a particular problem, and (4) an objective assessment of the outcomes of therapy.

This approach is not based upon one systematic set of concepts. Although it has many techniques, it has few concepts. It is primarily an inductive approach based on experiments, and it applies the experimental method to the therapeutic process. In initiating therapy with a couple, the behavioral therapist asks him- or herself, "What are the specific behaviors these partners want to change, and what new behaviors do they need to learn?" The attention to specificity necessitates a close and careful assessment of the couple's behaviors. Vague or general descriptions serve little use; the main therapeutic concern is to isolate the problem behaviors and then create means of changing them.

Behavioral marital therapy emphasizes acquiring new, more functional behaviors, strengthening and maintaining these behaviors, and at the same time eliminating dysfunctional behaviors. From the assessment of specific concerns, concrete treatment goals are established. Appropriate techniques then are chosen to accomplish these goals.

Since the problem behaviors are clearly and distinctly identified, treatment goals detailed, and therapeutic interventions delineated, it follows that the outcomes of therapy can be effectively evaluated. "Were the therapeutic goals achieved?" is a question that can be objectively and accurately answered. And behavioral marital therapy does entail such assessment of a couple's improvement and progress. Emphasis on evaluation of the treatment interventions, which allows a continual evolution and refinement of the therapeutic process, distinguishes behavioral marital therapy from most other approaches.

The Goals of Therapy

Therapeutic goals have a place of central importance in behavioral marital therapy. The general goal of therapy is to create new conditions for learning. The rationale is that all behavior, including dysfunctional marital interaction patterns, is learned. Because the patterns were learned they can be unlearned, and more functional and effective ways of responding can be acquired.

Goals should be realistic, should be agreed to by both the couple and the therapist, and should derive naturally from the assessment phase of therapy. Although goal setting is crucial in initiating therapy, it also requires continual evaluation and possible revision throughout the entire period of treatment. If either partner anticipates gaining benefits at the expense of his or her mate, or if either has excessively high expectations of him- or herself or the other partner, there needs to be a reassessment and revision of goals. This may involve clarifying conflicting values or possibly scaling down unrealistic expectations of what can be gotten from a marital relationship.

Behavior change in any area of the relationship is appropriate for goal setting. The goals chosen, however, should be specific, positive, and functional, and should have a likelihood of being attained. Setting goals that meet these criteria often necessitates the therapist's providing a framework from which couples can learn to effectively set goals. For example, goals that are functional include changing interactions or activities that are likely to occur frequently in the couple's life together and can offer natural sources of satisfaction and pleasure (Lieberman, Wheeler, de-Visser, Kuehnel, & Kuehnel, 1980). With a couple that is withdrawn and noncommunicative it would be more functional to work on end-of-the-day greetings than on how to acknowledge one another's birthdays more affectionately; birthdays come once a year, but seeing each other after work is a daily occurrence and can be a richer and more frequent source of pleasurable exchanges.

The Role of the Therapist

Since the primary goal of therapy is for a couple to learn new skills, the role assumed by the behavioral marital therapist is an active teaching and coaching one. For example, in assisting a couple to learn new interaction skills, the therapist would begin by giving a rationale as to why the skill is important and how it directly relates to their presenting problem. The therapist next instructs the couple on how to use the skill. Having fully explained the procedure, the therapist demonstrates both how to do it and how not to do it. The couple is asked to rehearse the procedure there in the session, after which the therapist provides feedback on how well they did. The feedback is positive and specific, followed by sugges- tions for improvement, if necessary. Once the couple has practiced the skill successfully in the therapy session, the therapist assigns the two homework of practicing the skill in the natural environment of their home. This homework is reviewed at the beginning of the next session.

The behavioral marital therapist's role as an active teacher involves a number of functions, two of which are considered especially significant. The first of these is the therapist's functioning as a reinforcer. Goodstein (1972) suggested in this regard that "the counselor rewards certain re- sponses . . . and punishes others. These rewards are approval, interest, and concern . . . [and] such reinforcement would be especially important when the client is trying out new responses or behavior that is as yet not regularly reinforced by others in the client's life" (p. 275). Often couples report that the new skills they are learning feel unnatural and contrived; when this is the case, the new skills initially are not perceived as reinforc- ing in terms of a benefit/cost ratio. The therapist's reinforcement, then, can be what increases the benefits of continuing to practice the skills relative to the costs long enough for their practice to become mutually reinforcing for the marital partners.

The second important function of the behavioral marital therapist is his or her role modeling for the couple. Bandura (1969) indicated that most of the learning that occurs through direct experience can also be acquired through observation of others' behavior. Couples can learn new behaviors through imitation of the social modeling provided by the thera- pist. Thus, the therapist must be aware of and utilize this crucial identifi- cation or modeling process in facilitating couples' adoption of more ap- propriate and adaptive interpersonal behaviors.

The Therapeutic Relationship

Behavioral marital therapists have conducted few research investiga- tions concerning the application of learning or social-influence principles to enhance the therapeutic relationship. Because of this scarcity of re- search, it appears, some critics characterize the relationship between the behavioral therapist and couple as overly technique oriented and too im- personal (Gurman & Razin, 1977). However, a number of behavioral mari- tal therapists, while not having researched specific relationship variables, have written of establishing good working rapport and proposed that it is a meaningful part of the therapeutic process (O'Leary & Turkewitz, 1978;

Wilson & Evans, 1976). This tenet of behavioral therapy can also be seen or implied from aspects of the therapeutic process that have been the subjects of research, such as the establishment of a good therapeutic relationship in order for the therapist to function as a reinforcer and role model.

It does appear that most behavioral therapists do not consider the therapist-couple relationship variables all-important, as some approaches do. Nevertheless, most behavioral marital therapists do assert that factors such as empathy, warmth, authenticity, and acceptance complement therapeutic efforts. In and of themselves, these factors are not seen as sufficient to effect successful therapy; rather, they are seen as secondary conditions to facilitate behavior-change strategies. These relationship variables have also been seen as setting the stage for therapeutic interventions to occur (Goldstein, 1973).

The relationship between the therapist and couple in behavioral marital therapy might best be characterized by the nature of the therapeutic contract they establish. This contract specifies what the therapist can provide and, in exchange, what the couple is expected to give in terms of fees, attendance, length of treatment, confidentiality, and treatment goals. The contract provides an objective, measurable means of clarifying and specifying mutual expectations and of affirming mutual commitment regarding treatment. The word *commitment*, as used here, is defined as "a promise or pledge to do something and also as an act of doing or performing something" (Lieberman et al., 1980, p. 36). The contractual process should encompass these definitions and demonstrate that both the couple and the therapist can, with adequate reinforcement from each other, respond to positive expectations.

The degree of formality of this therapeutic contract is dependent upon the therapist's and couple's preferences. These may include legalistic procedures, such as having signatures witnessed, or it can be kept anecdotal and simple. The main point to emphasize is that, whatever the form, the contract specifies the terms of the therapeutic relationship.

The Structure of Therapy

To maximize therapeutic effectiveness, it is important that therapists be prepared to conceptualize the present circumstances and future directions of efforts to be undertaken in therapy. Viewing the overall treatment process in terms of its present status and the manner in which it may be expected to change over time enables planning, continuing evaluation, and, if necessary, adjustment or readjustment of intervention strategies. This all greatly facilitates progress being attained as easily as possible and in the most efficient and effective manner.

O'Leary and Turkewitz (1978) have proposed four stages in which the social-learning approach to marital therapy can be conceptualized. These are: (1) courtship, (2) engagement, (3) marriage, and (4) disengagement. The parallel between the first three stages and a couple's own relationship process is obvious. The last stage, disengagement, is a necessary and eventual part of the therapeutic process—termination. Its counterpart, divorce, is typically a stage couples seeking assistance for their marital concerns want to avoid. These four stages and the basic procedures and concerns relevant to each are highlighted further below.

Stage 1: Courtship.   The courtship stage is primarily a time for establishing rapport and assessing a couple's presenting problems within a behavioral framework. During this stage the therapist decides whether he or she can be of assistance to the couple while the marital partners likewise decide whether the therapist can be helpful to them. The therapist should utilize relationship-building skills, exhibiting warmth, empathy, and acceptance of the couple so as to facilitate building rapport upon which to base later therapeutic efforts. Although assessment of presenting concerns and progress in dealing with them occurs throughout therapy, it is during this initial time that the therapist completes an in-depth assessment. (This assessment process is discussed extensively later in this chapter.)

The courtship stage is also a time when it is important to facilitate the couple in developing favorable therapeutic expectations. This is done essentially through therapist statements regarding the potential benefits the couple can derive from therapy. The therapist's conviction and optimism in expressing this view can do much to raise a couple's expectations. In addition, the fact that these statements can be based on objective assessment data allows the therapist to make his or her statements relevant to the concerns the partners have presented and to do so in a reasonable, realistic way. This produces much more trust in the therapist's judgment than would overly optimistic or unfounded statements suggesting therapy to be a cure-all for problem marriages. Thus, through an initial in-depth assessment, rapport building, and the development of favorable expectations for therapy, the therapist prepares a couple to make an active commitment to the upcoming treatment and, thereby, prepares them to become "engaged" in the therapeutic process.

Stage 2: Engagement.   During this stage, the therapist seeks to solidify his or her working relationship with the couple. Specifically, the therapist conveys a commitment to work with the partners in achieving their goals and states his or her expectations: that the partners will invest their time and effort in attempting to achieve their stated goals and will work to do so both in the therapy sessions and at home.

The therapist also seeks to solidify a better working relationship between the partners themselves. This begins with an analysis of the assessment data gathered during the courtship stage and is followed by recommendations for treatment. By presenting an analysis of a couple's relationship concerns in social-learning terms, most notably utilizing the concept of reciprocity, the therapist emphasizes a view that proposes mutual responsibility for current difficulties. The assessment data is related to the couple in a manner that does not attribute blame to either partner alone and is delivered as an objective and expert opinion. This tends to enlarge each partner's perspective and lead to a consideration of other views, thereby facilitating their acceptance of mutual responsibility for maintaining the current dysfunctional state in their relationship (Jacobson, 1981).

Another major aspect of the engagement stage is the development of the therapeutic contract. This contract seeks to ensure collaboration between the therapist and couple as well as between the partners themselves. The therapist provides the couple with an understanding of the treatment approach and, based on assessment information, with rationales for any intervention strategies he or she may propose. The couple is asked for a commitment (usually a written contract) to follow and implement the proposed treatment program and to do so in a mutually collaborative manner. Once the partners have committed themselves, most do act accordingly (Jacobson, 1981).

Finally, following the partners' agreement to commit themselves to the terms of the therapeutic contract, it is suggested that the first behavioral homework assignment be given. In the early sessions, it is important that treatment-intervention strategies and homework assignments be relatively undemanding and call for minimal collaboration. Successful therapy is predicated on partners ability to work collaboratively to improve their relationship. Even with agreement given to the terms of the therapeutic contract, partners' collaboration cannot be assumed; it should be gradually shaped and fostered by the therapist. By beginning with strategies and outside-the-session assignments with low risk and a high probability for success, the partners' working relationship can be enhanced. This prepares them for the more demanding challenges of therapeutic interventions to come.

For example, a beginning homework assignment we often propose in work with couples is one described by Azrin, Naster, and Jones (1973) called the "Reciprocity Awareness Exercise." Partners each are asked to list ten of their mutual behaviors that are helpful or pleasing and are verbally or physically expressed. Also, each partner is to list five behaviors of the other's that the first partner finds pleasurable and five behaviors of his or her own that the other partner perceives as pleasurable. During the next session, the partners read their lists aloud. The therapist assists them in stating the behaviors in concrete and observable terms. For instance, "My husband was wonderful Monday evening" might be better stated as "My husband surprised me Monday evening by asking me if I'd like to go out to dinner and then suggesting we go to a place that I like and he normally would rather not go to." This simple exercise begins teaching couples the importance of being observant of the positive rather than the negative aspects of their relationship. It also gives them practice in being concrete in describing behaviors, which is a crucial skill for carrying out most behavioral-intervention strategies. In addition, most partners report that they get pleasurable feelings from paying closer attention to the positive aspects of their relationship and they greatly enjoy receiving positive feedback from each other.

The assignment described exemplifies the value of homework outside the session. In this case, the goal of developing a collaborative working relationship between partners is obviously furthered by their participation in the exercise. This should be emphasized by the therapist; at the engagement stage, progress is meaningful not only in its own right but in raising the credibility and value of the therapist's proposals and enhancing the therapist-couple relationship.

The first two stages, courtship and engagement, generally take place in only the first two or three therapy sessions. The therapeutic process then proceeds to the most active and involved phase of therapy, the marriage stage.

Stage 3: Marriage.   Just as the marriage stage is the most involved and difficult part of a couple's relationship, it is the most lengthy part of the therapeutic process. It is during this period that intervention strategies are implemented and new relationship skills are learned. These include behavior-exchange procedures, problem-solving and communication-enhancement skills, and more, all of which will be expanded and elaborated upon later in this chapter in the section on techniques and procedures.

Stage 4: Disengagement.   Disengagement is actually not a separate phase as this stage distinction would imply. In reality, the couple "disengages" throughout therapy as the partners learn to cope in new and more efficient ways. However, during the final therapy sessions the therapist begins to noticeably withdraw active direction and influence. Correspondingly, the couple is given more and more responsibility for addressing independently the problems that arise and for utilizing relationship skills learned in previous sessions. The partners are also encouraged to analyze for themselves interactions that go poorly and to intervene appropriately when difficult circumstances arise. This fading of the therapist's influence allows both the therapist and the partners to evaluate whether the couple has the collaboration and intervention skills necessary to cope with problems that may present themselves following the termination of therapy. If they don't have the skills, review, reassessment, and additional reeducation may be necessary. If they do, the withdrawal of influence provides the partners with more confidence about the course of their relationship following the termination of therapy.

Throughout therapy, the therapist should be continually considering ways in which disengagement can be facilitated. The partners can then be gradually prepared to function adaptively on their own, the ultimate therapeutic goal.

Therapeutic Techniques and Procedures

One of the main contributions of the behavioral approach to marital therapy has been its development of proven efficient and effective techniques and procedures for alleviating marital dysfunction. Since the methods utilized are objectively measurable and are continually assessed throughout therapy, errors in diagnosis or applying specific intervention strategies immediately become evident. Either the partners improve or they don't. If necessary, ineffective procedures can be adjusted or eliminated and new alternatives tried.

It is important for techniques and procedures to be tailored to the needs of the couple. The methods we present, although they have been found highly effective for most couples, still are only general frameworks, to be modified to fit specific circumstances and situations. With this understanding in mind, let us first look at the techniques and procedures of the assessment process. These are followed by intervention strategies to relieve marital distress and enhance relationship functioning.

Assessment of Marital Functioning

An in-depth assessment of marital functioning can require a number of sessions. Assuming there is no immediate crisis (which would be dealt with prior to the assessment or concurrently with it), two or three initial sessions are typically devoted to assessment. In our practice, we use the first three sessions with a couple primarily for assessment, but also for building rapport and facilitating collaborative relationships. The first and third sessions are conjoint interviews; the first focuses on presenting concerns and background history, and the third is an assessment of the partners' communication and problem-solving skill repertoires. The second session is split; each partner is seen individually for half of the session to assess their motivation and give them the opportunity to express openly, and with assured confidentiality, any concerns, doubts, or comments about the relationship that they might be reluctant to reveal with their mate present. In addition, concurrently with these sessions partners are asked to complete various written assessment measures, and to take a measure of the other's observable behaviors in their home environment.

Before identifying specific assessment tools, we outline a four-point characterization of behavioral marital assessment, presented by Jacobson (1981) and summarized here to provide a further conceptual basis for understanding the process.

Point 1: Assessment is primarily concerned with identifying current behavioral excesses and deficits that have produced the present dysfunction. This is based on the idea that the common denominator in dysfunctional relationships is too few reinforcing behaviors, too many punishing behaviors, or both.

Point 2: Assessment involves the direct measurement of behavior, not a focus on personality dynamics or labeling according to hypothesized underlying constructs. This follows directly from Point 1. Describing and explaining the relationship between behaviors and the environmental reinforcement or punishment that maintains or prevents them is the basic concern of the behavioral marital therapist during both assessment and treatment.

Point 3: Treatment plans are a direct result of the initial assessment. This further emphasizes the critical importance of the initial assessment. Techniques and procedures are not applied on the therapist's subjective whim but are based on objective and observable data.

Point 4: Assessment is continuous and occurs throughout therapy. Assessment is continued after the initial assessment and formulation of a treatment program in order to provide both the therapist and couple with feedback as to the progress of their efforts. Errors in assessment or treatment planning are thereby readily detected and can be quickly remedied.

With these points in mind, we next present an examination of various means of collecting the assessment data. A review of the literature and our own clinical experience utilizing a behavioral approach suggests that the following categories are representative of relevant information-gathering tools.

Self-Report Measures.   Several areas important to marital functioning are amenable to assessment via self-report devices, which vary in degree of standardization and formality. Generally, these devices are used to obtain an index of the severity of a couple's problems and a generalized measure of marital satisfaction. Although self-report devices are of limited value in a behavioral assessment because they do not yield specific information regarding problem areas in the relationship, they do provide a reliable measure of global satisfaction and are normally an effective indicator of therapeutic movement.

Self-report measures can also be used to gain information concerning other relationship variables, such as motivation for therapy, areas of desired change, descriptions of problem areas and communication patterns, and more. The following list describes the battery of self-report measures that we use.

Locke-Wallace Marital Adjustment Test (MAT). This (Locke & Wallace, 1959) is the most utilized global measure of marital satisfaction in the field. It is a 15-item questionnaire that requires only 10 to 15 minutes to complete and less than 10 minutes to score for both partners. It is a general sampling device that briefly assesses various aspects of marriage, such as communication, sexual compatibility, affection, social activities, and value differences.

Areas-of-Changes Questionnaire (A-C). This measure (Weiss, Hops, & Patterson, 1973) asks couples to indicate which of 34 partner behaviors they would like to see changed, as well as how much change is desired and whether the direction of the change should be toward more or less of the behavior.

Feelings toward Spouse Questionnaire. This (Turkewitz & O'Leary, 1975) is an 18-item measure designed to evaluate the emotional quality of a marital relationship. Its purpose is to assess feelings that are not necessarily communicated directly. For example, "Do you feel positive about your spouse's personal successes?" and "How often do you look forward to being alone with your spouse?" The measure is valuable for pretreatment assessment and also provides a measure of changes in feelings that accompany or follow behavior changes resulting from therapeutic efforts.

Marital Status Inventory (MSI). This measure (Weiss & Cerreto, 1975) contains 14 true-false items that indicate the steps toward separation and divorce already undertaken by marital partners. The MSI provides valuable and necessary data to consider in assessing partners' motivation to attempt therapy, let alone to succeed in it.

Miscellaneous Measures. Other areas of importance can also be assessed by self-report measures. These measures are usually informal rather than standardized. For instance, in our work with couples, we feel that physical health is quite relevant to the success or failure of therapeutic efforts. For that reason, we use a simple questionnaire we ourselves designed to gather data concerning the date and results of partners' last physical examinations as well as past history and present suspicion of any problems (for example, with blood pressure, ulcers, depressed or listless feelings, impotence, or vaginismus). If anything of concern is presented, a physical examination prior to therapy is recommended.

Spouse Observation.   Weiss, Hops, and Patterson (1973) developed an instrument to assist couples in their collection of direct-observation data in their home environments. This instrument, the *Spouse Observational Checklist* (SOC), consists of about 400 items of partner behaviors grouped into 12 separate categories: affection, child care, communication, companionship, consideration, coupling, financial management, household responsibilities, personal habits, one's own and spouse's independence, sex, and work (school) activities. The task is for partners to check each item that occurs during a 24-hour period. The instructions can be varied so that partners record all behaviors that occur, or limit their recordings to behaviors that have pleasing or displeasing impacts. In addition, each partner is to give the relationship a daily rating on a scale of 1 to 7, based on overall satisfaction.

The SOC serves a number of critical assessment functions throughout the entire therapy process. It provides the daily frequency counts of relationship behaviors. Also, by correlating behavioral frequencies with daily satisfaction ratings, it identifies those behaviors that seem to be most important to the satisfaction of each partner. Finally, it provides an excellent means of monitoring therapeutic progress. By having partners continue daily recordings throughout therapy, changes in behavioral patterns being subjected to intervention strategies can be readily observed and, therefore, the effectiveness of those strategies evaluated.

Communication and Problem-Solving-Skills Observation.   Behavioral marital therapy emphasizes the importance of communication and conflict-resolution skills. A direct observational assessment of these skills is therefore an integral part of the assessment process. Yet, in collecting and evaluating information to plan for the modification of marital communication and problem-solving skills, therapists have been handicapped by the lack of relevant guidelines and procedures. For the practicing therapist, observation of these skills is by necessity often relatively informal and unstandardized (Jacobson, 1981).

We have found one device, the *Marital Interaction Coding System* (MICS, developed by Hops, Wills, Weiss, & Patterson, 1971), to provide a means of formal and standardized collection of information on communication and problem-solving skills. Used particularly by clinical researchers, the MICS comprises 28 categories that identify problem-solving statements, positive and negative interaction responses, and nonverbal behaviors that either facilitate or impede communication. Our use of the MICS is a modification of the research-oriented use.

In employing the MICS for assessment purposes, a couple is given 5 to 10 minutes to solve a minor problem in their relationship with the therapist observing and coding their interactions according to the MICS categories. (The session is also tape recorded, for later clarification of the results.) The result is 28 ratios—one for each category. Each ratio consists of the number of interactions in the category divided by the total number of interactions recorded for each partner.

To use the MICS the therapist must learn the coding system, a time-consuming task. However, the added information given in an objectively measurable manner makes pre-treatment assessment and post-treatment evaluation more meaningful and exact.

The Clinical Interview.   Compared with most other approaches to working with couples, the behavioral approach deemphasizes the therapist-couple interaction as a source of information. Most of the assessment data required is gotten more efficiently through the means just described. However, the interview does provide the therapist an opportunity to gain some types of information not always readily provided by the other procedures and measures. Also, the interview serves as a means to begin establishing rapport and facilitating collaboration and favorable expectations for therapy. In our work with couples, we utilize the interview for express purposes, the main ones being:

- to elaborate on those behaviors assessed through self-report and other measures;
- to identify the antecedents and consequences characterizing a couple's patterns of interaction;
- to determine whether there are other major concerns in addition to those already assessed;
- to gain a relevant developmental history of the relationship in order to determine historical antecedents of current functional and dysfunctional behaviors;
- to provide a setting wherein collaboration between partners themselves and between partners and the therapist can be fostered and favorable expectations for therapy facilitated.

Finally, in the assessment phase of therapy, individual difficulties of partners should be assessed and attended to. For example, extreme depression, drug or alcohol dependency, compulsiveness, and the like may need to be addressed before any marital interventions are attempted. If so, individual therapy is suggested as a prerequisite to working full-time on the relationship. If, however, the presenting problem is generally limited to the marital interaction, it is viewed more as a marital than an individual concern and is approached accordingly.

At the conclusion of the initial pretreatment assessment, the couple and the therapist meet to discuss evaluation findings and treatment planning. Then, assuming the couple adheres to the diagnosis and the therapist's recommendations for treatment, a specific intervention program is agreed to. Reaching this stage of the therapeutic process, we next explore the major intervention strategies that characterize the social-learning approach to marital therapy.

Intervention Strategies

As we have stressed, the social-learning approach to marital therapy posits the need to identify specific target behaviors. When behaviors have been identified to be modified or nurtured and enhanced, specific intervention strategies are planned and applied. Five main forms of intervention form the basis for behavioral-change techniques and procedures. They include: (1) behavior-exchange procedures, (2) communication-enhancement training, (3) problem-solving training, (4) marital contracting, and (5) homework assignments.

Behavior-Exchange Procedures. Behavior-exchange procedures rely heavily on the principle of reciprocity. Simply put, partners get what they give and give what they get. These procedures assume that each partner has resources and behaviors that are perceived as valuable and pleasurable to the other. The main goal of behavior-exchange procedures is to assist each partner in increasing the frequency of the behaviors of the other that are pleasurable. Although there are many variations of behavior exchange utilized in marital therapy, two basic steps are common to all of them (Jacobson, 1981). First, behaviors described by one or both partners as pleasurable are specifically pinpointed. Second, there is an attempt made to increase the frequency of these behaviors.

Numerous examples of behavior-exchange procedures are found throughout the marital-therapy literature. A typical example is one suggested by Lieberman, Wheeler, deVisser, Kuehnel, and Kuehnel (1980) called "Catch Your Spouse Doing Something Nice." This procedure involves having partners observe each other carefully and then clearly acknowledging, verbally or nonverbally, when "you catch him or her saying or doing something that gives you a good feeling." This procedure helps partners to develop and maintain an awareness of each other and to learn the value of positive reinforcement that is *immediate*. Instead of taking one another's good points for granted or not responding to them, as typifies many distressed couples' interactions, this procedure emphasizes the importance of overt, positive interactions and allows couples to experience them.

Behavior-exchange procedures are especially well suited for the early stages of therapy. They are not heavily demanding, and they tend to generate positive interactions that can be the foundation for later changes. However, as Jacobson (1981) has suggested, several factors need to be considered when utilizing behavior-exchange procedures early in the therapeutic process.

First, since many couples are probably only beginning to establish a collaborative stance toward working on their concerns, the intervention should not pressure either partner into any concessions in fundamental areas of disagreement. Behaviors to be exchanged should be clearly understandable and easily deliverable without any need for extensive negotiation or new skill development on the part of either partner. Second, since one of the initial purposes of behavior-exchange procedures is to develop a collaborative working relationship between partners, the procedures used at this point should not assume or depend upon a high degree of collaboration. Finally, the focus should be on increasing positive behavior rather than decreasing negative behavior. High-frequency or high-intensity negative behaviors are usually the major reasons for seeking therapeutic assistance. To attempt to reduce them this early in therapy would surely require aversive control tactics (punishment), which might only exacerbate most couples' already highly negative perceptions of each other and their relationship.

Communication Enhancement.   Communication enhancement training involves two main therapeutic goals: (1) helping partners reduce and
clarify misunderstandings that arise in their interactions and (2) increasing the appropriate expression of feelings.

1. *Clear Communication.* A common complaint among couples in
therapy is that "He/she doesn't understand me." There is some research
that suggests distressed partners actually do have more difficulty interpreting each other's statements (Kahn, 1970) and hold more discrepant
definitions for concepts significant to the marriage (Katz, 1965) than do
partners who are not distressed. When a message sent differs from the
message received, the confusion that occurs often leads to unnecessary
misunderstandings and conflict. Couples must frequently be taught to
counter this—to ask for clarifications and elaborations of one another's
communications.

In teaching couples the value of clearer communications, note that
the key to initiating a request for clarification is noticing when the reaction to a partner's statement is surprise or a negative feeling. If a partner
says something that puzzles or angers his or her mate, that mate should be
urged to stop the interchange and clarify the situation instead of assuming
the worst and reacting negatively. "Is this what you mean?" can interrupt
potentially escalating negative interchanges.

Training in empathic skills is also useful to clarify communication.
Partners can be taught to reflect what they hear their mate expressing—
both the feelings and the content of the speaker's statement. For example:

Wife: I had a miserable day at work today.
Husband: You're frustrated and tired [feelings] after such a hard day at
work [content].

In this illustration the husband, by reflecting the feelings and content
being expressed, is implicitly saying "I understand how you feel and
why," to which his wife will likely respond "Yes, that's exactly how I
feel." If he was wrong in what he heard she would likely correct him:
"No, I'm not tired, just frustrated and angry."

2. *Appropriate Expression of Feelings.* Often, couples in therapy are
all too comfortable expressing negative feelings and asserting themselves.
However, there are also many partners who will not share their feelings.
Distressed couples have been found to report more fear of expressing
their feelings than nondistressed couples (Bienvenu, 1970). O'Leary and
Turkewitz (1978) proposed several reasons why it is important to increase
expression of feelings by distressed couples.

First, in order for any behavior change to occur, the negative behaviors in need of change must be identified through the expression of
negative affect in regard to them. Second, expression of feeling (both
positive and negative) is often a desired behavior-change goal in its own
right as an antidote to partners' reports of feeling distant from one another. And third, if feelings are not expressed openly they often are ex-

pressed indirectly or nonverbally, thus not allowing partners opportunities to react to them. For example, a partner who displays anger by yelling frequently but claims that he or she is just "speaking loudly so I can be heard" and that nothing is wrong is taking a passive-aggressive stance that offers little specific opportunity to target or agree on a behavior needing changing.

Teaching the expression of appropriate feelings to reluctant partners involves a shaping process, wherein the therapist must at first only encourage the expression of feelings with little affect tied to them. For instance, the partner in the above example, obviously angry, might be asked to express and discuss his irritation or annoyance rather than the anger or rage actually being experienced. Gradually, as the partner learns to feel more comfortable in expressing his or her feelings, the level of emotion addressed can be increased. The same strategy can be used to increase the expression of both positive and negative feelings.

Systematic Training.   Numerous other techniques have been employed in helping couples learn communication skills. Most behavioral therapists, however, rely on a systematic method of training based on the concept of reinforced practice. This method has three basic components: (1) instruction, (2) behavioral rehearsal, and (3) feedback (Jacobson, 1981). In addition, of course, partners are encouraged to follow specific guidelines or rules for effectively communicating.

Instruction involves the therapist presenting an explanation of the specific communication skill to be mastered. The therapist then models the skill for the couple by asking each partner to role-play a situation, the therapist taking on the role of mate for each partner. Discussion of the new skill and questions by the couple about the therapist's use of it follow.

Behavioral rehearsal offers the opportunity for the couple to practice within the therapy session the skill they have just had explained and modeled, and have also discussed. Rehearsal also provides the therapist with feedback as to the couple's competencies in utilizing the new skills they are learning, indicating the extent to which they are assimilating the skills into their behavioral reportoires.

Feedback is the final step of the training sequence. Behavioral rehearsal is followed by the therapist noting desirable and undesirable aspects of partners' performances, with reinforcement offered wherever possible for efforts and improvements. The entire sequence is then repeated, or at least the behavioral rehearsal and feedback are repeated, until the couple seems to have acquired a basis for practicing and utilizing the skill outside the session.

Problem-Solving Training.   Problem-solving training can be a powerful treatment strategy for a wide variety of distressed couples. As noted in the preceding discussion of marital satisfaction, conflict resolution or problem-solving competencies are one of the basic indicators of nondistressed couples, and they contribute heavily to the maintenance of marital happiness.

Jacobson (1981) has outlined three stages of guidelines to utilize in teaching couples problem-solving skills: (1) establishing general guidelines, (2) defining the problem, and (3) reaching agreement. These stages and the most important aspects of each are highlighted below.

Stage 1: Establishing General Guidelines
   a. *Discuss only one problem at a time.* Focusing on one problem makes resolution easier than attempting to reach agreement on two or more simultaneously.
   b. *Paraphrase or clarify communications.* Each partner should be encouraged to begin his or her response to the other's remark by summarizing what the other has said. The speaker is then given the opportunity to note whether the summary is accurate. If not, the procedure is repeated. This ensures that each partner is carefully listening to what the other is saying and obviously reduces any miscommunication.
   c. *Avoid "mind reading."* Problem solving can be hindered by inferences about a partner's motivation, attitudes, or feelings. The focus should be on the specific behavior under discussion. Mind reading often leads to defensive reactions and interferes significantly with any collaboration partners may have nurtured so far.
   d. *Avoid abusive or aversive exchanges.* When problem-solving attempts are interrupted by negative reinforcement, hostile comments, or humiliation, little progress in the process can be made.

Stage 2: Defining the Problem
   a. *Begin with positive aspects.* An opening positive remark to any concern being presented increases the likelihood that the problem will be received in a spirit of collaboration. In addition, it helps reinforce the notion that the problem represents only one aspect of a partner's overall behavior and is not suggestive of that partner being a total failure or "rotten" mate. For example, instead of opening a problem discussion with "You didn't fix the broken chair as you promised to yesterday," a partner might instead state, "I appreciate all the work you've been doing around the house this weekend. The place is really shaping up nicely. My only concern is that broken chair you promised to get to."
   b. *Be specific.* Beginning with a vague definition of a concern can make problem solving impossible. For instance, "Things are a mess" offers little information as to what "things" need to be addressed. Problems are best defined in terms of precise

behavior. "Things are a mess" might better be "The kitchen sink is full of dirty dishes that need washing, and they prevent me from preparing dinner."

c. *Encourage expression of feelings.* When delineating a problem, partners should include description not only of the behavior but of the emotional effect of the problem on them. The listening mate will tend to be more sympathetic to a complaint when its negative impact is clearly understood. For instance, "I wish you would call if you're going to be late" might be extended with "because I worry that something may have happened to you."

d. *Acknowledge mutual responsibility.* It is important that both partners acknowledge their roles in perpetuating a problem. The majority of relationship concerns contain contributions from both partners; defining the problem as a mutual one increases the probability that both partners will be motivated to work toward a mutual solution. This need not suggest that the partners have equal responsibility for the problem's occurrence. However, the fact that the problem does have an effect on their relationship implies that both are involved in its continuance, by their action or inaction.

e. *Keep definitions brief.* The focus of behavioral problem solving is on solving problems, not on finding fault, uncovering the whys or hows, or unnecessarily elaborating on side issues, even though they are related. By defining the problem as efficiently and briefly as is possible, partners are able to move into the solution phase of problem solving and therefore to alleviate the distress the problem causes.

Stage 3: Reaching Agreement

a. *Keep discussion "solution focused."* To develop a solution focus for their problem-solving efforts, partners should utilize the technique of brainstorming. This involves trying to think of as many solutions to the problem as possible, no matter how unworkable, silly, or absurd they may appear at first glance. The solutions suggested should not be evaluated until as many as possible have been proposed; the initial part of the task is just to generate potential solutions. Once a list of solutions has been compiled, the obviously unworkable suggestions can be eliminated and then the advantages and disadvantages of the remaining suggestions can be evaluated.

b. *Base final solutions on mutuality and compromise.* This guideline reemphasizes the aforementioned need for collaboration. It should be stressed to partners that if the solution to a problem burdens them equally, resolution is easier, and their relationship can only benefit as a result.

c. *Make final agreements specific.* Any behavior changes agreed to as a consequence of the problem-solving process are best described concretely in terms of frequency, duration, and the conditions under which the new behaviors are to occur. This simply lessens the possibility of new problems arising from some misunderstanding of the final agreement.

Marital Contracting. Developing marital contracts between partners is an excellent means of utilizing the rewards naturally present in a marital relationship. It also represents the culmination of behavior exchange, communication enhancement, and problem-solving training; all are utilized in developing contracts. The purpose of the marital contract is to delineate interchanges between partners in terms of who does what and when. Actions and their consequences are clearly identified. The end product is an agreement (usually written) by both partners, understandable and acceptable to each.

Marital contracts generally have two main elements. First, there is a statement of agreement by each partner to engage in specified behaviors. Second, the positive or negative consequences of the specified behaviors are identified.

Lieberman, Wheeler, deVisser, Kuehnel, and Kuehnel (1980) developed an exercise for marital contracting. We have used a modified version of this exercise in our work with couples and found it to be easily understandable and usable by the couples who have tried it. This version of the exercise is outlined in Figures 4-1 and 4-2. Figure 4-1 presents the instructions given to couples; 4-2, a sample of a completed marital contract.

Homework. One or two hours a week of behavior-change efforts during therapy sessions cannot be expected to change a relationship that is dysfunctional. It is essential, therefore, that couples practice and use the skills learned during therapy sessions at home and on a regular basis. Regular and repeated practice of new skills at home can continue and even extend the effects of therapy between sessions. Thus, regularly com-

---

CONTRACTING EXERCISE

Marital contracting is a method for clarifying what each of you expects from the other and what each of you is willing to give in your marriage. Your therapist will lead you through a process of negotiation and compromise that will end with a contract. A properly developed and mutually agreed-upon contract should satisfy some of the unmet needs you and your spouse have in your marriage.

The basic steps you will follow in developing a *tentative* contract with each other are as follows:

1. Each of you chooses one, two, or three behaviors that you think will please your partner and that you might be willing to do for your partner. Ask yourself, "What does he/she want that I can offer?" Write these items in the responsibility column of your tentative contract, using the attached blank contract form.

2. Each of you asks the other for feedback on how pleasing each of these items would be if they were done.

3. Each of you then chooses one, two, or three behaviors that you think would please yourself. Put these items in the privileges column of your tentative contract, using the same contract form.

4. Each of you, in turn, explains why you think privileges your partner chose would please him or her.

5. Each of you, in turn, explains how difficult it would be to carry out the items you have listed in the responsibilities column of your tentative contract.

6. Each of you ranks the items in your privileges column as to their degree of desirability and the items in your responsibilities column as to their degree of difficulty. Ask yourself, "Which privileges do I want the most?" and "Which responsibilities will be the most difficult for me to carry out?"

7. Each of you then negotiates and specifies the dimensions of *how often, how much, when, where,* and *with whom* for each responsibility and corresponding privilege on your contract. Remember, compromise is essential. You may not get everything you want, and improvement comes in small steps.

Now write the *final* contract:

8. Once the terms of each of your contracts have been clearly stated and agreed upon, write them down on your final contract. Ask yourself, "Can I commit myself to the contract?" If each of you answers yes, sign the contract and specify the length of time it will be in effect before it is renegotiated (one week, two weeks). If either of you answers no to this question, begin again at Step 7. If the answer is still no, go back to Step 1 again.

FIGURE 4-1.   The contracting exercise directs the partners in developing their own contract. (*Adapted from* Handbook of Marital Therapy, *by R. P. Lieberman, E. G. Wheeler, L. deVisser, J. Kuehnel, and T. Kuehnel. Copyright © 1980 by Plenum Publishing Corporation. Reprinted by permission.*)

CONTRACT FORM

In return for accepting the following responsibilities, I, Mary, will enjoy the following privileges:

Responsibilities	*Privileges*
1. Greet Harry affectionately each day upon his arrival home.	1. Harry will do the same.
2. Express approval for something Harry does well once a day.	2. Harry will give me a 5 minute massage 3X a week.
3. Initiate sex once a week.	3. Harry will take me out to dinner once a week.

Contractor *Mary E. Jones*
Contracting Partner *Harry J. Jones*
Witness *C. Nelson*
Date *1-18-84*

Ground Rules

1. No privilege can be used until the corresponding responsibility is carried out. No cheating! First do your responsibility, then enjoy your privilege.
2. All clauses have been freely and mutually agreed upon; changes can be made only after renegotiation in the presence of the therapist.
3. Reciprocity requires giving something in order to receive something.

FIGURE 4-2. Completed marital contract form. (*Adapted from* Handbook of Marital Therapy, *by R. P. Lieberman, E. G. Wheeler, L. deVisser, J. Kuehnel, and T. Kuehnel. Copyright © 1980 by Plenum Publishing Corporation. Reprinted by permission.*)

pleted homework assignments are seen by behavioral marital therapists as an essential therapeutic procedure—one that correlates highly with the degree to which a couple's relationship improves as therapy proceeds.

One example of a homework assignment is a task developed by Stuart (1980). This is the "caring-days" technique. On specific caring days, couples are asked to work on making relationship changes by acting as if they do in fact care for one another. (They are forewarned, however, that they may not fully experience caring feelings until they have actually changed their behavior.) The focus is on getting partners to offer each other seemingly inconsequential, small, caring behaviors that build their commitment to the therapeutic process and to their relationship. A caring day offers an opportunity to realize that all behavior between the partners need not be negative.

There are several things that the therapist can do to facilitate completion of homework assignments by couples:

1. Provide couples with a rationale for the importance of repeated practice outside of therapy sessions.
2. When assigning homework, get specific agreement from the couple as to the when, where, and other conditions under which they will complete the assignment. This can be put in writing as an extra reminder.
3. Always review homework at the beginning of the next session, giving it prominent importance. Give time and attention especially to assignments completed rather than to why assignments may have not been completed.

Evaluation and Summary

In this chapter we provide an overview of the social-learning approach to marital therapy. We explore this approach from a theory and practice standpoint, supported by clinical and laboratory research data. Since the social-learning or behavioral approach has been used in treating marital dysfunction only in the last 15 to 20 years, it is still evolving in both theory and therapeutic technique; controlled research has and will likely continue to shape its development, and herein lies its main contribution to the field of marital theory and therapeutic practice.

The behavioral approach systematically subjects its therapeutic techniques and procedures to experimental validation. And, as evaluation efforts produce new data, its methodology undergoes a continual process of refinement and development. We feel that this form of development is very encouraging in a profession criticized for its relative inability to provide accountability. "How can you prove that what you're doing works and is worth its costs?" mental-health professionals are often asked. It is quite paradoxical that the one major approach to marital and family therapy that strongly seeks to empirically validate its methods and results finds itself widely misunderstood and often criticized by the very people who work in this field. We therefore conclude this section and consolidate some subsidiary but essential points of social-learning theory by responding to some commonly held criticisms and misconceptions of the approach.

Criticism 1: *Behavioral marital therapy deemphasizes the importance of the therapist-couple relationship.* Although it is often the case that behavioral marital therapists do not place a primary value on therapist-couple relationship variables, this does not mean that they function as robots who conduct therapy mechanically. As was discussed in the section of this chapter dealing with the therapeutic relationship between the therapist and couple, relationship variables are indeed seen as setting the stage for upcoming therapeutic interventions. In addition, behavioral marital therapists do stress fostering collaboration between partners themselves and between the partners and therapist. Although not termed *rapport,* isn't this collaboration one and the same as rapport? Thus, although not assigning relationship variables the major role in the therapeutic process, behavioral therapists do not deemphasize them to the degree that some critics propose. Obviously therapy is most effective when there is cooperation and a working relationship established between the therapist and couple—that is, when they are working toward the same goals.

Criticism 2: *Behavioral marital therapy assumes that couples entering therapy will collaborate in a mutual effort to improve their relationship.* It is noted in this chapter that a collaborative working relationship is necessary to the success of therapeutic efforts. However, it is also noted that this collaborative relationship is not assumed to be present in couples' initial therapeutic interactions. The therapist must actively work to foster it.

Criticism 3: *Behavioral marital therapy does not offer a couple insight.* The behavioral marital therapist who considers this criticism an accurate one would likely respond that insight isn't necessarily required. Direct behavior-change efforts are a more efficient and effective therapeutic focus. Besides, if the goal of insight is ultimately behavior change anyway, then behavioral marital therapy techniques that have proven results have the same effect as insight. If the goals are the same, should not the relative efficacy of the two methodologies be determined empirically?

Not all therapists agree that behavioral therapy omits insight. Some couples might think of insight into their problems as emanating from past historical antecedents; however, many couples express "insight" as a behavioral therapist might, recognizing the positive effects on their relationship of behavior-exchange, communication-enhancement, and problem-solving procedures.

Criticism 4: *Behavioral marital therapy ignores historical causes of present dysfunctional behaviors.* This criticism is often levied by those of the psychoanalytic school of thought, who assert that it is necessary first to discover the original causes of dysfunctional behavior in the past and, based on these causes, to induce insight in the marital partners. Then the behaviors will change. Behavioral marital therapists do acknowledge that maladaptive behaviors likely have historical origins. However, these therapists understand that maladaptive behaviors continue to occur because they are reinforced in the present. Therefore, the focus of therapeutic efforts is on the present. Learning new behaviors or changing currently reinforcing environmental stimuli is what is necessary for behavior change to take place.

Criticism 5:   *Behavioral marital therapy may change behaviors but it does not adequately address the importance of changing couples' feelings and emotions.* Some critics have argued that emotions must change before behavior change can occur. Behavioral marital therapists' point of view, conversely, is that if partners' behaviors are changed the emotions will change as a result. Empirical evidence has not borne out the criticism that emotional change must be a prerequisite for lasting behavior change.

The behavioral approach to marital therapy, like all other marital therapy approaches, has certain limitations. Yet, also like other perspectives, it has unique contributions to offer. As practicing clinicians, we have found these contributions to be plentiful and of effective assistance in working with couples. As with the psychoanalytic approach, one need not totally subscribe to behavioral theory and therapy in order to derive benefits from its concepts, techniques, and procedures.

References

Azrin, N., Naster, B. J., & Jones, R. Reciprocity counseling: A rapid learning procedure for marital counseling. *Behavior Research and Therapy,* 1973, *11,* 365–382.

Bandura, A. *Principles of behavior modification.* New York: Holt, Rinehart & Winston, 1969.

Bienvenu, M. J. Measurement of marital communication. *Family Coordinator,* 1970, *19,* 26–31.

Corey, G. *Theory and practice of counseling and psychotherapy.* Monterey, Calif.: Brooks/Cole, 1977.

D'Zurilla, T. J. *Marital problem solving: A cognitive-behavioral-relationship approach to marital therapy.* Paper presented at the Association for the Advancement of Behavior Therapy, New York, December 1976.

Goldstein, A. Behavior therapy. In R. Corsini (Ed.), *Current psychotherapies.* Itasca, Ill.: Peacock, 1973.

Goodstein, L. Behavioral views of counseling. In B. Stefflre & W. H. Grant (Eds.), *Theories of counseling* (2nd ed.). New York: McGraw-Hill, 1972.

Gottman, J. M. *Marital interaction: Experimental investigations.* New York: Academic Press, 1979.

Gottman, J., Markman, H., & Notarius, C. The topography of marital conflict: A sequential analysis of verbal and nonverbal behavior. *Journal of Marriage and the Family,* 1977, *39,* 461–477.

Gottman, J., Notarius, C., Markman, H., Bank, S., Yoppi, B., & Rubin, M. E. Behavior exchange theory and marital decision making. *Journal of Personality and Social Psychology,* 1976, *34,* 14–23.

Gurman, A. S. Contemporary marital therapies: A critique and comparative analysis of psychoanalytic, behavioral and systems theory approaches. In T. J. Paolino, Jr. & B. S. McCrady (Eds.), *Marriage and marital therapy.* New York: Brunner-Mazel, 1978.

Gurman, A. S., & Razin, A. M. *Effective psychotherapy: A handbook of research.* New York: Pergamon, 1977.

Hops, H., Wills, T., Weiss, R., & Patterson, G. *Marital interaction coding system.* Unpublished manuscript, University of Oregon, 1971.

Jacobson, N. S. Behavioral marital therapy. In A. S. Gurman & D. P. Kniskern (Eds.), *Handbook of family therapy.* New York: Brunner-Mazel, 1981.

Jacobson, N. S., & Margolin, G. *Marital therapy: Strategies based on social learning and behavior exchange principles.* New York: Brunner-Mazel, 1979.

Jacobson, N. S., Waldron, H., & Moore, D. Toward a behavioral profile of marital distress. *Journal of Consulting and Clinical Psychology,* 1980, *48,* 696–703.

Jacobson, N. S., & Weiss, R. L. Behavioral marriage therapy: III. "The contents of Gurman et al. may be hazardous to our health." *Family Process,* 1978, *17,* 149–164.

Kahn, M. Nonverbal communication and marital satisfaction. *Family Process,* 1970, *9,* 449–456.

Katz, M. Agreement of connotative meaning in marriage. *Family Process,* 1965, *4,* 64–74.

Lederer, W. J., & Jackson, D. D. *The mirages of marriage.* New York: Norton, 1968.

Lieberman, R. P., Wheeler, E. G., deVisser, L., Kuehnel, J., & Kuehnel, T. *Handbook of marital therapy.* New York: Plenum Press, 1980.

Locke, H. J., & Wallace, K. M. Short-term marital adjustment and prediction tests: Their reliability and validity. *Journal of Marriage and Family Living,* 1959, *21,* 251–255.

O'Leary, K. D., & Turkewitz, H. Marital therapy from a behavioral perspective In T. J. Paolino, Jr. & B.S. McCrady (Eds.), *Marriage and marital therapy.* New York: Brunner-Mazel, 1978.

Patterson, G. R. *Families: Applications of social learning to family life.* Champaign, Ill.: Research Press, 1971.

Patterson, G. R., & Gullion, M. E. *Living with children.* Champaign, Ill.: Research Press, 1968.

Patterson, G. R., & Hops, H. Coercion, a game for two: Intervention techniques for marital conflict. In R. E. Ulrich & F. Mounjoy (Eds.), *The experimental analysis of social behavior.* New York: Appleton-Century-Crofts, 1972.

Stuart, R. B. *Helping couples change: A social learning approach to marital therapy.* New York: Guilford, 1980.

Turkewitz, H., & O'Leary, K. D. *Positive feelings questionnaire: The relationship between positive feelings toward one's spouse and general marital satisfaction.* Unpublished manuscript, SUNY, Stony Brook, N.Y., 1975.

Walsh, W. M. *A primer in family therapy.* Springfield, Ill.: Charles C. Thomas, 1980.

Weiss, R. L., & Cerreto, M. *Marital status inventory.* Unpublished manuscript, University of Oregon, 1975.

Weiss, R. L., Hops, H., & Patterson, G. R. A framework for conceptualizing marital conflict, technology for altering it, some data for evaluating it. In L. A. Hamerlynck, L. C. Handy, & E. J. Mash (Eds.), *Behavior change: Methodology, concepts and practice.* Champaign, Ill.: Research Press, 1973.

Wills, T. A., Weiss, R. L., & Patterson, G. R. A behavioral analysis of the determinants of marital satisfaction. *Journal of Consulting and Clinical Psychology,* 1974, *42,* 802–811.

Wilson, G. T., & Evans, I. M. Adult behavior therapy and the therapist-client relationship. In C. M. Franks & G. T. Wilson (Eds.), *Annual review of behavior therapy: Vol. 4.* New York: Brunner-Mazel, 1976.

CHAPTER FIVE

Systems Theory

In this chapter we explore marriage and marital therapy from a systems-theory perspective. Although we primarily consider working with couples, systems theory as a therapeutic approach emphasizes the relationships between individuals, their marital system, family system, community system, and the other suprasystems of which they are a part. Marital relationships, although systems within themselves, are frequently viewed by systems theorists as simply subsets of the greater family system of which they are a part. Marital dysfunction is therefore often treated by working with the couple as well as with other significant family members—the entire family together. Indeed, systems theory as a theoretical orientation toward marital therapy is likely best considered as a family-therapy perspective on the couple subsystem. For this reason, and in contrast to the psychoanalytic and social-learning approaches, it is not completely valid to identify a freestanding approach to marital therapy emanating from general systems theory.

It has been our experience, however, that the marital "subsystem" (when viewed from a family-therapy focus) often holds the key to the entire family's functioning. In such circumstances, our emphasis is frequently on the couple alone. Further, numerous couples without children come to therapy, as well as couples whose extended-family members are greatly separated by geographic distances. In all these cases, we view an understanding of systems concepts as vital in work with couples alone. (Chapter 10 addresses family theory and therapy, giving conceptual information and general strategies and suggestions for working with couples together with their significant family members.)

Although all systems therapists are likely to view marriage from primarily a general systems theory formulation, it would be quite inaccurate to refer to a single systems-theory perspective. Such a label might be acceptable only if it were meant to imply the very broad application of general systems theory to understanding marriage and practicing marital therapy (as in Chapter 1's discussion of how systems properties operate within marriage). However, within this broad theory as it is applied by individual therapists there are significant differences, in the emphasis placed on various systems properties and their relevance in explaining the nature and origin of marital dysfunction, explaining partners' interactions, and delineating appropriate procedures for therapeutic intervention.

The historically prominent approaches to therapy from a systems perspective (with their primary focus on family therapy) as referred to by leading figures within the field (Green & Kolevzon, 1982), include those of Satir (1967, 1972), Minuchin (1974), Haley (1963, 1976), and Bowen (1976, 1978). Our review of the marital theory and therapy literature suggests that, among these four systems approaches, those of Murray Bowen and Jay Haley, although they are primarily family therapists, have been applied most directly to couples—to marital therapy per se. Although Minuchin's work has included some influential and significant contributions, little has been published regarding the systematic treatment of the marital subsystem in isolation (Gurman, 1978). Satir's work has been purported to represent more of an "eclectic melange" of systems- and non-systems-oriented principles and thus not to present as "pure" a systems orientation as others (Gurman, 1977, 1978).

We now examine systems theory and therapy applications from the perspective of Murray Bowen's Bowen theory and, similarly, from the point of view of Jay Haley's problem-solving therapy.

Bowen Theory

Murray Bowen was one of the first therapists to relate systems concepts to the study of marital and family relationships. He was originally trained in a traditional psychoanalytic model, and he utilized this approach in research on the treatment of severely disturbed individuals, particularly schizophrenics. While conducting his early research, Bowen noticed that patients made more progress when their families were involved as part of the treatment process. This insight gradually developed into a large research study at the National Institute for Mental Health in Washington, D.C. in 1954. As part of this study, Bowen began to hospitalize the whole families of his schizophrenic patients for observation and research. The families lived with the patients in the hospital for varying periods of time.

One of the major findings of this research was that the parents of schizophrenic children react poorly to anxiety, and, as a result, often have particularly tension-filled marital relationships. These poorly functioning marriages are characterized by emotional distance between the partners that tends to lead to "triangulation," in Bowen's terms, when a child is born into the system. *Triangulation* refers to a situation in which the marital partners are unable to relate to each other and so use a third person, in this case their child, to reestablish contact and some kind of homeostatic balance. It is as if this third person is needed to maintain a relationship between the marital partners.

Along with the notion of triangles, several other concepts emerged in the late 1950s and early 1960s to form the basic structure of Bowen's theoretical approach. Other concepts were added during the 1970s, and today the whole is known as Bowen theory (Bowen, 1976b; 1978).

Bowen (1976b) stated that it is inaccurate to consider his approach synonymous with general systems theory, although he does see the approach as fitting into the broad framework of general systems theory. Others, however, have noted the relationship of Bowen theory to the larger theoretical structure in finer terms. As Gurman (1978) put it, Bowen "clearly writes in terms consistent with the most fundamental characteristic of general systems theory that there is a set of principles which can guide our thinking about all systems, whether living or mechanical" (p. 511). We agree with Gurman and therefore feel it important to include Bowen theory here both because it represents a major contribution as a currently practiced approach to marital theory and therapy and also because it clearly falls within the framework of holistic or organismic theories encompassed by the general systems notion (Steinglass, 1978).

Major Concepts

Although Bowen theory is based upon a number of related concepts, it has as its foundation two main assumptions. One concerns the degree of anxiety and the other the degree of differentiation of self that individuals experience. Let us examine these two variables as a basis for proceeding to a discussion of Bowen theory's major concepts.

Degree of Anxiety. Anxiety or emotional tension can differ with respect to intensity, duration, and kind. In using a biological model to explain how anxiety is managed, Bowen suggested that all organisms can reasonably adapt to acute anxiety for short periods of time. However, when anxiety becomes sustained or chronic, the mechanisms normally able to cope with it no longer seem sufficient. If this occurs, the organism develops tension, within itself or its relationship system, and this tension results in symptom formation, dysfunction, or illness. How marital partners respond to the tension that is produced by chronic or sustained anxiety determines whether the marital system remains free from symptoms, dysfunction, and illness.

Degree of Differentiation of Self.   Bowen uses this construct to define the functioning and experience both of individuals and of relationships according to their "differentiation," or its opposite, "fusion." In the relationship domain, fusion or lack of differentiation is reflected in a family's "emotional stuck-togetherness" or "undifferentiated family ego mass." Bowen views the family as an "emotional relationship system"— that is, members are emotionally intermeshed. For Bowen, this process of emotional relating has more significance than does either verbal or nonverbal communication. He sees the fusion/differentiation context as one from which emotional processes arise that can dominate intellectual processes. Such dominance creates a highly emotional climate, in which poorly differentiated adults and emotionally ruled children have difficulty achieving independence. In order to avoid falling victim to the emotional force of the system and to be able to separate oneself from the system's emotionality, a member must be able to differentiate between intellectual and emotional functioning.

Therefore, in the individual domain, differentiation refers to the ability of an individual to distinguish between emotion and intellect. People in whom intellect and emotion are poorly differentiated—fused—are ruled by their emotions. They react in a relatively primitive, instinctual manner. They are usually less flexible and less adaptable than other people and very dependent upon those around them. They are readily prone to dysfunction when tension arises, and it is difficult for them to recover. By contrast, people in whom emotion and intellect are well differentiated are able to choose emotional and/or intellectual interaction rather than to simply react, thoughtlessly. They react in an adult manner, basing their reactions on choice. Well-differentiated people function relatively autonomously and, while under stress, are more flexible, more adaptable, and more independent of the emotionality around them than are those in whom emotion and intellect are fused.

In Bowen theory, individual and systems functioning is a consequence of the degree of fusion or differentiation achieved between emotionality and intellect. People with low levels of differentiation are unable to separate themselves from their family systems. On the other hand, well-differentiated individuals are able to separate from their family systems. And, the systems reflect members' degrees of differentiation.

Thus, the level of differentiation an individual possesses determines whether he or she is able to function effectively, independent of the family system. For example, the highly differentiated individual likely responds to a conflict between two other family members with the thought, "Well, that's between the two of them to work out," deciding this from his or her intellect. The poorly differentiated individual does not recognize a choice including that response but, rather, is emotionally drawn into the conflict in an attempt to "help out."

From presentation of these fundamental premises we proceed to discussion of how degree of anxiety and of differentiation of self apply in more specific conceptual terms.

Differentiation-of-Self Scale

Bowen conceptualized degree of differentiation of self along a scale ranging from low to high. In doing so, he developed four profiles of emotional-intellectual functioning. The scale is illustrated in Figure 5-1.

Low Differentiation of Self.   People whose differentiation of self is poor exist in a world dominated by emotion. They have difficulty distinguishing between what feels good and what is good. They are almost totally relationship oriented, devoting tremendous amounts of energy to seeking love, attention, and approval from others. They are unable to separate how they feel about themselves or events from how others feel about the same things. Any decisions they make are on the basis of what feels good immediately and how others evaluate the decisions. They have little energy or desire for independent problem solving. Thus, poorly differentiated people are likely to lead lives that move from one crisis to the next, in which they are dominated by emotionality and unable to differentiate fact from feeling.

Moderate Differentiation of Self.   People at a moderate level of differentiation can begin to differentiate between intellect and emotion. Although at this level lives are still guided by emotions, lifestyles are more flexible. When anxiety level is low, moderately differentiated people can function fairly well. When anxiety is high, however, functioning can resemble that of a poorly differentiated individual. Relationships continue to be of primary importance. Many people at this level are in a

Low Level of Differentiation of Self		*High Level of Differentiation of Self*	
Emotions and Intellect Fused		Emotions and Intellect Differentiated	
Low Differentiation	Moderate Differentiation	Moderate-to-High Differentiation	High Differentiation

FIGURE 5-1.   The differentiation-of-self scale.

lifelong quest for the perfect relationship. Most are either frustrated in not finding this perfect relationship or, if they feel it is attained somehow, they become so threatened by the emotional fusion they experience that they react with distance and alienation. Failing to achieve the closeness they desire, they become withdrawn and depressed, or seek closeness in other relationships. When the relationship systems of these people are unbalanced, symptoms and problems occur.

Moderate-to-High Differentiation of Self.   At a moderate-to-high level of differentiation, emotion and intellect are sufficiently differentiated for the two systems to function more cooperatively than at lower levels. When anxiety increases, the intellects of people at the moderate-to-high level are able to hold their own and not be dominated by the emotional systems. Thus, at this level people are able to make appropriate choices. They can participate in emotional events without having to fear that they will become victims of their emotions because they know they can extricate themselves with logical reasoning if the need arises. These individuals are less relationship directed and more able to pursue independently sought goals. Although not unaware of their relationship systems, they determine their life courses more from within themselves than from what others think.

High Differentiation of Self.   Bowen chose not to categorize the few individuals who have developed beyond "good [high] differentiation," calling this level of differentiation "more hypothetical than real" (Bowen, 1976b, p. 73). It would seem, however, that such people would be able to react to and function quite effectively in various emotional relationships and at the same time to maintain individuality.

It is important to note that any person, on any level of the continuum, may drop to a lower level in times of increased anxiety and tension. The manner in which an individual is able to eventually respond to this anxiety indicates his or her level of self-differentiation. Better differentiated people may react emotionally in times of crisis but, as tension decreases, recover rather quickly. Those whose differentiation is moderate to high may need assistance to make a similar recovery. In contrast, some moderately and most poorly differentiated individuals are plunged into such a state of emotional fusion by crisis that they need substantial assistance to recover, when recovery is even possible.

Triangles

When anxiety and tension are low, most two-person systems operate fairly calmly and stably. But when tension and anxiety increase beyond a level the two-person system can manage, a third person or object is frequently "triangled in" to act as a mediator or deflector in the relationship and thereby reduce the tension being experienced.

The classic example of triangulation involves the father-mother-child relationship. When there is tension between the parents, they project it onto the child. Instead of the parents arguing about a situation, the mother, for example, may find herself in conflict with her child. This frees the father from the original stressful relationship with his wife and allows him to realign himself with her in commiserating about her poor relationship with their child. Bowen labeled this phenomenon the "family projection process." It is through this process in childhood that individuals develop a low level of differentiation. The child, because of his or her young age, has not had the opportunity to differentiate him- or herself from the parents as yet. He or she simply reflects the parents' levels of differentiation. The child is at the mercy of the parents' emotional forces in times of stress. As the parents' emotionality rises, the child resonates this emotionality at the expense of his or her intellectual process. The degree to which family projection does or does not occur largely determines a person's place on Bowen's scale of self-differentiation.

Although the notion of triangulation was developed by Bowen in his research on families with schizophrenic members, it applies as well to families considered normal and to married couples who are childless (Gurman, 1978). For example, the childless couple may look to the extended family (mothers-in-law are traditionally "triangled in"), the community, a therapist, or "objects" such as religious beliefs, societal norms, or other external standards (as reflected in such axioms as "It's God's will"; "A partner should not criticize his or her mate").

Emotional Cutoff

Bowen proposes that in childhood all people develop a certain degree of emotional attachment to their parents and families of origin. All people have some degree of unresolved emotional attachment; however, the lower the level of differentiation, the more intense the unresolved attachment. As individuals grow to adulthood and leave their families, they must deal with the resolution of this emotional attachment. The manner in which it is resolved, or left unresolved, determines the "emotional cutoff." How well individuals are able to differentiate themselves from their original families and the degree of emotional attachment that remains compose a critical determinant of how they handle all subsequent emotional relationships.

Bowen suggested that there are various levels of emotional cutoff. Yet the degree of one's unresolved emotional attachment is roughly proportional to the degree of one's lack of differentiation, and these factors generally determine each other. Bowen identified a number of dysfunctional ways that individuals attempt emotional separation from their families: emotional isolation or withdrawal, physical distancing, and a combination of the two. These are all dysfunctional because the emotional dependency still remains, knowing no time or space boundaries.

Ideally, emotional cutoff is negotiated during late adolescence and early adulthood, when people normally leave their family systems and go out on their own. People with relatively high levels of self-differentiation encounter the least conflict in separating. Because they are well differentiated and independent, they are able to resolve the emotional attachments to their families and to form new attachments in other relationships.

Choice of a Marital Partner

According to Bowen theory, one's degree of differentiation of self determines choice of a partner. Moreover, this selection process does not occur accidentally: mating and marriage "are governed to a significant degree by emotional-instinctual forces" (Bowen, 1976b, p. 79). Bowen also proposed that level of differentiation and lifestyle pattern are largely determined by the time one leaves one's family of origin. Thus, individuals tend to repeat in all their future relationships the style of relating learned in the parental family.

As people seek potential marital partners, they select those most like themselves in level of differentiation. They believe that long-term intimacy is more likely when attributes are commonly shared. Of course, the partners are not consciously aware of their self-differentiation on similar levels. However, in the process of joining together they develop a lifestyle that is compatible with these levels. From the beginning of their relationship, this lifestyle determines the nature and kind of problems they encounter.

Marital Dysfunction

The daily pressures of partners' accommodating one another as well as having to cope with outside forces can cause stress sufficient to develop tension in a marital relationship. If the shared lifestyle of the couple is not differentiated enough to resolve the pressures, problems result from this tension. The lower the level of differentiation, the more intense the emotional fusion and therefore the difficulty. Some of the tension may be released through relationships outside the marital system or nuclear family, through contacts with the extended family or in the community (as in work, in church, or with friends). When the tension is too much for the system to release in this way, it turns in on itself in an attempt to reestablish homeostasis.

According to Bowen theory, there are a number of ways partners deal with fusion symptoms. The most frequent means is for partners to emotionally distance themselves from each other. Other than emotional distance, there are three major ways in which lack of differentiation in the marital relationship comes to be manifested in symptoms so as to reduce tension in the system: (1) marital conflict, (2) dysfunction in one partner, and (3) impairment of one or more children.

Marital Conflict.   The basic feature in the pattern of conflictual marital relationships is that neither partner gives in to the other. In these relationships each partner invests a great deal of energy in the other. At a particular moment, the energy may be emotional or intellectual, positive or negative; the core of the problem is that the self of each partner is focused mostly on the other. The relationship cycles through periods of intense closeness, conflict, and then making up, which begins another cycle of intense closeness. Partners whose feelings cycle in this manner have the most overtly intense of all relationships. Both the anger and negative feelings during conflict and the positive feelings of closeness are equally intense. The partners think of little but each other even when they are apart.

Dysfunction in One Partner.   Dysfunction in one partner is an alternative to outright conflict. It begins with one partner's adaptive posture to the dynamics generated by the couple's undifferentiated state. The partner who is adapting is unable to make decisions or take any responsibility for him- or herself. Adaptive partners' passivity and complacency are contrasted by their mates' active dominance. Adaptive partners subjugate themselves and become dependent on the direction of their dominant mates, constantly adapting ideas, emotions, and behaviors to please. The partners who are adaptive are those most susceptible to dysfunction. Any substantial increase in stress and anxiety in the relationship can initiate some form of dysfunction on the part of the adapting partner, such as a physical or emotional illness. Since many of these illnesses are socially sanctioned ("He/she can't be blamed for his/her illness."), and they do provide an effective means of reducing tension and maintaining balance in a marital system, they can become enduring and quite resistant to change.

Impairment of One or More Children.   When tension caused by a couple's undifferentiated state cannot be reduced entirely by marital conflict or one partner's dysfunction, impairment of one or more of the children may occur. In this case, the disturbance between the parents is transmitted directly or indirectly to one or more of the children. The child becomes the focal point of the problem and removes the locus of intensity from the parents' relationship.

The Therapeutic Process

The Goals of Therapy

The two most basic therapeutically relevant concepts of Bowen theory are *differentiation of self* and *triangulation*. The importance of the process of detriangulation provides the main focus of treatment. The degree of a person's differentiation of self is the critical factor in vulnerability to fusion within a system. It follows, then, that the primary goal of therapy is increasing marital partners' differentiation of self, both individually and from their families of origin. This is done through detriangulation.

For some, the process of increased differentiation through detriangulation occurs more quickly and easily than for others. The basic goal is perceived as attained, however, when both partners have gained a reasonable level of differentiation of self from each other and from their families of origin and have become more effective in coping with increases in anxiety and the resulting tension and crises that can accompany them.

The Role of the Therapist

In the view conceptualized in Bowen theory, the therapist is an active, directive model and teacher. The marital therapist is potentially the third element in the triangle; from that position, the therapist's role is to remain emotionally detached, and to intellectually model and teach the other two people in the triangle to develop higher levels of self-differentiation. This is accomplished through the therapist's use of four essential intervention strategies: (1) defining and clarifying the relationship between the partners, (2) the therapist's keeping him- or herself detriangled from the emotional system, (3) teaching the functioning of emotional systems, and (4) demonstrating differentiation by taking "I-position" stands during the course of therapy. These strategies are expounded upon in the discussion of specific techniques and procedures for treatment that ends the presentation of Bowen theory.

The Therapeutic Relationship

Bowen proposed that the therapist explicitly avoid getting intensely involved with a couple. Because of his emphasis on differentiation of self, Bowen suggested that the therapist should work to relate to each partner as an individual. During the therapy session, even though both partners are present, the therapist should speak to each partner separately. The other partner observes the interaction between the therapist and his or her mate but may not enter into the exchange.

Although this may appear to be primarily a focus on the individual, as in psychoanalytic theory, remember that detriangulation and development of greater self-differentiation is the major therapeutic goal. One means of achieving this goal is helping each partner take an "I-position"—an expression of individual differentiation. In addition, Bowen's theory holds that changing one member of a triangle creates circumstances that cause changes in the relationships in the triangle and thus leads to the other participants also changing.

The Structure of Therapy

Bowen's description of therapy is one in which the process proceeds through several identifiable phases. In the early phases of therapy, partners learn to know each other better, to differentiate themselves, and to deal with the reactions that their self-differentiation evokes in their mates. Bowen (1976a) described this process:

> Characteristically, one spouse begins to focus on self while the other pleads for togetherness. It is common for the differentiating one to yield to the togetherness pressure at least once before proceeding on a self-determined course in spite of the opposition. This results in a brief emotional reaction in the other, following which they both arrive at a new and slightly higher basic level of differentiation. This is usually followed by another fairly calm period, after which the other spouse focuses on self and takes the same steps toward differentiation while the former opposes with togetherness pressure. Thus, differentiation proceeds in small alternating steps [p. 399].

As early as possible the therapist also begins to assist partners in differentiating themselves from their families of origin. When partners can be successful at this the total process proceeds more rapidly, without the alternating pattern that occurs when there is less attention given to families of origin. Therapy may terminate when presenting symptoms are relieved, or it can continue toward a deeper, more satisfying resolution. If the couple is well motivated and the therapist is relatively successful at keeping him- or herself emotionally detriangled, it is usual for the couple to find more and more to work on and resolve (Bowen, 1976a).

Termination is usually reached when both partners have achieved a reasonable degree of differentiation from each other and from their families of origin, when they have learned enough about family systems so that one or the other is better able to react to crisis situations, and when they have some logical plan and motivation to continue working toward greater differentiation.

Note that assessment is an important aspect of the therapeutic structure. While it is not standardized, relying instead on the therapist's clinical judgment, it does center on core themes and dimensions for all couples. These assessment areas and the techniques and procedures with which to therapeutically intervene now become our focus.

Therapeutic Techniques and Procedures

Assessment of Marital Dysfunction

The role of assessment is basic to the therapeutic process because what is occurring in the system in terms of triangulation, projection, and levels of individual and family differentiation provides the therapist with information regarding partners' potential for change. Two specific concepts of Bowen's theory were noted by him to provide especially pertinent data in this regard: (1) multigenerational transmission process and (2) sibling position.

Multigenerational Transmission Process. This concept is in many ways a synthesis of several other concepts. In the view taken in Bowen theory, the development of individual dysfunction is a result of several generations of low-to-moderate differentiation, triangulation, family projection, and inadequate emotional cutoff. Typically, in one generation the parents project their lack of differentiation onto one of their children. This triangled child becomes the most dependent and least differentiated of the children. When this child marries, he or she usually chooses a partner with an equivalent low level of differentiation. The partners in this new generation in turn project their poor differentiation onto their children, in varying degrees. The maximally involved child emerges with a lower level of self-differentiation than the parents. A less involved child may emerge with about the same level of self-differentiation as the parents. A more independent child may have a higher level of differentiation.

As the third-generation children form their own families, there is movement to higher and lower levels on the differentiation-of-self continuum. Those who move higher may have more productive lives than their parents. Those who move down to a lower level encounter more difficulties and are less able to cope with life's crises. Thus, the multigenerational transmission process provides a longitudinal view of marital partners' families. In doing so, it gives the therapist an in-depth picture of partners' current levels of functioning.

Sibling Position. Bowen adapted the work of Toman (1961) concerning personality profiles of each sibling position in a family. The basic thesis of the sibling-position concept is that certain personality characteristics correspond with the birth order of each child in a family. Bowen theory uses this correspondence in comparing an individual's personality profile with the profile suggested by order of birth; unexpected differences in the two profiles help the therapist trace the level of differentiation and the direction of the family projection process from generation to generation. For example, if an oldest child has a profile more like that of a youngest, the disparity indicates that the oldest was the most triangled child. However, emotional immaturity is not the only indication of low level of differentiation. If an oldest child is extremely domineering in interpersonal relationships, this might also suggest a lower level of differentiation. By contrast, behavior that is calm, responsible, and rational is indicative of a higher level of differentiation.

A careful assessment of family history in light of the concepts of multigenerational transmissions and sibling position can provide the therapist with valuable data as to partners' present level of functioning and how they might be expected to respond in therapy.

Intervention Strategies

As pointed out in the discussion of the role of the therapist, Bowen postulated four main therapeutic intervention strategies: (1) defining and clarifying the relationship between partners, (2) keeping "self" detriangled from the emotional system, (3) teaching the functioning of emotional systems, and (4) demonstrating differentiation by taking "I-position" stands during the course of therapy.

Defining and Clarifying the Relationship between Partners.   To some extent all marital partners function in a "feeling world" in which they respond to the emotions of the other. As a marital relationship develops and becomes more intimate, partners quickly learn what subjects make their spouses anxious, and they therefore avoid these subjects. In turn, the avoidance creates a void in their interactions, which partners often attempt to resolve by "talking it out." But all too often this only stirs up emotional reactiveness and drives the partners apart.

Early in Bowen's therapeutic endeavors, he discovered this relationship between emotional disclosure and greater degrees of dysfunction. He began to discourage partners from interacting on emotional issues and instead had them speak only to him, in the calmest, most low-key and objective way possible. This technique resulted in clarification and definition of the relationship. Partners were each able to really hear what the other was saying without reacting emotionally, some for the first time in their relationship together.

The focus in this intervention strategy is on helping partners to become more aware of emotional responses and to define those that affect their relationship so as to be able to react more from intellect than from emotion. For example, when a husband speaking to the therapist becomes upset, the therapist asks the wife whether she is aware that her husband is upset, and asks her response to it. The therapist then asks the husband for his reaction to his wife's response.

Keeping Self Detriangled from the Emotional System.　Bowen proposed that partners' emotional problems resolve automatically if they can remain in contact with a third person who can remain free of their emotional field while still actively relating to each of them. The technique of staying detriangled thus rests on the ability of the therapist to relate to each partner, seeking a balance between being too close and too distant, too emotionally involved and too intellectually detached. The therapist's own degree of differentiation of self and knowledge of triangles are crucial factors in achieving this balance. If the therapist can attain this detriangled, balanced position and relate to a couple from it, the partners soon discover their emotional maneuvers to triangle in the therapist to be futile, resulting not in emotional involvement of the therapist but in their having to change. Bowen (1976a) described his own therapeutic stance in this regard:

> I attempt to back out emotionally to the point where I can watch the ebb and flow of the emotional process while always thinking "process," and without getting caught in the flow. Furthermore, there is usually a humorous or comical side to most serious situations. If I am too close, I can get caught in the seriousness of the situation. If I am too distant, I am not effectively in contact with them. The "right" point for me is one between seriousness and humor, when I can make either a serious or a humorous response to facilitate the process [p. 397].

Teaching the Functioning of Emotional Systems.　In a therapeutic process such as Bowen proposed, teaching or instruction is particularly necessary. This is especially so because the focus of therapy is on utilizing intellectual concepts to guide the effort to modify emotional systems. Thus, the therapist's intervention in an emotional triangle often involves didactic instruction about the process occurring, as well as means of learning to become better differentiated, to clarify values and ideals, and to resolve specific concerns.

Taking I-position Stands.　The basis for this intervention strategy is that when one partner is able to calmly and rationally state his or her own convictions and to act upon them without becoming involved in an emotional interaction as a result, the other is likely to do likewise. The more the therapist assumes the role of calm, rational participant and models it by exhibiting a high degree of differentiation, the greater the possibility that the partners will better understand the therapeutic goal of increasing differentiation and, seeing its effectiveness, will be encouraged to work toward it themselves.

The primary idea to convey is the difference between an I-position and a you-position. In the you-position, emotional reactiveness is automatic, reflexive, and uncontrolled. Partners functioning from this stand do not take responsibility for their actions. Instead they blame their mates for "making" them feel some unpleasant emotion (or alternatively, praise their mates for inducing good feelings). Partners functioning from an I-position are aware of the potential emotionality inherent in their relationship, but they step back from it, observe how the process is evolving, and control their reactions to it. Such people have the security of responsible, considered principles rather than dependence upon the approval or disapproval of others to guide them (Singleton, 1982).

Aside from the aforementioned intervention strategies, Bowen has written little regarding specific techniques. For example, his book *Family Therapy in Clinical Practice* (Bowen, 1978) has not even one chapter devoted to technique and only a few scattered comments on the subject. Singleton (1982), in discussing Bowen's work, suggested this lack to be a deliberate effort by Bowen to maintain therapists' primary focus on theory and their own personhood as opposed to technique. Singleton stated, in this regard:

> In working on his own self-differentiation, the consultant is doing within the clinical situation what he more importantly makes a life-long effort with his own family, both nuclear and extended. To the extent he has succeeded in becoming more relaxed and less reactive in important relationships in his own family, he will find it easier to do so with clinical families. Furthermore, he will work out his own techniques for putting this into practice based on his own beliefs and experiences. . . . While Bowen and those trained under him have many carefully developed techniques, imitation of them is meaningless without the underlying theory. Conversely, with the theory, a neophyte can gradually develop his own techniques which will work better for him than someone else's [p. 90].

Problem-Solving Therapy

Of all the major systems theorists, Jay Haley has written the most extensively on marital therapy. His approach to marital theory and therapy stresses a struggle for power and control in every relationship through the messages exchanged. He proposed that all symptoms are strategies for controlling a relationship when other strategies have failed. As a therapist, Haley's emphasis is on clarifying the nature of the power relationship. This intervention effort is aimed at teaching partners awareness of their actual intentions in maneuvering to gain power in their relationship. The new awareness allows the partners the opportunity to accept or change their behaviors.

Haley's approach to marital therapy has steadily evolved. He focused on marital therapy from a dyadic view in *Strategies of Psychotherapy* (1963b), presented the different stages of marriage over the life cycle in *Uncommon Therapy* (1973), and most recently, in *Problem-Solving Ther-*

apy (1976), emphasized a triangle concept that includes the dysfunctional couple and a third element.

Haley's problem-solving therapy falls within what have been termed the "strategic" approaches to family therapy. Haley (1973) defined strategic therapy as that in which the therapist initiates what happens during treatment and designs a particular approach for each problem. The strategic therapist takes responsibility for directly influencing people. Further, in order to bring about beneficial change, the strategic therapist wants to enhance at least temporarily his or her influence over the interpersonal system at hand. Haley has been identified as a prominent figure who subscribes to this approach (Stanton, 1981).

Major Concepts

Haley's theoretical and therapeutic conceptualizaton of marriage is based on the notion that relationships are defined by communications, which vary in their levels of meaning. His primary therapeutic assumption, however, is that any relationship is by definition a struggle for power and control. We now examine Haley's major beliefs that explain these fundamental concepts.

Marital Themes

Haley (1963a) described marriage as "a more or less voluntary relationship" (p. 183). He suggested that a marital relationship in which there is a balance between voluntary and compulsory aspects functions best. For example, a couple having achieved this balance defines the relationship as one of choice, yet the partners have sufficient compulsion to stay together when crises arise because of laws, social customs, or personal commitments.

Problems arise if the relationship is either too compulsory or too voluntary. However, the important consideration is not whether the relationship is actually too compulsory or voluntary by external standards but how partners themselves choose to define it. For example, if partners perceive themselves as having few compulsory ties and divorce is a readily available alternative, there may be too little compulsion in the relationship to hold it intact in times of crisis. At the other extreme, couples who feel forced to stay together because of children or strict religious beliefs may begin to believe that they are together only because they must be and not because they choose to be. Seeing a relationship as compulsory tends to encourage hostility and bad feelings, as well as their frequent expression.

Levels of Communication

Fundamental to Haley's approach is the idea that communication defines the nature of a marital relationship. When partners communicate, they have the potential to do so on two levels. One level consists of those messages that have a specific referent, and one only. That is, the message is about one thing and not about something else as well; "I am hungry" means simply that I desire food.

However, there is also a second level on which messages may be sent. There are usually various clues (such as voice intonations, facial expressions, and gestures telling how a message is to be taken. "I am hungry" may literally mean that the speaker desires food, but on a second level the speaker may mean "You make something for me to eat."

Problems arise when meanings in partners' communications are not shared. When a message sent (at both levels) is congruent with the message received, there is shared meaning. Otherwise, an interactional pattern that is dysfunctional is created. As partners develop their relationship, it is their interactional patterns, functional or dysfunctional, that create, reinforce, or allow for the changing of the rules by which they come to function.

Rules

Haley proposed that every situation a newly married couple encounters must be addressed by establishing explicit or implicit rules. There are three types of rules: (1) those that are recognized and able to be described; (2) those that partners do not initially perceive but, if pointed out, would acknowledge; and (3) those that an observer might see but the couples would likely refuse to recognize or acknowledge. A couple cannot avoid establishing these rules; whenever they complete a transaction, a rule has been established. For example, even if partners chose to be completely spontaneous with each other, they would still have established a rule that they behave in that manner.

A couple not only sets rules as a matter of course but necessarily also reaches agreement as to which of the partners makes rules for the various areas of their relationship. The first issue is always addressed together with the second; the process of rule setting always occurs within a context of resolving who is setting the rule. Thus, rule setting is another area in marriage where power and control issues predominate.

The process of resolving conflicts over making rules involves the establishment of a set of "meta-rules," or rules for making rules. For instance, some couples expressly avoid discussing aspects of their relationship (perhaps sexual issues). They have established a meta-rule about how to deal with those areas. Conflicts over establishing rules are heavily influenced by partners' learning experiences, especially in their families of origin. The transition to one's own family from a previous one requires considerable compromise and some inevitable conflict.

Defining Relationships

Looking at marriage in terms of establishing rules for living together is another way of describing marriage as a process of defining relationships. Any rule instituted by partners defines their relationship in one of two ways: as a complementary relationship or a symmetrical relationship.

A complementary relationship is one in which there is a leader and a follower, a giver and a receiver. Different sorts of behavior are exchanged in complementary relationships. Symmetrical relationships are those in which the same type of behaviors are exchanged—for example, both partners giving. The basic criterion for a symmetrical relationship is equality in relating.

Couples in relatively satisfying relationships respond to each other both in complementary and symmetrical ways in different areas of the marriage. Problems arise, however, when partners are unable to form either of the two types of relationships and the marriage becomes restricted to the other. This occurs as a result of negative past experiences with one type. For example, a marital partner whose parents only related to him or her as a child in a harsh complementary manner, never symmetrically, may rebel against behavior initiating even the slightest complementarity on the part of a mate. In such a situation, both partners are deprived of the various types of pleasurable interactions characteristic of the blocked style of relating.

Choice of a Marital Partner

Haley has published relatively little on the issue of marital choice. Presumably, individuals seek potential partners whose styles of interaction are familiar to them on the basis of past interpersonal experiences. This assumption is supported by a statement by Haley (1963a):

> The patterns which appear in a marriage existed in some form prior to the ceremony. People have a remarkable skill in choosing mates who will fit their needs, although they may insist later they married the unexpected. The girl who needs to be treated badly usually finds someone who will cooperate. If someone feels he deserves very little from life, he tends to find a wife who feels she deserves very little; both get what they seek [p. 185].

Marital Dysfunction

In Haley's frame of reference, conflict and dysfunction in a marital relationship can arise in four primary areas: (1) what rules to follow, (2) who is to set the rules, (3) attempts to enforce rules that conflict with each other, and (4) incompatibility between the process of working out conflicts and the conflicts themselves.

What Rules to Follow.   Haley suggested that the most easily resolved conflicts in marriage are those involving which rules to follow. Although disagreement on various aspects of a couple's relationship may cause considerable difficulty, compromises that resolve these matters can be reached. Such problems involve relatively little emotional involvement; they are more "disagreement" than actual conflict.

Who Is To Set the Rules.   Although most disagreements are about which rules to follow, conflicts that are especially emotional revolve around who is to make the rules. This concern is not as easily dealt with through compromise. When partners focus on who is to make the rules, they often behave as if basic human rights are at stake. The question of rights involves a complicated procedure that often provides the impetus for either conflict or reconciliation.

For example, a husband might welcome advice from his wife if she offers it in just the right way or if he has asked for it. If so, he cooperates in a complementary relationship. However, he may angrily oppose such a relationship if she offers advice authoritatively or insists on his adhering to her advice. Similarly, this wife might be quite willing to treat her husband as an equal, but if he demands it she may reverse her desire to do so. Thus, the struggle for perceived control presents itself as the major issue.

Attempts to Enforce Rules that Conflict with Each Other.   At times, partners may each communicate about rules on a different level. In doing so, they can offer each other messages that define one type of relationship at one level of communication and an incompatible type of relationship at another level of communication. The conflicts this can produce are difficult to resolve and often provoke reactions that tend to perpetuate the struggle.

For example, a husband insists that his wife not be so passive and that she assert herself more with their children instead of always doing what they tell her to do. However, by asserting herself with the children she passively accepts her husband's command. Two conflicting sets of rules, and therefore types of relationship, are being imposed.

Incompatibility between the Process of Working Out Conflicts and the Conflicts Themselves.   A final kind of potential marital conflict can occur when there is incompatibility between the meta-rules partners establish for resolving disagreements about rules and the rules themselves. Consider, for instance, a situation wherein a couple has established a meta-rule that disagreements will be resolved through mutual compromise and discussion. However, when disagreement arises on an issue that is particularly anxiety producing for the husband he withdraws from the discussion, choosing not to confront the issue. His behavior defining the relationship as complementary on this issue is incompatible with the meta-rule to handle disagreements symmetrically. The result is mutual dissatisfaction and discord in the relationship.

The Therapeutic Process

The Goals of Therapy

In order to adequately comprehend the goals of therapy from Haley's perspective, it is necessary to first conceptualize the levels and nature of change as defined by the Mental Research Institute group of which Haley is a prominent member. The group has defined two levels of change (Watzlawick, Weakland, & Fisch, 1974). "First-order" change is an allowable sort of moving about within a nevertheless relatively unchanging system in a way that makes no difference to the family. "Second-order" change is a shift that actually alters the system. To be successful, therapy must bring about second-order change.

In regard to differentiation of the two levels of change, Stanton (1981) offered the example of a family who came to therapy for treatment of a son who was failing in school. As therapy progressed, the son's grades improved. However, at the same time a sister's school performance deteriorated. Even though there appeared to be basic change because the son showed improvement, the family system itself was never really altered, as evidenced by the daughter subsequently being substituted as a problem. This constitutes a first-order change.

If the son had started to make academic progress (without manifesting new problems) and his sister remained at her pretreatment level (or better), it would have been more likely that second-order change had occurred; the system itself and the son's apparent position in it would have been changed, with the implication that the family no longer required him to behave dysfunctionally (Stanton, 1981).

For Haley, "the main goal of therapy is to get people to behave differently and so have different subjective experiences" (Haley, 1976, p. 49). In his view, couples in difficulty tend to perpetuate their distress by attempting to deal with it, ironically, in such a way that it continues provoking only first-order changes. These attempts tend to maintain the system's current patterns—that is, a state of homeostasis. Haley's focus is on this repeating sequence of conflict-laden behavior. In order to facilitate behavior change that will result in a new homeostatic setting for the system (second-order change), the therapist must not only shift or expand the types of relationships a couple is experiencing but also induce a change in the manner in which they work to maintain the stability of their marital system. Effecting these changes requires influencing the relationship's homeostatic mechanisms so that the system itself undergoes change. As a means of doing so, Haley (1979) noted that "one can plan a therapy in which crisis is induced, thereby forcing the whole system to reorganize. Or one can start small change and persistently push it until the change is so amplified that the system must change in order to adapt to it" (p. 41).

The Role of the Therapist

Couples who present themselves for marital therapy are essentially seeking a more satisfying means of perpetuating their relationship. The therapist assists in this endeavor in a number of ways: (1) by encouraging that discussion be used to resolve conflict rather than previous ineffective means, such as silence or withdrawal; (2) by being a reasonably impartial advisor and judge; (3) by assisting couples to examine motivations they may have but are not immediately aware of; (4) by making manipulative maneuvers explicit and therefore more difficult to employ; (5) by facilitating couples' ability to deal with sensitive topics; and (6) by using paradoxical communications (Haley, 1963a).

Haley (1976) placed the primary responsibility for change in the system on the therapist. He proposed that the therapist utilize brief, intensive interventions, being active and directive from the outset and asserting control from the first session. In doing so, the therapist's focus should be on the present and on ways to organize the members of the system to change what is happening. Also, when working with a couple, the therapist should organize what is said and done so that the therapeutic process is aimed at achieving specific objectives. A final consideration in the therapist's role is the critical importance of being aware of his or her own philosophy of life and marriage. The therapist must have seriously thought through and appraised his or her own feelings regarding the issues of separation and divorce as well as regarding responsibilities within the family group. The self-appraisal of relationship-responsibility issues serves as a necessary guideline for effective therapeutic interventions. Simply not offering counsel on these issues does not avoid them; the therapist's beliefs will be communicated somehow—most likely as a second-level communication. Unless therapists have clarified their own thinking, couples' sensitive marital concerns may be met with responses that are confused, biased, or uncertain.

The Therapeutic Relationship

Haley's method recognizes the importance of the therapist's establishing a warm, trusting relationship with a couple. However, in order to be an effective teacher and model, the therapist must be perceived by the couple as potent and credible in terms of his or her expertise. The therapist's role is directive and controlling. The therapist must thrust him or herself into the system and, by assuming control of the system, force the system to redefine its presently prevailing power mechanisms.

In Háley's view the marital unit is a triangle, with the third element activated in times of crisis "to intervene and stabilize it" (Haley, 1976, p. 153). Haley proposed that the therapist replace or become the third party in this triangle and stabilize the dyad. Of course, the therapist must also be able to effectively exit without the couple becoming unstabilized and again seeking a third party.

Haley's method uses directives to intensify and bond the therapeutic relationship. He stated in this regard:

> By telling people what to do, a therapist becomes involved in the action. He becomes important because the person must either do or not do what the therapist says. If the directive is something the people are to do during the week, the therapist remains in their lives all week. They are thinking about such things as: What if we don't do it? What if we only half-way do it? What if we change it and do it in our own way? and so on. When they come back for the next interview, the therapist is more important than if he had not given a directive [1976, p. 49].

Thus, the therapeutic relationship is seen by Haley as a complementary one. It is akin to a teacher/facilitator-student relationship, and as such is positive and growth producing.

The Structure of Therapy

There are six basic stages in Haley's therapeutic progression. Theoretically, these stages occur in sequence and are spread over several sessions. However, because Haley's problem-solving therapy is a brief and intense process, all of the stages might occur immediately in the initial session and then be repeated in subsequent sessions when appropriate. For example, in a first session the therapist might progress from initial greetings and exchanging introductions to direct intervention. Subsequent sessions may also require some initial social exchange as a prelude to more anxiety-arousing efforts. The therapist should implement any or all of the stages as necessary, with the understanding that the final three are the most productive in achieving behavior change.

1. *Social Stage.* In this stage the family is greeted and made comfortable. Haley (1976) proposed that "therapy is more effective and more rapid when more people are involved in the interviews" (p. 15). When the therapist can observe a couple interacting with the significant others in their family lives, especially children, a better understanding of the marital system is possible. At least in the first sessions, as many significant members of the couple's family as possible are encouraged to take part in therapy.

The therapist uses this stage to define the situation as one in which all the members are involved and important. This is accomplished by getting responses from each member present, encouraging all to take part. In succeeding sessions, the social stage allows participants a time to reacclimate and prepare themselves to take part in therapeutic efforts. During this initial phase, the therapist is observing family members' interactions, both verbal and nonverbal, in order to gather information on how to begin the next stage.

2. *Problem Stage.* This stage begins the shift to the work of therapy; the situation is defined no longer as social but rather as purposeful. Again, all present are encouraged to participate in the discussion. It is at this time that the therapist inquires why the couple/family is here or what the problem is. The therapist's observations continue to be important for planning upcoming interventions. How everyone acts and what they say communicates such therapeutic concerns as who is given responsibility for the problem, the participants' motivation for therapy, and the relative stability of aspects of the system.

3. *Interaction Stage.* The interaction stage focuses on getting the couple/family to elaborate on their presenting problem. At this time, the therapist removes him- or herself as the center of conversation. Instead of being the person each participant speaks to, the therapist focuses them on speaking to each other. In this manner, the therapist is able to observe from a third-person perspective how the couple/family interacts in a potentially stressful situation. This is necessary because family members cannot tell the therapist about their sequences and patterns of behavior; the members often don't know what these are. Only by observing how the members behave with each other is this information gained. The interaction stage provides the therapist the opportunity to observe.

4. *Goal-Setting Stage.* At this point, it is important to gain a clear statement of what changes everyone would like to derive from therapy. It is essential that this statement be put in a form that makes it solvable. The discussion that occurs during this stage involves negotiating how to make the presenting problem operational. For example, to say that the couple is unhappy provides little information useful in solving the problem; the way in which the unhappiness manifests itself and the reactions to it are the problem. In addition to the advantage of spelling out the problem in allowing it to be solvable, clearly specifying the problem also allows the therapist to know whether he or she has succeeded in dealing with it. Again, all participants are encouraged to be involved. Identification of goals, mutual satisfaction with them, and a commitment to their attainment constitute the primary objectives of this phase of therapy.

5. *Intervention Planning Stage.* The intervention stage of the process relates to the therapist directly. This is when he or she develops and plans the intervention strategies that will be used in upcoming sessions. These strategies are based on the information that the therapist has gathered from observations and from the goals expressed by the couple/family.

6. *Intervention Stage.* In this stage the therapist gives specific direc-

tives to the couple/family in order to involve him- or herself in the system's action and to structure the system in the direction of change. These directives are tasks that participants are asked to engage in. They may be metaphoric, as in the case of an activity that resembles the target behavior but has a goal that is easier to achieve, or they may be paradoxical and phrased in such a way as to be irresistible because of the double bind in which they place the recipient.

The therapy process is terminated when the couple/family and the therapist perceive the therapeutic goals as being attained.

Therapeutic Techniques and Procedures

Guidelines for Therapy

How the therapist approaches working with couples about their marital concerns is determined by many factors. What to do with a specific couple is determined by the unique circumstances of that particular couple's concerns. Haley (1976) proposed, however, that there are some general rules that point out what the therapist should avoid, and that can be applied to most cases.

1. *Avoid minimizing problems.* To minimize a problem suggests to a couple that the therapist does not understand their situation. Further, small problems are often analogous to larger ones.

2. *Avoid abstractions.* Discussion of specific behaviors is necessary in order to devise specific directives that will lead to change.

3. *Avoid being in a constant coalition with one partner.* At times, for a specific therapeutic purpose, the therapist may side with one partner. However, by constantly joining one partner against another the therapist can help perpetuate the very problems he or she is attempting to change. Maneuvers such as one partner gaining the therapist's support against the other, are likely the same maneuvers used outside of therapy to maintain the problematic interactions in the relationship.

4. *Avoid debates about life.* Philosophical issues raised by a couple should be shifted back to more concrete immediate issues. Therapy is not a time to discuss the meaning of life but, rather, a means by which two people learn to relate in more productive ways.

5. *Avoid the past.* The past is past. The present and future are where more adaptive and satisfying modes of relating, and changes leading to them, are possible.

6. *Avoid thinking that problems are identical.* Every couple's ecology is different. It is disrespectful to partners to assume that their problem is the same as one experienced by the therapist or another couple.

7. *Young therapists should not try to appear wiser than they are.*

Beginning therapists are often young and unmarried. These therapists should seek a stance to work from that is acceptable to couples that are older and have more actual marital experience. For example, it's usually reasonable to say that "You obviously know more about your marriage than I do. But, as a trained observer, I can offer you an objectively informed view of some of your concerns."

8. *Avoid unformulated goals.* Specific goals provide the basis for planning intervention strategies and thus facilitating behavior change. Without concretely specified goals to work toward, therapy cannot meaningfully proceed.

9. *Avoid forcing a couple to ask explicitly what they want from each other.* Asking a couple to say everything "right out in the open" is an abnormal way of communicating; partners who feel they have been told to behave in a way they would rather not may resist the directive. It is often better to make a request using "indirection." For example, instead of suggesting that a wife directly ask her husband for something, the therapist might say "I would like you to ask your husband for what you want, but in such a way that it takes him awhile to understand what you mean."

10. *Avoid crystallizing power struggles.* Although Haley's theory stresses the importance of power struggles in the clinical setting, it is best to conceive of dealing with marital problems in terms of clarifying the issues rather than as struggles for power. The former emphasis opens more options for consideration. Emphasizing power can limit alternatives to either winning or losing; other available outcomes may be more appropriate but be blocked by a focus on power.

11. *Multiple therapists can make the marital relationship more difficult to change.* Haley notes that "one therapist can do therapy more successfully than two, and one is more economical. Usually cotherapy is set up for the sake of uncertain therapists, not for the case" (Haley, 1976, p. 167).

12. *Avoid allowing irreversible decisions.* Therapists should strive to see that couples allow room for change, negotiation, and flexible alternatives. If a partner appears about to say something that will force him or her to defend an indefensible position, the therapist should intervene and not allow it. (Distraction is an effective intervention strategy.)

Assessment of Marital Dysfunction

Formal diagnosis or standardized assessment of marital functioning is given little value in Haley's work with couples. Rather, assessment of dysfunctional communications is an ongoing observational procedure that occurs as therapy progresses. Haley (1976) proposed that "the best diagnosis *for therapy* is one that allows the social group to respond to attempts to bring about change" (p. 12; the emphasis is Haley's). Thus, in order to gain assessment data, the therapist must intervene with a therapeutic act and then observe the reactions and responses of those present. This is the means of gathering data to use in formulating therapeutic hypotheses and then treatment plans.

Intervention Strategies

Haley (1963a, 1963b, 1976) identified three basic intervention strategies to utilize in the therapeutic setting.

Being Present.   The mere presence of the therapist is an intervention in itself. By involvement in a couple's system as a fair participant, the therapist's presence requires the partners to deal with each other differently; each partner must respond to both the therapist and his or her mate rather than just to the mate. For example, the wife who utilizes avoidance and withdrawal to deal with her husband finds these maneuvers ineffective with the therapist present. Instead of being unable to do anything about this avoidance behavior, the husband is enabled to discuss it with the therapist to prove his point. It is hoped the wife will learn the ineffectiveness of her tactic and change her behavior to a more adaptive manner of responding.

In addition, couples who have difficulty accepting either complementary or symmetrical relationships are affected by the presence of the therapist. The therapist's modeling of effectively workable symmetrical relationship behaviors with one partner can set a new model for a reluctant mate to implement. Further, the couple opposed to any form of complementary relationship interactions in their marriage will find that their acceptance of the therapist as an authority figure, and therefore the acceptance of a complementary relationship, becomes part of the process of accepting this type of relationship at times with each other.

Relabeling.   In Haley's view, symptoms occur when one partner "is in an impossible situation and is trying to break out of it" (Haley, 1973, p. 44). That partner is locked into a sequence of behaviors within the marital relationship and cannot see a way to alter it through nonsymptomatic means. In relabeling seemingly dysfunctional behavior as reasonable and understandable, Haley emphasizes the positive. For example, if a wife is questioning her husband's constant outbursts of anger towards her, Haley might relabel the husband's behavior as "overconcern" about their relationship's well-being. In doing so, Haley is simply following the principle that communication defines the nature of a marital relationship and partners have the ability to communicate on two levels. It is the second-level message (the meta-communication) that qualifies what takes place on the surface level. Therefore, the significance of any behavioral event changes depending upon the context in which it takes place. Through relabeling, Haley changes the context, thereby freeing the partners to behave differently in a new context.

Paradoxical Interventions. Haley believes that dysfunctional interaction patterns are utilized to maintain homeostasis in a marital system and are therefore "functional" (for the purpose of maintaining a homeostatic balance) to a couple, even though that couple may express serious concern about the relationship. Because of the functionality of their dysfunctional behavior, partners usually resist any attempt to get them to actually change that behavior. In utilizing paradoxical interventions Haley attempts to force couples to abandon their old dysfunctional behavior patterns by getting them to engage in a power struggle with the therapist. The focus is on getting marital partners to resist the therapist and to change as a result.

The main difference between relabeling and paradoxical interventions is that relabeling is implicit and paradoxical interventions are explicit. Relabeling does not require overt behavior change. It may be successful without the active cooperation of the couple. If the relabeling by the therapist is not disputed, then the meaning and effects of the symptomatic behavioral sequence have already been altered. Paradoxical interventions, on the other hand, prescribe behavior.

It is assumed in Haley's view (1976) that couples who come for help are also resistant to any help being offered. The result of the resistance is frequently a power struggle, with the therapist attempting to assist a couple to improve but unstabilizing their homeostatic balance in the process. The partners, working to maintain that balance, try to get the therapist to fail. They do so even though, realizing something is wrong in their relationship, they continue in therapy.

In paradoxical interventions, the couple is in effect directed to "disobey" the therapist. Should the partners follow the therapist's instructions and continue the prescribed behavior, they do the therapist's bidding, and, therefore, give the therapist power; the therapist gains control by making the symptom occur at his or her direction. If the partners resist the paradoxical instruction, and therefore the therapist, they move toward "improvement" (and in the long term also toward doing the therapist's bidding). The confusion that occurs regarding how to resist leads to new patterns and perceptions and thus to change—at the very least the confusion can help to achieve a certain amount of detachment from the disturbing behavior (Hare-Mustin, 1976).

Thus, the couple told not to change often defies the therapist's directive; the partners begin to change to prove the therapist wrong in assuming that they could not change. For example, Haley might tell partners who fight continually and unproductively to go home and fight for two hours each day. The issue becomes one of power and control between the couple and the therapist. The couple works not to fight; people do not like to make themselves miserable because someone else tells them to do so. Further, it is assumed that in many cases the symptom presented (here, fighting) originally evolved as a way of gaining interpersonal advantage and that, if the symptom instead places the partner or partners at a disadvantage, it will disappear.

Haley (1976) outlined eight stages of the paradoxical intervention: (1) a client-therapist relationship is defined as one to bring about change, (2) a problem is clearly defined, (3) goals are clearly defined, (4) the therapist offers a plan, usually with a rationale, (5) the therapist gracefully disqualifies the current authority on the problem—likely one of the partners, (6) a paradoxical directive is given, (7) the response is observed and the therapist continues to encourage the "usual" behavior—no "rebellious" improvement is allowed, (8) the therapist avoids taking credit for any beneficial change that occurs, such as symptom elimination, and may even display puzzlement over the improvement. Haley (1963) stated that the basic rule is "to encourage the symptom in such a way that the patient cannot continue to utilize it" (p. 55).

Thus, in order to most appropriately utilize paradoxical interventions to facilitate change in a marital system, the therapist must provide a framework within which change is possible. Then, within that framework, the therapist encourages the partners to continue their usual behaviors but to do so in a way that makes their continuing an ordeal. The cure becomes more troublesome than the dysfunctional behavior.

In concluding this presentation of Haley's approach, particularly the use of paradoxical interventions, we recommend keeping in mind the important point offered by Papp (1979). He cautioned, "If motivation is high enough and resistance low enough for a family to respond to direct interventions, such as logical explanations, suggestions or tasks, there is no need to resort to a paradox" (p. 11). We understand this to suggest some likelihood of negative effects when paradoxical interventions are used with well-motivated couples.

Evaluation and Summary

This chapter examines the theoretical conceptualizations and therapeutic approaches of two major systems theorists, Murray Bowen and Jay Haley. In Bowen theory, current behaviors are considered to be the result of a long process over many generations of patterned relationships that are to a great degree both predetermined and self-perpetuating. The long process is perpetuated because people tend to choose for marital partners those who have baseline levels of differentiation similar to their own, and because families rarely change dramatically from generation to generation. Bowen's approach suggests a view of the concepts of organization and control different from the conceptualization put forth by Jay Haley. Whereas, in Haley's view, the basic patterns of marital interaction are expressed in communication exchanges between partners, Bowen looks for their expression in family themes developed over many generations. Further, in Bowen theory, the historical data are particularly important in helping individuals within a marital relationship to delineate the heritage they are either benefiting from or struggling against. Although Bowen theory shares with Haley's view an interest in context as it determines and structures behavior, the two define *context* differently: Bowen theory considers it to be context in history; Haley's problem-solving therapy emphasizes level of communication.

Green and Kolevzon (1982) proposed that, while a general-systems-theory perspective perseveres in the marriage-and-family-therapy profession, increasing specialization has resulted in considerable diversification among systems-oriented approaches. A number of attempts at profiling the nature of this diversification have been made (Guerin, 1976; Madanes & Haley, 1977; Olson, 1970; Olson, Russell, & Sprenkle, 1980). Efforts have focused on ordering the field by emphasizing unit of treatment (Olson, 1970), theoretical perspective (Guerin, 1976), and typologies on which therapists vary (Madanes & Haley, 1977). In contrast, a study of members of the American Association for Marriage and Family Therapy found that their goals for therapy seemed to reflect ideas that were not the property of any one specific orientation (Sprenkle & Fisher, 1980).

The diversification reflected in the AAMFT study results obviously allows for more flexibility in the expansion of current knowledge and, thereby, perhaps also allows current theorists to avoid some of the pitfalls experienced when psychodynamic theory was being built (Schaefer, 1976). On the other hand, negative consequences also may stem from diversity. For example, Minuchin has warned of the dangers inherent in the proliferation of the many "family therapies." He has cautioned that each of the major proponents has been "merchandising" his or her own techniques rather than focusing on the "commonality of thinking" within the field and that, in the process, the proponents of specialized theories impede the development of a unified theory of practice (Simon, 1980).

Gurman (1978) proposed that Bowen theory merges perceptually into psychoanalytic object-relations theory in terms of both theoretical conceptualization and clinical intervention. He also proposed a significant technical overlap with much of contemporary behavioral therapy. Further, whereas the basic pattern of marital interaction may be expressed in the communication of couples regarding rules for their relationship, the same pattern seems to be expressed as well in historical data gleaned from family interactions over multiple generations. In noting this "composite" viewpoint, Gurman stated:

Bowen theory may be the only currently existing approach to marital therapy that has the potential, in some modified form, of simultaneously (a) operating out of a developmental framework, (b) paying explicit attention (though in different words) to the rules and meta-rules of intimate relationships, and (c) implementing therapeutic change strategies that are rather readily teachable, which center on current observable transactions, and which include a significant didactic-educational component. Stated otherwise, Bowen therapy seems to offer a treatment capable of using some of the best of what psychoanalytic, communications, and behavioral therapies have to offer [1978, p. 517].

In his review of marital and family therapy for the decade of the 1960s, Olson (1970) commented that "the search for *the* theory of marital therapy is slowly changing to the realization that there needs to be considerable exploration of various theoretical approaches before a more integrated and comprehensive approach can be developed" (p. 516). Given that more than a decade of exploration and refinement of theoretical approaches has occurred since Olson's statement, and the fact that recently Minuchin (Simon, 1980) called for "commonality of thinking," perhaps another cycle in the development of marital therapy has been completed. However, instead of renewing a search, perhaps that "commonality of thinking" and "integrated and comprehensive approach" will naturally be synthesized, utilizing Bowen theory as its base. We suggest the possibility to be a viable one.

References

Bowen, M. Principles and techniques of multiple family therapy. In P. J. Guerin, Jr. (Ed.), *Family therapy: Theory and practice.* New York: Gardner Press, 1976a.

Bowen, M. Theory in the practice of psychotherapy. In P. J. Guerin, Jr. (Ed.), *Family therapy: Theory and practice.* New York: Gardner Press, 1976b.

Bowen, M. *Family therapy in clinical practice.* New York: Aronson, 1978.

Green, R. G., & Kolevzon, M. S. Three approaches to family therapy: A study of convergence and divergence. *Journal of Marital and Family Therapy,* 1982, *8,* 39–50.

Guerin, P. J. (Ed.). *Family therapy: Theory and practice.* New York: Gardner Press, 1976.

Gurman, A. S. Much vigor, little rigor. *Contemporary Psychology,* 1977, *22,* 67–68.

Gurman, A. S. Contemporary marital therapies: A critique and comparative analysis of psychoanalytic, behavioral, and systems theory approaches. In T. J. Paolino, Jr. & B. S. McCrady (Eds.), *Marriage and marital therapy.* New York: Brunner-Mazel, 1978.

Haley, J. Marriage therapy. *Archives of General Psychiatry,* 1963a, *8,* 213–234.

Haley, J. *Strategies of psychotherapy.* New York: Grune & Stratton, 1963b.

Haley, J. *Uncommon therapy.* New York: Norton, 1973.

Haley, J. *Problem solving therapy.* San Francisco: Jossey-Bass, 1976.

Haley, J. Ideas that handicap therapy with young people. *International Journal of Family Therapy,* 1979, *1,* 29–45.

Hare-Mustin, R. Paradoxical tasks in family therapy: Who can resist? *Psychotherapy: Theory, Research, and Practice,* 1976, *13,* 128–130.

Madanes, C., & Haley, J. Dimensions of family therapy. *Journal of Nervous Disorders and Disease,* 1977, *165,* 88–98.

Minuchin, S. *Families and family therapy.* Cambridge, Mass.: Harvard University Press, 1974.

Olson, D. Marital and family therapy: Integrative review and critique. *Journal of Marriage and the Family,* 1970, *32,* 501–538.

Olson, D. H., Russell, C. S., & Sprenkle, D. H. Marital and family therapy: A decade review. *Journal of Marriage and the Family,* 1980, *42,* 973–994.

Papp, P. Paradoxical strategies and countertransference. *American Journal of Family Therapy,* 1979, *7,* 11–12.

Satir, V. *Conjoint family therapy.* Palo Alto, Calif.; Science and Behavior Books, 1967.

Satir, V. *Peoplemaking.* Palo Alto, Calif.: Science and Behavior Books, 1972.

Schaefer, R. *A new language for psychoanalysis.* New Haven: Yale University Press, 1976.

Simon, R. Conclusion of an interview with Salvador Minuchin. *Family Therapy Practice Network Newsletter,* 1980, *3,* 5–10.

Singleton, G. Bowen family systems theory. In A. M. Horne & M. M. Ohlsen (Eds.), *Family counseling and therapy.* Itasca, Ill.: Peacock, 1982.

Sprenkle, D. H., & Fisher, B. L. Goals of family therapy: An empirical assessment. *Journal of Marital and Family Therapy,* 1980, *6,* 131–154.

Stanton, M. D. Strategic approaches to family therapy. In A. S. Gurman & D. P. Kniskern (Eds.), *Handbook of family therapy.* New York: Brunner-Mazel, 1981.

Steinglass, P. The conceptualization of marriage from a systems theory perspective. In T. J. Paolino, Jr. & B. S. McCrady (Eds.), *Marriage and marital therapy.* New York: Brunner-Mazel, 1978.

Toman, W. *Family constellation.* New York: Springer, 1961.

Walsh, W. M. *A primer in family therapy.* Springfield, Ill.: Charles C. Thomas, 1980.

Watzlawick, P., Weakland, J., & Fisch, R. *Change: Principles of problem formation and problem resolution.* New York: Norton, 1974.

CHAPTER SIX

A Comparative Case Study

Chuck and Mary were both in their early thirties, and were the parents of two children, ages 3 and 1. Chuck and Mary were what most people would consider an average middle-class couple. In their sixth year of marriage, they faced a serious crisis in their relationship. Mary felt isolated; Chuck felt trapped; both felt that they had little in common except the children and a mortgage. Their relationship became little more than alternate arguing, withdrawing, sulking, and pouting over their situation.

Chuck and Mary described their marriage as having deteriorated continuously, but more quickly in the year preceding their seeking therapy. In the beginning of their marriage they felt relatively happy and content with each other, shared a number of common interests, and had a satisfactory sex life. However, for the past 12 months or so they had experienced a recurrent cycle of bitter, hostile conflicts in which Mary was critical and demanding and Chuck withdrawn and silent.

Mary felt that Chuck had become less and less available to her, worked too many hours, and didn't seem to understand or appreciate the magnitude of her mothering and housekeeping responsibilities or the stress that they caused. Mary described the situation:

> *Marital responsibilities should be shared, and I don't feel ours are. I knew when we first discussed having children that there would be added constraints placed on me, but I feel completely tied down to the house and kids! I don't like it. I now realize I'd rather work and have the freedom I had before the kids came along. Chuck works long hours and hard at his job, but too hard. I know we need the money, but I rarely see him. Even when he's not at work, he's not home—not mentally, anyway. He's always bringing work home from the office or getting ready to play golf, or just lying there watching television. Marriage just isn't supposed to be like this.*

Chuck felt that Mary was impossible to talk to, and that when they did converse she was always critical and demanding. He saw withdrawing from her as his only defense against her constant criticism and self-pitying complaints. He stated, about their current circumstances:

> *I just don't understand Mary. I can see her desire to get out of the house more or get a job as legitimate. We could sure use the money, anyway. But doesn't she realize that it's important for the kids to have their mother around? After they start school, she can get a job. She wanted the children too. I know I could share more in the household chores and taking care of the kids, but my God, with working 10 to 12 hours a day and still having to bring work home from the office, what does she expect of me?*

When the topic of separation and divorce finally came up between them, Chuck and Mary were hit with the realization that their marriage was in deep distress. Mary discussed their situation with a close friend, who suggested to Mary that she and Chuck seek professional help. Chuck agreed.

If Mary and Chuck presented themselves for marital therapy to a psychoanalytic object-relations-oriented therapist, what experiences might they have? What experiences might they expect with a therapist whose approach was in terms of social-learning theory? With a therapist who utilizes the Bowen theory? Or with a therapist implementing Jay Haley's problem-solving therapy?

The purpose of this chapter is to illustrate how these four perspectives might be used in working with the same couple. The couple—Mary and Chuck—and their marital relationship and accompanying circumstances are addressed from each of the four approaches presented in the preceding three chapters.

Before reading on, review the introduction to this section of the book, in which the functions of theoretical models are discussed. We note there the three functions that are essential to the success of any therapeutic efforts: (1) providing the therapist a means for organizing information in order to form hypotheses to guide the course of therapy, (2) offering an understanding of adaptive and maladaptive behavior, and (3) suggesting a conceptual foundation for developing and determining the appropriateness of specific intervention strategies.

How might each of the approaches serve the three essential functions? As you formulate explanations in terms of each theory, using the background material provided, consider the following questions: What aspects of the partners' individual and relationship behaviors represent the primary focus for therapeutic efforts? What are the major theoretical concepts that explain the existence of their problems? What are the general goals for therapy? How might the therapist proceed, and what would be the therapist's role in the therapeutic process? What might be some of the characteristics of the relationship between the couple and the therapist? What techniques and procedures might the therapist employ during the course of therapy?

We feel that presenting this single case study from the four viewpoints discussed in this section of the book is of particular value to illustrate not only the differences between the approaches but also, in highlighting compatible concepts and practices, to point up the similarities. This comparative case study thus offers a means of both differentiating and integrating the approaches presented, and, in doing so, assists in more clearly comprehending and conceptualizing the therapeutic applications of each model.

Psychoanalytic Theory

The psychoanalytic object-relationship approach primarily focused on the unconscious intrapsychic determinants of Chuck and Mary's behavior. The general goal of therapy involved the restructuring of both partners' perceptions of, expectations of, and reactions to themselves and each other. Intrapsychic growth and awareness were seen as the means to this end.

The initial session with the therapist was one in which Chuck and Mary were seen separately. From the second session on, they were seen together. The first two sessions were spent in gathering diagnostic information concerning the partners' commitment and motivation to change and the type of change they sought, as well as in an in-depth appraisal of each partner and their respective contributions to their marital dysfunction. Questions regarding dreams, fantasies, childhood memories, and the history of their relationship, as well as agreements made regarding it, formed the basis for the initial interviews.

In subsequent sessions, both Chuck and Mary were encouraged to continue to share and expound upon these and other experiences including crises and other major events in their lives. Both began to see connections between their present problems and respective early childhood experiences. The exploration involved memories of past relationships with parents and significant other people in their lives. Both experienced old feelings and also uncovered some long forgotten emotions tied to early traumatic events. Some of the therapist's questions included: What was your reaction when you felt you weren't loved? As a child, what did you have to do with your negative feelings? Could you express your angry, hostile, hurt, or fearful emotions? What effects did your relationship with your parents have on you? What did you learn from them about marriage?

In addition, the therapist suggested strongly that Mary and Chuck expend more effort in negotiating, as two adults, an exact and more satisfying agreement about responsibilities for family finances, household tasks, the children, and for each other. Time was spent during sessions learning to negotiate more effectively and to solve problems with instructions to continue at home.

Chuck came to see how his withdrawal from Mary's critical and demanding behaviors was a reflection of his fear of any kind of fighting and especially fighting with women. With the therapist's assistance, he related this fear to his childhood memories of his parents' constant fighting and bickering. His conceptualization of male-female relationships was a product of what he had learned through his early experiences with his parents: his father appeared to be the weak one who always lost, while his mother was a strong, overly domineering woman who could and did hurt his father. Chuck identified with his father's behavioral pattern, and he generalized his fear to all women, including Mary.

At the same time, Mary recognized how her criticism and demanding attitude were responses to anticipated rejection. She reported how upset she got if anyone was late for an appointment with her and the rage she sometimes felt as a result of having expectations disappointed. She was able to link these feelings with her recollection of her mother as a cold, largely unavailable woman. Since childhood, in situations in which Mary sensed that she might be deprived of a desired goal, she had feared rejection and responded with criticism, demands, and anger.

Through the therapist's interpretations, both Mary and Chuck came to see how their relationship interactions represented a reenactment of the relationship patterns of their own parents, in which essentially reserved fathers had been diminished and their selfhood suppressed by rather cold and powerful mothers. Under stress, their own marriage fell under the shadow of this shared image of the rejecting mother.

Mary and Chuck both initially viewed the discovery of this reenactment as most ironic; consciously, Mary saw in Chuck a warm, accessible man like her father was, but stronger. Chuck saw in Mary an emotional and caring woman who would not do to him what his mother had done to his father. At the unconscious level, however, it was discovered how each had chosen a partner ready to play the exact role that repeated the feared parental pattern of interaction. The strength in Chuck that Mary desired would always disappear just when she most sought it—that is, when she feared rejection. She would then behave like both their mothers had, and so provoke in Chuck the withdrawal that she feared. It was through analyzing and interpreting this transference-countertransference manifestation between Chuck and Mary that the therapist was able to lead them to consider how this maladaptive marital interaction pattern was essentially a replaying of internalized childhood "objects" rather than a relationship between an adult man and woman.

Using interpretation as the primary intervention, the therapist was able to thus diminish the amount of fantasy and increase the reality of Chuck and Mary's perceptions. Further, in utilizing an object-relations model, the therapist was able to explain the couple's interaction by noting discrepancies between the relationship they sought and the one they actually maintained. The therapist skillfully took note of elements of dependency and coercion in the couple's undesired interactions that indicated childhood origins. In pointing these out, the therapist was able to provoke further exploration of those origins. With Chuck and Mary, the therapist's identification of these inappropriate perceptions and behaviors (the technique of making the unconscious conscious) opened the way for their abandonment.

Finally, after Chuck and Mary came to clearly understand and reexperience how they had been shaped by past object relations, they exerted increasing control over their present functioning. In doing so they were increasingly able to be self-observing and self-analyzing and, therefore, able to cope better with the recurrence of past marital stresses as well as any new tensions.

Social-Learning Theory

In the initial session with the therapist using social-learning theory Chuck and Mary were made comfortable and asked to present their major concerns. The therapist then explained what they might expect to occur if they chose to work on these concerns in therapy. The therapist asked them to consider these thoughts for the next two weeks, during which the sessions would be devoted to assessing various aspects of their individual and relationship behaviors. The assessment process was outlined, and the two were given a rationale for things they would be asked to do during the two-week period.

Also during the initial sessions, Chuck and Mary were assisted by the therapist to translate some of their general goals into concrete, specific ones. For example, Mary's "unhappiness" was more clearly delineated through such questions put by the therapist as: What do you mean by unhappiness? What can you do to narrow down that broad goal to one that's more specific? When do you feel happiest? What specific behaviors of yours indicate to you that you're happy? Throughout therapy this specificity was continually stressed.

Following the assessment sessions, taking into consideration the assessment information and the couple's stated goals, the therapist provided Chuck and Mary with recommendations as to how therapy might proceed. It was explained that the emphasis would be on learning new and more functional behaviors with which they could interact in a more positive manner. Their past difficulties and experiences would not be explored, except to the extent necessary to modify their dysfunctional learning; no attempt would be made to uncover or work on childhood experiences, as Chuck and Mary, like many other people, had thought a necessary part of therapy. As the therapist told them, their present behaviors were causing their problems, and it was on the present that therapeutic efforts would focus. By learning more adaptive interpersonal and coping behaviors, they would be able to respond to each other more appropriately and to experience greater satisfaction in their relationship.

Mary and Chuck were then asked for a commitment to work with each other and with the therapist. This involved signing a written contract outlining mutual commitments and goals, recommending procedures, and specifying that the contract would be in effect for 12 sessions. At the end of that time, evaluation of progress would be formally assessed and discussed, and either therapy would end or a new contract would be developed.

The major treatment interventions utilized with Mary and Chuck over the next 12 weeks included:

Behavior-Exchange Procedures.   Chuck and Mary were obviously in a cycle of negative interactions about what each didn't do. Mary saw Chuck as not being home enough and not sharing household responsibilities, the child rearing, and more. Chuck perceived Mary as communicating little to him except in complaints, criticism, and demands. Beginning with an initial homework assignment, for which each was to observe and record at least one positive behavior of the other every day for a week, they were progressively taught to change their focus to more positive aspects of each other's behavior. This included not only observing and thus identifying positive behaviors but also acknowledging to each other that they were pleased, at the moments the pleasing behaviors occurred. The therapist explained the importance of these new behaviors in terms of the value of immediate reinforcement. Chuck and Mary agreed and noted they enjoyed the good feelings each got in hearing about their own positive behaviors and commenting on the other's. They reported that they had even begun to independently initiate doing things to please each other much more often as a result.

Communication-Enhancement Training.   During times of disagreement especially, Chuck and Mary's ability to actively and appropriately talk and also listen to each other broke down completely. Mary became punitive and demanding, Chuck silent and withdrawn. In order to reestablish the balance of power in their interactions, the therapist worked with Chuck on becoming more assertive and able to more readily express his feelings. The therapist worked with Mary on minimizing her critical statements and questions, which sounded like demands, by maximizing her ability to communicate in a simple, calm, and clear manner. Both partners were taught to use more empathic statements so as to heighten their understanding of one another as well as to feel more understood by one another.

The new communication skills were practiced during the sessions, with the therapist modeling the skills during role-play situations by playing the role of one of the partners, and also by providing feedback concerning the couple's display of these behaviors. Chuck and Mary then worked on the skills at home, reporting back to the therapist each week on their progress or problems in using these interaction skills.

Problem-Solving Training.   These training procedures consisted of Chuck and Mary learning to negotiate and compromise on critical issues and, more commonly, on ordinary issues as well. For example, because Mary felt tied to the children and the house, Chuck agreed to watch the children by himself every Wednesday evening and Saturday morning, allowing Mary to engage in activities outside the home. Mary joined a Wednesday evening/Saturday morning bowling league. Competing with and associating with other people also gave Mary a greater opportunity for positive feedback from people other than Chuck and thus an opportunity to increase her self-esteem and positive feelings. Both partners agreed that they needed to incorporate more social and recreational activities into their weekly schedule, as a couple as well as with the children.

As a part of and consequence of the problem-solving process they were using, Chuck and Mary learned to develop and make use of marital contracts. As the therapist had explained, these contracts were a concrete way of indicating that each understood the nature of their behavior-change agreements and were committed to making these changes. Mary and Chuck noticed particularly that, for them, putting agreements in writing added incentive and commitment to carry through on their promises.

At the end of the 12 weeks agreed to in the original therapeutic contract, Chuck and Mary decided to go it alone for awhile. Their relationship had certainly improved, as was evidenced by another formal assessment and by their own informal observations and feelings. Both felt fairly confident in their newly acquired skills and ability, as they put it, to "seek out the positive."

Systems Theory: The Bowen-Theory Model

Utilizing Bowen's therapeutic model, the therapist started by first addressing a series of questions to Chuck, then a series of questions to Mary, then to Chuck, then to Mary, alternating between the two of them. By means of questioning, the therapist attempted to identify specific reasons for Chuck and Mary coming to therapy. They were also asked to pinpoint some specific short-term goals. Early in the first session, when Chuck made a comment directly to Mary, the therapist quickly interrupted him. It was asked that during therapy sessions they speak one at a time and only to the therapist. It was also requested that they attempt to phrase their comments in the calmest, most objective way they could.

The therapist initially took a careful history of Chuck and Mary's individual family backgrounds. During this process and in subsequent sessions, the therapist talked at length about triangles and one-to-one relationships. The therapist gently but firmly encouraged both Chuck and Mary to spend as much time as possible between sessions contacting, thinking about, and developing new, differentiated relationships with members of their extended families.

The therapist initially came across to the couple as rather aloof and authoritarian. The therapist seemed to be somewhat detached, in the continual emphasis on speaking calmly and objectively along with virtually complete deemphasis of how the partners were feeling. However, Mary and Chuck soon came to effect the same calm, rational climate in their own relating in therapy that the therapist was modeling. This calmer climate eventually generalized to much of their interactions at home, also.

The therapist usually began each session by asking one of the partners, for example Chuck, to report on what kind of progress he had made since the last session, and to do so in the most objective manner possible. The therapist would then turn to Mary and ask what her thoughts were while Chuck was talking. After Mary responded, the therapist would turn to Chuck and ask what his thoughts were when Mary was talking. The therapist constantly urged each partner to take I-position stands and, by doing so, to assume responsibility for statements and actions. Some session time was normally spent in the therapist teaching Mary and Chuck how emotional systems function; through this instruction, the partners learned how to handle more effectively the crises that can arise in their relationship.

Special attention was given to defining the "automatic" emotional responses of both Chuck and Mary that seemed to operate largely outside of their immediate awareness. Chuck and Mary learned rather quickly how a number of minor emotional stimuli on the part of either of them often triggered major emotional responses in the other—and mostly negative responses, at that. For instance, it was discovered that whenever Chuck shrugged his shoulders in a certain way while they were having any type of disagreement, Mary immediately became incensed. The therapist assisted them in becoming aware of the stimulus and response, defining them in as much detail as possible, and working to notice their occurrence and deal with it, with more reason than emotion. In doing so, Chuck and Mary were able to diffuse this problematic interaction. Thereafter, when disagreements were being discussed, Chuck worked to not shrug his shoulders, and Mary strove to react intellectually, rather than emotionally, when the behavior did occur.

Thus, Chuck and Mary came to observe and know each other better. However, as they tried out new behaviors, focused on themselves, and took personal responsibility for themselves to a much greater degree, there were times when they were at odds. In these instances, one partner seemed to be seeking a greater sense of self and the other seemed to want to prevent this from happening. Through the therapist's continued stress on responding to these pressures in a less emotional and more intellectual way, both Chuck and Mary were eventually able to express themselves and react more independently. In achieving this, they saw their relationship improve significantly. They were then functioning through choice, and not as before in emotionally reactive and hostile or withdrawn ways. Both recognized the need to continue these efforts on their own when therapy ended, and they left with a well-considered plan to do so.

Systems Theory: Problem-Solving Therapy

In the initial session with Mary and Chuck, the therapist who used problem-solving therapy[1] discussed with them the nature of their main problem and had them identify a concrete, specifically stated goal for therapy. At the end of the first session, the therapist asked Chuck and Mary what the consequence would be if their relationship significantly improved in the ways they stated they would like it to. They replied that it would be wonderful. The therapist expressed some doubt and suggested that the couple go home and consider during the coming week what changes in their lives would occur if they had a relatively happy marriage. The therapist's attitude implicitly communicated that something could definitely be done to make this happiness a reality. However, the therapist's attitude also conveyed doubtfulness about proceeding before Chuck and Mary were sure of the consequences of doing so.

When Chuck and Mary returned a week later, they said that they were unable to come up with any possible adverse consequences to improvement of their relationship. The therapist, however, introduced some potentially adverse consequences. Mary was addressed first. It was pointed out that some women can tolerate success, while other women cannot. Mary responded that she thought she could stand being a successful wife. She was uncertain whether the therapist was joking, as was Chuck, but the therapist gave no indication. The therapist then asked whether becoming a successful wife might not make her more successful than her mother; perhaps she could not tolerate that. Mary responded that she could certainly stand being more successful than her own mother, who, she said, had a terrible marriage with her father.

---

[1] In this study, the focus within problem-solving therapy is on paradoxical interventions.

When Mary began to expound upon remembrances of her parents' poor relationship, the therapist quickly shifted to the question of what Mary would do with herself during the day if her marriage were more satisfying. It had been revealed that Mary sat for hours each day, bemoaning her sad circumstances. Clearly she would have more free time if the marriage became a happy one. Had she considered what she would do with that time and what she would think about if she didn't have marital problems to worry over?

The therapist then shifted to the similar consequences of Chuck's becoming a successful husband. Later, the therapist dealt with the consequences for the two of them if they became a happily married couple. They had not been going out together very often. Where would they go if they began doing things together, and who would decide? Chuck said he thought they could tolerate going out together. So did Mary, mentioning that she often wanted to go out with Chuck, but never did.

A similar discussion of consequences centered on what Chuck and Mary would talk about in the evening if they didn't have complaints to ventilate and problems to discuss. Both Chuck and Mary decided they could find something to talk about besides their problems.

The following session, Mary began by mentioning that she was able to think less about what she had seen as their marital problems and thus hadn't sat around sulking over them. She noted that she liked having the extra time and was able to do other, more enjoyable things with herself. Both Chuck and Mary spoke about having gone out twice together in the previous week and having thoroughly enjoyed themselves. They clearly indicated to the therapist, without explicitly saying so, that they could tolerate a satisfying relationship.

The therapist reported puzzlement that their problem had resolved itself and pleasure that Chuck and Mary had done so well. Credit was given to them for the change. An appointment was set for two weeks later to be sure that everything was all right. In two weeks, Chuck and Mary returned reporting that all was well and continually improving.

Summary

This chapter looks at the theoretical and therapeutic concepts of psychoanalytic, social-learning, and systems-theory approaches to marriage and marital therapy from an "in-action" perspective. The case study of Chuck and Mary illustrates how each of these approaches might be implemented in a clinical setting. Of course, the case reports are compacted, edited versions of the total interaction and so present only the highlights, or crucial aspects, of all that would actually occur.

We point out, in particular, the psychoanalytic object-relations therapist's emphasis on the intrapsychic components of Chuck and Mary's behaviors developed during early childhood yet, at the same time, this therapist's utilization of practical problem-solving and negotiating strategies. Note that these practical strategies were used early in therapy with the couple's immediately pressing concerns, very pragmatically. This follows our observation that the psychoanalytic marital therapist is psychoanalytic in theoretical understanding but also, at times, quite eclectic in practice.

The social-learning therapist's focus on functional analysis, positive tracking and control, and skills training was clearly evident. Likewise, the Bowenian emphasis on detriangulation, differentiation, emotional cutoff, and a calm yet controlling posture on the part of the therapist was apparent in that therapist's work with the couple.

Finally, the therapist implementing Jay Haley's concept of a paradoxical stance provided a fine example of this approach. The therapist's ability to support Chuck and Mary in the idea that they could stand having a satisfying relationship, while at the same time motivating them to prove it, well displayed the therapeutic skills Haley advocates.

Following Section Two's exploration of major theoretical approaches to understanding marriage and practicing marital therapy, we are ready to focus in Section Three on pragmatic and procedural aspects of working with couples.

Comprehensive Marital Therapy

In the previous section, Section Two, we focus on specific theoretical orientations and how these provide an understanding of marriage and a model for marital therapy. Ideally, theory should assist therapists in making sense of what they are doing in work with couples. In order for therapy to do this, a therapist's use of intervention strategies should be closely related to a theoretical model. However, developing an effective, efficient therapeutic position that is also practical is often more complicated than merely accepting the tenets of a given theory.

It is our belief that the therapeutic position, with accompanying intervention strategies, that a beginning therapist can utilize best is one in which he or she is qualified and confident, as well as one with which the therapist is comfortable. We have found that qualification, confidence, and comfort are most easily attained when a therapist first gains a clear comprehension of a number of the major theoretical positions that have been discussed in the literature and tested in practice. Only then is one selected—one with which the therapist can identify and in which he or she can develop expertise. Yet the primary theoretical position employed

153

should ideally be one not only selected through the therapist's informed choice but one that is appropriate to the unique needs of the individual couple in therapy.

Quite often the best strategy for choosing a therapeutic orientation to use with a particular couple is to consider which interventions best fit their immediate situation. Therefore, after a beginning therapist has developed expertise in one major approach, we advocate that he or she pursue a systematic integration of therapeutic strategies. Unfortunately, some beginning therapists overreact to this opportunity to expand their therapeutic repertoires. They become overly eager to try out new therapeutic interventions, treating them almost as if they were a bag of tricks. Others, who have deviated too far from their primary mode of practice, become confused and anxious over not knowing what to do in a given situation. These therapists often try out various ideas and interventions in a hapless, helter-skelter manner.

We believe that marital therapists should have sound reasons for using a particular technique or intervention strategy and that these reasons should emanate from the primary theoretical position they adopt. After all, that position provides therapists with an understanding of what constitutes marital adjustment and what therapeutic goals to pursue in order to assist couples in achieving it. However, we also find that, with an appropriate perspective from which to conceptualize the process of marital therapy, the foundation therapists have developed can be expanded to integrate techniques and intervention strategies from other approaches.

To aid such expansion, Chapter 7 presents a process-oriented, atheoretical way of conceptualizing the course of marital therapy. This is a practical working model with which to utilize the concepts and procedures of one's primary theoretical position and to integrate ideas and interventions not normally associated with that position. And, toward an integration of fundamental techniques, Chapter 8 discusses general therapeutic intervention strategies for dealing with specific skill deficits that often cause couples to present themselves for marital therapy. It also considers some other areas of a more contemporary nature. Chapter 9 addresses special problems that can arise during therapy; we advocate procedures to facilitate their solution. Chapter 10 looks at family theory and therapy—a means of understanding and treating marital distress and related family concerns by involving significant family members in the therapeutic process.

CHAPTER SEVEN

A Process Model of Marital Therapy

Married couples are both unique and predictable. They are unique in the sense that therapists can rarely anticipate the kinds of controversies and concerns that a particular couple will present. Experienced therapists admit that they are frequently surprised by the variety of topics couples introduce. At the same time couples are predictable, in the sense that many problems and distressing situations are widely shared. Every marital partner has been upset, angry, confused, depressed, indecisive, or felt overwhelmed at one time or another. Expressing these concerns and doing something constructive about them is quite difficult for many couples. Thus the need for trained professional assistance.

As married couples are both unique and predictable, so are the theoretical approaches marital therapists utilize to assist couples in coping with their concerns and developing more satisfying relationships. We have seen in our discussion of psychoanalytic, social-learning, and systems approaches in the preceding chapters that each orientation has aspects unique unto itself, just as all have commonalities as well.

Marital therapists, like couples and the therapeutic approaches, are unique. We believe that marital therapists are specialists in their own settings who can and will successfully select the therapeutic strategies likely to be most effective with individual partners and couples and who can integrate these strategies within the primary theoretical approach taken—if they have the proper framework to do so. Regardless of a therapist's primary philosophical or personal leanings, be it toward a psychoanalytic, social-learning, or systems approach, or some other not presented in this book, given a practical "process-oriented" outline to keep in mind, this integration is possible. And frequently it is the most appropriate tack to pursue.

Some therapists do not base their work on any one theoretical approach at all and simply utilize concepts, techniques, and procedures from a variety of different viewpoints. This is commonly referred to as an "eclectic" approach to marital therapy. Because this approach is not based on one basic set of theoretical constructs, it requires considerable flexibility, versatility, and experience on the part of the therapist. The therapist who employs an eclectic approach must always strive to be consistent and comprehensive when incorporating theoretical aspects and therapeutic practices from different approaches. In particular an eclectic approach requires increased self-awareness, because in order to be effective therapists must understand why certain procedures appeal to them and why some do not.

As mentioned previously, it is our belief that marital therapists should have in-depth expertise in one major theoretical orientation and should utilize that orientation as their primary focus for conceptualizing marital adjustment and specifying therapeutic goals to pursue over the course of their marital therapy efforts with couples. This has been the approach that we have taken and have encouraged our students and supervisees to take.

In our work with couples, we have provided services to a broad population of people, in terms of chronological, cultural, economic, and geographic diversity. We have had to respond to the wide variety of needs they have presented. In the early peer and professional supervisory sessions of our work with couples, it was sometimes suggested that adherence to our primary theoretical orientation with a particular couple was meeting our needs rather than the couple's. It wasn't that what we were attempting to do was necessarily inappropriate but, rather, that a technique or intervention strategy not usually associated with our primary position was more appropriate.

In response to these suggestions, and out of a desire to maintain the concrete and structured framework that our primary theoretical orientation provided for guidance in our practice, we identified the process variables that are inherent in most all approaches for conducting marital therapy. That is, we identified variables in the overall process that characterize it no matter what the therapeutic orientation applied. In doing so, we were able to outline a basic framework with which we could maintain our primary theoretical focus and simultaneously integrate strategies from other approaches, when that seemed to be the appropriate path to pursue with a particular couple.

It is this process-oriented framework that we present here. It is by no means itself an eclectic approach, although it could be utilized by an eclectic therapist. Nor is it directly based to a significant degree on any one theoretical orientation (although it could be employed in order to implement only the major concepts and practices of any specific approach). Rather, this framework is simply a nonspecific, atheoretical way of conceptualizing the course of marital therapy; that is, it is a framework for the "process" of marital therapy, from beginning to end. We perceive it and employ it as a practical, working model with which to utilize the concepts and procedures of our major theoretical orientation and to integrate particular procedures from other approaches.

The Use of a Process Model

Throughout the preceding chapters, we have utilized the term *process* when discussing what occurs between a therapist and couple in therapy—the therapeutic process. The term *process* communicates much about the essence of what happens in this interaction; it refers to an identifiable sequence of events taking place over time, and it implies that the events occur in a progression of stages. For example, in the healing process of a serious physical injury, such as a broken arm, there are certain identifiable stages. Likewise, as discussed in Chapter 1, there are describable stages in the development processes of individuals and marriages over their respective life cycles. The stages in these processes are relatively common to all individuals and marriages, even though what occurs within each of the stages is unique with any individual or couple.

As with other processes, the marital-therapy process has identifiable and progressive stages. And the marital-therapy process has a second tenet as well; as a general rule, each stage's goals can be successfully accomplished only to the degree that the goals of the preceding stage have been successfully accomplished. For example, if in the first stage a therapist is not able to establish a relationship and stimulate open and honest communications with a couple, assessing their concerns in the second stage will be virtually impossible.

If the therapist is lost in the process, the couple, too, will be lost. The process model of marital therapy provides the map the therapist needs. With it a therapist can identify what stage of therapy corresponds to the work being done with a couple. Familiarity with the concepts and procedures of at least one and preferably a number of major theoretical approaches allows a therapist to proceed through the model. Obviously, then, knowledge of the map is no substitute for basic knowledge of theoretical concepts and therapeutic procedures; such basic knowledge is necessary to utilize the model. However, when a therapist needs to integrate into a primary mode of practice procedures from other approaches, there is no substitute for having a plan of action into which to fit them. The process model offers a therapist this guide.

To understand marital therapy as a process, it is important to identify the therapeutic goals that a therapist and couple normally seek to attain. Therapeutic goals are of two types: outcome goals and process goals. Outcome goals are the desired results of therapy. They are the objectives the partners want to achieve as a consequence of their efforts in therapy. By contrast, process goals are the objectives the therapist considers necessary to accomplish for the outcome goals to be realized, For example, an outcome goal might be improved communication between two partners; a related process goal is their acquiring communication skills. Thus, the process goal of the therapist's teaching (or the couple's learning) is instrumental in bringing about the outcome goal of improved communication.

Some process goals are specific to individual couples, their outcome goals, and the types of interventions needed to attain those outcome goals. Certain process goals, however, appear to be essential for all couples and amount to stages in the therapeutic process. For the therapist, each stage is characterized by one of these general questions:

• How can I stimulate open, honest, and full communication about the problems that need to be discussed and the factors and background related to those concerns?
• How can I identify the difficulties this couple is experiencing in terms of clear and accurate outcome goals?
• Having identified the outcome goals, what specific procedures can I employ to help achieve the desired goals?
• How do I evaluate the procedures employed, so as to know when they are effective or how to vary or replace them?
• How do I know when the goals have been achieved and therapy is to be ended, and how can I best communicate this?

The stages corresponding to these questions, in like order, are as follows:

1. Establishing a relationship.
2. Assessing a couple's concerns.
3. Applying intervention strategies.
4. Assessing progress and overcoming obstacles.
5. Ending therapy.

We now discuss each of these stages of therapy.

The Stages of the Process Model

Establishing a Relationship

Prior to the first therapy session, a therapist and couple are relative strangers. If therapy is to be a helpful and worthwhile experience, the couple and the therapist must first come to know each other at a level deeper than a casual acquaintanceship. They must learn to respect and accept each other, trust each other, and be able to communicate openly and provide information to each other. For the therapist, this first stage of our process model requires that several critical tasks be performed.

Structuring Therapy. Structuring is a means of increasing a couple's readiness to participate in the therapeutic experience. Most simply stated, it involves teaching partners to be good clients. It is especially important for unsophisticated couples who know very little about therapy. Structuring is a matter of providing a couple with information as to what services the therapist will render and, in exchange, what will be expected of the couple in such matters as fees, attendance, confidentiality, potential length of treatment, and outside-of-session tasks.

Structuring sets initial limits for the couple-therapist relationship. Often, in therapy, one or both partners attempt to manipulate the therapist in various ways; this may be symptomatic of their basic problems. By establishing guidelines for therapy at the outset, the therapist can begin to restructure dysfunctional interactional behaviors in the first session. It is critical for the partners to understand that therapy does not consist merely of friendly conversation, acceptance, and support. It is work, in which the conversation has a specific purpose. Cooperation and focus on common therapeutic objectives are essential if benefits are to be derived from therapeutic efforts. Thus, small talk is best kept to a minimum and attention is best devoted to those variables that are interfering with a couple's progress in achieving their desired relationship goals.

Building Rapport. Establishing an effective therapeutic relationship with a therapist requires amounts of time and effort that vary with each couple. For couples who have never had a trusting relationship with anyone, developing such a relationship may take considerable time. In some cases it is easier for one partner to become involved in such a working relationship than it is for the other. Even so, regardless of theoretical orientation, most all marital therapists would agree that rapport is an important element in establishing an effective working relationship. Therapist-couple rapport helps form the supporting structure and conduit for a couple's acceptance of the intervention to come in later stages.

In our discussion of the therapist as a person in Chapter 2, we note that the research of Rogers, Gendlin, Kiesler, and Truax (1967) and that of Truax and Carkhuff (1967) provides evidence that therapists' ability to function in several core emotional and interpersonal dimensions has a significant influence on their therapeutic effectiveness. Displaying these dimensions—empathy, respect, and genuineness—is vital to the establishment of a working rapport with couples. Similarly, from social-influence theory has come data to suggest that certain "relationship enhancers" significantly affect the level of therapist-client rapport (Goldstein, 1980).

In 1968 Strong wrote what proved to be a landmark article regarding social-influence theory and the therapeutic relationship. Corrigan, Dell, Lewis, and Schmidt (1980) have summarized the great quantity of writing and research emanating from Strong's original work. They outline Strong's major points as follows:

> Based on cognitive dissonance theory (Festinger, 1957), Strong hypothesized that counselors' attempts to change clients' behavior or opinions would precipitate dissonance in clients. Clients could reduce dissonance by one of five means: (a) change in the direction advocated by the counselor, (b) discredit the counselor, or (c) discredit the issue, (d) change the counselor's opinion, or (e) seek others who agree with the client. Strong suggested that counselors could increase the likelihood that the first alternative (the client changing) would occur by reducing the likelihood of the second and third (discrediting the counselor and/or the issue) [p. 396].

One particularly influential variable in whether change is induced is the client's opinion of the therapist, especially on three counts (Corrigan et al., 1980): "Strong postulated that the extent to which counselors are perceived as expert, attractive and trustworthy would reduce the likelihood of their being discredited" (p. 396).

1. *Therapist Expertness.* Strong (1968) suggested that, from the clients' point of view, a therapist who is expert is (in the terms of Hovland, Janis, & Kelley, 1953) "a source of valid assertions" (p. 21). The expert therapist has some skill, information, or special ability to help. Strong (1968) further stated that perception of a therapist as expert is influenced by "(a) objective evidence of specialized training such as diplomas, certificates, and titles, (b) behavioral evidence of expertness such as rational and knowledgeable arguments and confidence in presentation, and (c) reputation as an expert" (p. 216).

Egan (1982), reflecting Strong's (1968) points, outlined three general sources of client-perceived expertness: role, behavior, and reputation. Role expertness is based in the therapist having an identified profession and such credentials as degrees or certificates attesting expertise, as well as such symbols as offices, titles, and name plates.

Expertness is communicated to clients by the behavior of therapists who are active, listen intently, talk intelligently, display quiet confidence in offering alternatives, and exhibit high levels of empathy, respect, and genuineness. These behaviors tend to suggest an "aura of competence" to most clients (Egan, 1982).

Expertness is attributed through reputation when clients are aware of either direct or indirect testimony of therapist expertise. This testimony may be from former clients who found the therapist to be of assistance or colleagues who perceive the therapist to be a quality referral. A reputation for expertness may also emanate from a therapist's association with a prestigious institution or organization.

2. *Therapist Attractiveness.* Strong (1968) proposed that clients' perceptions of therapist attractiveness are based on "perceived similarity to, compatibility with, and liking for" the therapist (p. 216). Therapists may appear attractive to clients for a number of reasons: physical characteristics, general appearance, or, as was noted as significantly influencing perceptions of expertness, for reasons of role, behavior, and reputation.

Some elements in therapists' attractiveness are relatively unchangeable, although there do exist ways for therapists to increase their attractiveness to clients. Some steps can be taken to make oneself more attractive physically; however, greater change in attractiveness is possible by changing behavior, or by exhibiting some behaviors and not exhibiting others. Egan (1982), utilizing common sense and a research base, suggested that the following behaviors on the part of therapists increase attractiveness to clients:

- Attending intently to clients.
- Being friendly and warm.
- Being empathic.
- Not engaging in judgmental behavior.
- Being active rather than passive during therapeutic sessions.
- Communicating attitudes similar to the clients'.
- Disclosing personal information in moderate amounts, especially when self-disclosure indicates associations with clients.

3. *Therapist Trustworthiness.* Strong (1968) proposed that a therapist's perceived trustworthiness is based on his or her "(a) reputation for honesty, (b) social role, such as physician, (c) sincerity and openness, and (d) lack of motivation for personal gain" (p. 217). Trustworthiness has the same general sources as does attractiveness. For example, clients might see a therapist as trustworthy (or untrustworthy) because of physical characteristics, general appearance, role, behavior, or reputation, or any combination of these.

As with attractiveness, therapists can increase their trustworthiness in the eyes of their clients by exhibiting some behaviors and not exhibiting others. Egan (1982) identified the following means by which therapists might increase their perceived trustworthiness:

- Strike contracts with clients and live up to the provisions.
- Maintain confidentiality.

- Be sensitive to clients' needs and feelings.
- Demonstrate genuineness, sincerity, and openness.
- Be realistic but optimistic about clients' abilities to cope with their concerns.
- Be willing to give information or feedback to clients that might benefit them.
- Be open to clients' feedback.
- Avoid behavior that might indicate ulterior motives such as selfishness, superficial curiosity, personal gain, or deviousness.

Fostering Open Communication.   The third important task of a therapist during this first stage of therapy involves helping a couple to develop a system of effective communication. This entails each partner learning to communicate clearly and accurately so that the messages sent can be received as intended. In marital therapy, patterns of defensive and guarded communication between partners are often readily evident. Being asked to share feelings, beliefs, and perceptions about problems in the relationship risks attack and criticism from one's partner as well as possibly having to assume responsibility for those problems. This can be quite threatening to one or both partners, and each client has his or her own defensive way of coping with threat: one may attack directly; the other may dodge and defend by subtle attack. Nevertheless, if therapeutic efforts are to be effective, open communication must be facilitated and defensiveness reduced. Each partner must learn to listen actively and nondefensively to the feelings, perceptions, and needs of his or her mate. Applying these skills where there has been turmoil and frustration can be a difficult undertaking.

One example of faulty communication skills is many couples' establishment of shortcut communications between the partners, which leads them to infer messages incorrectly.

Wife: Why do we always have to do what you desire every Saturday evening? Every week we seem to wind up in a bar before the end of the evening.

Husband: I don't know why you're saying I drink too much. And, if either of us is selfish, you are. Think about all of the times. . . .

The wife did not say that her husband drinks too much, nor that he is selfish, yet those are the messages he reacts to. The husband's shortcut understanding and anticipation of where his wife's statement is leading motivates a defensive reaction on his part. He attempts to defend against the perceived attack by counterattacking.

To facilitate more open communication, the therapist must assist partners directly or indirectly in correcting maladaptive communication patterns. The therapist must help them to think about what they want to say, to say things accurately, and also to check by way of feedback from the other whether the communication is accurately received. One primary means for the therapist to foster clear communication is to model appropriate and open communication him- or herself. By communicating clearly and specifically in interactions with a couple, the therapist can foster improved communication continually. In addition, the therapist should maintain a clear understanding of the couple-to-therapist messages by clarifying the partners' statements on a regular basis, thus modeling for them another important communication skill.

Assessing Couples' Concerns

This second stage of our process model involves two major tasks for the therapist. The first task is an exploration into primary alternatives to the present marital situation; they are identified and analyzed. These alternatives include: improving the relationship; maintaining the relationship as it is, smoothing rough edges but not eliciting basic change; or terminating the relationship. The second major task is an evaluation of the general and specific dynamics of the dysfunction in each partner's behaviors, in their interactions within the relationship, or both. As is discussed, when dysfunction includes severe psychopathology special measures can be taken.

Exploration of Alternatives.   Eisenberg and Delaney (1977) have suggested that an exploration of available alternatives is a critical step in early marital therapy efforts, necessarily preceding any meaningful intervention strategies. This exploration includes identification and analysis of the following alternatives to a couple's present marital situation:

1. *Improving the Relationship.* What are the parameters within which each partner is willing to consider changing? What are the expectations that each partner has for him- or herself and his or her mate? How realistic are the partners concerning these options and expectations?

2. *Maintaining the Relationship.* On occasion couples may decide to maintain a marriage even though it is a relatively dissatisfying one. The reasons may include financial considerations, religious convictions against divorce, social pressures, and other forces that similarly impinge upon marital partners.

3. *Terminating the Relationship.* Termination of a relationship may be either separation or divorce. Questions to consider include: Are the frustrations and losses of staying in a bad relationship worth enduring for any reason? Who will leave? How will the procedure be carried out? How will responsibilities for children, finances, and other joint interests be divided?

It is often valuable for the therapist to meet individually with each partner to review the possible alternatives available. Frequently, the only alternative discussed when a therapist meets with both partners is improvement of the relationship. When given the opportunity in an individual session with the therapist, a partner may propose another alternative, such as divorce. Some reasons for this discrepancy are feelings on the part of one partner that the other would be unable to handle the idea of divorce, would flatly reject the suggestion at that time, might overreact emotionally or physically in a hostile and violent manner. On other occasions, perceived religious, social, or normative constraints block the raising of divorce as an alternative. The therapist's exploration of alternatives with partners during the period of assessing their concerns is intended to establish boundaries within which a couple will be willing to move. With these boundaries established, the process of therapy can proceed with all parties aware of the levels of motivation and commitment involved. The absence of these boundaries can create circumstances wherein therapeutic efforts are consistently met with resistance, restraint, or rejection.

Determination of Dysfunction.   The second major task of a therapist in this second stage of our process model is an evaluation of the general and specific dynamics of dysfunction in each partner's behaviors, in their interactions within the relationship, or both. Walsh (1980) recommended that a determination of dysfunction in any family (marital) unit be multifaceted, incorporating four basic aspects. One aspect is the partners' immediate pressing concerns, along with short-term goals dealing directly with these concerns. A second aspect is the more general dysfunction that may be manifested by partners' immediate concerns, and the long-range remediation of this dysfunction. A third aspect involves an evaluation of each partner's individual personality dynamics. The fourth aspect is the dynamics of the marital unit as a whole.

In order to assess these variables, the therapist first attempts to identify and isolate specific concerns that have brought the partners into therapy. Once this is done, short-term goals can be established. Temporary resolution of the most pressing immediate concerns can free a couple to deal with their more general dysfunctional behaviors and interactional patterns. And then, to deal specifically with the more general dysfunctional variables, long-term goals can be formulated.

When Severe Psychopathology Is Suspected.   In assessing a couple's concerns, it may become evident that one or possibly both partners display symptoms suggesting severe psychopathology. This might be, for example, a schizophrenic or major affective disorder. It is critical that such an evaluation be corroborated and appropriate treatment be instituted. This is best handled by referral for psychiatric evaluation and intervention. If a partner were extremely paranoid, manic, or depressed, marital therapy efforts could only proceed successfully when control of the symptoms had been achieved (for example, through the use of prescribed psychotropic medication).

In most cases, it is necessary to treat both the psychiatric symptoms suffered by individual partners and the relationship problems that are likely concomitant with, and perhaps related to, these symptoms. Some marital problems may be related to the causation of individual illness, some may be secondary to it, and others may not be clearly connected. Whatever the circumstances, marital therapy can proceed simultaneously with continuing psychiatric treatment once symptomatic control has been attained. Simultaneous therapy is best conducted when there is a coordinated effort between marital therapist and psychiatrist, with open lines of communication.

Applying Intervention Strategies

Although major intervention efforts cannot occur until some type of assessment has been conducted, the therapist actually begins the change process from the very first session. The techniques and procedures utilized to establish a relationship with a couple, to explore alternatives, and to determine dysfunctional dynamics can all be intervention strategies if implemented as such. Further, the therapist's mere contact with a couple can facilitate their interacting more adaptively, through the modeling of appropriate interactional behaviors and encouragement of partners to use them.

Based on the successful completion of the tasks of the first two stages (establishing a relationship and assessing a couple's concerns), in the third stage the therapist can begin to intervene systematically. There are two primary tasks for a therapist in this intervention stage. The first task involves the planning of appropriate strategies; the second task is the actual implementation of the intervention strategies planned.

Planning Interventions.   Following the partners' decision concerning the future of their marital relationship, the therapist is in a position to plan appropriate intervention strategies. The interventions are planned so as to best assist the couple in moving toward the general goal they have chosen as a result of their decision to improve, maintain, or terminate the relationship. The therapist's task is to plan the kinds of interventions that will assist the couple in achieving their goal.

If a couple decides to improve the relationship, usually the act of deciding to improve their marriage in itself contributes to positive changes. The decision signals a reaffirmation of the importance of the marriage to each of them and this source of motivation to change becomes a valuable asset. Intervention strategies can be planned to alleviate the areas of dysfunction identified during the assessment stage as well as to facilitate the expression of more satisfying and enhancing individual behaviors and relationship interactions.

Whatever the partners' reasons, a therapist might conclude that their decision to maintain an unsatisfactory relationship is generally a poor one. However, under certain circumstances, this may simply be a couple's least unattractive alternative. In such a case, the therapist's interventions can be planned so as to assist the couple with the skills basic to maintaining a relationship of any sort: to openly communicate with each other, to interact as cooperatively as possible, and to offer and receive the feedback necessary for a relationship that is at least minimally satisfying. The therapist may also attempt to intervene in areas of the relationship or in partners' lives individually so as to help them in coping as effectively as they are able with the stresses and tensions that likely arise quite frequently in their marriage.

Some couples decide, as a consequence of considering possible alternatives to their present circumstances, to end their marriages. Such a decision does not necessarily negate the usefulness to them of therapy. Ending any relationship, and especially a marital relationship, is generally a traumatic experience, involving intense emotional reactions. Some partners experience hurt and rejection. Others feel they have failed and are in some way inadequate. Still others have guilt reactions for having gone against religious or societal norms they value. Partners may wonder about the ability to support themselves or function alone in the future. And the impact that the termination of a marriage has on children, relatives, and friends is also a difficult issue partners must deal with. The therapist can plan intervention strategies to increase the effectiveness of partners' (or former partners') responses to any intense and negative reactions they have to ending the marriage. Strategies can also be designed to aid partners in coping with the reactions of children, relatives, and friends. Finally, the therapist can assist partners to develop realistic expectations about the procedures involved in ending their marriage as well as what may lie ahead.

Implementing Interventions.   The ways in which a therapist can intervene to help a couple change are many. It is our personal and professional belief that any ethically acceptable technique or method that either aids in changing attitudes, beliefs, and behaviors that are maladaptive or in enhancing those that are adaptive is appropriate. We present a number of strategies we commonly utilize that are often related to more than one theoretical approach. These by no means form an exhaustive list. In fact, a list of intervention strategies based on not only the fundamental modes favored by numerous theoretical orientations but on the variations of them made to tailor language and concepts to the intellectual, educational, and cultural backgrounds of individual couples would never be finished. We therefore offer the following six strategies as a sampling, to aid in better conceptualizing this stage of our process model of marital therapy.

1. Reenactment. One intervention that a therapist can utilize to provide a framework from which change can emanate is reenactment. Having partners describe recent examples of conflict situations allows the critical variables in the development and continuance of these conflicts to be highlighted. Often, this offers partners an opportunity to view their circumstances more objectively and assists them in considering alternative ways of behaving. At times, the therapist may actively interpret the dynamics present in the couple's description of their interaction and suggest specific alternative behaviors. Whether the therapist chooses to directly and actively manipulate a situation or to guide more indirectly is dependent upon the partners' capabilities. If partners are unable to creatively resolve conflict issues with the indirect assistance of the therapist—if indirect manipulation does not work—the therapist should become more active and directive. Thus, the manner in which the therapist intervenes utilizing a reenactment strategy will be somewhat dictated by the needs and abilities of each individual couple; the therapist may function differently with different couples and, as well, with the same couple at different times. In this way, the therapist not only provides maximum assistance in specific situations but also models flexible conflict-resolution and problem-solving behaviors. That is, the therapist exhibits to the couple verbally and nonverbally, directly and indirectly, that different circumstances require different responses, and thus emphasizes the value of flexibility as a key element in harmonious, constructive relationship growth.

2. Encouragement. A general intervention that can occur throughout therapy but is especially beneficial when working for specifically delineated change is to offer encouragement. For the therapist to express a positive attitude ("I know you can do it") can have a significant impact. Partners who act in dysfunctional ways often perceive themselves to be inadequate, and lack self-esteem. Encouragement as an intervention focuses on such beliefs and self-perceptions, entailing a search for assets and providing feedback so that partners become aware of the strengths from which they can behave admirably. In a too-often mistake-centered culture like ours, this approach can alter the norm. The therapist who facilitates partners' utilization of their strengths allows them to function in a more adaptive and satisfying manner.

3. Acting "As If." This action-oriented intervention is used with partners who complain "If only I could. . . . " The strategy consists of suggesting to a partner or partners that they should act "as if"; that is, they should behave as they wish they could but don't believe they can at the present. Partners frequently protest that this would only be an act, and they would feel phony. These protests can be responded to by showing partners that all acting is not a phony pretense; they can try on a role as a person would try on new clothes. The person wearing the new clothes is still essentially the same person but, with a new outfit, may feel and even behave differently. Thus, in essence, one who acts "as if" functions in a more satisfying and adaptive manner.

4. Communication Checks. Although communication between partners is dealt with during the relationship stage, it is vital that the new behaviors be continued and expanded upon. One means of the therapist intervening to facilitate this is through the use of communication checks. The therapist can, when appropriate, continually intervene to check his or her perception of what has been communicated during the session. By modeling this behavior and encouraging partners to utilize it, assumptions and inaccurate perceptions can be immediately identified and corrected. Partners can also be instructed to practice using communication checks outside of therapy sessions and to make them a commonly accepted and anticipated part of their mutual interaction. Checking one's perception is a learned behavior. The more practice partners have, the more likely they are to continue the behavior in the future.

5. Role Expectations. Realistic role expectations in a marriage are an important asset in working to make that relationship a satisfying one. Unrealistic expectations are eventually found to be unattainable and become negative expectations. Then, partners become discouraged and their pessimistic outlooks become self-fulfilling, which contributes to the development and maintenance of dysfunctional behaviors and interaction patterns. The therapist can intervene by facilitating identification of realistic expectations that the partners have for one another, as well as the tasks each sees as a function of their roles. Partners can be assisted to negotiate various aspects of their roles in order to achieve mutually satisfying positions including, for example, what tasks are entailed and what consequences will follow if they are not completed. The key element is collaboration. Both partners must perceive themselves as having contributed to the establishment and maintenance of satisfying and functional roles that are necessary for the well-being of their relationship.

6. Marital Rules. Like role expectations, mutually acceptable and workable rules in a marriage can be critical in making the relationship a rewarding one. Rules can range from the relatively general to the very specific. General rules relate to overall goals the couple has set; these rules may deal with mutual respect, love, understanding, and other broad fundamentals. It is important that the behaviors by which these general rules are seen as being carried out be specified. For example, a rule that a couple love one another might specify such behaviors as doing tasks for each other without being asked, offering physical caresses frequently, or making positive comments to each other as often as is appropriate. More specific marital rules might concern household responsibilities, financial matters, and social activities. Whatever the rules' subjects, the simple goal in establishing them is to facilitate the couple's organizing daily living patterns. Rules can establish guidelines for the most efficient and effective organization and functioning of a relationship, and the inevitable results are less conflict and greater satisfaction.

Assessing Progress and Overcoming Obstacles

Progress toward goals in therapy is most often judged in relation to the effectiveness of the intervention strategies implemented to bring them about. From the initiation of any intervention, evaluation should be an ongoing endeavor. If at any time both the therapist and couple agree that a strategy is not providing movement toward a stated goal, it is vital that the situation be reviewed and that any changes needed be implemented. However, we caution that it can take some time for the effectiveness of some strategies to become evident.

Assessing progress is often difficult because, except where obvious behavioral change can be observed, verifiable criteria on which to base decisions may not be apparent. In addition, it is often necessary to look hard at behavior changes that do seem apparent; some partners mistakenly report positive effects only to please the therapist, or from fear of appearing inadequate in some way because of the strategy's breakdown. This problem points up the critical importance of successfully accomplishing the tasks of earlier stages in order to accomplish tasks called for in the later stages of our model. Specifically, assuming an open, honest working relationship was established in the first stage of the model, evaluation of progress in this fourth stage will be conducted much more easily. With a good working relationship the therapist and couple together can objectively seek criteria for evaluating intervention strategies, and, also together, can validate these criteria, rather than taking effectiveness for granted. Here, too, time is an important consideration. Ups and downs must be expected during the course of therapy, and new behaviors, as well as attitudes, feelings, and thoughts, all take time to stabilize.

Based on the evaluation of progress, the therapist and couple may decide to continue with current strategies, revise the current strategies, or replace them with new procedures. Perhaps goals also need to be revised or replaced. Or, if the strategies were effective and goals met, termination of therapy is the next step to consider.

If progress in therapy is not as desired, the reason may be any of a large number of sources of resistance. Solomon (1969) identified more than 25 sources of resistance possible within a family-therapy setting. We have found, although not as exhaustive a list as that offered by Solomon, the following categories of frequent impediments to marital-therapy efforts: unrealistic expectations, transference/countertransference reactions, family secrets, and third-party influences.

Unrealistic Expectations. What couples expect from marital therapy and what their therapists expect may vary widely. And the expectations of either a couple or therapist may be unrealistic. Of course the therapist must recognize and deal with unrealistic expectations on both his own part and the couple's, but only the couple's become a focus in therapy.

Couples' Expectations. Common unrealistic expectations that couples have include the idea that one's partner or other people (often children) will change and the belief that the therapist will bring about desired changes magically, with little or no effort on the couple's part.

Typically one partner blames the other, attributing the major portion of the relationship's problems to that mate. In this case, the expectation is that the therapist will change the partner who's responsible and the marriage will improve as a result. In some cases this expectation may be somewhat realistic; one mate may indeed be disturbed or may regularly act in ways that displease the other. However, it is unrealistic to expect that the therapist can or would work to get one partner only to change his or her behavior to suit the desires of the other partner. The therapist must assist the complaining partner in understanding that relationship concerns are reciprocal in nature. Assuming that a partner is uncooperative, the therapist could suggest ways for his or her mate to influence the partner's behavior. These might include better communication, frank discussions, disclosure of personal wishes, and negotiated agreements. Obviously these suggestions require considerable effort—and a change in behavior—on the part of the mate wishing his or her partner to change.

Perhaps most detrimental to progress in therapy is the unrealistic expectation that change should occur with little effort on the part of the couple. For many couples this expectation reflects experiences with medical practitioners who place patients in a passive treatment role. For others, the expectation derives primarily from a philosophy of low frustration tolerance: "Life should be easy"; "I shouldn't have to do anything that is hard or uncomfortable." Frequently the first indication of this unrealistic expectation is a couple's reluctance to engage in outside-of-session assignments, and particularly behavioral assignments. Understandably, couples are often reluctant to attempt behaviors that are different from those they are used to. The two main reasons for the reluctance that stems from low frustration tolerance are the extra effort perceived to be involved and an attempt to avoid fear—especially fear of feeling uncomfortable or anxious (Wessler & Wessler, 1980). The therapist must first assist a couple to deal with their reluctance and then establish more realistic expectations before attempting to implement further goal-directed intervention strategies.

Therapists' Expectations. It is often tempting to attribute responsibility for lack of progress to the couple in therapy. Although a couple can indeed impede progress, so can the therapist. Since the therapist, as the expert provider of therapeutic services, has the major responsibility for the therapeutic relationship and interaction, lack of progress may be due to the therapist's problems in developing this relationship and in the interaction that takes place.

Like couples, therapists at times also have unrealistic expectations for what can be accomplished through a therapeutic relationship, and these expectations can interfere with a couple's progress. For example, one expectation of many beginning marital therapists is that a couple will improve markedly in a few sessions. This may be the case for some couples; however, for many other couples change takes much longer. Believing change will occur quickly, a therapist may attempt to cover too wide a variety of a couple's concerns during a single session, or overload a couple with outside-of-session assignments. Naturally the result is opposite what the therapist intends. To counter the expectation of quick progress, remember that the common term *short-term psychotherapy* does not itself refer to just a few sessions. Rather, the phrase came into use primarily as a contrast to classical psychoanalysis, which can last for years.

Another unrealistic expectation with the potential to impede therapeutic progress is that what seems to be true actually is true; specifically, that what a therapist is likely to assume is occurring in the therapist-couple interaction need not be verified. Most problems with interventions relate to the therapist not checking out his or her assumptions. For example, almost all therapists engage in some type of explanation at times— explanation of the therapy itself, the rationale for a procedure, and so on. A major assumption that may go unchecked is, "The couple understands me." Often a couple doesn't, and, for various reasons, the partners do not ask for further explanation. Thus, after offering a brief explanation, or at points during a explanation that is complex, it is important for the therapist to ask, "Does this make sense to you?" However, even when a couple responds "yes," it would be prudent to check even further. For example, the therapist might go on to direct that the partners "Tell me how this applies to you." If a couple doesn't understand, it will be readily apparent.

Transference/Countertransference Reactions.

As discussed in Chapter 3, on psychoanalytic theory, the therapist is likely to be the object of combinations of attitudes, feelings, and actions that one or both partners have long vested in people significant in their lives, and that may be positive or negative in tone. Some reactions of partners to the therapist may be quite useful and may facilitate therapeutic progress. However, to the extent any reactions are inappropriate and block progress, it is critical to the success of therapy that they be examined. Since a transference reaction is assured to be a carryover from significant past relationships, intervention might include calling attention to the apparent earlier situation, clarifying the unspoken communication involved, exploring the degree of appropriateness of the past interaction to the present interaction, and then identifying a more appropriate response to the current situation. This type of discussion can be most productive if it is utilized to help partners clarify the way this and similar kinds of interactions, especially between the two of them, may affect their present and future functioning.

While marital partners might experience intense transference reactions toward their therapist, the therapist too may develop inappropriate reactions toward one or both partners, and these may likewise be of such intensity and nature that they inhibit therapeutic efforts. It is vital that the therapist be able to recognize and deal with such reactions. For example, the therapist may act toward one of the partners as though he or she were the therapist's own present or former mate.

Management of a countertransference reaction involves, primarily, the therapist's awareness of personal values and conflict areas in him- or herself. Personal therapy is often of assistance; and professional peer or supervisory consultation is strongly urged. Therapists must remember that their views are not universally applicable, and that, as long as the solutions of the partners in therapy are viable, those solutions should be supported.

Family Secrets.   Individual marital partners may have secrets; these might even be known to their mates, but not openly acknowledged. A secret can involve overt behavior, such as an affair, or thoughts and feelings that one partner believes the other is not aware of. When one partner appears to be blocking therapeutic efforts for some reason that's not clear, the therapist should look into it. We often request a session or two with each partner to work intensively on some "individual concerns" as a rationale for broaching the topic of a possible secret. If, in one of these individual sessions, new information is made known that seems important to the success of marital therapy efforts, the therapist assists this partner in deciding whether to reveal it to the other. Glick and Kessler (1974) have reported that bringing these secrets (or pseudosecrets) into the open frequently results in a "clearing of the general artificial atmosphere and eventually, if not immediately, a sense of relief and greater mutual understanding" (p. 100).

If such disclosures are encouraged, the therapist should be prepared to deal with shock waves (or pseudo shock waves) at the time the secret first emerges. At such times, the value of the sharing of the secret, rather than the impact of the secret itself, is an effective focus. For instance, identifying the discloser's sharing of an affair as a demonstration of remorse and desire to make the future with one's marital partner more satisfying can emphasize the positive aspects of such a disclosure.

One caution: not all revelations of family secrets will facilitate therapy efforts. If a secret does not seem of value in assisting a couple to attain the therapeutic goals, it is best left as it is, untold. Complete honesty is not necessarily a prerequisite for total or even partial marital satisfaction, especially as concerns past events, which can't be changed. When a therapist considers whether an issue need be shared, this paraphrase of Buddha is valuable: "Before one speaks the following questions should be asked of oneself: is it true, is it necessary, and is it timely."

Third-Party Influences.   Occasionally, it may become apparent that some third-party influence (a friend, relative, or other professional) is strongly influencing one or both partners in a manner contrary to the direction of therapy efforts. At such times, a short-term therapeutic intervention entails having the third party come to a therapy session. There the third party's influence can be explored in a more direct manner; it can be considered as to its potential benefits and deficiences with regard to marital therapy efforts and the couple's present and future marital satisfaction. If a couple is seeing specified mutual therapeutic goals and the third party's influence is evaluated objectively in light of those goals, the probablity is that the influence wielded will be reduced. The presence of the third party in a therapy session also assists that person to reevaluate his or her position and preferably to assume a more neutral, if not supportive, stance, at least temporarily.

A second form of third-party influence is of a less direct nature. In the presentation of systems theory, in Chapter 5, we describe triangulation; by this dynamic, a third party is employed to serve as a distraction—a scapegoat—for a couple from their mutual marital difficulties. For example, the most convenient target for a couple's scapegoat is their child or children. The scapegoated child may become either a source of great irritation (for example, through rebelliousness, poor school performance, or inadequate abilities) or of great pride and vicarious satisfaction (as by achievement in sports, school, social endeavors). No matter whether the focus is positive or negative, the result is the same; it keeps a couple from having to deal directly with each other.

Barnard and Corrales (1979) proposed a didactic approach as the preferred intervention when triangulation impedes therapeutic efforts. Utilizing a diagram in Figure 7-1, an explanation is given to a couple of how two people in conflict can involve a third party to serve as a distraction from their relationship problems and how, in doing so, the two delude themselves into thinking there is no other problem. It is pointed out that without the third party friction significantly increases between the two marital partners.

The illustration and explanation are usually sufficient to help marital partners begin to accept the conflict between them as their own. This intervention can be utlized to create what might be termed healthy guilt between the partners and can motivate efforts to change their relationship, thereby eliminating the need for a scapegoat (Boszormenyi-Nagy & Spark, 1973).

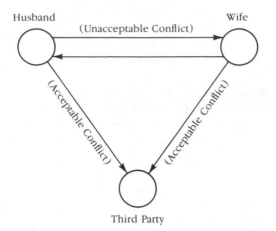

Husband   Wife
(Unacceptable Conflict)

Third Party

FIGURE 7-1.   In triangulation, marital partners refocus their own conflict on a third party. (*Adapted from C. P. Barnard and R. G. Corrales,
in* The Theory and Technique of Family Therapy, *1979. Courtesy of
Charles C. Thomas, Publisher, Springfield, Ill.*)

Ending Therapy

By this fifth stage in the therapeutic process, the couple has either
achieved the goals set or is making significant progress toward them. The
therapist begins to take a less involved role in the therapy efforts as the
partners assume more and more responsibility for their present and future
behavior. The partners have begun to generalize their new insights and
behaviors to all aspects of their lives, in and outside of their relationship.
They are no longer focusing the greater part of their energy on coping
with present conflicts. A productive problem-solving procedure has been
established and is being utilized. The couple is optimistic about the future, and is actively involved in planning for it. By another description,
termination is indicated when the couple and therapist are able to observe the following behaviors (Walsh, 1980):

1. Partners have internalized new attitudes and beliefs and exhibit new
   behaviors.
2. Conflicts that arise between the partners can be resolved in a mutually
   satisfying manner.
3. Partners have set realistic long-term goals for their relationship and for
   themselves.
4. The couple expresses optimism about future plans.

Termination need not be presented as a major event. In fact, to play it
down is probably better than to place any special emphasis on it. If a
couple's reaction suggests that ending therapy is a traumatic event, the

partners probably are not ready to terminate; this reaction indicates over-reliance on the therapist to fulfill some perceived need, which can then become a focus for therapy.

Usually, it is best to terminate therapy gradually. This is ordinarily done by increasing the length of time between sessions; a couple seen weekly for most of the course of therapy can be seen every other week and then once a month. Occasionally a six-month or one-year follow-up is suggested. This allows long-term evaluation of therapeutic efforts and also gives a couple the sense of an ongoing relationship, and one that leaves the door open, should that be necessary.

Finally, it can be expected that both the therapist and couple approach termination with some mixed emotions, particularly if the therapeutic relationship has been a close one. The therapist may feel sad about no longer seeing the couple but also, and more important, feel a sense of satisfaction that the couple has progressed so far. The couple is also likely to feel sad, as well as a bit apprehensive about the future. In addition, though, they are likely to feel confident that the relationship concerns as well as life's problems generally can be dealt with in a more effective and autonomous manner.

A Case Study

As is stressed in preceding chapters of this book, conceptualizations of a couple's functioning from a systems perspective are based on the assumption that individual behavior can be understood only in the context of the couple as a whole—of the system. Though individual behaviors are considered in this perspective, they are viewed as important only in that they represent part of the system's functioning. Thus, the goal of a systems-oriented therapist's interventions is not to change the individual behaviors of the partners but, rather, to alter the structure of the system. For example, a systems therapist might seek change in the partners' interaction patterns.

By contrast, the social-learning approach has historically focused on the behavior of the individual and on the environmental events that precede, shape, and maintain that behavior. Thus, the behaviorally oriented marital therapist typically focuses not on the organization of the couple system but on descriptions of individual behaviors, and on the manner in which partners control the contingencies for those behaviors (Linehan & Rosenthal, 1979). This often involves remedying specific skills deficits of one or both partners (Foster & Hoier, 1982).

A common experience of beginning therapists that we have observed in supervising their work with these two approaches has been aptly summarized by Birchler and Spinks (1980), who reported:

Simply put, there was an enormous gap between systems theory and its application. The systems approach often led to lengthy, aimless therapy which relied for its success upon the intuition of the therapist. The behavioral approach, on the other hand, was frequently experienced as overly structured, and many therapists were uncomfortable with inattention to process and failure to deal with underlying issues [p. 9].

It is in such cases, when therapists seek a means by which to integrate valued concepts and procedures from more than one approach, that our process model has proved most useful. Let us return to the case of Chuck and Mary presented in Chapter 6 and consider how a therapist whose primary orientation is in social-learning theory would integrate systems concepts in work with the couple.

In seeking to establish a relationship (the first stage), the therapist spent the initial session developing rapport, making the couple as comfortable as possible. To begin structuring therapy, the therapist asked Chuck and Mary to present what they saw as their major problems. The therapist explained to them the course that therapy would likely take and asked that they consider possible implications for the next few weeks, during which sessions would be devoted to assessing various aspects of their individual and relationship behaviors.

Chuck and Mary were also assisted in communicating more clearly, especially in expressing difficulties. Outlines of their general problems were translated into more specific, concrete issues. Goals, too, were specified more precisely.

In assessing the couple's concerns (the second stage), not only were the behaviorally oriented assessments considered, but the therapist formulated some systems hypotheses, especially relating to the rules by which the marital system operates and the homeostatic mechanisms the couple might employ to resist positive change. Following the assessment sessions, and so taking into consideration the assessment information as well as the couple's stated goals, the therapist provided Chuck and Mary with specific recommendations as to how therapy might proceed. These recommendations were primarily behavioral in nature and focused on the idea that their present behaviors were causing their problems and that, correspondingly, by learning more adaptive interpersonal and coping behaviors they could experience greater satisfaction in their relationship. A commitment was given in a written contract to work toward agreed upon goals for 12 sessions, at which time progress would be assessed and discussed.

In applying intervention strategies (the third stage), the following behavior-oriented treatment procedures were planned and implemented:

1. Behavioral exchange.
2. Communication-skills training.
3. Problem-solving training.

It was during the intervention stage that certain systems issues noted during the assessment phase came to be an integral consideration in the progress of therapeutic efforts. They came up in Chuck and Mary's having a great deal of difficulty agreeing about how to discipline their children. Normally, in working with a behaviorally oriented therapist, the couple would likely work on the difficulty with communication-skills and problem-solving training, as were indeed planned. However, in this case the therapist recognized issues of the use of power and control within the system and judged that their influence on Chuck and Mary's behavior warranted a specific intervention. It seems the rules the couple had implicitly established for disciplining the children were such that a complementary relationship was defined, with Chuck the leader and Mary the follower. And Mary was no longer satisfied with the position of follower. Having assessed the possibility that at some time during therapy this dynamic might cause resistance, the therapist waited to see if such problems developed. They did: Chuck and Mary began to have difficulty in completing joint homework tasks, they argued about how each felt about their presenting problems, and the crises between sessions increased.

In assessing progress so as to overcome obstacles (the fourth stage), the therapist first considered all other possible explanations for Chuck and Mary's resistance. Had the therapeutic relationship been firmly established? Were any expectations of the couple unrealistic, causing interventions to be premature or poorly timed? Or were homework tasks inappropriately designed? In ruling out these possible explanations, the therapist narrowed the analysis to the systems issue as the impediment. Accordingly the therapist digressed from the behavioral plan and dealt with the systems issue; Mary was assisted in relabeling what she saw as Chuck's negative, controlling behaviors as "overconcern for the children" rather than as usurping of her parenting role. The relabeling changed the context in which Mary viewed Chuck's behavior and thereby freed her to behave differently. This systems intervention was a brief one, yet it allowed the behavioral plan to be successfully accomplished in a more efficient and effective manner.

At the ending of therapy (the fifth stage), Chuck and Mary decided to pursue improvement on their own. The interval between sessions was gradually increased, at first to two weeks and then to a month. By that time, as evidenced by another formal assessment and the couple's own optimism and satisfaction, therapy had been successful.

Although in this case the therapist integrated systems concepts with a social-learning approach, such other combinations as social-learning theory with psychoanalytic theory or systems concepts with psychoanalytic theory (or some other blendings of theories) could equally be applicable.

Summary

In this chapter we present our process model of marital therapy, consisting of five identifiable, progressive stages: establishing a relationship, assessing a couple's concerns, applying intervention strategies, assessing progress and overcoming obstacles, and ending therapy. These stages are examined, significant aspects of each discussed, and a case example offered.

We propose that, regardless of marital therapists' primary theoretical orientations, they can function more effectively and with a greater diversity of couples if they have a framework that enables them to incorporate ideas, techniques, and methodology from a variety of theoretical orientations and to integrate them within the primary theoretical position and mode of practice. Having such a framework allows therapists to be flexible and still be consistent in their work with couples.

Our feeling is that if therapists know where they are going, they will get there faster and more efficiently. The model we offer in this chapter is the cognitive map for such direction. With this map, therapists can always be aware of where they are going in terms of process.

Some couples move through the therapeutic process and successfully end it in a relatively brief time. Others require more extensive remedial and developmental efforts and may be in therapy for longer periods. Regardless of the duration or the major theoretical approach employed, the process of therapy is essentially the same. In other words, successful, effective therapeutic endeavors always involve progressive movement from establishing a relationship to its ending by means of the turmoil and exhilarating change effected in the consecutive intervening stages.

References

Barnard, C. P., & Corrales, R. G. *The theory and technique of family therapy.* Springfield, Ill.: Charles C. Thomas, 1979.

Birchler, G. R., & Spinks, S. H. Behavioral-systems marital and family therapy: Integration and clincial application. *American Journal of Family Therapy,* 1980, *8,* 6–28.

Boszormenyi-Nagy, I., & Spark, G. *Invisible loyalties.* New York: Harper & Row, 1973.

Corrigan, J. D., Dell, D. M., Lewis, K. N., & Schmidt, L. D. Counseling as a social influence process: A review. *Journal of Counseling Psychology Monograph,* 1980, *27,* 395–431.

Egan, G. *The skilled helper: Model, skills, and methods for effective helping* (2nd ed.). Monterey, Calif.: Brooks/Cole, 1982.

Eisenberg, S., & Delaney, D. J. *The counseling process* (2nd ed.). Chicago: Rand McNally, 1977.

Festinger, L. *A theory of cognitive dissonance.* New York: Harper & Row, 1957.

Foster, S. L., & Hoier, T. S. Behavioral and systems family therapies: A comparison of theoretical assumptions. *American Journal of Family Therapy,* 1982, *10,* 13–23.

Glick, I. D., & Kessler, D. R. *Marital and family therapy.* New York: Grune & Stratton, 1974.

Goldstein, A. P. Relationship-enhancement methods. In F. J. Kanfer & A. P. Goldstein (Eds.), *Helping people change: A textbook of methods* (2nd ed.). New York: Pergamon, 1980.

Hovland, C. T., Janis, I. L., & Kelley, H. H. *Communication and persuasion: Psychological studies of opinion change.* New Haven: Yale University Press, 1953.

Linehan, K. S., & Rosenthal, T. L. Current behavioral approaches to marital and family therapy. *Advances in Behavior Research and Therapy,* 1979, *2,* 99–143.

Rogers, C., Gendlin, E. T., Kiesler, D. J., & Truax, C. B. *The therapeutic relationship and its impact.* Madison, Wisc.: University of Wisconsin Press, 1967.

Solomon, M. Family therapy dropouts: Resistance to change. *Canadian Psychiatric Association Journal,* 1969, *14,* 21–29.

Strong, S. R. Counseling: An interpersonal influence process. *Journal of Counseling Psychology,* 1968, *15,* 215–224.

Truax, C. B., & Carkhuff, R. R. *Toward effective counseling and psychotherapy: Training and practice.* Chicago: Aldine, 1967.

Walsh, W. M. *A primer in family therapy.* Springfield, Ill.: Charles C. Thomas, 1980.

Wessler, R. A., & Wessler, R. L. *The principles and practice of rational-emotive therapy.* San Francisco: Jossey-Bass, 1980.

CHAPTER EIGHT

Therapeutic Intervention: General Strategies and Specific Suggestions

In our Chapter 7 presentation of the course of marital therapy from a process-oriented perspective, we identify five distinct stages. The third stage, "Applying Intervention Strategies," is the part of the therapy process in which techniques and procedures are planned and then implemented in order to assist a couple to address the concerns they have expressed in the second stage.

There are almost an infinite number of therapeutic intervention strategies that can be used with couples. Each major theoretical orientation evolves its own interventions, and there are also many interventions independent of any major theory that are specialized for particular circumstances. The specialized interventions are necessary because of skill deficits on the part of one or both partners; facilitating skill acquisition at times calls for interventions beyond the immediate scope of the theoretical frameworks presented in Chapters 3, 4, and 5.

There are interventions far more specialized than those offered in this chapter; we undertake a brief examination of intervention strategies to utilize in the following pursuits: communication training, conflict management, parent consultation, sex therapy, and divorce therapy. We also consider some strategies in areas of a more contemporary nature for couples in today's society: women's issues, dual-career marriages, and marriage enrichment.

Communications Training

For a marital relationship to function effectively, partners must be able to establish and maintain clear communications together. This fact is plainly evidenced in a survey conducted by Beck and Jones (1973) wherein poor communication was by far the major problem reported by couples seeking therapeutic assistance (see Figure 8-1).

Because of the critical importance of clear and constructive communication between marital partners, a number of major therapeutic approaches have evolved whose primary focus is on teaching couples more appropriate ways to communicate. In *The Mirages of Marriage,* Lederer and Jackson (1968) proposed that a lack of clarity in communications between marital partners is the major cause of marital distress. In addition

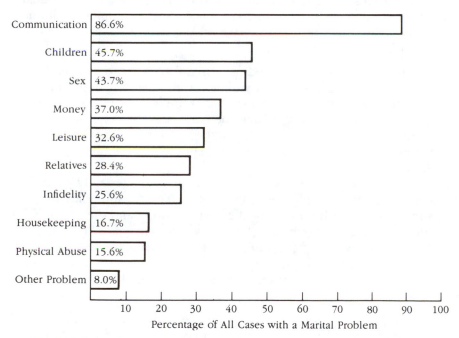

FIGURE 8-1.   The ranking of marital problems reported in the case loads of 266 U.S. family-counseling agencies. (*Reprinted from* Progress on Family Problems: A Nationwide Study of Clients' and Counselors' Views on Family Agency Services, *by Dorothy Fahs Beck and Mary Ann Jones, by permission of the publisher. Copyright © 1973 by Family Service Association of America, New York.*)

to teaching couples more effective styles of communicating, their method involves encouraging couples to reconsider the validity of their beliefs about marriage. Lederer and Jackson proposed that certain "mirages" or myths about marriage contribute significantly to marital distress. They advocated open, honest communications and "quid-pro-quos" ("something for something"), in a step-by-step process of bargaining that helps each partner satisfy his or her unconscious need and expectation of being equal in the relationship.

Virginia Satir proposed in *Peoplemaking* (1972) that there is a positive relationship between marital satisfaction and a couple's ability to communicate effectively. Her method involves teaching couples to express affect, send I-messages, and recognize and tolerate partner differences. It also includes assisting couples in recognizing and responding to four types of maladaptive communication styles that she termed blaming, placating, computing, and distracting. The work also deals with the "you," "me," and "us" aspects of relationships. Satir found that improving communications between partners increases partners' self-esteem and smooths functioning of the "us" aspects of relationships.

The Minnesota Couples Communication Program (Miller, Nunnally, & Wackman, 1976b) focuses on four major styles of communication, as well as on the intentions and behavioral characteristics associated with each style. These four styles are:

1. Cognitive emphasis with low disclosure, characterized by friendliness, sociability, conventionality, playful intent, chitchat, and descriptiveness.
2. An emphasis on feeling with low disclosure, characterized by tendencies to persuade, direct, blame, demand, defend, assume, compete, withhold, evaluate, advise, praise, and speak for others, with a focus on the use of absolutistic words such as "should," "ought," "always," and "never."
3. A cognitive emphasis with high receptivity, characterized by tentativeness, elaboration, exploration, speculation, search, and reflection, with a focus on a search for causes, the past or future, and the use of words such as "maybe," "perhaps," "probably," "could," and "might."
4. An emphasis on feeling and high disclosure, characterized by an active awareness, acceptance of responsibility, self-disclosure, understanding, caring, and cooperation, with a focus on self and the here and now.

Marital partners are taught to recognize their own and their mate's particular communication styles and to try out other, possibly more effective styles. In addition, partners learn to speak for themselves and to make appropriate statements of feeling and intention.

Stuart (1980) presented a more detailed skills-based approach for assisting couples to communicate effectively. He proposed three basic goals for couples' communications training: building partners' skills in

(1) making their desires known, (2) understanding their mate's requests, and (3) bargaining toward a common understanding. Stuart's program consists of a five-skill training sequence for reaching these goals: listening, self-expression, request-making, feedback, and clarification. In teaching the skills to couples Stuart suggested that therapists treat the set as cumulative rather than each skill as discrete; the first-mentioned skills are prerequisites for those that follow.

We present Stuart's training sequence in detail because we have found it to be a simple and understandable yet practical skills program that couples readily respond to.

Listening

The ability to listen is likely the most basic skill necessary for effective communication between marital partners. Because individuals are constantly sending messages (assuming that, as widely held, all socially relevant behavior is communication), it is the listener who actually determines whether communication takes place (Patton & Griffin, 1974).

Nierenberg and Calero (1973) have identified poor listeners as those who:

1. Reject the speaker's words as uninteresting, already known, too simple, or too complicated.
2. Attend to aspects of the speaker's manner and appearance rather than the words that are being said.
3. Stop attending to the overall message and instead concentrate on a single word or phrase.
4. Know in advance what they think they will hear.

In other words, poor listening involves inattention to content, distraction, obsession with a single aspect of the message, and attention to inner thoughts instead of the speaker's words. By contrast, according to Stuart (1980), good listeners are characterized by the following:

1. They fully commit themselves to listening.
2. They physically and mentally prepare themselves to listen.
3. They wait for the speaker to completely finish speaking before expressing their own ideas.
4. They use analytic skills to supplement, not to replace, listening.

Together, these skills allow an individual to receive information in relatively undistorted form, and they provide the listener with the ability to help the speaker feel accepted and understood.

Stuart identified a series of brief exercises for use during and between therapy sessions to teach couples the four components of good listening in the preceding list. Often, just a simple set of recommendations is the impetus marital partners need to begin to listen more effectively. In the exercises that follow, the first recommendation involves identifying any biases or hidden assumptions each partner may hold. What are some of the things that each expects the other to do quite frequently? Does one expect to be put down? Does the other expect to be ignored? If so, one partner may hear constant put-downs while the other feels constantly ignored regardless of messages sent. Stuart proposes that the therapist have couples write down for themselves those things they think the other will say in a given situation. In doing so, self-fulfilling prophesies can be identified and explained. Also in these exercises couples are taught to orient themselves toward one another for greater listening effectiveness. The therapist should be prepared to coach couples as to when and how long to speak and when to listen, asking each partner to practice repeating and paraphrasing selected messages of the other's, to actively communicate their listening ability.

Self-Expression

Self-expressive statements are those that assist marital partners to better orient themselves in relation to one another. Self-expression allows each partner to make sense of his or her own experiences by putting those experiences into words (Miller, Nunnally, & Wackman, 1975). Stuart suggested that marital partners can best learn effective self-expression by being taught specific rules to follow for expressing themselves. These "rule statements" are described here.

The "I-Rule."   Self-statements best begin with the personal pronoun *I.* "I" statements are expressions of self-responsibility; they are clear, based upon personal awareness, leave room for the awareness of others, and encourage the disclosure of differences (Miller, Nunnally, & Wackman, 1976a). "I" statements can be contrasted with "it" statements (which externalize responsibility; the listener finding it difficult to respond because the speaker has not accepted ownership of what is being said), "you" statements (which are almost always accusatory and lead to defensiveness; they involve an effort to shift responsibility for the statement's impact from the speaker to the listener), and "we" statements (which mean by definition that the speaker is talking for both him- or herself and for the listener as well). For example, consider the following statements:

- "I am angry."
- "It makes me angry."
- "You make me angry."
- "We are angry."

Only in the first statement, "I am angry," does the speaker communicate his or her own experience and take sole responsibility for the accuracy of the message.

The "Statement" Rule.   Self-expressions should be in the form of statements rather than questions whenever possible. Stuart (1980) proposes that questions are "efforts to elicit a commitment from the other person without the speaker's taking responsibility for a position first" (p. 225). Further, questions, especially those beginning with "why," very frequently are accusatory and seek to put the one to whom they are directed on the defensive (for example, "Why did you do that?"). Questions therefore prevent the speaker from having to take responsibility for what he or she says, while putting the speaker in a "one-up" position and holding the listener in a "one-down" position.

The "Say-Ask," "How," and "Two-Question" Rules.   When a question must be asked, it is best for it to be preceded by a self-statement, to begin with *how,* to be followed by a second question seeking amplification of the answer to the first. The say-ask rule of preceding questions with self-statements increases the level of responsibility the speaker takes for his or her messages and thus lowers any need for defensiveness on the part of the listener. The use of *how* to begin questions contributes to the development of a problem-solving orientation between partners rather than of the accusatorial exchange that is created by "why" questions. Further, the two-question rule in which the speaker is ready with a request for more information from the listener avoids the possibility that the answer will be used as a setup for an immediate attack. It also expresses the asker's interest in the answerer's response. Consider the following conversation:

Partner A: How have things been going?
Partner B: Very well, thanks.
Partner A: Well, they're not going too good for me. This morning. . . .

Now compare that conversation with this one:

Partner A: How have things been going?
Partner B: Very well, thanks.
Partner A: Were you able to progress much more on the business venture we spoke of last week?

In the first conversation, it is clear that Partner A was using Partner B's answer as a means of moving to a self-statement rather than to convey any real interest in B's response. The second conversation shows how a follow-up question can display a genuine feeling of interest in B. The use of the second question is likely to elicit a far more positive reaction than did the sequence in the first conversation.

The "Now" Rule.   Self-expressions are best kept present oriented. Any tense other than the present can create a distance in verbal communication by which the speaker divests him- or herself of at least part of the responsibility for the words that are spoken (Nierenberg & Calero, 1973). Thus, staying in the present increases openness and reduces potential defensiveness.

The "Simplicity-Speaks-the-Truth" Rule.   It is important that self-statements be made directly, openly, and honestly—free of any verbal excess. In this respect, Nierenberg and Calero (1973) cautioned against the use of phrases that tend to manipulate the listener into the frame of mind desired by the speaker. For example, "softeners" (such as "You're going to like what I'm going to tell you") can be employed to create a positive reception; "foreboders" (Don't worry, but . . . ") can create anxiety in the listener; and "downers" ("You haven't heard this yet, but . . . ") can build up the position of the speaker. These manipulations and others like them maneuver the listener into expressing the reaction desired by the speaker—regardless of the true impact of the main message.

Request Making

In regard to request making, Stevens (1971) noted:

> Most demands are not expressed openly and directly. Usually I don't want to take responsibility for my demands, so I hide and disguise them in sweet requests, suggestions, questions, accusations, and countless other manipulations. I would like you to satisfy my desires without having to ask you. If I demand directly, I run the risk that you might refuse [p. 110].

Stuart suggested that request making requires two types of skills: (1) framing the request properly, and (2) appropriately timing its delivery. Requests should be framed so that they meet all of the rules of self-statements. In addition, they are best begun with "I want" rather than "I need," a want being something that one desires but is not absolutely necessary to his or her survival. *Want* places less pressure on the listener to comply than *need,* which often contributes to a reluctance on the part of the listener to comply. After all, it is more pleasurable to do something for one's partner out of desire than out of demand.

Apart from choosing the proper words, the proper time is also a critical variable in making requests. For example, the best time to discuss buying new clothes may not be the day when a pile of bills arrives. It is important for both partners to learn when to temporarily set aside their desires in deference to the desires or needs of the other.

Stuart suggests that it is not difficult to assist couples to learn appropriate ways to phrase their requests; most people are aware of the value of such strategies as simply saying "please." He does, however, note that difficulty does often arise in helping couples learn when to express their desires. It is important therefore that marital therapists work to teach couples how to read one another's readiness or receptivity cues. One means of doing this is to have each partner assume the responsibility of telling the other when he or she is willing to put him- or herself at the disposal of the other. One partner might ask the other if there is anything he or she would like done, or one might tell the other that he or she would like to spend some time discussing what each might do to lessen the other's responsibilities or add pleasures to the other's life.

Feedback

All people need feedback if they are to function at any task successfully. Positive and negative feedback determine the success or failure of any performance. However, the true value of feedback lies in its influence on future behavior. Stuart (1980) offered the following example in this regard:

> Jerry has felt that Pat has been quite aloof, and he would like to have a greater feeling of closeness to her. He could wait several weeks and tell her that he felt she had been distant for some time, in which case he will have gone on suffering with a gnawing sense of isolation. However, he could also tell her immediately that he would like to feel closer to her, moving into a request that she sit on the sofa with him for a while and talk about things they could do together to gain an opportunity for sharing and the closeness it could bring. In this way, feedback about Jerry's present feelings can be used to help Pat make changes that can have an immediate and positive effect [p. 233].

Stuart identified six primary characteristics of effective feedback statements:

1. Feedback statements should begin with "I."
2. Feedback statements should refer to specific behaviors.
3. Feedback statements should stress the positive aspects of behaviors; if they do not stress positive aspects, they are best phrased as requests for specific positive changes.
4. Feedback statements should use language that reflects what people do—*process language* (for example, "He spends time at the golf course that he could spend at home")—rather than static labels—*terminal language* (for example, "He's stubborn."). Process language addresses things that can be changed and is therefore more constructively received.
5. Feedback statements should be expressed as soon as possible after the behaviors to which they refer occur. This keeps the feedback present oriented.
6. Feedback statements should be offered at an appropriate time and in the way that is most likely to be comprehended.

Training couples to give appropriate feedback should be a therapeutic focus both during and between sessions. Couples should be asked to practice between sessions the skills they learn during sessions. During sessions, the therapist can encourage partners to give nonverbal feedback by smiling, nodding, or pointing an index finger at the other partner in response to any preferred verbal or nonverbal behavior. These gestures can then be paired with verbal expressions about perceived positive behaviors between partners. The therapist can continually offer suggestions on how partners can improve the way their feedback is expressed and also praise the efforts and improvements made.

At the same time partners are being trained in giving feedback, they should also learn how to better receive it. With the goal of giving a constructive response, partners can be taught to ask themselves several silent questions when receiving feedback:

• In what ways is the feedback positive?
• How is the fact that the feedback was offered an indication that my partner is concerned about what I am doing?
• How does the feedback help me to see how I might perform well in the future?

If the answers to these questions are found, the chances are that the reaction to the feedback will be positive.

Clarification

Virtually all approaches developed to teach couples more effective communication skills include training in clarification responses. Gottman, Notarius, Gonso, and Markman (1976) labeled the process of marital partners seeking clarification of each other's messages "validation." Miller, Nunnally, and Wackman (1976a), in their Minnesota Couples Communication Program, termed this skill "confirming/clarifying." These approaches define what Stuart called clarification in terms of its objective: to check out the meaning of another's message until some consensus as to its mutual meaning is achieved. This refers to nonverbal as well as verbal messages.

Marital therapists can begin teaching couples to make clarifying responses in the very first therapy session. This process occurs through the therapist's modeling of two primary responses: (1) questioning for additional information necessary to understand the speaker's message (for example, "I'm not sure I understand what you're saying. Could you express that thought in another way?"), and, when the speaker does as requested, (2) paraphrasing or restating the meaning of the speaker's message that is understood and asking for verification.

When most marital partners seek clarification, they omit the first step. The original speaker then feels unjustly challenged and needlessly misunderstood when his or her words are fed back incorrectly. Asking the question first indicates the listener's interest in really hearing what the speaker has to say.

In teaching a couple to clarify messages, the therapist can request that the partners practice the two-phase clarification process modeled, urging each to first ask for a clear meaning and then to restate the message received. In this practice, the speaker is questioned for additional information until the listener can accurately paraphrase in his or her own words (rather than the words of the original message) what the speaker has said. It is also important that the therapist stress the speaker's responsibility to attempt to send messages in a manner that is truest to the intended meaning. Both partners should be encouraged to avoid any tendency to become hypercritical of themselves or their partners, which can engender hostile and competitive exchanges and turn skill building into an angry contest. Therefore, the therapist must constantly give constructive feedback and act as a model for couples to follow in their effort to achieve an effective repertoire of communication skills.

Conflict Management

Failure to deal with conflict constructively has been viewed as the single most powerful force in dampening marital satisfaction (Cuber & Harroff, 1965), if not the most prominent cause of marital failure (Mace, 1976). This does not mean that marriages are or should be centers of complete consensus and harmony to the exclusion of any argument, anger, or conflict. Some conflict is inevitable in every relationship. Therefore it is important that couples have at their disposal a set of well-rehearsed strategies for managing conflict. Before presenting some guidelines for managing conflict, however, let us consider some common practices that tend to increase the amount of conflict in relationships. These practices have been identified by one pair of writers as "alienating fight tactics" (Lamanna & Riedmann, 1981).

Alienating Fight Tactics

Alienating fight tactics are behaviors that tend to create distance between marital partners. These tactics don't resolve conflict; they increase it (Lamanna & Riedmann, 1981). Some of the major forms of alienating fight tactics are fight evading, gunnysacking, mind raping, and stereotyping. Each of these is defined and further described here.

Fight Evading.   Fight evading involves avoiding conflict at all costs, and thus refusing to accept one's own or a partner's hostile or angry emotions. Partners who engage in fight evading are likely very insecure about the stability of their relationship. They avoid conflict by several maladaptive means, such as:

- Leaving the house or the scene when a fight threatens to occur.
- Turning sullen and refusing to talk.
- Derailing potential arguments by whining, "I can't take it when you yell at me."
- Flatly stating, "I can't take you seriously when you act this way."
- Employing the "hit and run" tactic of filing a complaint, then leaving no time for an answer or for some resolution (Bach & Wyden, 1970).

Partners seeking to evade conflict at all costs often say that they avoid conflict because they don't want to hurt their mates. More likely, however, they are mistakenly attempting to protect themselves. As suggested by Crosby (1976), "a great deal of dishonesty that ostensibly occurs in an effort to prevent pain actually occurs as we try to protect and shield ourselves from the agony of feeling our own pain, fear, fright, shame, or embarrassment" (p. 157–158). Regardless of the intent, evading conflicts can make partners who need to work out and resolve dissatisfactions in their relationships feel worse, not better.

Gunnysacking.   Gunnysacking occurs when partners keep grievances secret while "tossing them into an imaginary gunnysack that grows heavier and heavier over their shoulders" (Lamanna & Riedmann, 1981, p. 297). Gunnysacking has been considered a predominantly feminine tactic, but in recent years it has become prevalent among men as well (Bach & Wyden, 1970). A typical negative result of gunnysacking occurs when partners do argue; they reach into their gunnysacks and drag irrelevant and past occurrences into their present disagreement. Consider the following example given by Bach and Wyden (1970, p. 18–19):

He: Why were you late?
She: I tried my best.
He: Yeah? You and who else? Your mother is never on time either.
She: That's got nothing to do with it.
He: The hell it doesn't. You're just as sloppy as she is.
She (getting louder): You don't say! Who's picking whose dirty underwear off the floor every morning?
He (sarcastic but controlled): I happen to go to work. What have you got to do all day?
She (shouting): I'm trying to get along on the money you don't make, that's what.
He (turning away from her): Why should I knock myself out for an ungrateful bitch like you?

The immediate issue, the wife's lateness, is never resolved. In fact, it appears to have been forgotten (or itself gunnysacked to be used as future ammunition in another conflict). Obviously, gunnysacking does nothing to help partners feel better about themselves or their relationship.

Mind Raping.   Mind raping involves making assumptions about the thoughts, feelings, and motives of one's partner and then telling that partner what he or she thinks or feels or ought to think or feel (Bach & Deutsch, 1970). In mind raping, partners assign feelings and motivations to their mates, often correcting and rejecting their partners' own statements about themselves. Consider the following illustration:

Husband: Why didn't you pick up the batteries for my transistor radio on your way home like I asked you to this morning?
Wife: I don't know. Work was so hectic today. It just slipped my mind.
Husband: Oh, sure. It slipped your mind because you weren't listening when I told you I needed to use my radio this evening and that the batteries were dead. You don't need the radio so you just conveniently chose to worry only about yourself. You just don't care about me.

It is possible that the wife's forgetfulness was intentional and an instance of passive-aggressive behavior; the husband's perception may have been correct. Still, mind raping only increases the intensity of the conflict and does nothing to solve the problem.

Stereotyping.   Stereotyping occurs when one partner places a diagnostic, racial, or cultural label on his or her mate in order to make a point. For example, one common stereotyping tactic is to label one's partner either unfeminine or unmasculine. When threatened by a partner's expressions of anger and dissatisfaction, a husband might try to divert hostility by responding "This is the sweet bride I married?" or a wife could say "You're not being a man!" (Lamanna & Riedmann, 1981).

Stereotyping alienates partners. It indicates an attempt by one partner to depersonalize the other. Stereotyping is a sign that a partner is giving up trying to understand the other as a unique person. To label one's partner as a type inevitably lowers self-esteem and leads only to exchanges or insults or worse.

Constructive Responses to Conflict

The alienating fight tactics just described are likely to intensify conflict and push partners apart; managing conflict requires responses to conflict that are constructive—that bring partners closer together. In another work (Huber & Baruth, 1981), we described a series of guidelines to assist couples in improving their responses to conflicts. Our approach proposes that couples not avoid marital conflicts but rather accept that they will occur and attempt to resolve them mutually when they do. Resolution is not the same as compromise (which is frequently suggested as a solution in conflict situations). Resolution is achieved when both partners feel that each has gained something; in contrast, compromise is a process in which both partners give up something. The pursuit of resolution can be encouraged by teaching couples the ideas and process behind Dreikurs' (1946) four directives for conflict resolution: (1) create mutual respect, (2) pinpoint the issue, (3) seek areas of agreement, and (4) mutually participate in decision making. All unresolved marital conflicts involve a violation of one or more of these principles.

Create Mutual Respect.   Mutual respect allows neither fighting nor giving in. Fighting violates respect for one's partner; giving in violates respect for oneself. Mutual respect involves acknowledging that the first step in resolving conflict lies in understanding and accepting one another's points of view and the value of mutual, not individual, "winning."

To begin to resolve a conflict in their relationship, partners must learn to ask themselves whether their mates are less worthy of their respect because of their different points of view. Usually, what creates conflict is not what's in contention but the attitudes partners hold toward it. And, to keep a conflict going, both partners have to actively cooperate. To stop it, only one partner needs to withdraw. This does not mean that one partner must give in; if, instead of arguing, either starts looking for the real reasons behind their respective destructive behaviors, progress can be made.

Pinpoint the Issue.   In any conflict partners experience, it is important that they learn to pinpoint the fundamental issue. This usually is not what partners are ostensibly arguing about. The real issue is their troubled marital relationship. A partner who resists a request that the other partner perceives to be completely reasonable may be resisting not the request but what is perceived as an attempt at domination or control. Whether partners argue over money, friends, in-laws, children, or other topics, underlying each disputed issue is the problem of personal involvement on the part of each partner—such concerns as who is right, who is being treated unfairly, who wins, and whose personal status, prestige, or superiority is threatened.

Dreikurs, Gould, and Corsini (1974) suggested that the underlying issue in most conflicts is one of the following:

- A threat to personal status ("Why should I give in?").
- A question of prestige ("What will he/she/they think?").
- A matter of superiority ("If I'm not on top, I'll be on the bottom").
- The right to decide ("Why should I let him/her decide for me?").
- The right to control ("If I don't boss him/her, he/she won't do it right").
- The right of judgment ("Whose way is the best way?").

- The idea of retaliation ("He/she won the last time").
- The wish for revenge ("I'll get even this time").

By not recognizing the critical role of personal involvement in marital conflict, partners often escalate mere disagreements into unresolvable battles. By learning how to pinpoint and deal with the real issue, a couple takes a crucial step toward meaningful conflict resolution.

Seek Areas of Agreement.   Conflicts signal agreements to fight. Therefore, to resolve any conflict, partners must make a new agreement. Instead of agreeing to argue, which amounts to attempting to dominate or abuse, partners can learn to agree to work toward a more friendly, peaceful means of interacting. Few couples realize that any type of mutual interaction, whether it be conflict or closeness, is based on agreement, on full cooperation and accord.

Two people cannot experience conflict without having communicated their intention to fight and then gained each other's cooperation and support to do so. Even if only one partner, understanding this, refuses to continue his or her role in the agreed-to conflict, hostility will be reduced. The agreement to fight can be changed even if only one partner simply does what he or she alone can do, instead of pointing out what his or her mate should do, to end the discord. Reaching a new agreement ultimately comes down to each partner's declaring "This is what I'm willing to do, no strings attached." It should be emphasized to couples that reaching agreement can be relatively simple if each of them is prepared to change his or her own role and behavior.

Mutually Participate in Decision Making.   Couples must mutually participate in making decisions that affect them both. This participation should not be limited to the decision-making process itself but should apply also to equal sharing of responsibility for any decision made. Dinkmeyer, Pew, and Dinkmeyer (1979) offered a situation illustrating the consequences of violating this principle:

> A husband came and announced to his wife, rather emphatically and enthusiastically, that he had made arrangements for them to spend a weekend at a resort motel and had also made reservations for dinner at a fine restaurant. He was quite surprised and disappointed when his wife didn't show the enthusiasm he had expected. What he didn't realize was that, by acting without consulting her, he had shown little respect for his wife and violated the principle of participation in decision making [p. 245].

Decision making can be viewed as an unequal, superior-inferior relationship wherein one partner (the superior) decides, while his or her mate (the inferior) is given no role in the process, only informed of the outcome; or alternatively it can be a joint venture, in which both partners contribute to the process and take responsibility for participating in any decision made. Identifying decisions involving both partners as decisions to be mutually decided upon can have a dramatic impact on the way in which those decisions are made and implemented.

Johnson (1972) presented a decision-making strategy for the cooperative resolution of conflict situations. We have found an adaptation of this process to be an effective outline for couples to utilize. This strategy is described in the accompanying box.

STEPS TO A COOPERATIVE RESOLUTION OF MARITAL CONFLICT

Considering the conflict situation and the attitudes that operate in regard to it:

1. How do you define the problem between yourself and your partner? (Remember to consider fundamental issues that may be underlying the problem.)
   HUSBAND:
   WIFE:
2. What behavior or behaviors of yours contribute to the problem?
   HUSBAND:
   WIFE:
3. How appropriate are the behaviors just described to the situation in which the problem occurs?
   HUSBAND:
   WIFE:
4. What is the most succinct definition of the problem?
   BOTH:
5. What are the areas of difference between the two of you?
   BOTH:
6. What are the areas of commonality or agreement between the two of you?
   BOTH:
7. As explicitly as possible, state the behaviors of your partner that you find unacceptable in the conflict situation.
   HUSBAND:
   WIFE:
8. What events triggered the conflict?
   BOTH:
9. Each of you speaking for yourself, what are the things you need to do in order to resolve the conflict?
   HUSBAND:
   WIFE:
10. What are some possible mutually desirable goals for the resolution of this conflict? (How would you like things to be different?)
    BOTH:
11. Identify possible solutions to the problem.
    BOTH:
12. What might be the outcome of implementing each of the possible solutions just identified?
    BOTH:
13. To implement each possible solution, what cooperative interaction needs to take place and what responsibilities need to be shared?
    BOTH:
14. Which solution would be the most constructive?
    BOTH:
15. How will you know whether the solution is effective and the conflict resolved?
    BOTH:

IMPLEMENT THE SOLUTION!

The Marriage Conference

If couples are experiencing intense conflict, the therapist might suggest that they attempt a series of marriage conferences (Dinkmeyer, Pew, & Dinkmeyer, 1979) as a beginning step in managing their concerns better. This involves partners making a series of appointments with each other. Each appointment should be for half an hour and in a place where the two will not be disturbed. If they have significant conflict, a minimum of three appointments, two or three days apart, is recommended. Some couples report disappointment when using the marriage conference for the first time. This is frequently a result of not following the directions closely. It is suggested that the procedure not be altered until the couple has had some experience with it. It is often advisable to have a couple conduct their initial marriage conference during a therapy session, with the therapist present to respond to any question they have regarding the process.

At the time of the first marriage conference appointment and as a result of previous agreement (flipping a coin is a good approach), one partner becomes the speaker for the first 15 minutes, while the other partner listens silently and refrains from interrupting, making facial expressions, or in any way interfering with what is being said. Partners are asked to avoid any potential distractions, such as television, radio, eating, drinking, or smoking. The only source of stimulation should be the speaker's voice. During the first 15 minutes, the speaker is free to say whatever he or she likes, or, alternatively, to say nothing and remain silent. The speaker may utilize the time as he or she chooses. At the end of exactly 15 minutes, the process is reversed; the partner who was the speaker becomes the listener. At the end of the second 15 minutes, the conference is completed.

Partners should not discuss any controversial items that come up during a conference until the next marriage conference; rather, they should simply consider what they might do to correct the situation by changing their own behaviors. Noncontroversial items can, of course, be discussed between conferences. At the second conference the procedure is repeated, except that the order in which the partners speak and listen is reversed.

Marriage conferences provide a means of clearing the air in a distressed relationship without partners having to fear new conflict or escalation of an old conflict situation. These conferences also assist partners in looking to themselves to see how they can change their own behavior rather than looking to their mates to change.

Parent Consultation

In our discussion of marital life-cycle development in Chapter 1 we note that having children can radically change the manner in which spouses live with and relate to each other. Often, when partners become parents, the new, parental roles dominate the marital relationship. Crises concerning children therefore frequently affect spouses' ability even to coexist. This fact is echoed in Table 8-1, in which children appear as the second greatest concern reported by couples as a major marital problem when seeking therapeutic assistance.

When work with a couple relates to their children, many factors come into play. In most instances, however, a child is not meeting the expectations of his or her parents in some way. It is critical that the therapist first determine how realistic these expectations are, and whether the child is developmentally ready—physically, emotionally, socially and intellectually—to meet them. Parent-consultation intervention strategies are based on the premise that positive changes can best be facilitated and maintained if parents' attitudes, beliefs, and behaviors are modified simultaneously with the attitudes, beliefs, and behaviors of their children. Assuming parents' expectations are realistic, there are a number of therapeutic intervention approaches a therapist might consider.

We present the two parent-consultation approaches we feel currently have strong popular as well as professional support: (1) the Adlerian model, and (2) Parent Effectiveness Training. Two other intervention approaches, the systems and social-learning models, we do not address here, although they are widely accepted also. One, the social-learning approach, we see as quite similar in its interventions to those advocated by the Adlerian model, but it is more difficult to convey to couples and have effectively implemented. And, as Okun and Rappaport (1980) suggested, one can view and assess parent-child functioning from the other approach—a systems framework—and set systems goals, and yet utilize Adlerian and Parent Effectiveness strategies successfully. Hence, our focus is limited to the Adlerian and Parent Effectiveness Training approaches.

The Adlerian Model

This approach, advanced by Alfred Adler early in this century in his work *Individual Psychology,* views children as social beings who are motivated to find a place of importance at home, at school, and in the world at large. All behavior is viewed as purposeful and goal directed, indicating the various means each person has devised to gain status and significance. When children feel worthwhile, they function in a positive, fulfilling manner; low self-esteem and discouragement, however, result in unproductive and destructive methods of gaining a feeling of importance and belonging. Thus, as Adlerians see it, destructive behavior is a consequence of a child's mistaken notions about the way one can gain status and a sense of significance.

Children's mistaken notions or "goals of misbehavior" have been classified into four major categories (Dreikurs, 1957): attention, power, revenge and display of inadequacy.

1. *Attention.* The child misbehaves in order to get attention from those around him or her. The child sees attention (negative attention, if positive attention cannot be gained) as proof of his or her acceptance and importance.
2. *Power.* The child wants to be in control. Misbehavior involves attempts to engage others in power struggles; being thus in control is seen as attaining significance. Engaging others in arguments is one method of provoking power struggles.
3. *Revenge.* The child misbehaves to get even. He or she feels hurt by others and sees hurting them in return as a way to feel better about him- or herself.
4. *Display of Inadequacy.* The child misbehaves in order to appear disabled. In this manner he or she elicits both overprotection and fewer demands.

Most parents would not readily recognize one of these goals in a child's misbehavior. However, parents can be taught to identify the goals, by applying two kinds of information: (1) how they feel in response to the child's misbehavior, and (2) the child's response to attempts at correcting the misbehavior. After accurately identifying a child's goal, parents can learn to respond so as to modify the behavior in a more positive, constructive direction. This process is outlined in Table 8-1.

Regardless of which of the four goals a child might pursue, the primary intervention focus is on teaching the parents to block the child's misguided, destructive efforts and, more important, to simultaneously encourage and reward cooperative, positive, and responsible behavior. The major technique advocated by the Adlerian model to facilitate and maintain positive behaviors is encouragement. Encouragement is perceived not as simple praise but as a process of assisting children to become aware of their own worth. Recognizing a child's attempts at mastery of the environment and expressing appreciation of effort, as well as achievement, can contribute significantly to a more positive focus. In contrast, responding relatively more to the behavior that is destructive or unsuccessful leads to discouragement.

The Adlerian techniques recommended to block misguided behavior include the use of natural and logical consequences. Natural consequences are those that follow naturally from a child's behavior without any direct intervention. For example, if a child touches a hot stove there is no need for parents to point out the child's mistake. The pain from touching the stove is the natural admonishment inherent in the situation and a sufficient warning to the child. Logical consequences are those arranged by the parents when suitable natural consequences either will not occur

TABLE 8-1 Elements in Recognizing and Correcting the Four Goals of Misbehavior

GOAL OF MISBEHAVIOR	"A" What the Child Does	"B" What the Teacher/Parent Do and How They Feel	"C" What the Child Does as the Consequence	What the Child Is Saying	Some Corrective Measures
ATTENTION	Active and passive activities that may appear constructive, destructive.	Annoyed; wants to remind, coax; delighted with "good" child.	Temporarily stops, disturbing action when given attention.	"I only count when I am being noticed or served."	—Ignore —Answer or do the unexpected —Give attention at pleasant times
POWER	Active and passive activities only destructive in nature.	Provoked, angry; generally wants power challenged—"I'll make him do it." "You can't get away with it."	Intensifies action when reprimanded; child wants to win, be boss.	"I only count when I am dominating, when you do what I want you to."	—Extricate self —Act, not talk —Be friendly —Establish equality —Redirect child's efforts into constructive channels
REVENGE	More severe active and passive activities.	Hurt, mad—"How could he do this to me?"	Wants to get even, make self disliked; intensifies action in a hurtful fashion.	"I can't be liked, I don't have power, but I'll count if I can hurt others as I feel hurt by life."	—Extricate self —Win child —Maintain order with minimum restraint —Avoid retaliations —Take time and effort to help child
INADEQUACY	Passive activities that defy involvement.	Despair—"I give up."	No reprimand, therefore, no reactions. Feels there is no use to try; passive.	"I can't do anything right, so I won't try to do anything at all; I am no good."	—Encouragement (may take long) —Faith in child's ability

Note: From Focus on Guidance, by J. Carlson and B. Faiber, Copyright © 1976 by Love Publishing Company, Denver, CO. Reprinted by permission.

or might be dangerous. For instance, if a child is late for dinner, he or she doesn't eat. The effectiveness of consequences depend heavily upon their being implemented in a calm, nonpunishing, nonsarcastic, and nonhumiliating way. The attitude is simply, "This is the reality of the situation." Whenever possible, children should be urged to participate in determining logical consequences.

Finally, the Adlerian model proposes that parents and their children have regularly scheduled discussions called family councils to both discuss problems and plan recreational and other pursuits. The discussion is held in a democratic manner, with parents and children having equal voices. In addition, each person is expected to respect the others' rights and to receive respect in return. Utilizing family councils, parents and children learn to live in a cooperative, mutually satisfying way. Thus in the Adlerian model the therapist's goal is to facilitate parents' utilization of more appropriate ways of interacting with their children. Specifically, the Adlerian model might be seen as a framework for parent reeducation; this reeducation, in and of itself, is a therapeutic intervention.

Parent Effectiveness Training

In attempting to facilitate their children's growth and well-being, many parents find themselves in a dilemma. On one hand, imposing structure and limits on their children is problematic; failure of minor structure often prompts stricter measures, which frequently lead only to increased resistance and, at times, rebellion. On the other hand, permissiveness is similarly ineffective, because it leads to a do-your-own-thing attitude and to anarchy. Thomas Gordon (1970) has characterized this syndrome of authoritarianism versus permissiveness as a win-lose struggle and, as a response, developed Parent Effectiveness Training (PET) with its no-lose problem-solving approach.

The PET no-lose approach is very similar to the joint-decision-making procedure used so often by business and labor. Gordon (1970) describes it as follows:

> Parent and child encounter a conflict-of-needs situation. The parent asks the child to participate with him in a joint search for some solution acceptable to both. One or both may offer possible solutions. They critically evaluate them and eventually make a decision on a final solution acceptable to both. No selling of the other is required after the solution has been selected, because both have already accepted it. No power is required to force compliance, because neither is resisting the decision [p. 196].

A major point from Gordon's (1970) credo for adult-child relationships is his statement that "I respect your needs, but I also must respect my own. Consequently, let us strive always to search for solutions to our inevitable conflicts that will be acceptable to both of us. In this way your needs will be met, but so will mine—no one will lose, both will win'' (p. 305).

The basic procedure in this no-lose method of conflict resolution involves first a definition of the problem and a determination of whose problem it is, then intervention. The first is accomplished by assessing whether the problem behavior (the child's) is acceptable to the parent. If it is acceptable to the parent, either the child "owns" the problem or there is no problem. If the child's behavior is not acceptable, the parent "owns" the problem. Thus, the person who owns the problem is the one who feels disturbed by it—the one whose desires are not being met. Identification of problem ownership determines subsequent intervention strategies. For example, a child keeps interrupting a parent's conversation with a friend. The parent does not want to be interrupted; the child's behavior is unacceptable to the parent. Confronted with this behavior, the parent, not the child, must help him- or herself. The parent is responsible for taking action.

Three primary intervention strategies are advocated in PET (Gordon, 1970): active listening, use of I-messages, and no-lose problem solving.

Active Listening.   This strategy involves teaching parents to communicate with children in a way that helps a child understand, accept, and deal with his or her feelings. For instance, if a child comes home crying and talks about a fight with another child, the parent would decode that message to identify the underlying feeling and would respond, "You feel angry at Johnny because he started a fight with you." This message, both acknowledging feeling and clarifying reason, facilitates further discussion and exploration of the problem in a number of ways:

- Catharsis is fostered.
- The child feels freer to express and experience negative feelings.
- A warmer relationship is promoted between parent and child.
- The child is influenced to be more accepting of parents' thoughts and ideas.
- The focus is kept on the child, helping him or her to become more self-directing, independent, and responsible.

The effectiveness of active listening depends to a large degree on the absence of judging, lecturing, preaching, criticizing, moralizing, and communicating from other stances that tend to generate defensive reactions and prevent discussion, exploration, and problem solving.

Use of I-messages.   This strategy involves showing parents how to confront their children and express their frustrations effectively without giving you're-not-OK messages. For example, when a child plays music so loud that it interferes with the conversation of her parents in the next room, one of the parents could utilize an I-message, such as "I feel kind of cheated. I want to spend some time talking in the next room, and with the stereo so loud we can't hear each other." That message is much more conducive to finding a mutually acceptable solution to the problem than an accusatory, evaluative you-message, such as "Can't you be more considerate of others? Why must you blast that stereo so loud?" I-messages are less apt to provoke resistance, and by simply stating a situation's effects without accusation they facilitate children taking responsibility, signaling trust that the child will respect a parent's needs and offering a chance to behave more constructively. Further, by communicating directly and honestly with I-messages, parents model and encourage similarly honest, direct communication on the part of their children.

The No-lose Method of Problem Solving.   This intervention procedure involves six separate steps. Although some conflicts are worked out without going through all the steps, by following the set of all the steps parents are much more likely to have successful experiences.

Step 1: Identify and define the conflict.
Step 2: Generate possible alternative solutions.
Step 3: Evaluate the alternative solutions.
Step 4: Decide on the best acceptable solution.
Step 5: Work out ways of implementing the solution.
Step 6: Follow up to evaluate how well the solution worked.

The first two interventions, active listening and use of I-messages, can require a therapist to provide parents extensive skill training. Parents must learn to identify feelings precisely and to express themselves assertively. And, often considerable time must be spend unlearning use of ridiculing, shaming, threatening, moralizing, criticizing and other stances that provoke defensiveness and prevent mutual exploration and problem solving. The primary purposes of these two interventions are to foster a working rapport, to define problems accurately, and to nurture self-esteem and mutual respect rather than damage them. Often, the use of active listening and I-messages alone can solve many problems. More intensive conflicts call for the use of the no-lose problem-solving method.

Using the no-lose method parents can, after having defined the problem with their child, suggest "What can we do about this? Let's look at all of the possibilities." Together they then list different ways by which the problem might be solved. All potential solutions are considered. The next step is for the parents and child to decide which of the alternatives they can all accept and how they will implement it. They then act on their decisions. If neither the parents nor their child can find a solution that's mutually satisfying, they have to try again; neither imposes his or her solution on the other. Thus, the PET approach advocates negotiation and conflict-resolution skills without the use of power.

Sex Therapy

Sex therapy as a specialized intervention within marital therapy today is primarily a behaviorally based approach that focuses on treating and curing specific sexual dysfunctions. Probably the most popular and best known approach to sex therapy is that pioneered by Masters and Johnson (1970). Their approach is essentially a short-term treatment program that relies heavily on behavioral techniques.

Masters and Johnson identified four major sexual dysfunctions, which are held to have either an organic or psychosocial basis.

1. *Male Impotence.* Male impotence is considered either primary, when the male has never been able to achieve or maintain an erection of sufficient quality to perform sexual intercourse, or secondary, when the male at one time was able to engage in intercourse.
2. *Premature Ejaculation.* This dysfunction occurs when the male ejaculates before his partner has time to become satisfied. (The time required depends in part upon the female partner's orgasmic responsiveness.)
3. *Female Orgasmic Dysfunction.* This is a condition in which the female either has no response whatsoever to sexual stimuli or becomes aroused and lubricated but has difficulty reaching orgasm.
4. *Vaginismus.* Vaginismus is a spasm of the vaginal muscles that prevents the male from penetrating.

Masters and Johnson have found that these sexual dysfunctions have a psychological basis in about 90% of their cases and that sexual dysfunction primarily reflects a relationship problem rather than individual pathology. Reasons for sexual dysfunction range from a simple lack of knowledge about body and sexual functioning, or misinformation, to emotional immaturity, repressive childhood influences, midlife crises, environmental stresses, and performance anxiety. However, when investigating the basis for sexual dysfunction it is always important to take into account potential congenital and medical factors; certain diseases and types of medication can affect both sex drive and sexual functioning. Individual differences and preferences are also important to examine.

A basic assumption of the Masters and Johnson approach is that there is no such thing as an uninvolved partner in a relationship in which some form of sexual dysfunction exists. Consequently both partners are always treated conjointly, emphasizing that any dysfunction is a problem for the couple as a unit rather than for only one element of that unit. Another major aspect of Masters and Johnson's approach includes the use of a male-female co-therapy team to work with both partners, based on the premise that a dual-sex team can alleviate potential misinterpretation due to male or female bias. The importance of complete medical and sexual histories is also stressed. Not only are the chronologies of sexual experiences considered but, more important, so are sexually oriented values, attitudes, beliefs, feelings, and expectations. Additional procedures stress open communication, pleasuring, and information giving in an educational milieu. The behavioral focus of therapy attempts to include all aspects of sexual senses—visual, taste, auditory, tactile, olfactory, and spatial.

According to Masters and Johnson, one primary reason for sexual dysfunction is that a partner (or both partners) is critically observing his or her own sexual performance instead of completely allowing him- or herself to experience the giving and receiving of erotic pleasure. They term this "spectatoring." Masters and Johnson proposed that in order to fully enjoy and functionally participate in an intimate sexual encounter it is necessary to suspend all the distracting thoughts and anxieties about being evaluated (or evaluating oneself) for one's sexual performance that constitute spectatoring.

Masters and Johnson have developed a number of techniques and procedures particular to specific dysfunctions. However, there is one procedure that is advocated for all situations. This procedure, "sensate focus," involves a couple receiving instructions on learning to touch and explore each other's bodies and discovering what each other's sensate areas are, but without feeling pressed for sexual performance or orgasm. As intercourse is forbidden at the outset, the pressure to engage in intercourse is removed from the situation. The couple is instructed to pick a place and time when they can freely relax and not be distracted or disturbed. They are asked to focus on learning the pleasure that communicating both verbally and nonverbally about their likes and dislikes can bring. Initially genital contact is forbidden; eventually, genital areas are included and intercourse is allowed. Sensate focusing provides partners an opportunity to assume responsibility for their own sexuality. In addition, it tends to revitalize sensitivity and pleasure in giving and receiving, often alleviating other, dissatisfying aspects of a relationship through enhanced focus on positive interchanges between partners.

As described, the Masters and Johnson approach is an educational one in which a couple is taught to relax and attend to giving and receiving erotic stimuli. This process is carried out through a series of gradual and progressive sexual tasks requiring both partners' individual responsibility for communicating their desires and their mutual cooperation in seeing that these desires are achieved. Therapists who are influenced by the Masters and Johnson model usually propose that a couple seeking sex therapy agree to work on other basic relationship concerns also. Although it is possible to treat sexual dysfunction without treating the relationship, most therapists would want to be sure that other relationship concerns are being treated concurrently so that the results of sex therapy efforts are meaningful and long lasting.

One currently popular advocate of treating other relationship concerns concurrently with sexual problems is Helen Singer Kaplan (1974), who has developed a modification of the Masters and Johnson techniques that includes both psychodynamic and behavioral procedures in the treatment of sexual dysfunction. Kaplan proposed a number of immediate causes of sexual dysfunction in a couple attempting intercourse, including the inability to communicate openly about sexual feelings and experiences, simple sexual ignorance, fear of failure, excessive demand for performance, and exaggerated need to please one's partner. Kaplan also suggested that there may be various intrapsychic conflicts within one or both partners impeding the attainment of satisfying sexual experiences. Such intrapsychic hindrances may be early sexual trauma, repressed sexual thoughts and emotions, or feelings of guilt and shame. Finally, Kaplan noted as a third set of psychological determinants of sexual dysfunction those that arise from the basic marital interaction patterns of partners. These include various forms of marital discord, lack of trust, and power struggles between partners, as well as efforts to sabotage any type of pleasurable experiencing. Any one or a combination of these problems or conflicts can lead to concerns resulting in sexual dysfunction for one or both partners.

Unlike Masters and Johnson, Kaplan suggested that only one therapist, rather than two, treat a couple. Couples are treated conjointly once or twice per week with no time limit placed on the overall treatment program. Combining psychoanalytic and behavioral theories and techniques, treatment goals involve both insight and behavioral changes. As in Masters and Johnson's approach, couples are assigned various sexual tasks, such as taking turns stimulating or "pleasuring" one another's erotic areas without demands on the part of either partner for orgasm or coitus. Treatment is terminated when presenting symptoms are eliminated and the couple is achieving relatively satisfying sexual functioning.

Masters and Johnson have reported a very high overall success rate for their procedures. This is even more meaningful when their stringent criterion for success is considered—no recurrence within five years of treatment. The greatest success of the approach has come in treating premature ejaculation in men (97.8%); for secondary impotence the success rate is lower (73.7%), yet it is still quite high when compared to that for other therapeutic endeavors. Likewise with women, a success rate of 83.4% for primary orgasmic dysfunction (never having achieved an orgasm) is very impressive. Kaplan reported similar results for rapidly relieving a wide variety of sexual dysfunctions. As she pointed out, though, while recent sex-therapy advances constitute considerable progress in understanding and treating couples' sexual concerns, it is no cure-all for a marriage rife with distress and discord.

Divorce Therapy

Throughout this chapter we address intervention strategies that presuppose partners want their current relationship to continue. But, despite this preoccupation with maintaining and enhancing marital relationships, at times separation and divorce may be preferable treatment goals. In some instances, although initial treatment goals are to improve the relationships, these objectives appear increasingly to be unrealistic, either because change has not been sufficient for the couple to want to continue the relationship or because one or both partners remain insufficiently satisfied even though obvious positive changes have taken place. In such cases and others as well, it is not always correct to assume that preservation of the marriage is the optimal therapeutic path. Further, it is foolish to automatically consider any marital therapy effort that ultimately ends in a couple divorcing as a failure. In fact, if measured by outcome, much of what is offered as marital therapy might better be advertised as divorce therapy; with increasing frequency, couples are entering therapy with consideration of divorce as their prime concern (Stuart, 1980).

Unfortunately, some marital therapists act as if divorce is the ultimate enemy, and keeping couples together is the only possible therapeutic path to take. This is particularly characteristic of therapists who utilize a success/failure standard, with continuance of marriages as the measure of marital therapy outcomes, rather than an improvement standard relating to individual partners' personal satisfaction. To the extent that marital therapists align their interests with the perpetuation of marriages regardless of the particular interests of the individuals involved, their effectiveness is questionable (Jacobson & Margolin, 1979).

Although some couples may have already decided to terminate their relationships before entering therapy, most couples do not consciously enter marital therapy with that intent. Even so, in almost all cases where there is severe marital distress there comes an early period when one or both partners begin to consider the possibility of ending their relationship rather than attempting to continue it. Divorce is seen as a feasible alternative for resolving their relationship problems. In some cases, one partner makes this decision before the other is even aware of the magnitude of their problems. This often leads to some desperate attempts on the part of the reluctant partner at holding the marriage intact, and it frequently results in a hostile and difficult divorce. In other cases, the idea of divorce is so anxiety provoking for both partners that they rush into therapy for help and are highly motivated to eliminate the discord and improve their relationship. Thus, whether divorce is overtly mentioned or not, the divorce or maintain the marriage question is a source of ambiguity and struggle, and very much alive for both the therapist and couple.

The Decision to Divorce

Ultimately, as seems obvious, the decision to divorce belongs to the couple. However, this is not always a particularly useful guideline, since the feasibility of a couple in therapy reaching a decision independent of their therapist's influence is highly unlikely. Most partners want an informed comment on their relationship and its prognosis. In so doing they prime themselves to be influenced by the therapist, and they become sensitive to the cues the therapist provides concerning his or her opinions about the marriage.

Jacobson and Margolin (1979) urged therapists to develop a conservative posture on questions concerning a couple's decision either to separate or commit themselves to working on the relationship. They proposed that partners should be respected as individuals, and that one who leans toward terminating marriage should not be cajoled into therapy. The position taken by Jacobson and Margolin is that it is incumbent upon therapists not to ignore their potential for biasing a couple's decisions, as well as to adopt a strategy that is as unencumbered as possible by their personal views about the desirability of therapy or separation.

Of course, value judgments will always be present for both therapists and couples. Our society as a whole is undergoing a period of rapid change regarding beliefs about marriage and divorce. Most individuals have relatively strong positions on these issues, although they may never have verbalized them clearly to themselves or others. In reaching decisions regarding divorce, it is important that therapists and couples examine their own values relating to the ethics and mores of marriage and divorce. Walen, DiGiuseppe, and Wessler (1980) cited a number of questions they found facilitated the clarification of relationship values:

- Is marriage better than no marriage?
- Is a bad marriage better than no marriage?
- Should couples stay together regardless of how dysfunctional their relationship is?
- Does this reflect a bias in favor of marriage?
- Are you tolerant of different living arrangements, such as open marriage or communal marriage?
- Do you believe that affairs are always destructive to marriage?
- Do you readily encourage couples to separate?
- Does this reflect a belief in the value of divorce?
- Do you believe that people are capable of making their own decisions?

The Divorce Process

When the decision to divorce has been made, the task of the therapist is to help one or both partners adaptively cope with the decision and its effects. Framo (1978) defined the goal of divorce therapy as being "to help a couple disengage from a marriage with a minimum of destructiveness to themselves and their children, and with the personal freedom to form new relationships" (p. 77).

In the past decade, several analyses of the process couples seem to experience in ending their marriage have been offered. The majority of these analyses suggest a stage conceptualization of the divorce process. These range from Weiss's (1976) two-stage progression of transition and recovery, through Bohannan's (1970) six-station conceptualization, involving emotional, legal, economic, co-parental, community, and psychic divorce, to Froiland and Hosman's (1977) comparison of the divorce process to the stages of mourning delineated by Kubler-Ross (1969) for loss due to death: denial, anger, bargaining, depression, and acceptance.

In considering treatment interventions to implement in divorce therapy, Kaslow (1981) stated that "every known therapeutic approach has been adapted to working with individuals and couples in every stage of the divorce process" (p. 682). To clarify strategies and also utilize what others have implemented successfully, Kaslow developed a "diaclectic model of divorce" and delineated three major periods in the divorce process. For each period he identified the feelings couples can be predicted to experience as well as the actions and tasks they must confront if they are to move forward (see Table 8-2).

Gurman and Kniskern (1981) supported Kaslow's approach in stating:

> In our view, the existence of such a "broad spectrum" of treatment approaches about divorce problems reflects the undeniable fact that there have been developed essentially no intervention strategies or treatment techniques that are *specific* to the emotional, behavioral and interpersonal difficulties caused by separation and divorce. On the other hand, as Kaslow makes clear, there are rather predictable stages in the divorce process, with similarly predictable emotional tasks to be addressed by the patient. Knowledge of such normative patterns in the divorce process is crucial for a therapist working with such patients, regardless of the particular treatment operations he/she chooses [p. 682].

We agree with Gurman and Kniskern's observations regarding Kaslow's model. It offers a general intervention strategy by which therapists can help partners (and former partners) identify and react appropriately to those feelings likely to be expected and can also assist the partners in confronting and completing the requisite actions and tasks that lie before them. The specific treatment techniques utilized in doing so can be those most compatible with the therapist's basic theoretical assumptions.

Divorce Mediation

Kressel and Deutsch (1977) surveyed 21 highly experienced divorce therapists and found most of them critical of lawyers for the following

TABLE 8-2   Kaslow's Diaclectic Model of the Divorce Process

Divorce Period	Feelings	Requisite Actions and Tasks
Predivorce: Deliberation Period	Disillusionment Dissatisfaction Alienation	Confronting partner Quarreling Seeking therapy Denial
	Dread Anguish Ambivalence Shock Emptiness Chaos Inadequacy Low self-esteem	Withdrawal (physical and emotional) Pretending all is okay Attempting to win back affection
During Divorce: Litigation Period	Depression Detachment Anger Hopelessness Self-pity	Bargaining Screaming Threatening Attempting suicide Mourning
	Confusion Fury Sadness Loneliness Relief	Separating physically Filing for legal divorce Considering economic arrangements Considering custody arrangements Grieving and mourning Telling relatives and friends
Postdivorce: Reequilibration	Optimism Resignation Excitement Curiosity Regret	Finalizing divorce Begin reaching out to new friends Undertaking new activities Stabilizing new life style and daily routine for children
	Acceptance Self-confidence Energy Self-worth Wholeness Exhilaration Independence Autonomy	Resynthesis of identity Completing psychic divorce Seeking new love object and making a commitment to some permanency Becoming comfortable with new life-style and friends Helping children accept finality of parents' divorce and their continuing relationship with both parents

Note: Adapted from "Divorce and Divorce Therapy," *by F. W. Kaslow. In A. S. Gurman, D. P. Kniskern (Eds.),* Handbook of Family Therapy. *Copyright © 1981 by Brunner/Mazel, Inc., New York. Reprinted by permission.*

reasons: (1) for advocating an adversary process that hinders amicable divorce settlements; (2) for becoming unwitting pawns in the escalation of marital conflict; and (3) for compromising objectivity in financial considerations, especially where a contingency-fee agreement has been made. The legal aspects of divorce often entail partners entering a system with built-in adversary roles. Under this adversary system, lawyers advocate their own clients' interests only. Anxious to get "the most for their client," opposing attorneys often ignore questions of what might be in the best interest of everyone concerned.

A relatively new approach formally called "structured mediation in divorce settlement" has come to the fore in recent years in some areas of the country. Developed by Coogler (1978) and promoted by the Family Mediating Association (FMA), divorce mediation is geared to resolving the following types of issues: property division; terminating dependency upon the relationship; and continuing the ongoing business initiated by the partnership, such as responsibility for any children born to the couple. In participating in a divorce mediation process, partners must follow a specified procedure and agree on a value system. This is something most have been unable to do during their marriage, but, in order to utilize the services of the mediator, they must agree to follow the "marital mediation rules." This entails establishing a mutually acceptable value system and an orderly procedural process for reaching settlement.

The divorce mediator is a trained, neutral third party who does not decide controversial issues. Rather, the mediator stresses, his or her role is to assist the two parties to responsibly make their own decisions and commit themselves to honoring them. Coogler (1978) cites the following as advantages of structured mediation:

- The issues to be decided are clearly defined.
- The issues are limited to those that need to be resolved in order to reach settlement.
- Procedural methods are established for collecting and examining factual information.
- All options for settlement of each issue are systematically examined.
- Options are selected within socially acceptable guidelines.
- Consequences likely to follow selection of each option are examined.
- Uninterrupted time for working toward resolution is regularly allocated.
- Impasses are promptly resolved by arbitration.

The stated goals of the FMA are to improve the quality of family life by offering cooperative methods of conflict resolution to those who are divorcing. The divorce mediation procedure is being used to negotiate written settlement agreements for those who intend a legal separation, for those who want a binding civil contract that will later become part of a divorce decree, and for those who want to revise an existing divorce decree. The FMA offers professional training, certification for competence in using the methods, and consultation for establishing mediation services.

Kressel, Deutsch, Jaffe, Tuckman, and Watson (1977) did an in-depth analysis of nine complex divorce cases, each mediated according to Coogler's innovative procedures. Their findings are based on two primary data sources: audiotapes of each couple's mediated sessions, and extended, separate interviews conducted by the researchers 3 to 12 months after completion of the mediation and finalization of the divorce.

The obstacles to effective mediation were found to be:

1. High levels of internal conflict (emotional ambivalence and sometimes volatility).
2. Scarcity of divisible resources.
3. Naive negotiators.
4. Discrepancy in relative power—the wife frequently being "ignorant" about financial documents and arrangements.

Kressel, Deutsch, Jaffe, Tuckman, and Watson concluded that, in order for one to be competent to handle the strategic problems in divorce mediation, he or she should:

1. Take a premediation course in divorce negotiations covering money management and tax law, as well as the psychology of the divorcing process.
2. Learn an "advocacy" model of mediation in order to be able to deal with and compensate for the unequal power balance between the parties.
3. Learn how to deal with the emotional issues that surface, perhaps also recommending individual or couples group-therapy session.

We have found the structured mediation model to be a viable alternative to the traditional legal-adversary model for those couples who are able to appropriately participate in it. The more partners can resolve their conflicts and arrive at a mutually acceptable settlement through negotiation, in a calm and just atmosphere, the better their chance of achieving a divorce that ultimately is amicable. This is even more important when children are present, and ongoing respect for each other's input as parents can be continued.

Women's Issues

Whether viewed as a positive or negative phenomenon, the women's liberation movement (some call it a revolution) has had an undeniable impact on virtually all institutions of our society. The 1970s have been labeled by some U.S. historians as the decade of the emerging woman. The effects are visible in politics, with continuing efforts to ratify the Equal

Rights Amendment (ERA); in religion, with ordination of women to unprecedented roles of leadership; in schools, where efforts are being made to reduce teaching of sexist attitudes; and certainly in the economy, with more women seeking jobs and advancing. The institution most affected by the redefinition of women's roles is, perhaps, the family—and by direct implication marriage therapists are at the cutting edge of this revolution.

In the late 1960s (and the beginning of the 1970s), Masters and Johnson (1966) released empirical evidence on human sexuality. Dr. Masters' stern admonition that no man can understand how a woman feels about her sexuality and that no man could ever fully understand the experience of a woman's orgasm added impetus to the search by male therapists to find female co-therapists. "The women's movement, historically coincident with the Masters and Johnson work, focused additional social pressure on the professions to utilize women" (Golden & Golden, 1976, p. 11). The "liberation" of women had multiple effects in all forms of therapy involving women. Lassen (1976) referred to the treatment of a nonorgasmic female in which the therapist helped her experience her sexual and relationship needs in terms of pleasing herself instead of pleasing others, and stated: "This therapeutic shift almost always has spillover into the rest of her life, and she begins to move in the direction of more independence, more self-confidence and more insistence on getting what she wants out of life" (p. 33). According to Wolman (1976), the women's liberation movement has affected millions of women, many if not most of whom would not necessarily acknowledge direct participation in social or political activities. The profound effect of changes so widespread cannot be fully assessed at this point, but the women's revolution has added depth and dimension to psychotherapy with married couples. As the primary consumers of psychotherapy, these women, who have realized they need more for themselves and their families, have challenged the fundamental assumptions of the theory and practice of therapy.

Turmoil seems likely between couples influenced by women's liberation. Worthington (1976) identified as a key element of successful therapy "an undeniable belief, shared by husband, wife, and therapist, that the couple is willing to compromise because, above all else, they want and need a successful marriage" (p. 7). He proposed a three-pronged approach to identifying goals for marital therapy:

> The first prong is the wife's ability to identify the source of her inner turmoil. The second prong is the husband's ability to understand the manifestations of this conflict and his willingness to change himself. The third prong involves conjoint therapy to help the couple to work together to rebuild their marriage [p. 7].

Perlman and Givelber (1976) suggested that, although couples rarely begin therapy because of explicit concerns about women's liberation and subsequent role conflicts, the theme of the changing status of women runs through all couples' treatment. The therapist must be attuned to the implications of this theme for therapy with couples and also to the possibility that the theme may be used as a red herring to disguise other marital conflicts that are more salient.

For example, the "traditional" woman defines herself in terms of her husband and children and fulfills herself through them; the "liberated" woman defines herself through her own achievements. When a woman shifts in self-definition and her husband does not, both internal and interpersonal conflicts are likely to result (Perlman & Givelber, 1976). Women involved with the movement, however, are reported to be better patients (Wolman, 1976). Perhaps this is because the new feeling of liberation reduces the unrealistic belief that the therapist has "the" answer. Wolman (1976) cited five reasons for his belief that women's liberation is one of the best things that could have happened to the psychotherapy of married couples:

- The female has options not available before.
- Couples' peer groups force them to examine their relationship.
- One partner in therapy is more likely, now, to bring the other.
- The self-esteem of the female partner is not in need of repair in so many cases.
- The husband is no longer in the defensive position inherent in stereotyped relationships.

Silverman (1975) offered further explanation, describing how women are challenging the status quo of bland, routine, and personally degrading marriages.

> When women have more confidence in themselves, men who base their masculinity on feminine servitude will be challenged and finally unmasked as inadequate individuals; . . . the women's liberation movement can stimulate many of these women into thinking more critically about their situation and will give support to those who became disenchanted with their original submissive role [p. 40].

The support lent by women's liberation might be viewed as either positive or negative by therapists; although such challenges of the status quo create turmoil in a number of relationships, whether this is positive or negative is, of course, a value judgment. Nevertheless, surely the entire matter is of concern to marital therapists.

Therapists' accurate understanding of themselves and the issues is imperative if clients are to be helped through crises arising from or influenced by women's liberation. As in all therapy, marital therapy seems impossible when a therapist has less than a full understanding of his or her personal stands on relevant issues, as well as knowledge of specific techniques for assisting couples to assess their beliefs.

Dual-Career Marriages

The past few years have seen many changes in the attitudes and life patterns of marital partners regarding their careers. A career differs from a job in that a career holds the promise of advancement, is considered important in itself and not just as a source of money, and demands a higher degree of commitment (Rapoport & Rapoport, 1971). In a dual-career marriage, partners do not have just two jobs, or one job and one career. Instead, the dual-career aspect implies two married individuals who are each committed to following a lifestyle that supports, encourages, and facilitates—not just tolerates—the career pursuits of both partners. The growth offered by dual-career marriage is a reality for an increasing number of couples, and, as with most forms of growth, too often it is accompanied by pain.

Dual-career marriages can be hectic and tense. Most often the tension emanates from difficulties in juggling schedules, chores, and child care. For example, consider the complaints of a husband named Ken:

> *I'm fed up with my wife's attitude since she's gone to work. Ann never liked staying home with the kids, and she had always let me know about it too. For seven years, she complained about her lack of fulfillment. When I suggested that she go back to pursue her old career in nursing she rejected the idea, saying that a mother should be home while her children are young. But last year, she did return to nursing. I thought she'd be happy. Well, she isn't. Now all I hear is how tired she is, how much work she has to do at work. She never has time to cook anymore, take the kids to the park, or do anything—except complain. When I try to talk to her about it, she gets furious. Last night, in the middle of an argument, she said that she'd spent the last seven years waiting on me and the children, and now it was my turn. What does she mean by that?*

Clearly, a dual-career relationship presses both partners to make adaptations. Couples must learn to reallocate traditional gender-oriented activities. In doing so, they must also learn to adapt emotionally to the expectations and stresses these new roles are likely to bring. When couples are unwilling or unable to reassess or reorient their roles, the problems that occur can be particularly difficult.

The problems most frequently manifested in dual-career-couples' relationships, and exemplified in the above illustration of Ken and Ann, are usually a result of overload. Overload results from having too many roles and too many demands simultaneously (Hall & Hall, 1979). It is most often experienced by women when child care, house care, and husband care responsibilities conflict with career obligations and desires; the result is a highly stressful situation. Whichever responsibility or obligation a woman chooses to meet, she can find herself feeling anxious, tense, or guilty about omitting some other equally important task. Table 8-3 illustrates some common overload reactions of wives and mothers who also actively pursue career goals.

The reactions identified in Table 8-3 are all immediate responses; the long-term effects can be more serious. Frieze, Parsons, Johnson, Ruble, and Zellman (1978) found that sustained overload ultimately leads to complete demoralization and fatigue. Fewer men may experience overload than do women; however, the men who do experience it can be just as seriously affected as are women. Men may feel hurt, left out, or distant from their wives. Many feel that they suffer because of their wives' devotion to careers. For example, Hall and Hall (1979) quoted one recently divorced husband as saying, "I could handle Kim working okay, but I couldn't handle being second in her life. . . . When I realized her job was more important than me, I cut out" (p. 221).

When dual-career couples present themselves for marital therapy, their concerns are likely to revolve around some form of disagreement (Lawe & Lawe, 1980). A state of imbalance exists in their relationship. This imbalance reflects role conflicts regarding what is to be done, when

TABLE 8-3   Overload Reactions of Dual-Career Women

Overload Reaction	*Wife-Mother's Response*
1. Omission: temporarily omitting certain demands	1. Forgetting to pick up the cleaning; not hearing a child's request while talking on the phone
2. Queuing: delaying response during high overload period	2. Promising a child that Mother will talk about his or her problem after dinner; telling someone to call back after the children are asleep
3. Filtering: neglecting to process certain types of information while processing others	3. Neglecting household tasks or elaborate food preparation to take care of children's needs
4. Being less discriminating: responding in a general way to a number of demands	4. Preparing common meals that disregard the food preferences of different family members; having a common bedtime hour for children of different ages; not responding to the unique personality needs of each child
5. Employing multiple channels: processing information through two or more parallel channels at the same time	5. Talking to children or husband while cooking or ironing; changing a diaper while talking on the phone
6. Errors: processing demands incorrectly	6. Confusing the date of a meeting or social engagement; burning the dinner; yelling at a child for somethng that she or he had gotten permission to do
7. Escape	7. Going to a movie; falling asleep; leaving home

Note: From Women and Sex Roles: A Social Psychological Perspective, *by I. H. Frieze, et al. Copyright © 1978 by W. W. Norton and Company, New York. Reprinted by permission.*

the task is to be done, and who is to do what. Disagreement may result from philosophical differences or perceptual differences, or from partners' differing beliefs regarding husband-wife roles. A husband may believe that it is his wife's responsibility to take care of the household chores, regardless of any additional responsibilities she assumes in her career. Disagreements may also reflect partners being pressed for such basic requirements as sufficient money, time, or space (Frey, 1979).

While most couples are under the mistaken assumption that their disagreements are negative and should be avoided, the therapist's initial task is to point out that disagreements may be beneficial, in the sense that they can expose issues, increase effective problem solving, bring about emotional involvement, sponsor creativity, clarify objectives, and increase cohesiveness (Palmores, 1975). One typical area of disagreement relating to overload issues is the accomplishment of household chores. For instance, returning to the example of Ken and Ann, Ken may have felt that it was acceptable for Ann to have a career as long as no imposition was made on him, meaning that he should not have to take on any additional responsibilities. Ann felt that she had as much right to a career as Ken and that domestic tasks should be shared. She originally attempted to negotiate with Ken, but he would not talk about her dissatisfaction and was angry that she brought it up. While the surface issue of household chores may seem to have been the major source of disagreement, such other, underlying issues as power and control and values and beliefs may have been root sources promoting and maintaining the disagreement. Ken continuously strove to control what he believed to be appropriate behavior for Ann according to his values, whereas Ann continuously strove to invalidate Ken's position. How such a disagreement continues or is resolved is likely to be determined by the nature of the communication flow between the two partners. If each attempts to manipulate and maneuver the other covertly, then it is likely the focus of their conflicts will take the form of surface issues, such as household chores. If, on the other hand, partners are facilitated in making their communications more overt, greater understanding, negotiations, and potential resolution are more likely.

The initial focus in assisting couples to make their communications overt is on the previously discussed skills in communications training and conflict management. But beyond these communication and conflict-management skills, couples need to learn simple problem-solving and negotiation procedures. Several steps seem important to consider in this regard. The initial step is assisting couples to form clear definitions of their primary sources of disagreement and to determine what they are mutually willing to do to resolve them. The second step involves determining means by which each partner can contribute to formulating agreement. This calls for generating a list of strategies and alternative strategies. Such strategies involve breaking problems into smaller units, ranking these units in terms of importance, and then mutually negotiating and agreeing upon a plan of action. Implementation of the selected plan is the third step; however, prior to implementation all tasks and role behaviors should be clearly defined in terms of who is to do what, when it is to be done, and how this behavior will bring about an agreement. In other words, before the solution is put into practice the partners should be in accord about the nature of the disagreement, the purpose and objectives for any agreement, and what desired outcomes may be expected. The implementation stage should be compared to an experiment in which new behaviors and problem-solving strategies are being tested to determine their effectiveness. And, as with an experiment, if original strategies do not bring about desired results, readjustment and retesting are always an option.

Finally, some relationship factors may be particularly important in two-career marriages. Maples (1981) found five "successful ingredients" characterizing dual-career partners' relationships. These five ingredients are identified and briefly explained to conclude this discussion.

1. *Flexibility.* Flexibility relates to partners' ability to give a little to get a lot. In order to reach mutually satisfying conclusions, partners must allow themselves to weigh both intellectually and emotionally all the alternatives that go into decision making.

2. *Mobility.* Success in a career often demands that an individual move to a different location. And successful negotiation of relocations, which can be crucial to continuing marital satisfaction, may have to include such options as one partner relocating alone or with one or two of the children until such time as the other partner is able to follow. If distances between locations are reasonable (for example, between Washington, D.C. and New York), some couples may end up in "weekend marriages."

3. *Independence and Interdependence.* A dual-career relationship is severely strained when one partner desires a dependent relationship. But between two relatively independent partners there usually develops a healthy interdependence. For example, such partners seem able to seek out one another's advice while feeling free to act upon it or not.

4. *Common Interests.* Although the interdependency of the partners' relationship may be based in independence more than dependence, opportunities are still needed for mutual leisure-time activities. These activities may revolve around children, especially since, due to career pressures, dual-career parents are unable to spend as much time with their children as are traditional parents. (As a therapist may remark, "It is the quality, not the quantity of time that counts.") For those without children, or whose children are on their own or are involved in their own activities, an effort to participate produces many forms of mutually pleasing leisure-time activities.

5. *Self-Actualization.* To allow and encourage one's partner to pursue career activities that can result in status and salary higher than one's own can be tremendously threatening. This is especially the case with traditionally oriented males. Perceived competition can be a threat, and that readily negates the possibility of self-actualization within the relationship. However, in a successful dual-career marriage partners take pride in one another's achievements, viewing them not in a negative light but as a positive reflection of themselves and their relationship.

Marriage Enrichment

The marriage-enrichment movement began in the late 1950s in the Catholic Church. Father Gabriel Calvo, a priest in Spain, assembled couples for weekend retreats in order to "encounter" one another in depth (Mace, 1977). This service came to be organized as Marriage Encounter, now the largest organized enrichment program, with national and worldwide branches.

In America, the growth of marriage-enrichment programs can be traced similarly to religious organizations. In the early 1960s, David and Vera Mace (pioneers in American marriage enrichment, and joint executive directors of the American Association of Marriage Counselors from 1960 to 1967) were hired by the Quakers for assistance in this area. In 1964 Leon and Antoinette Smith began similar work for the United Methodist Church that ultimately established leadership training programs in each state. The Catholic program, Marriage Encounter, was brought to America in 1967 and became worldwide in 1973. Dr. Margaret Swain began work called Family Clusters for the First Baptist Church in Rochester, New York, in 1970. Paul and Ladonna Hopkins began marriage enrichment work with the Christian Church (Disciples of Christ) in 1971, and the Church of God began using the Parent Effectiveness Training program by Thomas Gordon in 1973. Jewish marriage enrichment began in 1974 (Smith, Shoffner, & Scott, 1979). Many of the organizations offering marriage encounters are associated directly with religious groups; others, though not directly associated, are directed by theologians. For example, The Association of Couples for Marriage Enrichment (ACME) is directed by Dr. David Mace, who also directs the Department of Pastoral Care at Baptist State Hospital, Winston-Salem, North Carolina.

Marriage enrichment is viewed by most practitioners as preventive mental-health care for the enrichment of relationships that partners expect to continue. This new field takes its place along with education and counseling as a professional service to couples and families. In Mace's view (1979), enrichment is beyond the services offered by education or counseling, in the sense that enrichment is possible in marriages that have been made stable by education, counseling, or both. Pursuing the enrichment experience is seeking to improve the healthy marriage and is "not a mere dutiful acceptance of the *status quo,* but a mutual concerted effort to change the *status quo*" (Mace, 1977, p. 521). The effort thus involved is what seems to transcend the therapeutic effects attributed to counseling. Some feel that the problem-oriented approach of therapists and counselors may be detrimental to enrichment experiences and hold that enrichment leaders require specific training for that position (Smith, Shoffner, & Scott, 1979). Mace (1979) countered, however, by proposing that most of the basic marriage-enrichment concepts and procedures can be applied in a counseling setting. He contends that in his 40 years of marriage counseling and 15 years of enrichment experience he saw no significant differences in the two groups of clients. The same conflicts and dissatisfactions are below the surface in marriages submitted for en-richment but have been sealed off from sensitivity. The difference he did note between the two sets of couples is that the pathology is no longer hidden among those seeking marriage counseling.

Goals

Whether addressed generally or in great detail in particular programs, the goal of marriage-enrichment programs is expressed in the name—to enrich marriages. Mace (1977) aptly pointed out that churches have a doctrine of getting married without a doctrine of marriage itself, except for the case when a marriage boils over into public view in the form of a divorce, fighting, or the need for counseling. Hof, Epstein, & Miller (1980) listed goals that seem to be generic: self-awareness, empathy, self-disclosure, increased intimacy, development of relationship skills (com-munication and problem solving), and building conflict-resolution skills. Mace (1977) stated that the lack of effective communication skills and the inability to creatively use conflict account for the majority of marital fail-ures among reasonably normal people. The view of the field espoused by L'Abate (1979) reflects an academic contribution. His detailed program for marriage and family enrichment training is based at Georgia State Uni-versity in Atlanta. L'Abate described his program as one for preventive mental health, as quasi-therapeutic (and amenable for use along with therapy), as diagnostic, and as capable of generating a body of research about the field. This mental-health theme is often repeated by the advo-cates of marital enrichment. Sauber (1974) advocated using the marital enrichment model as a means of improving public mental health. One can see with little difficulty the parallels between the goals of marital therapy and of marriage enrichment programs. The primary differences seem to be the functional level of the marriage that partners perceive and the techniques used by the therapist/trainers.

Techniques

There seems to be wide agreement that a marriage-enrichment group should be led by a married couple team and that a minimum portion of the encounter be experiential (Mace, 1979). One initial concern is the time schedule. Three schedules are most often used to accommodate the training. The most popular is the intensive weekend retreat. Spaced training periods are useful for relationship-skills training, with ongoing support-group activities encouraged after the intensive or spaced encounter. The experience of each group usually differs as the leader assists the couples to assess where the marriage is, where it is going, and what skills are needed to enrich it. Mace (1979) identified three rules in marriage-enrichment programs that foster experiential involvement: (1) no opinions are accepted, only experiences; (2) confrontation is not allowed, only support; and, (3) diagnosis or peer counseling by participants is discouraged. One experience common to most enrichment groups is dealing with resistance by participants to sharing "private" areas of their relationships and to identifying any pathology in a marriage that may be employed by individuals for personal gain. Hof, Epstein, and Miller (1980) proposed a sequential model for marriage-encounter groups:

1. Motivate the participants to expend the effort necessary.
2. Reduce resistance they use as "secondary gains."
3. Build relationship/communications skills.
4. Generalize from the enrichment experience to the home environment.
5. Maximize longevity of the positive gains.

A caution often given to participants of marriage-encounter groups is to beware of the "reentry" crisis; the outside world does not experience the enrichment the participants do and so may be unwilling, initially, to accept a couple's commitment to change.

Concerns

Critical analysis of marriage-enrichment programs has been reported by several writers, including both critics and advocates of the movement. These analyses are generally critical of marriage-enrichment programs on two issues: the ethics of recruitment and the lack of methodological research to substantiate success claimed for the programs. Smith, Shoffner, and Scott (1979) reported six concerns relating to ethical issues:

- There may be coercion to change when a couple may desire the status quo.
- Leadership training and the relationship of couple-leaders to each other are often questionable.

- Participants may believe that this program is a panacea for marriage ills, both self- and other-caused.
- Enrichment may not bring participants closer together as advertised—in fact, they may decide to separate.
- Enrichment programs foster the belief that peak emotional experiences will make life better.
- Even though the programs are preventive, they can't prevent all conflict or other marital problems.

DeYoung (1979) attended a marriage encounter group as a participant observer and, as a result, encouraged the therapeutic professions to become more involved in examination of questionable recruitment and proceedings of such groups. Specifically, he noted that the second half of the experience was an attempt to proselytize for the local church group, that the minimal enrollment fee of $10 was a come-on for a hidden sermon delivered during the encounter on "giving till it hurts," that clannishness was encouraged among those who have been "encountered," that social and occupational problems of marriage were not addressed, and that teachings were male centered. He did report that marriages seemed to be strengthened by the experience.

The lack of methodological research has been recognized by several writers. Hof, Epstein, and Miller (1980) pointed out that outcome reports are usually self-reports and that benefits may be illusory. Control groups are reported by most critics as inadequate or nonexistent. Gurman and Kniskern (1977) reported that since "the majority of studies have used unrelated control groups and appear to offer evidence of meaningful change as a result of these enrichment experiences, several methodological deficiencies are common to these investigations, and therefore a cautious optimism about the efficacy of these programs is suggested" (p. 3). In one study, with a small but well-controlled group, the experimental couples did report a significant increase in marital adjustment and, even more significantly, greater actualized relationships (Killman, Julian, & Moreault, 1978).

In conclusion, marriage enrichment is a popular movement that apparently is successful at doing what its name claims—enriching marriages. Many seem to feel that it does not do all that it claims to do, and others cannot accept the claim of success without scientific research to substantiate it. If attendance is any measure of success, however, some substantiation exists. As of 1976, approximately half a million couples had participated in the American version of Marriage Encounter (Koch & Koch, 1976). And, as discussed, though Marriage Encounter is the largest such program, it is by no means the only one. Religious organizations were major customers of the early practitioners and are now offering packaged programs for order by local churches.

Many practitioners herald this movement as a new professional area in the applied family field, along with the family life and counseling (Smith, Shoffner, & Scott, 1979), a new field of family psychology (L'Abate, 1979), and a new field along with education and counseling (Mace, 1979). Marital therapists trained in marital-enrichment skills would ostensibly be able to aid couples to surpass healthy marriage and reach enriched marriage. Marriage enrichment seems to offer a popular group method to do much of what most marital therapists do at some point in the course of therapy with individual couples.

Summary

Following the Chapter 7 discussion of the course of marital therapy in a process-oriented, five-stage framework, in Chapter 8 we concentrate on the third stage,—applying intervention strategies. The intervention strategies we survey in this chapter we have found to address effectively some major issues couples bring to the attention of marital therapists, involving skill deficits. Our major purpose in examining these interventions is to highlight the specialized approach to certain treatment issues regardless of a therapist's primary theoretical orientation. We note that the necessity of these specialized interventions is due to the fact that certain couple concerns involve specific skill deficits on the part of one or both partners. Facilitating couples' acquisition of these skills calls for more specific and focused intervention than derives from the theoretical perspectives in Chapters 3, 4, and 5. Although there are many more specialized interventions than space limitations allow to be discussed here, we do offer introductory overviews of procedures with which to respond to needs in several areas: communications training, conflict management, parent consultation, sex therapy, and divorce therapy.

We also discuss some relevant concerns and intervention strategies emanating from three areas of a particularly contemporary nature: women's issues, dual-career marriages, and marriage enrichment, While these areas are in the midst of their own evolution and currently changing in scope, we point out several implications each has for marital therapists and the couples with whom they work.

References

Bach, G. R., & Deutsch, R. M. *Pairing.* New York: Avon, 1970.

Bach, G. R., & Wyden, P. *The intimate enemy: How to fight fair in love and marriage.* New York: Avon, 1970.

Beck, D. F., & Jones, M. A. *Progress on family problems.* New York: Service Association of America, 1973.

Bohannan, P. The six stations of divorce. In P. Bohannan (Ed.), *Divorce and after.* New York: Doubleday, 1970.

Carlson, J., & Faiber, B. Necessary skills for parenting. *Focus on Guidance,* 1976, *8,* 2–3.

Coogler, O. J. *Structured mediation in divorce settlement.* Lexington, Mass.: Lexington, 1978.

Crosby, J. F. *Illusion and disillusion: The self in love and marriage* (2nd ed.). Belmont, Calif.: Wadsworth, 1976.

Cuber, J. F., & Harroff, P. B. *Sex and the significant Americans.* Baltimore: Penguin, 1965.

DeYoung, A. J. Marriage encounter: A critical examination. *Journal of Marital and Family Therapy,* 1979, *5,* 27–34.

Dinkmeyer, D., Pew, W. L., & Dinkmeyer, D., Jr. *Adlerian counseling and psychotherapy.* Monterey, Calif.: Brooks/Cole, 1979.

Dreikurs, R. *The challenge of marriage.* New York: Hawthorn, 1946.

Dreikurs, R. *Psychology in the classroom.* New York: Harper, 1957.

Dreikurs, R., Gould, S., & Corsini, R. J. *Family council.* Chicago: Henry Regnery, 1974.

Framo, J. L. The friendly divorce. *Psychology Today,* 1978, *11,* 77–80, 99–102.

Frey, D. Understanding and managing conflict. In R. Eisenberg & M. Patterson (Eds.), *Helping clients with special concerns.* Chicago: Rand McNally, 1979.

Golden, J. S., & Golden, M. A. You know who and what's her name: The woman's role in sex therapy. *Journal of Sex and Marital Therapy,* 1976, *2,* 6–16.

Frieze, I. H., Parsons, J. E., Johnson, P. B., Ruble, D. N., & Zellman, G. L. *Women and sex roles: A social psychological perspective.* New York: Norton, 1978.

Froiland, D. J., & Hosman, T. L. Counseling for constructive divorce. *Personnel and Guidance Journal,* 1977, *55,* 525–529.

Gordon, T. *Parent effectiveness training.* New York: Plume, 1970.

Gottman, J., Notarius, C., Gonso, J., & Markman, H. *A couple's guide to communication.* Champaign, Ill.: Research Press, 1976.

Gurman, A. S., & Kniskern, D. P. Enriching research on marital enrichment programs. *Journal of Marriage & Family Counseling,* 1977 *3,* 3–11.

Gurman, A. S., & Kniskern, D. P. (Eds.). *Handbook of family therapy.* New York: Brunner-Mazel, 1981.

Hall, F. S., & Hall, D. T. *The two-career couple.* Reading, Mass.: Addison-Wesley, 1979.

Hof, L., Epstein, N., & Miller, W. R. Integrating attitudinal and behavioral change in marital enrichment. *Family Relations,* 1980, *29,* 241–248.

Huber, C. H., & Baruth, L. G. *Coping with marital conflict.* Champaign, Ill.: Stipes, 1981.

Jacobson, N. S., & Margolin, G. *Marital Therapy: Strategies based on social learning and behavior exchange principles.* New York: Brunner-Mazel, 1979.

Johnson, D. W. *Reaching out: Interpersonal effectiveness and self-actualization.* Englewood Cliffs, N. J.: Prentice-Hall, 1972.

Kaplan, H. S. *The new sex therapy.* New York: Brunner-Mazel, 1974.

Kaslow, F. W. Divorce and divorce therapy. In A. S. Gurman & D. P. Kniskern (Eds.), *Handbook of family therapy.* New York: Brunner-Mazel, 1981.

Killman, P. R., Julian, A., III, & Moreault, D. The impact of a marriage enrichment program on relations factors. *Journal of Sex and Marital Therapy,* 1978, *4,* 298–303.

Koch, J., & Koch, L. The urgent drive to make marriages better. *Psychology Today,* 1976, *10,* 33–35.

Kressel, K., & Deutsch, M. Divorce therapy: An in-depth survey of therapists' views. *Family Process,* 1977, *16,* 413–443.

Kressel, K., Deutsch, M., Jaffe, N., Tuckman, B., & Watson, C. Mediated negotiations in divorce and labor disputes. *Conciliation Courts Review,* 1977, *15,* 9–12.

Kubler-Ross, E. *On death and dying.* New York: McMillan, 1969.

L'Abate, L. *An attempt at prevention: Marriage and family enrichment programs.* New York, N. Y.: Paper presented at the 87th annual convention of the American Psychological Association, 1979. (ERIC Document Reproduction Service No. ED 184 047).

Lamanna, M., & Riedman, A. *Marriages and families: Making choices throughout the life cycle.* Belmont, Calif.: Wadsworth, 1981.

Lassen, C. A. Issues and dilemmas in sexual treatment. *Journal of Sex and Marital Therapy,* 1976, *2,* 32–39.

Lawe, C., & Lawe, B. The balancing act: Coping strategies for emerging family lifestyles, In F. Pepitone-Rockwell (Ed.), *Dual-career couples.* Beverly Hills, Calif.: Sage, 1980.

Lederer, W. J., & Jackson, D. D. *Mirages of marriage.* New York: Norton, 1968.

Mace, D. Marriage and family enrichment—a new field. *Family Coordinator,* 1979, *28,* 409–419.

Mace, D. Marriage enrichment: The new frontier. *Personnel and Guidance Journal,* 1977, *55,* 520–522.

Mace, D. R. Marital intimacy and the deadly love-anger cycle. *Journal of Marriage and Family Counseling,* 1976, *2,* 131–137.

Maples, M. F. Dual career marriages: Elements for potential success. *Personnel and Guidance Journal,* 1981, *60,* 19–24.

Masters, W. H., & Johnson, V. E. *Human sexual response.* Boston: Little Brown, 1966.

Masters, W., & Johnson, V. *Human sexual inadequacy.* Boston: Little Brown, 1970.

Miller, S., Nunnally, E. W., & Wackman, D. B. *Alive and aware: Improving communication in relationships.* Minneapolis: Interpersonal Communications Programs, 1975.

Miller, S., Nunnally, E. W., & Wackman, D. B. *Couple workbook: Increasing awareness and communication skills.* Minneapolis: Interpersonal Communication Programs, 1976a.

Miller, S., Nunnally, E. W. & Wackman, D. B. Minnesota couples communication program (MCCP): Premarital and marital groups. In D. Olson (Ed.), *Treating relationships.* Lake Mills, Iowa: Graphic, 1976b.

Nierenberg, G. I., & Calero, H. H. *Meta-talk: Guide to hidden meanings on conversations.* New York: Simon & Schuster, 1973.

Okun, B. F., & Rappaport, L. J. *Working with families: An introduction to family therapy.* North Scituate, Mass.: Duxbury Press, 1980.

Palmores, U. *A curriculum on conflict management.* La Mesa. Calif.: Human Development Training Institute, 1975.

Patton, B. R., & Griffin, K. *Interpersonal communication: Basic text and readings.* New York: Harper & Row, 1974.

Perlman, C., & Givelber, F. Women's issues in couples treatment: The view of the female therapist. *Psychiatric Opinion,* 1976, *13,* 6–12.

Rapoport, R., & Rapoport, R. *Dual-career families.* Baltimore: Penguin, 1971.

Satir, V. *Peoplemaking.* Palo Alto, Calif.: Science and Behavior Books, 1972.

Sauber, S. R. Primary prevention and the marital enrichment group. *Journal of Family Counseling,* 1974 *2,* 39–41.

Silverman, J. The women's liberation movement: Its impact on marriage. *Hospital & Community Psychiatry,* 1975, *26,* 39–40.

Smith, R. M., Shoffner, S. M., & Scott, J. P. Marriage and family enrichment: A new professional area. *Family Coordinator,* 1979, *28,* 87–89.

Stevens, J. O. *Awareness: Exploring, experimenting, experiencing.* Lafayette, Calif.: Real People Press, 1971.

Stuart, R. B. *Helping couples change: A social learning approach to marital therapy.* New York: Guilford, 1980.

Walen, S. R., DiGiuseppe, R., & Wessler, R. L. *A practitioner's guide to rational-emotive therapy.* New York: Oxford University Press, 1980.

Weiss, R. *Marital separation.* New York: Basic Books, 1976.

Wolman, R. N. Women's issues in couples treatment: The view of the male therapist. *Psychiatric Opinion,* 1976, *13,* 13–17.

Worthington, E. R. *Post separation adjustment and women's liberation.* Washington, D. C.: Paper presented at the 84th annual convention of the American Psychological Association, 1976. (ERIC Document Reproduction Service No. ED 143 908).

CHAPTER NINE

Therapeutic Intervention: Special Problems and Their Solutions

Much of what has been presented in the preceding chapters has been based in the assumption that couples who enter marital therapy are relatively willing to cooperate in the therapeutic process. This is usually the case, and initiating and maintaining a working relationship with such couples presents no major problems. However, not all partners participate in therapy willingly.

Some partners, if given the choice, would not talk about themselves, behave differently, or be in therapy at all. In many situations, one partner comes, reluctantly, only because he or she is pressed. And, in some situations, partners come willingly, but with misguided expectations: that the therapist will show only their mates to be in the wrong and that their mates are responsible for any change required in the relationship.

Those partners who enter therapy under pressure or with misguided intentions are likely to exhibit attitudes and behaviors that tend to limit progressive therapeutic movement. They often come to sessions with an orientation toward self-protection, being defensive and quick to place blame for any problems somewhere outside of themselves. Many resent the mates who pressed them to come to therapy and transfer that resentment to the therapist. Often such partners perceive no need for help and therefore do not view the therapist as a helping person.

Problems that such partners present in initiating or maintaining therapeutic progress are expressed in a variety of ways. Some people show defiance: "I don't want to be here and I don't have to cooperate." Others exhibit their defiance in passive-aggressive ways: continually leading the discussion away from themselves to some irrelevant topic, being unwilling to communicate anything beyond brief and inadequate answers to direct questions, or sitting silently and with a disgusted demeanor. Still others, so as to be free of any responsibility, try to manipulate the therapist into providing all the effort.

Clearly, marital therapists encounter some genuinely difficult clients. The problems posed by some of these clients occur fairly often in therapy, and obviously they can interfere with therapeutic efforts. If therapy is to be of any benefit, they must be dealt with successfully. In this chapter, we identify some of these special problems and also suggest procedures to facilitate their solutions and prevent their recurrence.

The Battle for Structure

Marital therapy actually begins before a couple is ever seen. It begins with the initial contact made with the therapist, usually by telephone. Whitaker (Keith & Whitaker, 1980) claimed that therapy always begins with a "battle for structure"; that is, it begins with a fight over who controls the context of therapy. He proposed that a couple must capitulate to the therapist's mode of operating. The therapist is the expert from whom the couple is seeking assistance, and thus it is appropriate that the therapist has leverage over those factors necessary for therapeutic effectiveness to evolve.

There are a number of issues on which a couple can stage a battle for structure with a therapist. The most common include who decides the content of therapy and the manner in which it is to proceed. Couples often test a therapist, evaluating whether he or she has the determination to withstand the manipulations they use to maintain their present homeostatic balance. Barnard and Corrales (1979) compare this testing often seen in the beginning of therapy with that of preadolescents who want to be reassured that, if self-control is lost, their parents can be firm enough to take over. Within an umbrella of trust thereby established, the youths or, presumably, the marital partners, can begin to take initiative toward more constructive action. Barnard and Corrales offered the following thoughts for therapists to consider in this regard:

> It is helpful to keep in mind that families [couples] enter therapy with ambivalent feelings. They are hurting very much, desirous of change, and yet

afraid that change may mean the loss of what little they have in terms of acceptance, affirmation, and identity. They come in half convinced of therapy and half scared. If they sense that the therapist means business, they are more likely to bring in the affect and the energy they need to achieve therapeutic change. At this point, some families [couples] abandon the therapist and shop for one who is willing to play simply a supportive role, to be a listening board for their frustrations [p. 107].

For all the reasons couples enter therapy uncooperatively, it is critical that the battle for structure yield an immediate victory for the therapist. A clearly understood initial agreement should be made with the contacting party. This agreement should delineate who shall be in attendance (preferably both partners) and details of time, fees, and purpose. When reluctance is apparent, the therapist should be resolute in stating that if therapy and positive change in the marriage are considered important, arrangements can be worked out. Of course, tact and realistic flexibility must characterize the therapist's response to such potential reluctance. Nevertheless, the importance of agreeing to a set of criteria before treatment efforts are initiated should not be minimized.

Although a battle for structure may appear to end, the same dynamics may recur, in other forms. Let us proceed to consider several more potential difficulties.

The Absent Partner

When only one partner presents him- or herself for therapy and suggests that marital concerns are the primary problem, it is important to convey the idea that, ideally, both partners in the relationship should participate in therapy. Often, however, the partner who arrives alone protests vigorously that the other will not participate in therapy. An absent partner's receptivity to therapy can be promoted in a number of ways.

One major assumption the therapist can make is that a partner absent at first will invariably come for at least one session. The therapist should first attempt to determine the circumstances surrounding the partner's absence and assist the partner who's present to confront them productively. This entails finding out how the present partner approached the topic of marital therapy with his or her mate; have there been threats, attempts at coercion, or ultimatums? Or, conversely, has the absent mate not been informed of his or her partner's desire to seek therapeutic assistance? It is sometimes discovered that the issue of marital therapy has not been discussed between the spouses, and the absent partner is unaware that his or her mate is seeing a marital therapist.

We have often been surprised after hearing about an absent partner to find how much he or she differs from the description we had been given, even knowing that, especially if the partner offering the description was angry and upset, it was likely quite biased. A more important difference for the success of therapy, however, is that when both partners are present, their individual and joint contributions to the marital problems can be recognized and confronted.

When the absent partner has not been informed of his or her mate's appointment for therapeutic assistance in marital concerns, it is critical to ask permission to get in touch with the absent partner. This can often be done by telephone immediately during the session. It can be valuable to winning the cooperation of the absent partner to point out that only he or she can speak for him or herself, and that it is important to hear what he or she has to say. The analogy might be used that speaking to only one partner about a marital relationship is like seeing two actors on a stage but hearing the lines of only one of them. In our experience, the absent partner can usually be persuaded to come in for at least one session. And most often, once this first step is taken and a cooperative relationship develops and takes hold, therapy with both partners can commence.

Occasionally, an absent partner's reluctance to join the other in therapy is based on the conviction that the marriage is too rife with discord to attempt change. Separation or divorce is seen as the only alternative to the present situation. One way to counter this discouragement is to agree that terminating the relationship is a viable alternative to consider, but that other options are also open. It might be suggested that before such a critical decision is finalized a period of time should be agreed to within which every effort will be made, with professional assistance, to improve the relationship. Without such efforts, the possibility that the marriage might have improved and endured as a result of therapeutic aid will never be resolved; with such a trial period, any decision to continue or terminate the relationship can be a more clear and definite one. Should the eventual decision be to end the marriage, the therapeutic effort can help to reduce any feelings of guilt or hostility and to make the separation an amicable one.

If the situation between partners has been one in which threats have been made or ultimatums stated to no avail, it may be necessary to work temporarily with the sole willing partner. During this time the willing partner can be trained to approach the other in a more positive, nonthreatening way. The therapist can stress that marital therapy is not a treatment process only for couples considered sick but a developmental and preventive educational experience that focuses on improving relationships. It can be explained that marital problems result less from each partner's personality problems than from how partners' interests, needs, and desires coincide or clash. And, therefore, the focus of therapy efforts will be on improving the marriage, not assigning blame. Basic communication skills, such as empathic expression and assertiveness rather than aggression or passivity, can be taught to assist the partner who is present to convey these notions to the other partner.

Whether the partner who is present can learn to approach his or her mate in a more persuasive manner regarding therapy or the therapist must initiate contact, the critical factor is to get the absent partner to come in for a session. However, if all efforts to involve the absent partner fail, the present partner should be encouraged to continue therapy on his or her own. He or she can work on coping better within any limitations imposed by the relationship and be assisted in making decisions regarding future courses of action.

Stressing the importance of seeing both partners requires treading a fine line. If the therapist identifies dual participation as an absolute necessity rather than an ideal circumstance, the partner who is present may assume that nothing can be gained by individual therapy. He or she may thus miss an opportunity to learn to cope better within the marriage, to identify ways he or she can improve it, or to get individual assistance. In contrast, the opposite extreme of stressing individual therapy as an alternative may not stimulate sufficient effort to involve the absent partner. Therefore, whenever marital therapy seems indicated but one partner is absent, the therapist should have clearly in mind the partners' options and the limitations they varyingly impose. One major option to consider is one-partner therapy.

One-Partner Marital Therapy

Marital therapy with only one member of a marriage has been reported less effective than conjoint therapy (Brock, 1978; Gurman & Kniskern, 1978), but, when one partner is totally unable or unwilling to come, it becomes necessary. Brock (1978), recognizing the need for a one-partner marital therapy approach, developed and tested an alternative intervention similar to conjoint therapy that required professional involvement with only one partner. That one partner was trained in self-disclosure and empathic understanding skills; the partner then trained his or her mate in the same skills over a five-week treatment period. Results indicated that it is possible to train one partner as a relationship change agent and that such intervention is potentially helpful to couples in which one partner is not able to participate in sessions with the therapist.

A similar type of intervention was reported by Scheiderer and Bernstein (1976) in which one partner became a "behavioral engineer" (with the therapist as a consultant). Using an extended behavior-modification model, the partner working with the therapist completed four major assignments:

1. Accurately assessing problems in the marriage, including behaviors that might be changed.
2. With the therapist, formulating a treatment plan and weighing the probable consequences.

3. Being responsible for implementation of the plan, including the responsibility for required self-change.
4. Reassessing the relationship after completion of the plan.

In a setting where conjoint therapy clearly was not possible—a correctional institution—Freedman and Rice (1977) made use of one-partner marital therapy as the only variation of marital therapy feasible. They reported that letters, phone calls, tapes, and visits complemented with professional assistance functioned much like the therapeutic technique of "letting one spouse speak uninterruptedly while the other's task is to listen intently, to paraphrase what he or she has heard, and then to respond again without interruption from the partner" (p. 180). They listed a number of tactics that therapists might consider under these conditions:

• Forestall any drastic actions by the inmate such as divorce.
• Increase the inmate's feeling of control and potency.
• Perform marital therapy in the manner noted.
• Perform individual therapy to complement the marital therapy.
• Help the inmate and his or her partner get more aid in the community.
• Assist in a loosening of ties if separation becomes likely.

We have found all the aforementioned considerations to be potentially useful when one-partner marital therapy is the most practical path to pursue.

Resistance

In the context of marital therapy *resistance* refers to a lack of agreement between the goals of the couple and those of the therapist. As such, it is often manifested in a couple's opposition to the therapeutic process, which the therapist needs to reduce as much as possible. Resistance usually occurs in response to one or both of two primary issues:

1. Opposition to the basic concepts of the overall therapeutic approach being employed.
2. Opposition to one or more of the intervention strategies being attempted.

Whenever resistance is detected, it is important to interrupt the therapeutic process and attempt to negotiate a new set of goals that are acceptable to all parties. Therapy can then proceed. There will be times, however, when negotiation leads to an agreement that consensus regarding the goals for therapeutic efforts is not possible. In this case, referral to another therapist or termination is indicated (Dinkmeyer, Pew, & Dinkmeyer, 1979).

Resistance is present to some degree in all couple-therapist relationships. Because it is so prevalent, therapists should be aware of the potential for it—especially in initial therapy sessions. Any indication of resistance arising should be dealt with immediately. However, by taking preventive measures, the therapist can reduce the likelihood of resistance occurring significantly.

Lieberman, Wheeler, deVisser, Kuehnel, and Kuehnel (1980) proposed a number of activities therapists can implement to prevent or overcome resistance to therapeutic efforts. These include providing an orientation and rationale concerning therapeutic procedures, facilitating favorable expectations, offering an opportunity for catharsis, employing what's called a customer approach, and making therapy special, each of which is described here.

1. *Orientation and Rationale.* A potentially resistant couple should be carefully oriented to the overall therapeutic process as well as specific intervention strategies as they are planned. It is important that the rationale be understood and accepted by both partners. Therapy can progress only if it deals with specific issues that partners recognize as important and want to work to change. No movement can occur until the goals of therapy, and the means of achieving those goals, are spelled out and mutually agreed upon.

2. *Favorable Expectations.* The key variable in facilitating favorable expectations for therapy is the therapist's attitude, expressed in both verbal and nonverbal ways. The means of expression include at least words, tone of voice, gestures, and facial expressions. The therapist can convey a sense of optimism by looking forward to working with a couple and by proposing that therapy will be challenging, worthwhile, and fun. Anecdotes and positive statements quoted from former clients can also contribute to an optimistic outlook.

3. *Catharsis.* Catharsis involves giving partners an opportunity to ventilate their accumulated feelings of hurt or anger and to express any complaints or accusations they feel are relevant before structuring therapy and setting goals. Some couples need to express their negative ideas and emotions before they can become receptive to identifying and agreeing to work on goals that can prevent similar emotional upheavals occurring in the future. An additional use of a couple's catharsis in early sessions is in the therapist's identification of particularly upsetting situations and behaviors that can be targeted for change efforts, thus helping to create a closer goal alignment between therapist and couple.

4. *Customer Approach.* The customer approach involves a therapist's active and vigorous solicitation of a couple's desires, hopes, fears, and wishes for the therapeutic experience. The therapist works to have both partners clearly and understandably identify their major concerns and formulate specific goals for therapy. Common therapist questions when employing a customer approach include: "What would you like to get out of marital therapy?" "What would you like to see changed?" "How might we work together to improve your present relationship?" Discrepancies be-

tween the goals of the couple and the therapist and possible resistances are thus kept to a minimum.

5. *Making Therapy Special.* A final way of preventing or overcoming a couple's resistance to marital therapy is to establish this experience as different from other attempts to improve the relationship that may have failed in the past. Many couples who have problems sufficient to bring them into therapy have tried a variety of approaches for dealing with their difficulties; these include speaking to family and friends, reading self-help books, or even prior therapeutic endeavors. If previous attempts the couple made to resolve their problems included methods similar to those of the present therapist, it might be pointed out that his or her approach is more comprehensive and intensive. In addition, the therapist can have the couple explain or show how they attempted certain procedures that didn't work. Almost all reasonable methods and suggestions for improving a marital relationship have some validity. The usual reason for their lack of effectiveness in improving some aspect of a relationship lies not in the procedure as much as in a couple's implementing the methods incorrectly, inconsistently, or for too short a period of time. By stressing the value of the therapist as an expert and objective third-party observer who can offer feedback and follow-up, the current therapeutic experience can come to be seen as a special one.

Inappropriate Behavior

It sometimes happens that one or both partners display behavior inappropriate to the therapeutic setting and even highly obstructive to the therapy process. Violent outbursts, hostile and embarrassing remarks, or fear- and anxiety-producing behaviors can take place in the midst of a session. And occasionally a partner may come to a session under the influence of alcohol or drugs. It is important that the therapist be prepared to respond to such situations.

The primary element in preventing or dealing with these potential problems is to anticipate their occurrence and prepare in advance means of appropriately responding. Four such preventive measures are:

1. Screening couples for marital therapy.
2. Specifying guidelines for sessions.
3. Stimulating positive interactions between partners.
4. Identifying support services.

Screening Couples for Marital Therapy.   Particularly in an initial interview, a therapist may encounter two partners who are so obviously hostile and uncommunicative with each other that any attempt to form a collaborative relationship seems futile. Some partners simply have no motivation whatsoever to continue their marriage, or they are unable to listen or to speak in a calm and rational manner or are simply unwilling to comply with the guidelines proposed as a basic structure for therapy. When the therapist's attempts to counter this resistance are unsuccessful, individual therapy for each partner or referral to another form of treatment might be suggested.

Specifying Guidelines for Sessions.   As discussed in the part of this chapter on structure, guidelines for sessions should be specified at the beginning of, or even prior to, the first session. In these guidelines, such therapeutic considerations as confidentiality, acceptable behaviors, punctuality, regular attendance, and sobriety during sessions are identified and agreed to. The guidelines may well be tested, and it is critical that the therapist maintain them, specifying that partners who cannot accept these minimal limits are not likely to benefit from conjoint marital therapy.

For example, a couple may begin to interact in a hostile or violent manner during a session, so much so that the therapist cannot persuade them to respond to each other with a calmer, less defensive manner. Once the therapist recognizes that the tone of the session is destructive, he or she should take immediate action, stating that "Given the present emotional atmosphere, I would like to see you individually." It is vital that the therapist be firm and directive when destructive behaviors are occurring between partners at a nonstop pace. The therapist should then act, standing up and leading one of the partners to the door. Crisis intervention procedures suggest that when antagonists are immediately separated de-escalation and conflict resolution have a greater opportunity to take place (Lieberman et al., 1980). After the therapist sees each partner individually, a decision can be made to return to a conjoint situation or, if either partner has too little control over his or her emotions and behaviors to allow that, it may be necessary to recommend continuation of individual therapy, with conjoint therapy as a future goal.

Stimulating Positive Interactions between Partners.   Another means of preventing inappropriate behaviors from arising is for the therapist to work to make each therapy session a stimulating and positive experience for both partners. These characteristics may be the opposite of the atmosphere to which the two are accustomed; many couples find it easier to argue rather than agree. Others see the prospect of separation and divorce as less painful than expending the effort necessary to improve their troubled relationship. To stimulate positive perceptions of therapy, the therapist must make sure partners receive positive feedback on all that can be so acknowledged. Noting improved performance, positive suggestions made, or independent efforts at change attempted will significantly preempt destructive interchanges. Professionals who have observed this procedure often comment that it seems enjoyable for couples and therapists alike. Maintaining a positive atmosphere helps keep couples motivated, involved, and working toward improving their relationship rather than being concerned about protecting themselves from further pain (Lieberman et al., 1980).

To keep sessions positive, therapists should also be ready to quickly intervene if overtly destructive behaviors are displayed by one or both partners. One such behavior includes unnecessarily negative remarks—comments that may be factual but deal with particularly sensitive issues, often regarding something that can't be changed; the partner who raises the issue of a past mistake or embarrassing situation that cannot be changed does so to punish the other. In order to provoke change, the therapist can take action to identify and explain this self- and relationship-defeating behavior. The partner whose negative behavior is discouraged can then be encouraged to respond positively by the therapist's making it a point to reward positive behaviors, not destructive actions.

Identifying Support Services.   Finally, if inappropriate behavior during a session becomes destructive to the point of danger for the couple, the therapist, or someone else, the therapist must consider involving the police or some other protective agency. It is vital that the therapist already know what resource services are available and under what circumstances they may be called upon, and have the necessary telephone numbers readily available. The likelihood that most therapists will ever have occasion to thus call for protection is minor. However, should a therapist be unprepared, there is the remote possibility that he or she would be caught without knowing what to do or where to turn. Serious consequences could result. Problems rarely escalate to dangerous levels if appropriate preventive procedures are implemented early in therapy.

Premature Termination

At times, a couple may seek to terminate therapy before successful goal attainment has occurred. Premature termination can occur at any time during the therapeutic process. Frequently couples showing little motivation or commitment to work to improve their relationship may communicate an inclination to terminate from the very beginning of therapy. Some may communicate their rejection of therapy and the therapist as a source of help at later stages. One mechanism is for a couple simply not to return for later sessions. Another is for the partners to tell the therapist directly that they feel therapy is not of much benefit to them so they see no point in continuing. Occasionally such a statement by a couple may be appropriate—therapy indeed is not being of any significant benefit. But, especially when change is difficult for a couple to experience, such a statement may suggest that the couple is fearful about the impact therapy may have on them, or that they are simply not putting forth the necessary effort to change. Obviously, when these conditions hold, benefits do not accrue.

The initial response of a therapist when confronted by a couple choosing to prematurely terminate therapy should be to identify his or her own thoughts and feelings about the couple's rejection of therapeutic assistance. Under such conditions, apprehension and anger directed toward the couple are often potential therapist responses. Beginning therapists especially are apt to respond with anxiety, because rejection by a couple is often evaluated as reflecting therapist ineffectiveness. The therapist's goal is to be successful in assisting couples to achieve therapeutic objectives; being told that therapy is not being of assistance may represent a serious block to goal attainment for therapists, leading to feelings of frustration, anger, and anxiety. Ironically, these maladaptive emotional responses are sure to interfere with a therapist's effectiveness. Thus when such stress occurs in the therapist-couple relationship it is important to deal with it openly rather than to avoid dealing with it. Responding to stress in the relationship is far more likely to result in favorable consequences than will the avoidance of existing stress (Eisenberg & Delaney, 1977).

Assuming a therapist is aware of the impact that a couple's rejection has on him or her and copes with it effectively, the next step is to elicit discussion regarding what is involved in the couple's decision to terminate therapy. For example, one approach to a couple in this regard is, "You've stated that you don't see our work together as having been of much benefit to you. I'd like you to know that although I'm disappointed to hear this, I am glad that you did tell me. I do feel that it's important that we explore how you came to arrive at the conclusion." Depending on the couple's ensuing response and any further discussion, the therapist can then decide whether the couple's criticisms are valid or whether they are statements of resistance. If they are statements of resistance, the therapist should attempt to intervene, using the strategies previously discussed in the section on client resistance. If it is decided that the criticisms are valid ones, the therapist must reevaluate his or her therapeutic approach in working with this couple. Where intervention strategies have been inappropriate or inefficient, the therapist must be willing to change. Communicating this willingness to the couple may avert their premature termination. Otherwise, a referral to another therapist whose orientation is more likely to suit the couple's desires is indicated.

On occasion, one partner alone may desire to prematurely terminate therapy. This can have a serious impact on the partner who has a desire to continue. The remaining partner should be assured that individual therapy can be helpful to him or her, especially if there is a perceived need for further assistance. The partner terminating often returns when his or her mate continues to attend therapy, exhibits the benefits of this attendance, and demonstrates a continued commitment to improve the relationship. Perhaps a partner terminating conjoint marital therapy wishes to be seen individually for problems that are unrelated to the marriage but that need to be resolved before marital therapy can be properly utilized; the option for individual therapy should always be offered by the therapist. The interventions that have been suggested for responding in the case of an absent partner can also be valuable procedures for the therapist to consider.

Other Behaviors that Block Progress

Some behaviors of a partner or partners pose special difficulties for the marital therapist. And for the beginning therapist, these behaviors often cause even more concern than others; the new therapist's lack of experience in intervening with these particularly unyielding behavioral patterns frequently causes him or her to feel frustrated and anxious, wanting to succeed and being blocked from achieving the desired objectives. Even for the experienced therapist, however, these difficult behaviors can create substantial blocks to progress within the therapeutic setting.

The Argumentative Partner

Therapists occasionally encounter a partner who displays an excessive amount of antagonism during therapy sessions. The partner's voice always seems to be on edge. The therapist feels fatigued by the therapeutic interaction—there seems to be almost more arguing than cooperating. This partner is an argumentative one, willing to make an issue of any point with which he or she even slightly disagrees. A therapist's initial response upon recognizing this argumentative pattern should be to stop him- or herself from engaging with the partner in any disputant interchange. In a sense, the therapist and partner are tugging at opposite ends of a rope. The therapist need only let go of one end to terminate the tug-of-war. The therapist should go through one or more sessions without attempting to suggest, advise, or convince the argumentative partner of anything. Suggesting ideas or possible change strategies to an argumentative partner only intensifies the potential for quarrelsome reactions. Instead, the therapist can work to attain that partner's cooperation, simultaneously progressing toward therapeutic goals; this is accomplished by focusing on the strength and power of the partner, intervening by seeking cooperation through questioning. For example, "What do *you* think you might do to cope more effectively in that situation?" "What might *we* come up with to help you deal with that difficulty?"

The "Yes-But" Partner

A partner who counters the therapist's ideas and recommendations with a "yes-but" response is demonstrating a more subtle form of argumentativeness. The partner presents him- or herself as needing assistance but then proceeds to show the therapist how ineffective the therapist's advice is, how suggested strategies will not work, and so on. The yes-but is actually an implicit no. By playing helpless, this partner attempts to render the therapist helpless. It is important that therapists examine yes-but responses and determine whether this form of resistance is attributable to their own behavior; are they off-task, or have they focused discussion on an irrelevant issue? If not, perhaps the most likely explanation for a partner's "yes-but" behavior is that he or she simply does not want to change. For instance, a partner may be fearful of changing and attempt to use a smoke screen, such as yes-but responses, to hide the fear from the therapist. Such a partner uses communication in order not to communicate (Beier, 1966).

With a yes-but partner, the therapist must first consider what the payoff is for the partner's behavior. It is important to identify the positive or negative consequences that maintain the dysfunctional beliefs regarding this behavior. In doing so, the therapist should confront the partner in a caring and responsible way. This confrontation can be followed by an invitation to the partner to explore what is occurring in the therapist-partner, partner-partner, or therapist-couple relationship to create a need for the resistant behavior. This can lead to the partner lessening his or her yes-but defensiveness. The therapist can go on to enumerate the strengths and capabilities the partner possesses but has not utilized effectively; although the partner still has to make a decision to work for change, listing personal resources subsequent to the confrontation and exploration of a yes-but behavioral pattern in itself challenges that partner to act in a more adaptive manner (Egan, 1975).

The "It's-Not-Working" Partner

Some partners who are very capable of changing burden themselves with the belief that immediately upon beginning therapy they should experience positive changes in their marital relationship. This impatience and short-term hedonism often is translated behaviorally into patterns of poor self-discipline and low frustration tolerance. For example:

Partner: I know what we discussed in the session makes sense, but when the real situation occurred, your suggestion didn't work for me at all.

When such an opinion is expressed, chances are the partner spent little time prior to the actual situation practicing the therapist's suggestion. By this neglect the partner puts total responsibility for his or her changing on the therapist. The expectation is that the therapist will come up with magical and immediate solutions to all problems presented.

It is possible that a therapist's suggestion to a partner was an inappropriate one. However, it is essential that the therapist never automatically assume responsibility. The partner should be asked to relay in some detail what exactly happened. The therapist should listen for any obvious flaws in the partner's handling of the situation. Assuming there were flaws in the partner's implementing of the therapist's original suggestion, the procedure can be explained again and rehearsed during the session until the therapist is assured of the partner's competency in using it. The partner should then be advised to practice the procedure and, should a similar problem situation arise, to make the procedure work. Simply, the therapist facilitates the partner's understanding that it may take several attempts for any procedure to work effectively, and that the responsibility to make it successful is ultimately the partner's.

The "Backlash"

When one marital partner has made the changes in his or her behavior that the other partner has been complaining about for a long time, it would be expected that the partner making the complaint would be quite pleased with the changes. Although usually this is precisely what does happen, at times the opposite occurs. This opposite reaction has been termed the backlash (Hauck, 1980). Hauck describes the nature of backlash in the following illustration.

> I recently talked to a husband who had a number of complaints about his wife. Through my counseling she decided that if her marriage was to succeed, she was going to have to give in to him on several important points. I persuaded her to do so, and lo and behold, he came back the next week saying that he had even fewer feelings for his wife than he did before.
>
> How to explain this phenomenon? First, the husband was irritated that the wife could change so quickly. He had been badgering her for well over a year to make those changes. I talked to her for half an hour and she went home and gave him the kind of attention and performed the sort of duties that he could not get her to do in a year's time. That bothered him.
>
> Secondly, the fact that she turned around and became a sweetheart in a matter of a few days did not give him the full opportunity he needed to drain the hostility from his system. He still had a number of things he had to tell her and hostilities he had to express. The moment she became nice she cut off his right to tell her how nasty she had been over the whole previous year and it simply left him more frustrated than before.
>
> Thirdly, during the time that the husband was complaining about his wife he developed a number of fantasies about how he might leave her, which other women he might take up with, and how life would be very pleasant with them. The moment she turned out to be a pleasing and loving person

those dreams were shot to pieces. That too was additionally frustrating [p. 232].[1]

Should a backlash response in one partner become evident, or preferably before such a reaction is seen, it is critical that the therapist convey to partners an expectation that some couples' relationships frequently deteriorate for a time after one partner makes significant improvements in his or her behaviors. The therapist can caution a couple not to judge the status of their relationship by such a backlash and further urge them to make sure they give themselves time to allow changes in the relationship to stabilize before any final judgments are passed.

Undoubtedly, there are numerous other special problems that therapists confront in working with couples experiencing marital discord. The following general strategies might be considered when encountering these problem situations.

- Be sure that intervention strategies to be implemented are appropriate for the capabilities of a particular couple and represent a clear and identifiable means of achieving agreed-to therapeutic objectives.
- Provide couples with a thorough rationale and orientation regarding any procedures, goals, and expectations for therapy efforts.
- Keep couples focused on positive gains and forward progress rather than problems, disappointments, and lack of success.
- Anticipate problems before they occur, and develop a repertoire of alternative strategies for occasions when they arise.

Clinical Supervision

To work with marital partners displaying the especially inappropriate, blocking behaviors just described is not easy. If therapists encountering such behaviors are to intervene effectively, they had better have a high level of frustration tolerance. In all probability, for whatever reason, most of these partners are seeking to avoid change. If these partners are to be engaged in the work of improving their relationships, the therapist must be able to facilitate their perceiving change as in their best interests. That is, the therapist must foster an understanding that partners' present behaviors, engaged in for the pleasure, excitement, or relief of the moment, will likely lead to only undesirable consequences in the long run.

The process of marital therapy can be emotionally and physically draining, but especially so for a therapist working with particularly difficult and problematic partner behaviors. It is when the behaviors create circumstances that a therapist has rarely if ever experienced, or has not

[1] From *Brief Counseling with RET,* by Paul A. Hauck. Copyright © 1980 The Westminster Press. Reprinted by permission.

developed appropriate modes of intervention with which to respond, that clinical supervision is most helpful, and in many cases necessary. Clinical supervision plays a crucial role in assisting therapists to understand marital partners' behaviors and the means of implementing appropriate intervention strategies. The clinical supervisor is a resource person and educator capable of assisting therapists to learn what is needed for their immediate and ongoing clinical development.

As a resource person, the supervisor may suggest specific strategies to deal with special problems. He or she may focus on basic therapeutic skills, such as the importance of establishing rapport or of properly assessing couples' concerns, that need to be reviewed or stressed more by the therapist. And the supervisor may propose alternative theoretical positions with which to clarify couple dynamics, or may refamiliarize the therapist with the predictable stages of marriage or of necessary tasks to be performed by a couple during the life cycle of their marriage.

In the educator role, the supervisor is removed from the therapeutic relationship between the therapist and marital partners and can assist the therapist in gaining a more objective view of the interactions taking place. This also places the supervisor in a better position to offer the therapist feedback on the tone of an intervention, apart from its content. The supervisor is in a position to be observant of subtle changes in the therapist's style or technique. All these variables can have significant impact on a therapist's ability to effectively respond to special problem behaviors. Clinical supervision, then, can constitute a key factor in the efficient and effective delivery of marital treatment services. We return to the topic of the supervision process in Chapter 11, in our discussion of professional and ethical issues in marital therapy.

Summary

In this chapter we look at a variety of special problems some couples' behaviors can create to block or retard therapeutic progress. We present some common and some not-so-common difficulties marital therapists may encounter. These include the battle for structure, the absent partner, one-partner marital therapy, resistance, inappropriate behavior, and premature termination. Other behaviors discussed here that can block therapeutic progress are the argumentative partner, the yes-but partner, the it's-not-working partner, and the backlash.

We discuss the basic nature of these problem behaviors and the impact they can have on the therapeutic process. We also consider specific intervention strategies that can be used to prevent or overcome the obstacles to therapeutic progress these behaviors represent. We stress the importance for the therapist of preventive measures and of anticipating potential problems so as to be able to respond in the most effective and efficient manner possible should they arise.

Finally, we explore the process of clinical supervision and stress its value to therapists in dealing with problems that may arise in therapy sessions. We further identify the supervision process as one in which marital therapists can be significantly assisted in maximizing their therapeutic understandings and skills.

References

Barnard, C. P., & Corrales, R. G. *The theory and technique of family therapy.* Springfield, Ill.: Charles C. Thomas, 1979.

Beier, E. G. *The silent language of psychotherapy.* Chicago: Adline, 1966.

Brock, G. W. *Unilateral marital intervention: Training spouses to train their partners in communications skills.* Philadelphia: Paper presented at the annual meeting of the National Council on Family Relations, 1978. (ERIC Document Reproduction Service No. ED 172 047).

Dinkmeyer, D. C., Pew, W. L., Dinkmeyer, D. C., Jr. *Adlerian counseling and psychotherapy.* Monterey, Calif.: Brooks/Cole, 1979.

Egan, G. *The skilled helper: A model for systematic helping and interpersonal relating.* Monterey, Calif.: Brooks/Cole, 1975.

Eisenberg, S., & Delaney, D. J. *The counseling process* (2nd ed.). Chicago: Rand McNally, 1977.

Freedman, B. J., & Rice, D. G. Marital therapy in prison: One-partner "couple therapy." *Psychiatry, 1977, 40,* 175–183.

Gurman, A. S., & Kniskern, D. P. Research on marital and family therapy: Progress, perspective and prospect. In S. L. Garfield & A. E. Bergin (Eds.), *Handbook of psychotherapy and behavior change.* New York: Wiley, 1978.

Hauck, P. A. *Brief counseling with RET.* Philadelphia: Westminster Press, 1980.

Keith, D. V., & Whitaker, C. A. Experiential/symbolic family therapy. In A. S. Gurman & D. P. Kniskern (Eds.), *Handbook of family therapy.* New York: Brunner–Mazel, 1980.

Lieberman, R. P., Wheeler, E. G., deVisser, L., Kuehnel, J., & Kuehnel, T. *Handbook of marital therapy.* New York: Plenum Press, 1980.

Scheiderer, E. G., & Bernstein, D. A. A case of chronic back pain and the "unilateral" treatment of marital problems. *Journal of Behavioral Therapy and Experimental Psychiatry,* 1976, *7,* 47–50.

CHAPTER TEN

Family Theory and Therapy

It may be possible to attribute too much influence to environmental factors, but it's almost impossible to take too broad a view when looking for environmental factors that may apply. Consider the experience of a seasoned investigator:

> Commander Robert Peary, on one of his polar expeditions, labored one whole day toward the north, driving his dogs briskly. When he stopped to check his bearings, he was astonished to find that he was actually much farther south than when he had started. He had been toiling all day on an immense iceberg drawn southward by the ocean current [Woodburn & Barnhill, 1977, p. 510].

This incident illustrates the value of considering the environmental context when attempting to implement therapeutic intervention strategies. In cases where the environment has a significant impact on a couple, the therapist who focuses treatment efforts exclusively on the marital dyad may find him- or herself in a position analagous to that of Commander Peary—laboring tediously in one direction only to find that labor offset by influences unforeseen. Therefore, it is often important to consider marital problems within a larger relationship context—within the family.

In examining marital concerns from this "larger view" (within a family context), Fogarty (1976) stated:

> In the long run there is no such simple matter as "marital crisis." The more one looks at it, the more complicated it gets, and the more people are seen to be involved. There are, so to speak, at least three, and usually more than three, people in a bed. One cannot examine the marriage without investigating the extended family. The relationships that a person has with his father and mother vitally influence the kind of marriage he will have. . . . In some families, marital conflict is thinly masked by the problem showing up in one or more of the children. When a father and mother in such a situation are asked about their relationship, they may state that the child is the problem, and that their marriage is average, normal or fine. The therapist may almost sense from the description that they are being defensive and protective [p. 332].

While we do not go as far as Fogarty proposes in perceiving all marital crises as emanating from the greater family interactions, we do recognize that significant others in a couple's environment can have a tremendous impact upon them. Those significant others in a couple's life tending to influence them most are the family members—their children, their own parents, in-laws, aunts, uncles, grandparents, and others. Further, with the rising divorce and remarriage rate, "blended families" have become increasingly common. Divorced people remarry, and the children from the previous marriages are blended into one family. These blended families result in the creation of new and greater extended families, made up of former spouses, new spouses, assorted grandparents, and other relatives as well as the children and their step-siblings.

These relationships and the additional roles and responsibilities they entail can create stressful circumstances for individual partners and their marital relationship. Therefore, at times it may be necessary to involve family members in the therapeutic process. In this chapter we examine family theory and therapy as another means of understanding and treating marital distress, as well as related family concerns. We begin by examining family theory, discussing the family as a system of interrelationships that passes through a series of developmental phases, some in a functional manner and others dysfunctionally. We next look at the process of family therapy—its goals, roles, relationships, and structure. Our discussion continues with techniques and procedures with which to implement a family-therapist focus and ends with the presentation of a case example.

It should be noted that our primary goal in developing and including this chapter in a book on marital theory and therapy is to provide you with a brief overview of theoretical concepts and therapeutic practices to illustrate the appropriateness, value, and utility of a family approach to therapy. Therefore, we are by necessity selective as to what we present. In our selectivity, we choose not to delineate among the many approaches to family theory and therapy that currently exist, which include not only the psychodynamic, behavioral, and systems orientations, but also Gestalt, Adlerian, rational-emotive, and client-centered therapies, transactional analysis and more. Rather, we focus primarily on a general systems perspective to family theory and therapy emanating from the writings of Haley, Jackson, Minuchin, Satir, Watzlawick, and others. Despite the fact that the perspectives of the latter writers differ, they do have sufficient overlap to be routinely combined under a systems rubric (Foster & Hoier, 1982; Levant, 1980; Stanton, 1980). Further, it is our perception that, as a theoretical perspective and therapeutic modality, family therapy is becoming progressively more synonymous with systems ideas and practices.

Family Theory

The Family System

A family is far more than simply a group of individuals occupying a common physical and psychological space. A family is a system with specific properties unto itself, and one that has developed rules, roles, and ways to communicate, negotiate, and problem solve so that its members can function effectively in the environmental context they share. Our presentation of the marital relationship as a system, as well as the basic concepts emanating from this viewpoint, apply equally to the family, since the couple is a subsystem of the greater family system.

All systems, regardless of their makeup or function, share the same general principles of organization and operation. We discussed a number of basic systems principles in our presentation on the marital relationship as a system, and we review here the basic principles and their relevance to family therapy along with some additional concepts to consider.

One primary principle, wholeness, pertains to the family's organizational structure and is based on the assumption that individual family members' behaviors can be understood only in the context of the family group as a whole. Though individual behaviors are considered, they are viewed as important only in that they represent part of the total system's functioning. Simply stated, in systems terms an individual's or subsystem's functioning cannot be fully understood without comprehension of its relationship to the overall system's functioning. Okun and Rappaport (1980) offered the following as illustrative of how wholeness transcends the sum of the system's component elements:

> Suppose Mr. Brown comes for treatment because he is having difficulties with alcoholism and that he is cured of his alcoholism. This cure may have an impact on every subsystem within his family and on the total family system

itself. For example, the subsystem of Mrs. Brown and her daughter Sally may be affected. Mrs. Brown may have to transfer her anger to Sally, since Mr. Brown will no longer be a feasible target. Sally, in turn, may act more aggressively toward her younger brothers, Johnny and David. David may begin to suck his thumb and whimper because of Sally's aggression, and Mr. Brown himself may express resentment that his family is not behaving appreciatively toward his giving up drinking. All members of the Brown family may change their characteristics, as well as their ways of relating, because of one person's change in behavior [p. 9].

As the example illustrates, the family as a system can be described as nonsummative. That is, the family cannot be fully comprehended by simply summing its subsystems; it includes and is greater than the sum of individual behaviors. In addition, subsystems can be assumed to be organized in a hierarchical manner. In family theory, marriages are conceptualized as comprising two individual subsystems, husband and wife, and in turn being a subsystem of the family system. Similarly, families are subsystems of an extended family system, the community system, and other systems of progressively higher level, called suprasystems. Also, a particular system may be affiliated simultaneously with multiple suprasystems. Therefore, a husband/father for example is a member of both a marital system and a family system, but at the same time he is a member of a community system; of a system of personnel, if he works; and likely of other systems as well (Steinglass, 1978).

Hierarchy within families is also inherent in a family pecking order, manifested by the distribution of power. The power base may be founded on generational differences, external systems (such as the society at large), the history of the particular family system (for example, a matriarchal tradition), or coalitions (such as a joint set of actions by two family members against a third). Hierarchical organization has a strong bearing on the manner in which influence is expressed, and it delineates peers, subordinates, and superiors in the family (Foster & Hoier, 1982).

The idea that the family system can reach the same final state from different initial conditions and in different ways is the principle of equifinality. Equifinality is most obvious as it relates to family rules. Jackson (1965) proposed that the family is a rule-governed system; its members behave in an organized, repetitive pattern of interactions with one another. Rules may be overt ("If you make breakfast, I'll get the kids ready for school") or covert (as when a father is the disciplinarian, and the mother is known as the soft touch). Daily living tasks typically operate by overt rules, but covert rules tend to dominate the psychological interaction between family members. With these rules delineating equifinality in operation, no matter what the situation the resulting dynamics are likely to be the same.

Whereas overt rules are consciously agreed upon, covert rules reflect both conscious and unconscious agreements. According to Jackson

(1965), these rules and not individual needs, drives, or personality traits are what determine family members' behaviors. Goldenberg and Goldenberg (1980) offered an illustrative example. Observe the rules that define the relationship between a wife and husband, who are dressing to go out to dinner with another couple, in this interchange:

Wife: I wish you would dress better. I'd like you to pay more attention to your clothes. Why don't you take your Christmas bonus and buy yourself a new suit?

Husband: I just can't spend the money on myself when you and the children need so many things.

Wife: But we want you to have something, too.

Husband: I just can't put myself first.

Goldenberg and Goldenberg explain the dynamics of the interchange in the following way:

> Notice how, contrary to appearances, the one-down behavior of the husband (whereby he humbly places his needs "one down" from those of the rest of the family) is quite controlling. What sort of relationship have they worked out? The wife is allowed to complain about her husband's appearance, but he retains control over the family's expenditure of money. He apparently does not intend to follow her suggestions, and, moreover, cannot be faulted because he is the good person sacrificing for his family (and probably making them feel guilty). This couple, caught up in a repetitive exchange that defines and redefines the nature of their relationship, in fact executes no action and eliminates the possibility of finding new solutions to their differences [p. 30–31].

Thus, understanding a family's rules allows one to more clearly comprehend functional and dysfunctional behavior patterns. The principle of equifinality suggests that it may be necessary to change these rules before any change in behavior will occur.

Based on the rules that guide interactions within a family system, another major systems principle, homeostasis, posits that the family system will seek to maintain itself in a steady state. Homeostasis is a self-regulation mechanism; it is the tendency to maintain behavior within certain limits or norms. According to Jackson (1965), deviation from the acceptable range of implicit family norms is a form of feedback to family members, who in turn interact with the deviating family member in ways that reestablish the homeostatic balance. By this means, "feedback loops" limit family interaction to typical sequences, which continue "as a matter of mutual accommodation and functional effectiveness" (Minuchin, 1974, p. 52). In a sense, therefore, family members behave as they do because their behavior serves some function within the family context and because negative consequences will accrue from behaving in a significantly different manner.

The homeostatic property of systems is especially important with respect to stress. The family defines limits as to how much stress it will tolerate. If a change in the system raises the level of stress beyond these acceptable limits, a homeostatic mechanism is employed to lower the stress.

When the tension or stress builds in a family system, particularly over an extended period of time, symptoms may be exhibited by one or several members. For instance, as tensions build between a father and mother the two may begin to argue over one of their children as a means of reducing the stress between the parents. By arguing over or being angry at the child, the couple can reduce the tension to an acceptable level. The therapist may need to block homeostatic mechanisms such as this until the family can tolerate a higher level of tension.

The principles of wholeness, hierarchical organization, equifinality, and homeostasis enable us to understand behavior based upon a family's interaction patterns. Before proceeding to the application of systems principles to family therapy, however, it must be pointed out that family interaction patterns evolve, over time, within the system. This evolutionary process is shaped by the developmental life cycle of the family.

The Family Life Cycle

Much like the individual and marital development life cycles described in Chapter 1, families too can be viewed as going through a developmental process. Each family has its own unique and peculiar rhythms and tempos, hazards and rewards, harmonies and dissonances; but by and large it is useful to adopt a longitudinal frame of reference in looking at families (Duvall, 1977). Haley (1973) proposed that family dysfunction results when there is a dislocation or interruption in the naturally unfolding family life cycle. Haley suggested that one or more family members exhibit psychiatric symptoms (for example, depression or anxiety) when such disruption occurs, signaling that the family is having difficulty mastering the tasks inherent in that stage of the life cycle.

An illustration of this symptomatic behavior was offered by Goldenberg and Goldenberg (1980):

> For example, a woman who suffers a postpartum depression following the birth of a child is commonly thought to be undergoing some intense, personal, intrapsychic conflict, possibly involving guilt and hostility turned in upon herself. The family view, on the other hand, is that the entire family is having difficulty dealing with this new phase in its development brought about by the introduction of a new member. The signs of that family disturbance may be most obvious in the mother in this case, but a closer look would reveal a number of role shifts and realignments in the family brought about by the baby's birth [p. 14].

Duvall (1977) has postulated eight typical stages through which intact families pass during the normal cycle of their development. This model has evolved over the last three decades and is the most often cited general family-life-cycle conceptualization in the literature. Figure 10-1 presents a capsule view of the Duvall model and its eight stages, pointing up the length of time spent in each stage; the duration of each stage has implications for housing, health care, home management, recreation, education, and numerous other family responsibilities and resources. Note particularly that for more than half of the family life cycle a couple is alone (before children are conceived and after they have grown and left home).

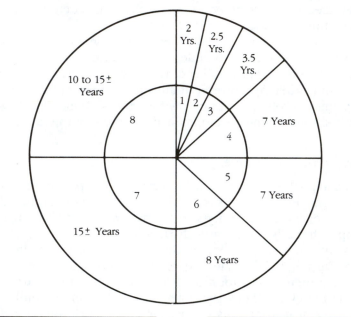

1. Married Couples (Without children).	5. Families with Teenagers (Oldest child 13–20 years).
2. Childbearing Families (Oldest child, birth–30 months).	6. Families Launching Young Adults (First child gone to last child leaving home).
3. Families with Preschool Children (Oldest child 30 months–6 years).	7. Middle-aged Parents (Empty nest to retirement).
4. Families with Schoolchildren (Oldest child 6–13 years).	8. Aging Family Members (Retirement to death of both spouses).

FIGURE 10-1.   The family life cycle by length of time in each of eight stages. Based upon data from the U.S. Bureau of the Census and from the National Center for Health Statistics, Washington, D.C. (*From* Marriage and Family Development, *5th edition, by Evelyn Millis Duvall. Copyright © 1957, 1962, 1967, 1971, 1977 by J. B. Lippincott Company. By permission of Harper & Row, Publishers, Inc.*)

Although as individuals we can each pass through life only once, it is possible to experience family life stages more than once. A family member may encounter one or more life stages, then leave that family and enter into another family relationship at the beginning or at a different level. Just as with individual- and marital-life-cycle stages, at each stage of the family life cycle families encounter critical transition points. Characteristic concerns and necessary learning tasks can be anticipated at each, and these experiences can be either successful or unsuccessful. How the tasks are dealt with is crucial to current functioning as well as future development. Table 10-1 presents Duvall's (1977) stages of the typical family's life cycle once more, in the framework of the developmental tasks that require mastery at each stage.

As developmental stages evolve, the family system needs to adapt and change. Changes may occur in terms of homeostatic shifts, subsystems expanding or contracting, and rule adjustments to accommodate the demands of a new stage. When these changes do not occur and a family does not accommodate the demands of developmental crises (or situational crises such as illness, a move to a new location, or the death of a family member), there may be a breakdown in the family's ability to cope with the stresses and tensions these events produce. For some families, these crises provide an opportunity to gain new understandings and skills. The family that learns to respond adaptively to a crisis situation emerges from it better able to cope with similar situations in the future. By contrast, the family that fails to gain the awareness and means necessary to react to a crisis in a functional manner may respond in a dysfunctional way and continue to do so in the future, manifesting one or more dysfunctional family behaviors.

Dysfunctional Family Behaviors

In a family that does not have effective ways of adapting to crises confronting it, symptomatic behavior or problems are typically manifested in one or more of its members in an attempt to adapt. We examine three common manifestations of dysfunctional behavior within a family: pathological communications, unclear boundaries, and scapegoating.

Pathological Communications.   For a family to function effectively, it must establish and maintain clear communication channels. Communication involves the sending and receiving of verbal and nonverbal messages. *Clear communications* implies the sending and receiving of clear, understandable messages among family members. In contrast, making assumptions, overgeneralizing, speaking in abstractions, and relying on connotations characterize unclear communication. When family communication patterns are unclear they breed dysfunction, which is usually manifested in symptoms in one or more members. The symptom bearer is,

TABLE 10-1   Stage-Critical Family-Developmental Tasks through the Family Life Cycle

Stage of the Family Life Cycle	*Positions in the Family*	*Stage-Critical Family Developmental Tasks*
1. Married couple	Wife Husband	Establish a mutually satisfying marriage Adjusting to pregnancy and the promise of parenthood Fitting into the kin network
2. Childbearing	Wife-mother Husband-father Infant daughter or son or both	Having, adjusting to, and encouraging the development of infants Establishing a satisfying home for both parents and infant(s)
3. Preschool age	Wife-mother Husband-father Daughter-sister Son-brother	Adapting to the critical needs and interests of preschool children in stimulating, growth-promoting ways Coping with energy depletion and lack of privacy as parents
4. School age	Wife-mother Husband-father Daughter-sister Son-brother	Fitting into the community of school-age families in constructive ways Encouraging children's educational achievement
5. Teenage	Wife-mother Husband-father Daughter-sister Son-brother	Balancing freedom with responsibility as teenagers mature and emancipate themselves Establishing postparental interests and careers as growing parents
6. Launching center	Wife-mother-grandmother Husband-father-grandfather Daughter-sister-aunt Son-brother-uncle	Releasing young adults into work, military service, college, marriage, etc., with appropriate rituals and assistance Maintaining a supportive home base
7. Middle-aged parents	Wife-mother-grandmother Husband-father-grandfather	Rebuilding the marriage relationship Maintaining kin ties with older and younger generations
8. Aging family members	Widow/widower Wife-mother-grandmother Husband-father-grandfather	Coping with bereavement and living alone Closing the family home or adapting it to aging Adjusting to retirement

Note: From Marriage and Family Development, *5th edition, by Evelyn Millis Duvall. Copyright © 1957, 1962, 1967, 1971, 1977 by J. B. Lippincott Company. By permission of Harper & Row, Publishers, Inc.*

in effect, being victimized by the poor communication methods of the entire family. In terms of homeostasis, the imbalance caused by stressful circumstances is righted at the expense of one of the family members. The individual's symptoms serve the purpose of restoring balance in the system. This victimization may not be purposefully or consciously pursued, but the sequence and results are typically predictable (Walsh, 1980). The process is illustrated in Figure 10-2.

Satir (1972) proposed that a family's communications can be either congruent or incongruent. Congruent communications lead to family harmony while incongruent communications result in dysfunction. *Congruent* in Satir's terms means direct, and stemming from current physical, intellectual, and emotional awareness on the part of each member in the family. Family dysfunction occurs when communications are not congruent. Dysfunctional families display little direct, realistic communication. Instead, they assign individual members characteristic stances, and particularly in crisis situations the members communicate from these stances more than from considered awareness. Satir (1972) identified four dysfunctional communication stances family members might adopt under stress:

1. *Placate*. Always agree, apologize, or give in to keep others from getting angry.
2. *Blame*. Dominate, accuse, or find fault, to put others on the defensive.
3. *Compute*. Remain detached, extremely reasonable, and calm so as to convey that the stressful situation is really harmless.
4. *Distract*. Act unaware and not involved so as to ignore the situation, behaving as though it were not there.

Each of these stances and various combinations of them can exist in dysfunctionally behaving families. Consider the following examples. A

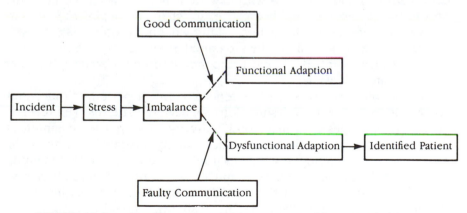

FIGURE 10-2.   Family communication patterns. (*From M. Walsh in* A Primer in Family Therapy, *1980. Courtesy of Charles C. Thomas, Publisher, Springfield, Ill.*)

blaming husband ("Why haven't you got dinner on the table?") and placating wife ("I was late getting home from work, but I'll make sure it doesn't happen again") complement each other neatly. In a blaming child, blaming wife, and computing husband triad, the child might complain strongly, "You two never let me do anything"; the wife might respond "Shut up and do what you're told," while the husband calmly and very reasonably interjects "Children that age are bound to be rebellious. It's part of being an adolescent." In neither example is anything really done to deal with the problem. These dysfunctional stances cannot be played out alone but must be used in interactions with others in order to reduce family tensions. For instance, a blamer needs a placater in order for the interaction to reduce stress.

In the Chapter 5 discussion of Haley's problem-solving therapy, it was described how individuals communicate on two levels. When a message sent is not congruent at both levels, a dysfunctional interactional pattern is created. Directly related to this conceptualization is the notion of another form of pathological communication, which has been termed the double-bind message (Bateson, Jackson, Haley, & Weakland, 1956). A double-bind message involves at least two people. It occurs when one person issues a statement to another that contains at least two messages or demands, one of which contradicts the other. The person receiving the messages is called to make a response but is doomed to failure whichever response he or she makes. On one hand, the receiver is getting a positive message from the sender. For example, a husband might actively seek to have sex with his wife. On the other hand, the receiver is also getting a contrary message—one that negates the positive one. The husband may have an intense fear of impotency that causes him to be highly anxious. Whenever the wife does respond to his initial positive message, he becomes anxious and begins to withdraw from her. However, he finds the idea of being impotent highly aversive, so when she begins to withdraw he again initiates sexual behaviors, asking what her problem is. The wife is caught in a double-bind; she's damned if she does, damned if she doesn't. And, worst of all, she must respond, for even no overt reply by her communicates a message.

As double-bind messages are repeated over a period of time, they contribute to increasingly dysfunctional behavioral patterns. The receiver of double-bind messages may continually try to search for meaning in double-bind situations and become increasingly frustrated. Or, he or she may finally give up trying, instead developing a general view of communication with the sender as senseless and a waste of time. A third alternative is to withdraw from the situation in order to block the meaningless material; the receiver escapes the situation by shutting out all communication from the sender. In its extreme form, this withdrawal becomes psychotic, extended to a shutting out of all communication from the environment (Walsh, 1980).

Unclear Boundaries. In effectively functioning families, clear boundaries exist between family members. Each family member has an individual feeling of "I-ness" along with a group perception of "we-ness." Each member retains his or her individuality, but not at the expense of losing a feeling of family belongingness. Minuchin (1974) stated in this regard that most families fall somewhere along a continuum between enmeshment (where boundaries are blurred) and disengagement (where boundaries are rigid and communication across subsystems becomes difficult).

Enmeshment refers to an extreme closeness and intensity in family interactions in which members are overdependent and overinvolved in each other's lives. The membership and functions of subsystems within an enmeshed family are so poorly defined that members cannot differentiate who does what when, or how things are to be accomplished. There are few clearly drawn lines of authority and responsibility. Since individual responsibility is discouraged, stress and tension that affects one member is dispersed and eventually affects all of the family members. For example, a father is late coming home from work; the wife calls his office, one child begins to cry, and the other sits very still, anxiously worrying.

In enmeshed families, children may act like parents and parental control may be ineffective. Excessive togetherness leads to an inappropriate lack of privacy as family members intrude on each other's thoughts and feelings, ever alert to signs of distress in one another. Family belongingness dominates all else, at the expense of each member developing a separate sense of self.

Disengagement, on the other hand, refers to an extreme separateness and autonomy resulting in little or no sense of family belongingness. Only minimal interaction occurs between subsystems. Communication is difficult, if not impossible. Family members feel isolated and are forced to function independently. There is little opportunity for the mutual support, shared experiences, and other interdependent aspects of normal family living. In times of stress for an individual family member, the enmeshed family might respond with excessive speed and intensity; the disengaged family might hardly seem to respond at all. Minuchin (1974) offered the following comparison in this regard: the parents in an enmeshed family become enormously upset if a child does not eat dessert; in a disengaged family, the parents feel unconcerned about a child's hatred for school.

In a disengaged family, boundaries are so inappropriately rigid that only an extreme level of individual stress can generate support from family members. Disengaged families tend not to respond even when a response is necessary, since individual members feel isolated from each other. Members of a disengaged family can rarely form functional relationships outside of the family, either, because they have gotten no experience within the family in how to relate.

It is important to remember that all families can be characterized with some degree of enmeshment or disengagement. It is when extreme enmeshment or disengagement develops into a chronic state that family dysfunction is present. Barnard and Corrales (1979) have explained this quite clearly:

> Clarity of boundaries does not mean unavailability; it allows for meaningful communication and movement between one subsystem and another. It also means that the subsystem has the capacity to close ranks temporarily in order to deal with an issue requiring a minimum of interference from other subsystems. For example, father and mother are available to their children for support, education, and play. But when they, as husband and wife, sense the desire for time alone, whether for recreation or for conflict negotiation, they are able to create the social space to perform such a function and to ward off unwarranted demands from the children [p. 30-31].

Scapegoating.   The desire for balance in families is universal. Adaptive, effectively functioning families seek appropriate alternatives when their desires are blocked or frustrated. They are open and creative in devising new strategies for coping with crises they confront. Families exhibiting dysfunctional behaviors have a similar desire for balance but are frustrated in achieving balance because of an inadequate problem-solving repertoire. As a result, they develop inappropriate and dysfunctional means of responding to stressful situations.

One characteristic of a disturbed family is that one individual, the "scapegoat," often carries the disturbance for the entire family. This does not necessarily mean that this scapegoated family member is less competent, adequate, or healthy than other members of the family. It means, simply, that he or she has been cast in the role of bearer of family problems (Bell, 1975). Stress can still throw the system out of balance, but when this happens the mechanism of focusing the stress on the scapegoat restores homeostasis.

An example of scapegoating is parents' displacing their anger and hostility toward each other onto one of their children (the "black sheep of the family"); they may thereby bring about harmony in the marital relationship, although at the expense of the child's emotional development. The child, in turn, may be willing unconsciously or consciously to sacrifice him- or herself to keep the family together. Scapegoated individuals can take on a variety of behaviors, depending on the particular role assigned. Hoffman (1971) has identified common scapegoat roles including "the mascot, the clown, the sadsack, the erratic genius, the black sheep, the wise guy, the saint, the idiot, the fool, the imposter, the malingerer, the booster, the villain, and so forth" (p. 296).

Goldenberg and Goldenberg (1980) caution that it is important to be aware that scapegoating is a mutually caused process, not simply one in which one member is victimized; all members, including the scapegoat, participate in the process. Further, different family members may take on scapegoat roles as family needs change and different crisis situations present themselves. As these mechanisms point up, for family therapy an understanding of systems concepts is critical. (In this case, circular causality, as described in Chapter 1, is the relevant concept.)

Family Therapy

Family therapy has been defined as "a psychotherapeutic technique for explaining and attempting to alleviate the current interlocking emotional problems within a family system by helping its members change the family's dysfunctional transactional patterns together" (Goldenberg & Goldenberg, 1980, p. 133). More simply stated, family therapy is a point of view that regards difficulties and dysfunction as emanating from family interactions rather than from any intrapsychic conflicts within one or more individuals. Individual symptoms are seen as reflections of stress arising within the larger family context. This stress can occur in response to difficulty in negotiating a developmental passage or when nondevelopmental crises occur (Okun & Rappaport, 1980).

A family therapist may initially become involved in working with a distressed marital relationship with a couple that presents only marital problems. However, the broader view may soon be taken that marital difficulties are fundamentally a reflection of a disturbed family system. Change the system—the family's characteristic pattern of interacting— and the marital partners' experiences and subsequent interactional patterns begin to change. Although most family therapists view marital distress from this framework, they might be expected to have different theoretical assumptions about the nature and origin of psychological dysfunction, perceptions of family interaction, and plans for therapeutic intervention. Kramer (1980) has described this situation as "many choices, much confusion." In doing so, he stated:

> The field has advanced and differentiated to the point where "schools" of family therapy can be identified. To do so, it is necessary to sharpen the differences while minimizing the similarities, because all of the family therapies have a common basis in the new paradigm—changing the family relationship system. The various schools have somewhat differing conceptualizations and techniques. Their short-term goals may be different depending on their concept of the best way to bring about change. However, the long-term goal of all the family therapies, simply stated, is symptom reduction and more effective individual and family functioning [p. 138].

We again remind you that this chapter and especially this section is meant to provide only an overview of family therapy and specific assumptions relating to its practice. Numerous approaches to family therapy currently exist, and we are selective in our presentation in order to offer a focused discussion of what we consider to be essential aspects and, thereby, to provide understandable guidelines for thinking about and working with the total family system. Our focus is on the long-term goal Kramer referred to in the preceding quotation. We urge you to consult references listed at the end of this chapter as well as those listed in the original sources themselves to gain a more detailed understanding of the theoretical and therapeutic assumptions advocated by systems as well as other major approaches to family therapy today.

The Goals of Therapy

The goals of family therapy may represent the values and basic beliefs of the therapist to some degree, but more often and to a greater degree the goals reflect norms prevalent in the culture of which the family is a part. Given this assumption, Bell (1975) has identified the goals of family therapy as encompassing a twofold process of (1) release, and (2) discipline. Release is the freeing of respective family members from any inhibitions they have about expressing feelings, wishes, ideals, goals, and values. Discipline refers to the development of new forms of expression that channel the spontaneous activities facilitated through release. The development of new expressive patterns allows activities that are helpful to the family's purposes to be perpetuated and activities that are destructive to be blocked.

Glick and Kessler's (1974) three broad goals for the family therapist reflect an emphasis on release and discipline similar to Bell's. Glick and Kessler proposed that the therapist attend to: (1) facilitating the communication of thoughts and feelings between family members, (2) shifting disturbed, inflexible roles and coalitions, and (3) serving as a role model and educator, teaching by example how to best resolve conflicts and concerns.

A more pragmatic distinction regarding the goals of family was made by the Group for the Advancement of Psychiatry (1970). They identified immediate, short-term, and overall long-term goals. Immediate goals are related to the family both as a system in its own right and as a context for the behaviors and experiences of its individual members. For example, first the therapist must attempt to discover whether and how the presenting problem is related to the family system; that is, the therapist must learn how family members and possibly other people are emotionally and behaviorally involved with each other. Second, the therapist must assess who the participants in family-therapy efforts might be.

Short-term goals vary over the course of therapy and are related to the therapist's technique. For example, a short-term goal of many family therapists, accomplished through active, directive interventions, is to show family members ways in which they communicate with each other, resolve differences, solve problems, or react to family crises. Another short-term goal might be to arouse an interest in continued participation in therapy, especially if particular family members came compliantly, or allegedly only for the sake of the symptom bearer.

Unlike immediate and short-term goals, overall, long-term goals generally evolve from the family therapist's basic therapeutic approach—the "school" with which he or she identifies. Some therapists let these goals emerge during the treatment process, so that the goals are a result of what happens in therapy. Other therapists have quite specific long-term goals from the start and begin working toward these goals immediately. Therapists of the latter grouping are apt to pursue some major goal with all families regardless of the presenting problem. Table 10-2 reflects this variation in goal-setting strategy, presenting the results of a survey of family therapists asked to indicate their primary goal from among eight classes of possible goals.

The Role of the Therapist

Robinson (1975) described the role of the therapist as helping a family as a unit to isolate and change those behavior patterns that support the appearance of symptoms in family members. Zuk (1971) described it as attempting to "shift the balance of pathogenic relating among family members so that new forms of relating become possible" (p. 213). These views convey an action-oriented role for the therapist. Therapists do need to bring unspoken messages into the open. They need to move people, work to change the ways family members interact, and alter the members' styles of communication.

Family therapy requires an active, directive therapist who encourages more functional interactions among family members. The family approach assumes that a family behaving in a dysfunctional manner has the resources and abilities to do what is necessary to function more adaptively

TABLE 10-2   Primary Goals Stated by Therapist with Families Actually in Treatment (N = 290)

Primary Goals	(a) With All Families %	(b) With Certain Families %	(c) Total %
1. Improved communication	85	5	90
2. Improved autonomy and individuation	56	31	87
3. Improved empathy	56	15	71
4. More flexible leadership	34	32	66
5. Improved role agreement	32	32	64
6. Reduced conflict	23	37	60
7. Individual symptomatic improvement	23	33	56
8. Improved individual task performance	12	38	50

Note: From Group for the Advancement of Psychiatry, Treatment of Families in Conflict. Copyright © 1970 by Jason Aronson. Reprinted by permission.

except for the fact that they are presently blocking themselves from doing so. Through active assertions, the therapist directs family members to interact with one another and thus to enact their normal transactional patterns. In doing so, the therapist gains information about how the family's interactions form a context wherein dysfunction can reside. As a result, the therapist is able to assess those maladaptive means the family utilizes for dealing with stress and tension. He or she can then intervene to: (1) raise the level of tension experienced in the family, so that its homeostatic mechanisms begin to be implemented; (2) block these mechanisms from operating; and (3) introduce new and more functional ways for the family to adapt to the level of tension experienced.

One example of active therapist intervention seizes on the mechanism employed to block anxiety. High levels of tension may be avoided in a family simply by changing topics when anxiety-provoking problems are raised for discussion. To block this homeostatic mechanism, the therapist might work to relabel the problem in terms more acceptable and less anxiety provoking for the family members. He or she might then introduce specific strategies to family members, providing them a means of changing so as to respond more functionally to the new relabeled problem. Finally, the therapist would assign outside-of-session homework tasks to assist the family to generalize their new ways of interacting to their home environment.

The Therapeutic Relationship

The thoughts, feelings, and behaviors of the therapist utilizing a family focus, as in any form of therapeutic focus, are seen as significantly influencing the progress and outcome of therapeutic efforts. However, from a family therapy perspective similar significance is also attributed to the way the therapist is affected by a family's interactions and emotional responses. Kramer (1980) described the reciprocal reactions present in the therapeutic relationship between therapist and family most aptly:

> These reactions bring to mind the classic physics experiment wherein the rising pitch of a violin shatters a goblet when the frequency of the sound vibrations exactly match the corresponding latent resonance of the glass. Families struggle with so many different conflicts that sooner or later their "vibrations" will evoke sympathetic vibrations in the therapist [p. 251].[1]

Family therapy thus offers a broad view of human behavior. The individual who manifests symptoms is seen as a family member whose disturbed behavior is simply an expression of his or her family's disequilibrium. Satir (1967) called this symptom bearer the identified patient and

---

[1] We agree with Kramer that the family can have an effect on the therapist; we also strongly emphasize that the reverse can happen, the therapist's actions provoking related frequencies as they evoke responses in areas of family interaction.

suggests that this individual's symptoms may in reality be a message that he or she is distorting self-growth as a result of trying to alleviate family pain. However, the identified patient does not remain the central focus for long. Rather, his or her problems are presented as an expression of dysfunction relating to the entire family. Individual problems are relabeled as relationship difficulties. Within such a family-therapy framework, the locus of pathology is not the individual but, rather, the individual in context (Minuchin, Rosman, & Baker, 1978).

As with the identified patient, the family therapist works as part of the system, not as an outside healer as in some approaches to the therapeutic process. In doing so, the therapist does not act as the focus of interactions between family members. By giving up the role of outsider, the therapist becomes a participant in the family social system, although remaining cautious not to become entangled in dysfunctional family alliances. As a member of the system, the therapist must be on guard not to adopt the others' beliefs about themselves (for example, that members are persecuted, exploited, or powerless) or the labels for individual family members (for example, denoting hopelessness, stupidity, or selfishness) that they apply (Goldenberg & Goldenberg, 1980).

The encompassing and involved therapeutic relationship (therapist + identified patient + family) sought in family therapy stands in contrast to the more separated and less involved relationship (therapist + identified patient − family) usually observed in traditional therapies. These relationships are illustrated in Figure 10-3.

The Structure of Therapy

Family therapy proceeds in stages, beginning with the therapist's initial contact with a family. Most therapists insist on seeing the entire family, although there are situations in which this either is not feasible (as with a couple whose children are grown and live too far away to partici-

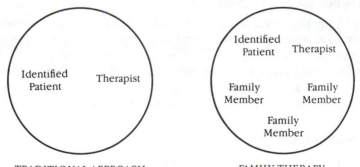

TRADITIONAL APPROACH   FAMILY THERAPY

FIGURE 10-3.   Configurations of people that characterize traditional and family-therapy approaches.

pate) or is impractical (as when children are very young). Some therapists, such as Minuchin (1974), proceed in a preplanned, systematic way. In order to treat a family displaying dysfunctional behaviors, Minuchin has developed an elaborate and well-structured therapeutic process. It has been described as "the most comprehensive expression in the field of family therapy to date" (Walsh, 1980, p. 50). Minuchin's therapeutic structure consists of three major steps:

1. Joining the family in a position of leadership
2. Unearthing and evaluating the underlying family structure
3. Creating circumstances that will allow for the transformation of this structure

In contrast, other family therapists, such as Satir (1982), approach therapy in a more spontaneous and experiential manner; it becomes more an encounter than a function of structure. Bell (1975) described a somewhat intermediate strategy:

> The sequence of these stages is not [so] clearly identifiable that each transition point to a succeeding stage can be identified and marked. In the social process of the therapy, behavior changes often begin with small anticipatory and experimental movements that become firmly established only after tentative exploration and trial confrontation with their consequences. Thus the stages are abstractions of interpersonal processes prevailing during time intervals in the therapy, rather than absolute and to-be-expected stages [p. 394].

As can be seen in the above three perspectives, the structure of family therapy is not a clear-cut matter. There is no consensus on how to proceed through therapy. Rather, each course of therapy reflects the individual therapist's dominant theoretical model within the general field of family therapy.

Implementing a Family-Therapy Focus: Techniques and Procedures

Because family therapy is an approach that regards problems as those of an entire family system, not of one member independently, therapeutic techniques and procedures naturally focus on the family and family interactions rather than individuals and individual behaviors. Before discussing specific interventions however, we consider the place of diagnosis in family therapy and present a general format for evaluating family functioning.

Family Diagnosis

Whether diagnosis is an integral part of treatment planning and goal selection or an irrelevant and counterproductive exercise in labeling left over from the medical model has been extensively discussed (Goldenberg & Goldenberg, 1980). Both views have supporters and detractors among family therapists. Our position is that, although diagnosis of individual family members is likely of little value within this framework, much can be gained by assessing the interactional experiences of the entire family. We agree with Bell (1975) in preferring to observe directly how family members relate to and interact with each other when they are together; according to Bell, diagnosis and treatment are conducted simultaneously throughout the entire therapy process. We find it hard to see how therapy could be conducted otherwise. Some therapists are more formal and structured in their diagnostic procedures, however; for them, diagnosis is an inherent part of establishing goals and planning treatment strategies.

It is important from a family therapy focus that diagnosis be conducted when the entire family or as many members of it as possible are together. Who speaks first? What kinds of messages are being communicated? What roles are assumed when tension is present? Blamer? Placater? Computer? Who appears to have the power and influence in the family? Are disagreements openly acknowledged and discussed or are they minimized or avoided? What is the general quality of the family's interaction: open? loving? hostile? During the course of assessment, general areas of importance to consider include (1) information-processing capabilities, (2) the nature of any stressful circumstances having an impact on the family, (3) the clarity of boundaries within the family, and (4) the present family developmental stage.

Information Processing Capabilities.   One of the most common problem areas for families is that of processing information. The manner in which families process information relates to how members perceive themselves and communicate their perceptions and how they receive like communications from others. Clear perceptions result in family members having an undistorted and realistic picture of what they can expect from others in the family, as well as of what is expected of themselves. Unclear perceptions are reflected in idealized pictures of these relationships or in denial of difficulties. Clear communications are evident when family members are able to express an entire range of feeling messages, both positive and negative (for example, both happiness and hostility), and a variety of content messages. Families exhibiting dysfunctional behaviors often operate with an overly rigid view and resulting strictures on the kinds of messages that can be expressed in the family (as exemplified by one member telling another, "Don't worry about it"). Also, such families often operate with an idealized image of how they should interact with each other (exemplified in the notion "He/she should be the one to discipline the children").

Stressful Circumstances.   Circumstances that affect functioning emanate from the external environment or from occurrences within the family system. Environmental stressors such as financial hardship resulting from inflation or even job loss may add additional stress to a family system that is not prepared to handle it. Likewise, internal family events such as physical illness, death, or divorce can generate tremendous stress within a family as the system seeks to reestablish homeostasis. Whether environmental or internal, these stressors may be reflected in symptoms developing in one or more of the family members.

Clarity of Boundaries.   A valuable initial indicator relating to the clarity of boundaries within the family is often members' willingness to come to therapy. For the members not only to come but to participate willingly suggests openness in the system (although extreme levels of reactions may indicate an enmeshed system). On the other hand, for members to be very reluctant and come only under strong coercion may indicate a disengaged system. An accurate estimation of the chronicity of present clarity of the family boundaries might also be sought in determining the family's amenability to change. Dysfunctional interactions that have been occurring for years are unfortunately chronic family patterns. Obviously, the shorter the time the dysfunctional patterns have been in operation, the better the prognosis for change.

Family Developmental Stage.   A family's developmental stage is determined by identifying the ages of the children and, if the identified patient is a child, his or her birth-order position. Duvall's stages of the family life cycle and the requisite tasks of each stage, as illustrated in Table 10-1, are helpful in determining developmental stressors. After establishing the appropriate developmental stage, the therapist is in a position to generate hypotheses regarding the nature of the family's difficulties. Is a couple having difficulty coping with the fact of being parents as well as spouses, with all of the adjustments required after the birth of the first child? Is a mother finding it difficult seeing her last child leave home to go out on his or her own? These and other possibilities can serve to guide the therapist's questioning and subsequent discussions with the family.

By conducting an assessment and gathering information, the therapist can better understand the functioning of a family system. By accumulating data and integrating it in a coherent picture, the therapist is able to formulate an accurate diagnosis and select one or a combination of interventions. We now examine some of the intervention strategies family therapists utilize.

Intervention Strategies

Family-therapy interventions require the therapist to utilize the transactions between family members, rather than the characteristics or behaviors of individual members, as the primary focus. Even when for one reason or another attention is directed to one individual, his or her behavior is addressed in relation to its power to affect and shape the behaviors of other members of the family system. Therefore, the sampling of techniques discussed intervene directly in a family's interaction. These interventions are reframing the symptom, prescribing the symptom, restructuring the system, and family sculpture.

Reframing the Symptom.   Symptoms accomplish functions in family systems: reframing them can render them unnecessary (Sluzki, 1978). Reframing symptoms devictimizes the identified patient and also helps family members recognize one another's pain. This intervention involves verbally relabeling motivations, intentions, and reasons for behavior so that perceptions of family interaction are altered. Reframing is seen not as an interpretation of behavior but as a strategy for restructuring family members' cognitions, in order to promote change in their interaction patterns (Jackson & Weakland, 1971). Successful reframing lifts a problem out of the symptom framework and into another that "positively connotes" both the symptom of the identified patient and the symptomatic behavior of the other family members, placing them all on the same level and avoiding coalitions of family members directed against each other (Selvini-Palazzoli, Cecchin, Prata, & Boscolo, 1978). For example, the poor motivation a boy's family perceives as the cause of his poor school performance can be reframed by the therapist as extreme exhaustion in school due to the boy's concern about the family's current stress. Although the poor-motivation label is not disqualified by the therapist, the new label addresses the entire system, as opposed to the child alone. This makes it easier to work on a family problem, not just the child's symptom. Such reframing also helps the other family members recognize the child's pain as a result of his desire to see the family function better.

Prescribing the Symptom.   Through prescribing a symptom to a symptomatic family member in the presence of the other members, the therapist can shatter the very pattern that perpetuates the symptom. This effect occurs through two means (Sluzki, 1978). (1) When one family member is told to "fake the symptom and fake it well" the other members are implicitly being told the resulting symptomatic behavior may be false, thereby inhibiting their prior responses that tended to reinforce and perpetuate the symptom. And (2) directing that the symptomatic behavior occur helps develop a consensus regarding the symptom-bearer's control over the symptom. The operation of the consensus in turn decreases his or her claim that the symptom occurs spontaneously. Simultaneously, the therapist's direction evokes its counterpart—that if the symptom can be produced through prescription it can be reduced in the same manner.

Bodin (1981) described a situation wherein symptom prescription was utilized to assist a husband and wife. The wife had been complaining of orgasmic difficulty and of her husband's anxious inquiries of whether she had climaxed. With both partners present, the therapist offered the following prescription:

> What I'm about to ask of you may not seem to make a lot of sense, particularly since you are so eager to make progress with this problem. However, since the problem has persisted for several years, a little bit longer shouldn't be too much of a sacrifice, particularly if it paves the way for progress. (Therapist turns and talks to wife—ostensibly.) Since you are not having an orgasm anyway, I'm going to make a small request of you, namely, that you somehow manage to go on, at least during the coming week, not to have an orgasm, but studying and mentally noting the process as you proceed. If by some mischance, you should happen to feel even the faintest beginnings of what might be an orgasm at any time during this coming week, for goodness sake keep that entirely to yourself no matter how much your husband presses you for details. After all, it's your orgasm, not his [p. 297]![2]

The result of this intervention was to relieve the wife of the anxiety resulting from her husband's emotional pressure. It also undercut the husband's motivation to continue subjecting her to his inquisition. And finally, the wife was thereby encouraged to interpret even the faintest tinglings as signs of success.

Restructuring the System.   In restructuring, a therapist challenges a family's current interactional style. Restructuring is aimed at unbalancing the family system and forcing the family to seek new alternatives and solutions. Minuchin (1974) pursues his therapeutic objectives with families primarily through restructuring, and he has identified a number of techniques in the implementation of this intervention. In general, he attempts to break down dysfunctional barriers and create more functional alliances.

An example of restructuring a family system is based on the commonly understood preference for parents to be closer to each other than to a child. When a therapist observes a parent who is overly involved with a child (that is, enmeshed), it is the therapist's obligation to restructure that family interaction (Blake, 1981). One means of doing so is first to distance the child from the overinvolved parent, then to temporarily transfer some of the child's attention to the therapist. In this way, the child is helped to go toward new relationships instead of being simply pushed out of an old one; the process is thus a more positive learning experience for the child. Figure 10-4 illustrates the steps of such restructuring.

---

[2] From "The Interactional View: Family Therapy Approaches of The Mental Research Institute," by A. M. Bodin. In A. S. Gurman and D. P. Kniskern (Eds.), *Handbook of Family Therapy*. Copyright © 1981 by Brunner/Mazel, Inc., New York. Reprinted by permission.

Family Sculpture.   Family sculpture is an intervention aimed at visually depicting a family's structure as seen through the eyes of family members (Duhl, Kantor, & Duhl, 1973). It facilitates the expression of each family member's experience in a single visual representation (Barnard & Corrales, 1979). To implement the strategy, one family member is asked to imagine the other members as malleable putty and to place them in spatial and postural relationships to one another. The "sculptor" places each family member as he or she views them, spatially representing their distance, their dominance, their clinging, or their need to individuate. The sculptor is asked to represent family members' emotional stances as well, for example touching their lips to create smiles or frowns, dramatically posing a desperate attitude, or highlighting the backs of different members. The sculptor then positions him- or herself in relation to the rest of the family.

Family sculpture may be utilized at any point during the therapeutic process. The request for a family member to sculpt is often made to cut through excessive verbalizations, when a family member sits silently

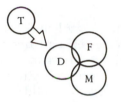

Stage 1.   Therapist enters family system of daugher, father, and mother

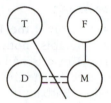

Stage 3.   Therapist blocks actions manifesting parent-child enmeshment

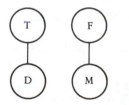

Stage 2.   Therapist joins with daughter

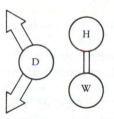

Stage 4.   Father and mother relate as husband and wife; daughter joins with peers and has more autonomy

FIGURE 10-4.   Restructuring involves challenging a family's lifestyle and seeing that it is reworked to be more functional. (*Adapted from M. Blake, "Family Therapy Techniques that Work,"* The School Counselor, *1981, 29, 157–162. Copyright © 1981 American Personnel and Guidance Association. Reprinted by permission.*)

through a session, or in the case of a family member who cannot easily express his or her thoughts verbally (Goldenberg & Goldenberg, 1980). Through reliance on physical communication, many of the intellectualizations and defenses of verbal communication can be circumvented. The actions performed may speak louder than words, frequently revealing to others for the first time what a family has felt but never before directly expressed.

Virginia Satir (1982) reported using family sculpture as a means of having all important parties present in spirit if not in body. The parties may include, in addition to the nuclear family, "the family of origin (grandparents and in-laws), significant others, household help, and even pets. When families are blended, this also includes in a fitting way and at the relevant time, ex-spouses" (p. 13). Family sculptures can be repeated at various times during therapy, to increase family members' recognition of how their perceptions are changing and thus of the therapeutic gains they are making.

A Case Study

This case involves the Howell family. Barbara Howell initiated contact with the therapist noting problems between herself and her husband, Jerry. The Howells had three children: Lynn, age 11; Laura, age 9; and Jerry, Jr., age 6. The therapist suggested that the whole family attend the first session. Barbara thought the request to include the children was odd but readily agreed as it relieved her of the need to find someone to stay with them while the couple met with the therapist.

During the initial meeting with the Howells, the therapist sought information about family interactions so as to begin to formulate some diagnosis.

Therapist (to Barbara): It must be tough at times with three young children.

Barbara: It sure is. They're constantly squabbling with each other, especially Laura and Lynn.

Jerry: Come on, Barbara. They're not that bad.

Therapist: Barbara, would you repeat to Jerry what you just said.

Barbara (with difficulty and looking down at the floor, directing her response to the therapist): He's not around that much. I'm always there and have to be the mediator.

Jerry: That's just how my brothers and I got along as kids. It's nothing. [At this point, Lynn and Laura begin poking at each other and Barbara tells them to behave; in moments they begin again, at which point Barbara goes over to the girls and sits between them. Jerry does nothing.]

In this first session the therapist escalated tension in the system in order to observe how the family reacted. Barbara had difficulty in disagreeing with Jerry, and Jerry pushed aside her concerns about the children's behavior as "nothing." By encouraging disagreement between Barbara and Jerry to surface during the session, the therapist was able to assess how different family members react to stress. Barbara and Jerry's communication with each other was poor, as shown by Barbara's inability to express herself assertively and Jerry's unwillingness to comprehend what Barbara was saying. This inability to communicate increased the distance between them.

When the therapist purposefully escalated tension between the parents, Lynn and Laura's bickering distracted their parents from their potential conflict, "rescuing" them with this inappropriate behavior. It is very likely that the children's bickering was often reinforced by Barbara through increased attention to them, even though the attention was negative. In using the children's interactions as the focus of her attention, Barbara was able to withdraw from potential conflicts with Jerry instead of the two partners directly and more functionally coping with the concerns confronting them. Lynn and Laura too needed to cope better with family concerns. As it was, none of these concerns could ever really be settled.

After observing the family's interactions, the therapist was able to formulate this tentative diagnosis and plan some initial treatment goals. Barbara and Jerry's disengagement and inability to communicate were primary concerns. They needed to form a closer coalition and to learn to send and receive each other's messages. And they especially needed to negotiate agreements that were more mutual. Jerry needed to become more aware and realistic in his parenting stances with the children; he acted less as a parent than as a bystander, leaving the disciplinary responsibilities all to Barbara. Therefore the therapist saw it as valuable to get Barbara and Jerry to act together in setting goals and limits for the children's behavior. This was a focal point through which the therapist felt Jerry and Barbara could begin to communicate and could form a closer coalition, thereby enhancing their marital relationship (as well as helping the children gain greater self-responsibility).

During the second session the therapist reframed the primary purpose of therapy as "working together to help the children," rather than as resolving Jerry and Barbara's marital conflict. At first, in considering the therapist's proposal that it was the children who needed assistance, Jerry took his usual "it's-nothing" stance. The therapist then took a very directive position with Jerry, saying that as an expert in human behavior he had observed similar "nothings" escalate into serious interpersonal deficiencies: "When children have difficulty relating within their early family, with siblings especially, it is often an early indicator of problems that will arise in later life. Many divorcing couples' behavior, for instance, can be traced to a lack of interpersonal-skill development." Although this was a rather extreme statement, it emphasized how responsible Jerry was for his children's future welfare, and how this was an excellent opportunity to "nip any problems in the bud." Jerry seemed somewhat hesitant, but he agreed to contract for a trial period of sessions. Barbara, with typical unwillingness to disagree, let the issues she considered marital to lapse. She did want Jerry's help with the children, anyway.

In reframing the situation as was done, the therapist restructured the family system by creating a natural coalition between Barbara and Jerry. In subsequent sessions, the therapist explained the importance of communicating more clearly with each other if they were to become an effective parenting unit. In doing so, each partner's perspective was considered and negotiations were entered into that resulted in greater mutual decision making in regard to the children's actions and responsibilities. The following dialogue illustrates therapeutic efforts during this period.

Therapist: How have you girls been getting along lately?

[The girls, Lynn and Laura, respond with quiet "OK's"]

Therapist: What have been your experiences with them this week, Jerry?

Jerry: They've been getting along well as I see it, but dinner dishes have been somewhat of a problem. Barbara's been screaming at them every night about the dishes. It's really aggravating for me to have to listen to it.

Barbara: I just can't get them to do the dishes after dinner unless I yell and scream. They play around with Jerry and I end up doing the dishes because it comes time for them to do their homework.

Therapist: Well, what could you two do about this, Barbara and Jerry?

Barbara: I could try not to scream so much so at least Jerry doesn't have to suffer too.

Therapist: Good, and Jerry?

Jerry: I don't know . . . perhaps I could tell the girls to get going on the dishes sometimes . . . .

Therapist: And possibly also that you'll play with them only after the dishes are done.

Barbara (to Jerry): That would be great. I'd appreciate your help a lot.

Jerry: OK.

From the hesitant manner in which Jerry approached this decision, it was apparent that Jerry was treading on new ground. The therapist's and Barbara's praise reinforced his effort, however, and he did follow through on his agreement. He also received additional support in the form of the positive reactions of the girls to his request that they finish the dishes before playing with him, which surprised him. Their reaction encouraged Jerry to support Barbara's requests of the children even more. Later interventions focused on providing the couple with more experiences in negotiating agreements, initially about the children but also concerning more specific couple's issues.

Summary

In this chapter, our focus is on family theory and therapy, particularly as a general intervention strategy that involves the others within a couple's immediate environment in the therapy process. Our examination begins with a look at how general systems and developmental-life-cycle concepts apply to the entire family. We also explore three common manifestations of dysfunctional behavior within a family: pathological communications, unclear boundaries, and scapegoating.

With this theoretical background, we discuss family therapy per se: the goals of therapy, the role of the therapist, the therapeutic relationship, and the structure of the therapeutic process. We then focus on specific techniques and procedures of family therapy. After stressing our belief in the value of family diagnosis, we briefly consider a general format to utilize in assessing family interactions. Subsequently, we describe a sampling of intervention strategies prevalent in the therapeutic repertoires of many family therapists: reframing the symptom, prescribing the symptom, restructuring the system, and family sculpture.

Finally, as a means of providing a clearer perspective on the applicability of family therapy when couples' concerns are the presenting problem, a case study is given. This points up in particular how the family therapist utilizes the transactions between family members, rather than the characteristics or behaviors of individual members, as the primary therapeutic forms.

This section, Chapters 7 through 10, concerns the practice of marital therapy, examining the pragmatic and procedural variables in working with couples. The understandings acquired from this section can be added to those gained from Section Two in the theory of marital therapy. In Section Four, we consider two other areas: the professional skills and knowledge involved in clinical accountability, and some of the major issues in current research in the field of marital theory and therapy.

References

Barnard, C. P., & Corrales, R. G. *The theory and technique of family therapy.* Springfield, Ill.: Charles C. Thomas, 1979.

Bateson, G., Jackson, D., Haley, J., & Weakland, J. Toward a theory of schizophrenia. *Behavioral Science*, 1956, *1*, 251–264.

Bell, J. E. *Family therapy.* New York: Aronson, 1975.

Blake, M. Family therapy techniques that work. *The School Counselor*, 1981, *29*, 157–162.

Bodin, A. M. The interactional view: Family therapy approaches of the Mental Research Institute. In A. S. Gurman & D. P. Kniskern (Eds.), *Handbook of family therapy*. New York: Brunner-Mazel, 1981.

Duhl, F. S., Kantor, D., & Duhl, B. S. Learning, space, and action in family therapy: A primer of sculpture. In D. Bloch (Ed.), *Techniques of family psychotherapy*. New York: Grune & Stratton, 1973.

Duvall, E. M. *Marriage and family development* (5th ed.). New York: Lippincott, 1977.

Fogarty, T. Marital crisis. In P. J. Guerin (Ed.), *Family therapy: Theory and practice*. New York: Gardner Press, 1976.

Foster, S. L., & Hoier, T. S. Behavioral and systems family therapies: A comparison of theoretical assumptions. *American Journal of Family Therapy*, 1982, *10*, 13–23.

Glick, I. D., & Kessler, D. R. *Marital and family therapy*. New York: Grune & Stratton, 1974.

Goldenberg, I., & Goldenberg, H. *Family therapy: An overview*. Monterey, Calif.: Brooks/Cole, 1980.

Group for the Advancement of Psychiatry. *Treatment of families in conflict*. New York: Aronson, 1970.

Haley, J. *Uncommon therapy. The psychiatric techniques of Milton H. Erickson*. New York: Norton, 1973.

Hoffman, L. W. Deviation—amplifying processes in natural groups. In J. Haley (Ed.), *Changing families: A family therapy reader*. New York: Grune & Stratton, 1971.

Jackson, D. D. The study of the family. *Family Process*, 1965, *4*, 1–20.

Jackson, D. D., & Weakland, J. H. Conjoint family therapy: Some considerations on theory, technique, and results. In J. Haley (Ed.), *Changing families: A family therapy reader*. New York: Grune & Stratton, 1971.

Kramer, C. H. *Becoming a family therapist*. New York: Human Sciences Press, 1980.

Levant, R. F. A classification of the field of family therapy: A review of prior attempts and a new paradigmatic model. *American Journal of Family Therapy*, 1980, *8*, 3–16.

Minuchin, S. *Families and family therapy*. Cambridge, Mass.: Harvard University Press, 1974.

Minuchin, S., Rosman, B. L., & Baker, L. *Psychosomatic families: Anorexia nervosa in context*. Cambridge, Mass.: Harvard University Press, 1978.

Okun, B. F., & Rappaport, L. J. *Working with families: An introduction to family therapy*. North Scituate, Mass.: Duxbury Press, 1980.

Robinson, L. R. Basic concepts in family therapy: A differential comparison with individual treatment. *American Journal of Psychiatry*, 1975, *132*, 1045–1054.

Satir, V. *Conjoint family therapy* (rev. ed.). Palo Alto, Calif.: Science and Behavior Books, 1967.

Satir, V. *Peoplemaking*. Palo Alto, Calif.: Science and Behavior Books, 1972.

Satir, V. M. The therapist and family therapy: Process model. In A. M. Horne & M. M. Ohlsen (Eds.), *Family Counseling and Therapy*. Itasca, Ill.: F. E. Peacock, 1982.

Selvini-Palazzoli, M., Cecchin, G., Prata, G., & Boscolo, L. *Paradox and counterparadox: A new model in the therapy of the family in schizophrenic transaction*. New York: Aronson, 1978.

Sluzki, C. E. Marital therapy from a systems theory perspective. In T. J. Paolino, Jr. & B. S. McCrady (Eds.), *Marriage and marital therapy*. New York: Brunner-Mazel, 1978.

Stanton, M. D. Family therapy: Systems approaches. In G. P. Sholevar, R. M. Benson, & B. J. Blinder (Eds.), *Handbook of emotional disorders in children and adolescents: Medical and psychological approaches to treatment.* Jamaica, N.Y.: S. P. Medical and Scientific Books, 1980.

Steinglass, P. The conceptualization of marriage from a systems theory perspective. In T. J. Paolino, Jr. & B. S. McCrady (Eds.), *Marriage and Marital Therapy.* New York: Brunner-Mazel, 1978.

Walsh, W. M. *A primer in family therapy.* Springfield, Ill.: Charles C. Thomas, 1980.

Woodburn, L. T., & Barnhill, L. N. Applying family systems therapy principles to couples counseling. *Personnel and Guidance Journal,* 1977, *55,* 510–514.

Zuk, G. H. Family therapy. In J. Haley (Ed.), *Changing families: A family therapy reader.* New York: Grune & Stratton, 1971.

Clinical Accountability

The field of marital therapy has received recognition as a significant part of the mental-health field. Along with this recognition comes the responsibility to be accountable for the services offered. This section deals with major issues leading to accountability—namely, the training of therapists, ethical behavior, and research.

In Chapter 11 we elaborate on some of the major issues associated with the training of marital therapists. These issues include curriculum, supervision, accreditation and licensure, continuing education, and professional associations. The remainder of the chapter focuses on ethical considerations pertaining to responsibility, confidentiality, client privilege, informed consent, and values.

In Chapter 12, we discuss research; this key element of accountability involves being able to support positive outcomes of marital therapy with a strong systematic research base. Rather than reviewing the multitude of studies that have been conducted in marital therapy, we center our discussion on some of the major issues affecting current research. Practical information is provided regarding the types of marital-therapy research, the general outcomes of marital therapy, some guidelines for clinical research, some guidelines for reading research, and the application of research to practice; also, suggestions are made for future research.

Section Four is perhaps the most important one in this book. The field of marital therapy is at a crucial stage of development in that people are asking for proof that therapy is effective. Both insurance companies and the government are concerned about paying for therapy people have received but for which there is no documentation of benefit. It is vital that therapists and researchers cooperate so that basic questions can be answered.

CHAPTER ELEVEN

Professional and Ethical Issues in Marital Therapy

No presentation of theory and therapy would be complete without discussion of some of the contemporary professional and ethical issues. Although there are a large number of relevant issues, we limit our discussion to those related to training marital therapists and to considerations of an ethical nature. The section on training includes curriculum, supervision, accreditation and licensure, continuing education, and professional associations. The section on ethical considerations focuses on responsibility, confidentiality, client privilege, informed consent, and values.

Training

Marital therapy has developed from individual psychotherapy and marriage education. A demand for marital therapy arose in both the United States and Europe shortly after the end of World War I. People began seeking assistance from professionals rather than relatives and friends in preparing for marriage and also in resolving marital conflicts. According to Nichols (1979), three marital therapy centers were opened in the United States by the early 1930s. A marriage consultation center was operating in New York under the direction of physicians Abraham and Hannah Stone. Two other centers not only provided services but also began training marital therapists. One of these centers was the American Institute of Family Relations in Los Angeles, directed by Paul Popenol, and the other was the Marriage Council of Philadelphia, directed by Emily H. Mudd. These centers in Los Angeles and Philadelphia were prototypes of the early marital therapy training in which self-taught therapists shared what they knew with others in a clinical setting. Most of these students already were trained in one of the established disciplines and sought additional knowledge and skill in marital therapy.

The current method of training marital therapists is not clearly defined. Some therapists are being trained at the post-degree level in institutes or through the American Association for Marriage and Family Therapy's (AAMFT) approved program. However, more therapists are receiving their training through graduate degree programs at colleges and universities. Nichols (1979) conducted a survey that identified doctoral programs at 7 universities and master's degree programs at 24 universities. The major growth in graduate training for many years to come is expected to be in two-year master's degree programs.

Curriculum

The experiences of the early marital therapists and their trial-and-error methods have provided invaluable information about the training of future therapists. There is a natural progression in the training of marital therapists that follows the development of theory in this field, and the progression is based on a tradition of training people first as psychotherapists who can work with individuals. As Leslie (1968) pointed out, "From the beginning, the AAMC [American Association of Marriage Counselors] insisted that marriage counseling is an advanced clinical specialty requiring skills not only in the diagnosis and treatment of individual problems, but in the far more demanding diagnosis and treatment of relationship problems" (p. 74). Harper (1953) too believes that marital therapists must be fully qualified psychotherapists who possess additional, specialized knowledge of the marital relationship. However, in requiring skills for working with individuals before the acquisition of skills for marital therapy, this approach to training is different from some others' in the field. One primary point of disagreement between Leslie's and Harper's approach (and our own) and some others' is whether graduates with master's and doctoral degrees would be viewed as having the preparation needed to begin working under supervision or as having a sanction to begin independent practice.

It is a difficult task, if not an impossible one, to design a program that includes all the training that a therapist might need. Restrictions such as the number of credit hours that are reasonable to expect a student to take are a major concern. Therefore, some decisions have to be made as to what to include or omit. In most training programs, the decisions are to balance the experiential and didactic learning modes; emphasize marital strengths rather than the medical model of illness; and prepare marital therapists with a broad base of knowledge and skills, in order to meet couples' developmental as well as crisis concerns.

Debate over what courses to include in a curriculum could continue at some length, but a definite program of study must be selected for each training program. The AAMFT-approved course of study includes the following six areas:

- *Human Development* (9 semester hours minimum). Courses in this area include developmental studies, personality theory, human sexuality, behavior dysfunction/psychopathology, and general concepts and principles in the psychotherapies. The purpose of this section is to assist therapists-in-training to gain an understanding of the normal and abnormal development of individual personality and models of individual psychotherapy.
- *Marital and Family Studies* (9 semester hours minimum). Courses in this area include the study of marital and family development, marital and family interaction, and communication theory and systems theory.
- *Marital and Family Therapy* (9 semester hours minimum). Therapists-in-training are expected to enroll in courses that give an understanding of couple therapies, structural family therapy (emphasizing the overriding dynamic structure within a family system), and transgenerational family therapy.
- *Professional Studies* (3 semester hours minimum). A course should be taken that covers the following topics: ethics, professional organization, family law/legislation, and independent practice/agency practice.
- *Supervised Clinical Work* (9 semester hours minimum). Therapists-in-training should be required to do individual, marital, and family therapy under clinical supervision.
- *Research Methodology* (6 semester hours minimum). Courses in research design, methods and instruments, statistics, and research in marital and family studies or marital and family therapy meet this requirement.

Supervision

After students are trained in the academic areas they need to study in order to become marital therapists, they are allowed to put theory and techniques into practice under very close supervision. The primary objective of clinical supervision is the skill development of marital therapists—providing marital therapists an opportunity to intervene more efficiently and effectively to assist couples achieve therapeutic goals. The focus is on the pragmatic issues of the therapist-couple relationship, such as how to be flexible and yet consistent when special concerns arise, couple dynamics and their impact on the current therapeutic flow, and transference-countertransference issues.

Clinical supervision is typically performed on an individual (one-to-one) or small-group (three to five members per group) basis. The group modality allows for the addition of peer interactions between therapists as well as supervision in a group learning milieu. Whether supervision is of an individual or group, the most common methods used are case review and analysis; utilizing the therapist's process notes, audio tapes, or video-tapes of sessions; direct or indirect observation of therapy through a one-way mirror; co-therapy in which the supervisor and therapist work together with a couple; and on-the-spot supervision in which a supervisor stays in direct communication with the therapist during the therapy session by earphone or telephone from behind a one-way mirror.

Supervision sessions are best scheduled regularly. Trouble-shooting supervisory sessions held on the run are sometimes necessary when crises arise; however, they don't offer a consistent and coordinated critiquing experience. Refinement and growth as well as effective crisis consultation are best achieved through ongoing supervision conferences. For example, should a crisis arise with a couple a therapist has discussed with his or her supervisor previously, the supervisor has an understanding and background from which to respond immediately. In addition, when supervisory sessions are a regular, ongoing process, the concerns a couple in therapy is likely to have can be anticipated and prepared for.

For purposes of supervision, marital therapists can be categorized in three distinct types, based on their levels of experience and expertise: beginning therapists, experienced therapists, and mature therapists.

Beginning marital therapists often have relatively narrow and rigid notions of the most appropriate manner of intervening when partners display especially difficult problem behavior. This is usually due to their inexperience. For example, a novice marital therapist may have the idea that confronting these problematic behaviors is the best intervention. However valid or invalid this assumption may be with a particular partner, a supervisor's familiarity with a variety of alternatives can give the beginning therapist a greater appreciation for the actual diversity of available interventions. In addition, natural therapeutic assets such as humor, vivid imagery, or interpersonal warmth and assertiveness can be modeled by the supervisor. This can aid the beginning marital therapist in appreciating the proper use of personal characteristics—in use of the self—in employing intervention strategies. It can also assist new therapists with the inevitable doubts about their suitability for clinical work, by reassuring them that they have within their own behavioral repertoires inherent therapeutic resources and qualities.

Experienced marital therapists have fairly well formulated, flexible sets of intervention strategies to deal with difficult partner behaviors that may arise during therapy. These therapists have likely encountered a number of difficult couples, overcome most of the anxiety that arises about intervening, and have gained a sense of confidence and responsibility. Supervision with the experienced marital therapist involves identifying and overcoming areas of clinical concern. The supervisor-therapist tasks are somewhat different for the experienced therapist than they were for the novice therapist; they involve sharpening, enhancing, and integrating the skills the therapist already possesses. Goals are much more specific. Also, the supervisor functions more as a consultant than as an educator. In doing so, the supervisor focuses on facilitating the therapist's use and refinement of skills and maturity.

Mature marital therapists are highly functioning clinicians; many probably fill supervisory roles themselves. Therefore, the process of clinical supervision with a mature therapist involves a rather open-ended relationship, with the supervisor and therapist functioning as co-equals. The supervisor serves as an ally, co-resource-person, and a peer who is able to share ideas and information on his or her own manner of responding to problematic partner behaviors. This is a creative and stimulating relationship for both parties, with particular potential for growth and enhancement of skills.

Kadushin (1973) pointed out a number of positive sources of satisfaction that can be derived from all levels of clinical supervision:

- A resource person is available to discuss client behavior.
- Critical feedback is provided.
- Clinical responsibilities can be shared.
- Discussion of the theory and practice of therapy is stimulated.
- Emotional support is made available.
- Professional development is enhanced.
- A forum for personal growth is provided.

Accreditation and Licensure

Accreditation and licensure are among the highest priorities of the marital therapy profession. The quality of training in marital therapy is regulated mainly by AAMFT through its Committee on Accreditation. The only purpose of this committee is the accreditation of graduate programs and post-degree training centers in marital and family therapy. In 1978 the Committee on Accreditation was recognized by the U.S. Office of Education of the Department of Health, Education and Welfare as the official body for accrediting educational and training programs in the field of marital and family therapy (Smith & Nichols, 1979). The *Manual of Accreditation* (AAMFT, 1977) contains not only a statement of training standards but also the procedures to be used by on-site visiting teams. At the time of this writing, there are ten accredited graduate programs and five accredited post-degree training centers (see Appendix A). Identifying quality accredited programs is essential for prospective students as they plan where they will receive their training in marital therapy.

Accreditation also plays a very important role in licensure, which is to protect the public from incompetent therapists. A regulatory board can determine whether individuals are competent to practice marital therapy much more easily when they have been trained at an accredited university graduate program or post-degree training center. Licensure is extremely important because of the whole issue of who can legally practice. Without requiring a license to practice, a state can neither control who will practice nor remove those therapists who violate the code of ethics under which they are permitted to practice. At present five states have passed licensure legislation: California (1963), Georgia (1976), New Jersey (1969), Utah (1973), and Virginia (1978). Three other states legally regulate marital therapy through certification: Michigan (1966), Nevada (1973), and North Carolina (1976). According to Nichols (1974), certification relates to the restriction of the use of a title, while licensure restricts a therapist's function. Licensure tends to be the more restrictive means of control, and it usually includes protection of title usage as well as function.

Specific requirements for licensure or certification can be obtained by contacting the responsible agency in each state. Some people who conduct marital therapy are exempted from licensure and certification as long as they perform this therapy in affiliation with a nonprofit community agency, governmental or other research program, or academic program. Also exempted are members of the clergy, attorneys, and physicians, provided they offer this service as part of a normal work load in their primary professions.

Continuing Education

Every marital therapist needs to develop a program of continuing education. Earning advanced degrees or licensure is only minimal assurance that an individual possesses the needed skills and knowledge; continuing education is a must to keep current with new knowledge in the field. Most professional organizations support efforts to make continuing education a mandatory condition for relicensing. In some cases it is still possible for some therapists to stop taking courses and seminars, or to stop receiving supervision; however, the ethics of the therapists who fail to keep current with new developments are highly questionable. Probably the best approach to continuing education is one allowing each therapist to develop individually the program of workshops, professional conferences, supervision, and other activities that is most useful. This personalized approach to continuing education would be much more meaningful than the meeting of requirements dictated by state regulatory boards to complete a designated number of hours in a specific area.

Professional Associations

Every marital therapist should be active in professional associations. Three of the best known are AAMFT, AFTA, and AASECT.

The American Association for Marriage and Family Therapy (AAMFT) is the largest organization for marital therapists, with more than 7000 members. Most of the members are master's level therapists from such diverse fields as psychology, psychiatry, social work, ministry, medicine, sociology, law, and education. All members must possess relevant academic training and supervised professional experience (see Appendix B). More information can be obtained by writing to AAMFT at the following address:

American Association for Marriage
and Family Therapy
1717 K Street NW, Suite 407
Washington, D.C. 20006

The American Family Therapy Association (AFTA) is the newest professional association in marriage and family therapy. There appear to be two major differences between AFTA and AAMFT. First, AFTA believes that marital therapy and family therapy are two distinct areas, and individuals trained in one specialty are not necessarily competent in the other. The second difference is that AFTA is oriented to the psychodynamic approach to therapy while AAMFT is oriented to systems theory and research. For more information about AFTA, write to:

American Family Therapy Association
30 Lincoln Street
Newton Highlands, MA 02161

The American Association of Sex Educators, Counselors, and Therapists (AASECT) has developed a certification program requiring academic training, supervised professional experience, and clinical experience. AASECT began its certification in 1974 and is still in the process of making decisions about some of the major issues, such as the nature of training and ethical standards. Write to AASECT for more information at:

American Association of Sex Educators,
Counselors, and Therapists
600 Maryland Avenue SW
Washington, D.C. 20024

It is important to note that such organizations as the American Personnel and Guidance Association (APGA), the American Psychological Association (APA), and the National Association of Social Workers (NASW) have many members involved in marital therapy; yet at present they do not have special divisions pertaining to the area. If these organizations are to continue to meet the needs of a substantial number of their members, divisions for marital and family therapy will have to be formed.

Ethical Considerations in Marital Therapy

Various professional associations involved with counseling, therapy, and other psychological services have established codes of ethics that provide guidelines for practitioners (see Appendixes C, D, and E). The guidelines offered by most associations, however, are minimal standards of ethical conduct. Each therapist must develop a personal code of ethics that goes beyond the codes of professional associations. It is important to note that marital therapists will be confronted with some situations that are quite different from those confronted by professionals in individual therapy. Margolin (1982) listed some ethical issues that confront a marital therapist in special ways, including responsibility, confidentiality, client privilege, informed consent, and therapist values. The remainder of this chapter is devoted to these ethical issues.

Responsibility

Most professional associations state that a therapist's primary responsibility is to the client. In marital therapy, the complication entailed is that the therapist is frequently involved in situations where helping one spouse might be harmful to the other. For example, a husband might want to become more socially active and attend community functions while the wife wants to continue to stay within the secure confines of her home. Or a couple may be in agreement on a goal to be achieved but in conflict over how to achieve the desired goal. The marital therapist must guard against the improvement for one spouse being achieved at the expense of the other. Some professionals use the systems approach to marital therapy because it allows them to identify the relationship, rather than the individuals involved as the client. Using this method, the therapist can help the relationship while, by focusing intervention on mutual benefit, minimizing favoritism to either spouse.

Although identifying the relationship as the client works well much of the time, there can still be problems involving conflicts of interest. The spouses are unlikely to receive equal benefit from therapy, and in most instances each spouse wants the other one to change as a way of improving the relationship; so even though the relationship may improve, one or both spouses might feel unhappy about the changes they had to make.

A situation that is very difficult for marital therapists is when one spouse wants to terminate the relationship and the other wants to keep the marriage together. What is best for the clients in this case? There is no way marital therapy can be successful when one spouse refuses to work on improving the relationship. Frequently what happens is that the therapist begins seeing each spouse individually or refers them to someone specializing in individual therapy. Each person then has an opportunity to resolve his or her own internal conflicts.

There are also some legal guidelines to follow in situations when the welfare of an individual takes precedence over the relationship. An example is when the therapist knows of or suspects spouse abuse. The primary objective for the therapist is to reduce the chance of physical harm. According to Margolin (1979), if this cannot be accomplished as part of the marital therapy, then it is the therapist's responsibility to help the threatened person find protection. The law is very clear in the situation when the therapist suspects that a spouse is abusing a child. The therapist is required to inform the authorities despite the possible consequences this action may have on the marital therapy. In general terms, a marital therapist's responsibilities involve balancing the needs of each individual and the needs of the marital relationship.

Confidentiality

Probably the most agreed upon tenet in therapist codes of ethics is that requiring confidentiality. Basically, *maintaining confidentiality* implies that the therapist has the responsibility not to divulge information obtained in a therapy session. However, when there is clear and imminent danger to the client or others, or when a specific requirement of the law takes precedence, the therapist may reveal information gained during a therapy session. The final decision to divulge confidential information and the consequences of this action rest with the therapist.

The marital therapist has some special considerations in the area of confidentiality that are not shared by colleagues involved in individual therapy. In work with two people, a decision has to be reached as to what degree of confidentiality, if any, should be maintained between the therapist and each partner individually. Some therapists elect not to keep any information given by one partner from the other person. This approach greatly discourages each spouse from sharing any information that might lead to a special relationship with the therapist and also exclude the other spouse. A therapist using this therapeutic approach will almost always conduct joint rather than individual sessions.

Another approach to confidentiality in marital therapy involves holding information obtained from each individual in absolute confidence. A therapist using this approach normally conducts many individual sessions with each spouse in order to obtain information that might not be presented in joint sessions. If the therapist believes that information given individually is essential to the resolution of marital problems, the spouse with the relevant information is encouraged to present it during a joint session.

A compromise between these two extremes of confidentiality is obtained when therapists indicate to their clients that, in general, confidentiality is not promised for either partner's information with regard to the other partner, although either client has the right to request that any particular information be kept confidential. It is important to note that, even though confidentiality is not promised, the therapist may choose to withhold some information. By this arrangement it is a matter of the therapist's discretion to divulge information from one partner to the other unless a specific requirement of the law takes precedence.

The most important consideration with regard to confidentiality is that clients be informed of the therapist's policy. Therapists who will not keep from one partner information given by the other must inform clients before any such information has been received. Clients should not be left to make assumptions, which may be erroneous. This is especially relevant when one or both spouses have previous experience in therapy that may have involved a different stand on confidentiality.

To some degree the therapist's position on confidentiality dictates how the marital therapy is conducted. That is, on one hand therapists who maintain the confidentiality of both spouses individually will probably have more information available to them but be severely limited in its use in joint sessions. On the other hand, therapists who do not grant confidentiality will probably not receive information that may be essential. The bottom line in how the issue of confidentiality should be handled is that a therapist must determine a policy that is compatible with his or her approach to conducting therapy, and this policy must be explained to the couple.

Client Privilege

The granting of privileged communication permits the therapist to refuse to reveal information learned during therapy sessions. It is important to note that the client is the holder of the privileged communication and therefore is the one who has responsibility for determining when this privilege is waived. This can be a very confusing issue for the marital therapist who works with more than one client at once. Does husband or wife hold the communication privilege, or do both? A few actual cases can help demonstrate the importance of this point.

Sugarman (1974) reported a situation in which a couple who had been seen by a marital therapist decided to divorce. The husband's lawyer subpoenaed the psychologist who conducted the therapy to testify about statements made in joint therapy sessions. The psychologist refused to testify because the wife would not waive her right to privileged communication. The state where this incident took place (New Jersey) did not have laws that protect the psychologist-client communication privilege. However, the judge ruled to protect the wife's privilege based on that state's laws for marriage counselors. According to Herrington (1979), a judge in Virginia gave a different interpretation in a similar situation in which a psychiatrist was the marital therapist. The judge ruled that the communication was not privileged because the statements were made in the presence of the spouse and not in private to the psychiatrist.

As these two examples demonstrate, guidelines for privileged communication in marital therapy are sketchy at best. The privileged-communication tenet covers only information stated in confidence, and therefore the impact of having the other spouse present is unclear. Marital therapists should certainly seek clarification of the legislation on client privilege in their states. The therapist should also make sure a couple beginning therapy is aware of the legal status of this issue, and he or she may wish to obtain a written agreement stating that neither partner will subpoena the therapist in the case of litigation at a later date.

Informed Consent

Standards for informed consent are not only necessary but highly desirable; clients deserve to have accurate information about therapy before a commitment is made. Basically, obtaining clients' informed consent implies they have made a conscious decision based on accurate information to participate in therapy. Margolin (1982) listed several types of information that should be discussed with clients before therapy begins:

- An explanation of the procedures and their purpose.
- The role of the person who is providing therapy and his or her professional qualifications.
- Discomforts or risks reasonably to be expected.
- Benefits reasonably to be expected.
- Alternatives to treatment that might be of similar benefit.
- A statement that any questions about the procedures used will be answered at any time.
- A statement that the person can withdraw his or her consent and discontinue participation in therapy at any time.

Informed consent should be obtained from both spouses. In situations in which one spouse begins therapy somewhat after the other partner has begun, informed consent should be obtained from each at the time each begins.

Consent should be obtained for therapeutic as well as ethical reasons.

A therapeutic agreement on the part of marital partners with each other and the therapist demonstrates that the decision to participate in marital therapy is made jointly and the responsibility is held mutually.

Values

In marital therapy, as in individual therapy, the values of the therapist have inescapable impact. There do not exist sets of values that are correct for all marriages. Therefore, to evaluate the needs of a particular couple, the therapist must remain flexible and open. However, therapists cannot simply ignore their own values. Margolin (1982) recommended that therapists (1) take time to become aware of their own values, (2) investigate how those values influence clinical practice, and (3) inform clients of personal values implicit in the therapist's mode of therapy. Therapist values related to preservation of marriages, extramarital affairs, and sex roles are of paramount importance in marital therapy and deserve special consideration.

When the question of whether to preserve a marriage arises, partners often ask the therapist's personal opinion about whether they should separate, divorce, or remain together. The Professional Code of the American Association for Marriage and Family Therapy (AAMFT) states: "In all circumstances, the therapist will clearly advise a client that the decision to separate or divorce is the responsibility solely of the client" (AAMFT, 1979). Many couples entering marital therapy have considered divorce and expect that the therapist can tell them what they should do. This presents a dilemma: should therapists make the decision for their clients or follow the AAMFT guidelines and help the clients make their own decisions? Wolpe (Yoell, Stewart, Wolpe, Goldstein, & Speierer, 1971) supports the need for the therapist to frequently make the decision for the client. On the other hand, Stewart believes that the decision will not be meaningful for the couple if the therapist makes it. A middle road for some therapists is to tell clients what they would do but to preface their remarks with the proviso that the opinion is personal rather than professional. The important point is that all marital therapists should know what values they hold relating to the preservation of marriage generally, because these values influence their approach to therapy.

Also arising frequently in marital therapy are issues relating to extramarital affairs. Therapists should not only know their own feelings about extramarital affairs but also know their clients'. If there appears to be a conflict of values that would impede therapy, then a referral to another therapist should be made. A study by Knapp (1975) showed that 43% of marriage counselors would be supportive of sexually open marriages for their clients; in fact, a few therapists would encourage one spouse to begin or continue an affair. The practice of encouraging an extramarital affair is highly questionable and, in several states, would be technically illegal. Most therapists discourage extramarital affairs or even withhold therapy until all extramarital relationships have ended. In cases where extramarital affairs are involved, the therapist and couple should reach a mutual agreement about whether to continue therapy or to stop it until the affairs end.

Marital therapists have some significant biases in the area of sex-role stereotyping of marital partners. The American Psychological Association (1975) found that marital therapists are especially susceptible to the following biases:

- Believing that remaining in a marriage rather than divorcing would result in better adjustment for a woman.
- Showing less sensitivity to a woman's career than a man's career.
- Continuing to believe that child rearing is the responsibility of the mother.
- Using a double standard for a wife's affair versus a husband's affair.
- Deferring to the husband's needs over those of the wife.

The task of the marital therapist is to expand the couple's awareness of any sexual stereotyping that may be affecting the marriage and yet not be too disruptive to the basic relationship.

Summary

In this chapter, significant professional issues related to the training of marital therapists and ethical considerations are discussed. There are basically two ways to become a marital therapist. The first involves being trained in a related profession and receiving additional training and supervision at post-graduate institutes or with AAMFT's approved supervision program. And the second approach to becoming a marital therapist is to receive graduate training at a college or university with a program in the field. The latter approach is growing in acceptance, and several universities are developing programs that will be accredited by AAMFT. Most of the programs will be at the master's level, with supervised experience being the cornerstone of the training process.

Professional and ethical issues will continue to be major concerns for years to come. Although most professional organizations have a code of ethics that broadly defines minimal standards, each individual must develop a more personalized code. Corey (1982) suggested the following guidelines to aid in formulating a personalized code of ethics:

1. Therapists must be aware of their own needs, what they are getting from their work, and how their needs and action influence their clients.

2. Therapists should have the necessary training and supervised experience in the use of assessment techniques and intervention strategies they employ.
3. Therapists should be aware of the ethical standards of their professional organizations and realize that many situations have no clear-cut answers; therapists have to exercise their own professional judgment.
4. Therapists should have some theoretical framework of behavior change to guide them in their practice.
5. Therapists must remember that their needs should not be met at the clients' expense.
6. Therapists need to be aware of the importance of continuing education as a way of updating their knowledge and skills.
7. Therapists should avoid any behavior that could jeopardize the therapeutic/professional relationship with clients.
8. Therapists are responsible for informing clients about confidentiality and other matters that may affect the therapist-client relationship.
9. Therapists must recognize their own values and beliefs and avoid imposing them on their clients.
10. Therapists must provide the information necessary for clients to give informed consent.
11. Therapists must be aware of the boundaries of their competence and, when they have reached their limits with a particular client, should seek supervision or refer clients to other professionals.
12. Therapists should strive to practice in their own lives the behaviors that they encourage in their clients.

References

American Association of Marriage and Family Therapy, *Manual of accreditation.* Upland, Calif.: AAMFT, 1977.

American Association of Marriage and Family Therapy, *Code of professional ethics and standards for public information and advertising.* Upland, Calif.: AAMFT, 1979.

American Psychological Association Task Force. "Report of the task force on sex bias and sex-role stereotyping in psychotherapeutic practice." *American Psychologist,* 1975, *30,* 1169–1175.

Corey, C. *Theory and practice of counseling and psychotherapy* (2nd ed.). Monterey, Calif.: Brooks/Cole, 1982.

Harper, R. A. "Should marriage counseling become a full-fledged specialty?" *Marriage and Family Living,* 1953, *15,* 338–340.

Herrington, B. S. Privilege denied in joint therapy. *Psychiatric News,* 1979, *14*(9), 1–9.

Kadushin, A. *Supervision in social work.* New York: Columbia University Press, 1973.

Knapp, J. J. "Some non-monogamous marriage styles and related attitudes and practices of marriage counselors." *The Family Coordinator,* 1975, *24,* 505–514.

Leslie, G. A. "The changing practice of marriage counseling: An introduction." In J. A. Peterson (Ed.), *Marriage and family counseling: Perspective and prospect.* New York: Association Press, 1968.

Margolin, G. "Conjoint marital therapy to enhance anger management and reduce spouse abuse." *American Journal of Family Therapy,* 1979, *7,* 13–23.

Margolin, G. "Ethical and legal considerations in marital and family therapy." *American Psychologist,* 1982, *37,* 788–801.

Nichols, W. C. *Marriage and family counseling: A legislative handbook.* Claremont, Calif.: American Association of Marriage and Family Counselors, 1974.

Nichols, W. C. "Doctoral programs in marital and family therapy." *Journal of Marital and Family Therapy,* 1979, *5*(3), 23–28.

Nichols, W. C. "Education of marriage and family therapists: Some trends and implications," *Journal of Marital and Family Therapy,* 1979, *5*(1), 19–28.

Smith, V. G., and Nichols, W. C. "Accreditation in marital and family therapy." *Journal of Marital and Family Therapy,* 1979, *5*(3), 95–100.

Sugarman, D. A. "Diary of a subpoenaed psychologist." *New Jersey Psychologist,* 1974, *24*(3), 13–18.

Yoell, W., Stewart, D., Wolpe, J., Goldstein, A., and Speierer, G. "Marriage, morals and therapeutic goals: A discussion." *Journal of Behavior Therapy and Experimental Psychiatry,* 1971, *2,* 127–132.

CHAPTER TWELVE

Research in Marital Therapy

As the field of marital therapy has emerged and subsequently become a part of the mental health field, the associated research has increased vastly. Especially because of the numerous research studies in marital therapy in recent years, it would not be feasible to review all that are relevant to the field in this chapter. However, there are more than 30 reviews of outcome research available to the reader. Gurman and Kniskern (1978) reviewed the entire field; Jacobsen (1979) and Jacobsen and Martin (1976) reviewed studies related to behavioral marriage therapy. Other reviews of interest concern studies of group marital therapy (Gurman, 1971) and marital-enrichment programs (Gurman & Kniskern, 1977). Because these comprehensive reviews are available elsewhere, our intent here is to focus on some of the major types of research, describe how therapists can use research findings, and suggest some areas that warrant future research.

The Design and Use of Research

Types of Research

There are many ways to classify research, but perhaps the simplest way is to identify it as basic or applied. Basic research is mainly concerned with the development of new knowledge and tends to be theoretical in orientation. Applied research is concerned mostly with assessing applications of existing knowledge. For example, once basic research had determined the major factors required for couples to communicate, applied research could develop ways to help couples communicate better and more efficiently.

Another classification of research is done in either the laboratory or the field. Laboratory research findings are usually viewed as theoretical and, therefore, usually associated with basic research. The primary purpose of laboratory research is to control those factors thought to be most relevant to a particular study. Laboratories for marital research are normally counseling centers, mental-health agencies, family-service centers, or other settings where the variables can be controlled. In marital therapy, laboratory research might be done, for example, to determine the effect of certain therapist attributes and styles on the therapeutic relationship.

Field research is usually conducted in noncontrolled situations and can test findings resulting from laboratory studies. For example, if laboratory research found that clients of certain backgrounds prefer therapists with similar backgrounds, field research (in this case, perhaps by therapists in private practice) could be used to determine whether case-load assignment on the basis of client/therapist background is really an effective way to assign clients to therapists.

Research can also be classified according to the methodology used in the study. Since any study can utilize several methodologies, the classifications in this system are not mutually exclusive. Some of the major methodological classifications are: survey, developmental, follow-up, correlational, case, and experimental studies. These are now described.

Survey studies usually gather relatively limited data from a large number of people, typically by using a questionnaire or interview. A survey that covers the entire population being studied is referred to as a census. A study that involves only a portion of the population is known as a sample survey. If a sample is used, inferences are made about the characteristics of the entire population on the basis of the sample population studied. In marital therapy, one example of a topic for survey research is the definition of the needs of couples who are likely to seek therapy.

Developmental research is either longitudinal or cross-sectional, depending on the survey technique used. In the longitudinal method the same sample of people is studied over an extended period of time. This method allows intensive studies of individuals and couples at various stages in their relationships. However, longitudinal studies have some inherent practical difficulties. First, a longitudinal study demands an extended commitment from an individual researcher or institution, requiring a number of years for completion. Second, the sample selected and variables chosen at the beginning cannot be changed after the study has matured. Third, keeping track of the location of the people in the sample and maintaining their cooperation for an extended period can be challenging.

Many of the practical difficulties of the longitudinal method are not present in the cross-sectional method. This approach might be used to study needs of couples that have been married varying lengths of time. It would identify needs of couples married one to three years, four to seven years, eight to ten years, and longer than ten years. The data gathered would be analyzed and conclusions reached as to the needs couples may have depending on the lengths of time they have been married. Usually, a much larger sample population can be used in studies that are cross-sectional as opposed to longitudinal, because in cross-sectional studies all the data is gathered at about the same time. A major disadvantage of the cross-sectional approach is the possibility that extraneous variables might create differences in the populations being studied. For example, in the research into needs of couples at various stages in their marriages, an extremely important variable could skew results; the couples who could not resolve their problems would probably have separated or divorced and so be excluded from the sample. Therefore, with the study design described, couples with possibly the greatest needs would be omitted.

Somewhat similar to the longitudinal method of conducting research is the follow-up study. Studies of this type are usually concerned with researching the subsequent development of subjects after a specified treatment or intervention. An example would be to follow up the participants in a marriage enrichment program in order to determine whether the experience has a lasting effect. Many treatments and programs appear to have been successful at their completion, but does this change last over an extended period of time?

Correlation studies are a frequently used type of research that is concerned with determining the extent of the relationship between two variables. For instance, on the basis of personal experience, a therapist may believe that there is a relationship between the age of a person at the time of marriage and the chance of a successful marriage. To test this belief or hypothesis, the therapist would have to select a sample from the target population and gather data. The age of each person would be obtained, and marital success would be measured, possibly by a test or self-report. The therapist would then determine through the use of the coefficient of correlation whether there is a relationship between age and marital success.

Correlation techniques are particularly useful in making predictions. If there is a correlation between two variables, then a prediction can be made of some aspect of one variable based on the other. For example, if the characteristics needed for a successful marriage were identified, the therapist would be able to predict the chance of a marriage succeeding based on the characteristics of the spouses.

Case-study research typically involves an intensive investigation of one individual or couple. Most case studies arise from efforts to solve problems. Freud is well known for case studies that began with his attempts to assist his clients in solving their personality problems. He felt that the relationships he observed between his clients and their environments might also be characteristic of other individuals with similar problems. He published detailed accounts of his therapy sessions with clients on the assumption that generalizations could be made from these studies.

The greatest advantage of a case study is the attempt to understand the whole person or situation in great detail. However, case studies have been criticized because of the possible effects on them of researcher bias and the questionable generalizability of findings. Still, it is a highly useful method that is valued by many therapists.

Experimental research begins with a population of subjects that can be randomly assigned to two or more treatment groups. The researcher wants to be able to say that the only significant difference between the groups is the treatment they received. For example, if a sample of couples experiencing marital difficulties is randomly assigned to two therapy groups designed to resolve the difficulties and one group makes more progress than the other, it can be assumed that variations in the therapy determined the varying levels of progress. It is also assumed that, if the groups were reversed, the group now receiving the less effective therapy would be the one to make relatively less progress. The random assignment in this method of study assures that every couple has as much chance of being assigned to one therapy group as to another. As a result, the characteristics of the couples assigned to each therapy group should be typical of the sample as a whole; this is critical to the validity of the study.

Outcomes of Marital Therapy

Probably the most frequently asked question in marital therapy is, "Does marital therapy actually make a difference?" Professionals entering the field must strongly believe that answer is "yes," but can this be documented through systematic research? Beck (1975) reviewed 32 controlled studies designed to measure the outcomes of marital therapy. In 23 of the

32 studies, significant gains were found on half or more of the criterion measures for the groups in marital therapy as compared to the control groups. Eight additional studies without control groups, and also data from the Family Service Association of America, are cited by Beck (1975) as additional evidence of the positive effects of marital therapy. In combination, these studies provide strong evidence that positive changes do occur in marital therapy.

Olsen, Russell, and Sprenkle (1980) and Gurman and Kniskern (1978) suggested that on the basis of studies of the outcome of marital therapy some definite inferences can be made. Their inferences are:

1. Conjoint marital therapy appears more effective than individual therapy for improving marital relationships.
2. No one school of marital therapy has been demonstrated to be effective with a wide range of presenting problems.
3. Therapist relationship skills are important regardless of the conceptual orientation or school of the marital therapist.

A major concern in outcome research involves the evaluation instruments. In the studies reviewed by Beck (1975), a wide array of instruments were used. The largest group of studies utilized a self-report approach; usually both husband and wife were asked to give their perceptions of their situation, and this information typically was gathered from each spouse before and after therapy. Significant positive gains were demonstrated in studies using each of the following instruments: the *Locke-Wallace Marital Adjustment Test* (short form), the *Taylor-Johnson Temperament Analysis,* the *Bienvenu Marital Communication Inventory,* and the *Locke-Williamson Marital Adjustment Test.* Some other instruments that appear well suited to the types of changes therapists report in marital therapy are the *Barrett-Lennard Relationship Inventory,* the *Azrin Marital Happiness Scale,* and the *Most Scale of Marital Friction and Satisfaction.*

Beginning therapists are strongly encouraged to become familiar with research in marital therapy. Research articles in professional journals should be read regularly, and other sources, such as Jacobsen's review (1978), should be explored.

Guidelines for Clinical Research

It is important for therapists, and especially beginning therapists, to have an understanding of the research done in their fields. Since most of the research in the marital-therapy field is of a clinical, or applied, nature, marriage therapists should know the steps this kind of research involves. Ary, Jacobs, and Razavich (1979) suggest the following guidelines:

1. *Statement of the Problem.* The researcher must start with a clear statement of the problem. This consists of clear identification of the vari-

ables involved in the study and a decision as to whether the study is to determine the status of these variables or to investigate relationships between the variables.

2. *Identification of Information Needed To Solve the Problem.* The information to be collected is listed, the nature of the information discussed, and the form the information is to take (such as test scores or responses to questionnaires) is specified.

3. *Selection or Development of Instruments for Gathering Data.* The most frequently used instruments are questionnaires, interviews, tests, and scales of various types. If no suitable instrument exists, the researcher must develop one.

4. *Identification of the Target Population and Determination of Any Necessary Sampling Procedure.* The researcher determines the group about which information is sought. If the entire target population would be too large, the researcher attempts to select a sample that will adequately represent the population.

5. *Design of the Procedure for Data Collection.* The researcher develops a schedule for obtaining the sample and collecting the information.

6. *Collection of data.* The procedure to collect data is implemented.

7. *Analysis of Data.* The data is examined to determine the answer to the problem stated in step one.

8. *Preparation of the Report.* The findings of the study are prepared so that they can be shared with others through a journal article, presentation at a professional meeting, or some other vehicle.

Guidelines for Reading Research in Marital Therapy

With such an abundance of research articles in the marital-therapy field, it is difficult to know which ones are worth reading. Harmon (1978) presented the following guidelines for evaluating research articles:

1. Read the abstract of the article (if there is one) and decide whether the article is of interest. If not, select another article and read the abstract.

2. The introduction should describe the purpose of the article; reports of experimental studies also include the hypothesis in the introduction.

3. In the introduction or in the methods section the important terms and concepts should be operationally defined.

4. If either the second or third step has been omitted, the article is probably difficult to understand. (You may want to stop reading the article and select another one.)

5. The methods section should include information sufficient to allow the reader to determine whether:

   a. The reliability and validity of the measures used are satisfactory.

   b. The subjects are appropriate for the study and the results can be generalized to other therapy situations.

   c. The research design tests the hypothesis or explores the question to be answered.

   d. The statistical analysis is appropriate for the problem.

   e. The methods seem logical.

6. The discussion, conclusions, and recommendations should seem consistent with the data; conclusions or recommendations that exceed the scope of the data probably are not valid.

Many studies do not meet these guidelines, and yet they are published. Of course, very few research studies, if any, are perfect. Because reading research articles is extremely important for staying current with developments in the field, therapists should be aware that imperfect research is published and be prepared to read critically.

There are several journals that report findings of marital therapy research. Four that are probably the most widely used sources are:

American Journal of Family Therapy
Brunner/Mazel, Inc.
19 Union Square West
New York, NY 10003

Family Process
Mental Research Institute
555 Middlefield Road
Palo Alto, CA 94301

Journal of Marital and Family Therapy
American Association of Marital and
Family Therapists
924 West Ninth Street
Upland, CA 91786

Journal of Marriage and the Family
Department of Sociology
Case Western Reserve University
Cleveland, OH 44106

Application of Research to Practice

Probably the most significant use of research findings is their application to the therapeutic relationship. Many therapists, however, find it difficult to use the research material they read in their professional journals. In this section we discuss three ways technical research findings can be translated into information useable by the practitioner.

Burr, Mead, and Rollins (1973) propose three different ways of using research, which they name the popularization, empirical, and theoretical methods. The popularization method involves changing research findings into a popularized form to be used by therapists. This method, although sometimes helpful, usually results in much of the precision in the research findings being lost and, therefore, may not be of significant value to the practitioner (Zetterberg, 1962).

The empirical method is the process of the practitioner reading research reports and, when encountering a client with a problem similar to that involved in the research problem, applying the research findings to the case (Tripodi, Fellin, & Meyer, 1969). Another way for therapists to use the empirical method is to review the literature for cases similar to ones with which they are working. Locating similar case descriptions, the practitioner attempts to use the findings to develop a solution for the case at hand.

The theoretical method is the process of going from technical research literature to theory and then from theory to practice (Zetterberg, 1962). The therapist analyzes the research findings through appropriate theory rather than, as with the empirical method, trying to apply the findings directly to a practical problem. In other words, a therapist who encounters a difficult case might find it advantageous to translate the problem into theoretical terms to find a solution, rather than attempting to find a solution directly in the empirical research.

At this point we present a case study and discuss its methods to help you better understand their application. Erickson (1954) described a case involving a young married couple, each partner of which had suffered from enuresis since childhood. Neither had told the other before their marriage, and following the wedding night both were surprised and relieved that the wet bed was not mentioned. This situation continued for several months until a chance remark led them to learn that the problem was shared. The enuresis continued, and the couple sought professional help. The therapist's recommendations included the following:

> Each evening you are to take fluids freely. Two hours before you go to bed, lock the bathroom door after drinking a glass of water. At bedtime, get into your pajamas and then kneel side by side on the bed, facing your pillows, and deliberately, intentionally, and jointly wet the bed. This may be hard to do, but you must do it, then lie down and go to sleep, knowing well that the wetting of the bed is over and done with for the night, that nothing can really make it noticeably wetter [Erickson, 1954, p. 171].

The couple was directed to follow the instructions to wet the bed every night for two weeks. Then, the night after the two weeks were up, they were to go to sleep in a dry bed. Their instructions for the next morning were to "arise, throw back the covers, look at the bed" (Erickson, 1954, 172). According to Erickson, the couple returned about five weeks later and reported that they had followed his instructions and after the two weeks of intentional bedwetting the bed remained dry.

Now, if therapists used the popularization method of applying Erickson's model, the result could be indiscriminately advising clients to effect the opposite of the therapeutic goals set. And if therapists used the empirical method of applying Erickson's research case study, they would have to wait until a couple with enuresis sought their help. Obviously this could take a long time to occur, if it ever did. However, the theoretical method would allow therapists to use Erickson's research almost immediately. To do this, a therapist would look for direct applications of the findings by first considering the theoretical principles Erickson used. One such principle is paradoxical intention, in which a behavior that seems in opposition to a goal is prescribed in order to actually move toward the desired goal (Becvar, 1978). In the case just presented, the goal was to stop wetting the bed. Erickson prescribed that they intentionally wet the bed, which was the behavior to be eliminated. After the two-week trial period the goal was achieved, and there was no longer a need to intentionally wet the bed.

This is a useful research case study because it illustrates effectiveness of the principle of paradoxical intention and also because it illustrates going from research to theory to practice. As a result of reading this study, therapists should not only have a better understanding of paradoxical intention but should become aware of how they can use it with many problems other than enuresis. Nevertheless, as with any use of any intention, therapists who do not have the skill and knowledge to use paradoxical intention should not attempt to apply this technique.

As discussed previously in this chapter, there are numerous types of research, and in the translation of research findings to theory the results become useful. However, if we use the empirical method most findings are not directly applicable to therapy, because of such limitations as differences in sampling and measurement, experimenter bias, and the technical nature of the operational definitions used.

In conclusion, while the popularization and empirical methods of applying research findings to practice may be of limited assistance, the theoretical method can be of significant importance to therapists. Through this method, the therapist does not attempt to apply findings from research studies directly to the clinical setting without first "going through" a theory. Research is viewed as support for or against the validity of a theory, and the information the therapist directly applies to the professional setting stems from the theoretical ideas supported by the empirical evidence (Burr, Mead, & Rollins, 1973).

Suggestions for Future Marital Research

According to Floyd (1976), research in the discipline of marital therapy is at a low state, and a new look at the need for empirical research studies is mandatory if the profession is to be accountable to the lay public. Not only is sound marital research difficult to find, but some topics are overresearched, while other important issues receive very little attention in the literature.

Blood (1976) suggested that the following topics have been very heavily researched: sex—premarital, marital, and extramarital; mixed marriages; class differences in family behavior; age at marriage; wives' employment; kinship; family power structure; family planning; parenthood as crises; child-rearing methods and the personality structure of children; the family life cycle; and divorce. He pointed out that researchers have concentrated on some of the most accessible, observable, and easily measured topics and it is time for researchers to study some of the more subtle and sophisticated aspects of marriage and marital therapy.

Among areas that Blood (1976) termed in need of further research are the following: dating; choosing a marriage partner; readiness for marriage in terms of personal maturity rather than simply chronological age; the effect of the women's movement on marriage; leisure-time companionship of husband and wife; and financial planning and decision-making processes.

Olsen, Russell and Sprenkle (1980) made the following recommendations for future outcome research:

1. Increased assessment of outcome by practicing therapists, which will require diagnosis and follow-up assessment.
2. Continued use of multiple outcome measures, including combinations of subjective, objective, and system-relevant measures.
3. Greater specifications of treatment procedures applied to a narrowly defined client group.
4. Continued effort to match treatment to relationship dynamics rather than to presenting complaints; that is, to match treatment to system rather than to symptom.
5. Investigation of the generalizability of treatment approaches to different settings.
6. Investigation of the generalization of treatment effects from the marital to parent-child subsystems and vice versa.

There has been a dramatic increase in the amount of research being conducted; the most important future direction is improvement of its quality. Such efforts as proper design and the use of control groups and of new, more generalizable samples are steps in the right direction. Longitudinal rather than cross-sectional research is needed to demonstrate the patterns of management within marriages. There is a need for data that will help us distinguish functioning and malfunctioning couples and marital systems. We need to know which intervention works best in what cases; whether co-therapy is effective; and the kinds of training that result in more effective therapists. And, certainly, there must be a greater integration of theory, practice, and research.

Summary

In this chapter we attempt to provide some understanding of the research associated with marital therapy. To accomplish this, we focus on the design and use of research—on the types of research and applications of research findings—and on suggestions for future research.

Several ways of classifying research are discussed, including whether it is basic or applied and done in the laboratory or the field, as well as according to the methodology used in the study. Some of the major methodological classifications are: survey, developmental, follow-up, correlational, case, and experimental studies. Most of the research in the marital-therapy field is of a clinical or applied nature, and eight guidelines for this type of research are presented. A summary of some of the outcome studies that support the effectiveness of marital therapy is included. In addition, suggestions are made to help therapists determine whether particular research articles are worth reading.

The importance of the practitioner being able to apply the findings of research is discussed, and three methods to accomplish this are presented. The first method is popularization, in which research findings are changed into a popularized form to be used by therapists. The second approach is the empirical method, in which research findings are used by therapists to help clients with problems similar to those described in research reports. The third and most appropriate model is the theoretical method, in which technical research literature is translated into theory and only then into practice.

We discuss future trends both in terms of methodology and suggested topics. On the methodological side, use of proper research design, use of control groups, and samples that allow for more generalization of findings are critical. Also, conducting longitudinal rather than cross-sectional research will give us a much clearer notion of what happens within particular marriages. Specific topics to be researched include such basic questions as: Is marital therapy effective? What is the most effective way to train therapists? Is co-therapy more successful than having only one therapist? Is group marital therapy effective? Other areas suggested for further research include: dating, choosing a marriage partner, decision making, and leisure-time companionship of husband and wife. The most important consideration for the future, however, is that we do not need an increase in the quantity of research but need drastic improvement in the quality of the research being conducted and reported in the literature.

References

Ary, D., Jacobs, L. C., & Razavich, A. *Introduction to research in education* (2nd ed.). New York: Holt, Rinehart & Winston, 1979.

Beck, D. F. Research findings on the outcomes of marital counseling. *Social Casework,* March 1975, 5 (3), 153–175.

Becvar, R. J. Paradoxical double bind in human relations training. *Counselor Education and Supervision,* September 1978, *18* (1), 36–43.

Blood, R. O. Research needs of a family life educator and marriage counselor. *Journal of Marriage and the Family,* Feburary 1976, *38* (1), 7–12.

Burr, W. R., Mead, D. E., & Rollins, B. C. A model for the application of research findings by the educator and counselor–research to theory to practice. *Family Coordinator,* July 1973, *22* (3), 285–290.

Erickson, M. H. A clinical note on indirect hypnotic therapy. *The International Journal of Clinical and Experimental Hypnosis,* 1954, *2* (3), 171–174.

Floyd, W. A. A new look at research in marital and family therapy. *Journal of Family Counseling,* Fall 1976, *4* (2), 19–23.

Gurman, A. S. Group marital therapy: Clinical and empirical implications for outcome research. *International Journal of Group Psychotherapy,* 1971, *21,* 174–189.

Gurman, A. S., & Kniskern, D. P. Enriching research on marital enrichment programs. *Journal of Marriage and Family Counseling,* 1977 (3), 3–11.

Gurman. A. S., & Kniskern, D. P. Research on marital and family therapy: Progress, perspective, and prospect. In S. Garfield and A. Bergin (Eds.), *Handbook of psychotherapy and behavior change* (2nd ed.). New York: Wiley, 1978.

Harmon, L. W. The counselor as consumer of research. In L. G. Goldman (ed.), *Research methods for counselors: Practical approaches in field settings.* New York: Wiley, 1978.

Jacobsen, N. S. A review of the research on the effectiveness of marital therapy. In T. J. Paolino, Jr. and S. McCrady (Eds.), *Marriage and marital therapy: Psychoanalytic, behavioral, and systems theory perspectives.* New York: Brunner-Mazel, 1978.

Jacobsen, N. S. Behavioral treatments for marital discord: A critical appraisal. In M. Hersen, R. M. Eisler, & P. M. Miller (Eds.), *Progress on behavior modification* (Vol. 7). New York: Academic Press, 1979.

Jacobsen, N. S., & Martin, B. Behavioral marriage therapy: Current status. *Psychological Bulletin,* 1976, *83*(4), 540–556.

Olsen, D. H., Russell, C. S., & Sprenkle, D. H. Marital and family therapy: A decade review. *Journal of Marriage and the Family,* 1980, *42* (4), 972–993.

Tripodi, T., Fellin, P., & Meyer, H. T. *The assessment of social research: Guidance for use of research in social work and social science.* Itaska, Ill.: Peacock, 1969.

Zetterberg, H. L. *Social theory and social practice.* New York: Bedminster Press, 1962.

APPENDIXES

APPENDIX A   American Association for Marriage and Family Therapy Listing of Accredited Graduate Programs and Accredited Post-Degree Clinical Training Centers

Accredited Graduate Programs	Prerequisite	Personal Therapy	Didactic Hours	Practicum Minimum Hours	Supervision Minimum Hours	Leads To	Accreditation Expires
Auburn University, Dept. Family and Child Development, Auburn AL 36849 ...Mary Lou Purcell, Ed.D.	B.A. and course in abnormal psych	Required	60 quarter hours	600-700	150	M.S.	1984
Brigham Young University, Marriage and Family Therapy Program, Provo UT 84602 ...Robert F. Stahmann, Ph.D.	B.A.; M.A. in MFT	Some dyadic counseling required	M.S. 30 + Ph.D. 60 + (semester hours)	300-600 M.S. (3 semesters) 600-900—Ph.D. (4-6 semesters)	200—M.S. 300—Ph.D.	M.S. Ph.D.	1986
East Texas State University, Marriage and Family Counseling Program, Commerce TX 75428 ...Alan J. Hovestadt, Ed.D.	M.A. + counseling experience	Recommended & available	60 + semester hours	1000	200 (1 hr in-div/2 hr grp/ per week)	Ed.D.	1984
Loma Linda University, Marriage and Family Therapy Program, Loma Linda CA 92354 ...Antonius Brandon, Ph.D.	B.A. inc. Human Growth & Dev. Int. & Cslg. Psy. Testing, Stat., Intro. to Personality Theories	Optional but recommended	84 units	500	60 indiv 140 group	M.S. in MFT	1987
Purdue University, Marriage and Family Therapy Center, CDFS Bldg, Lafayette IN 47907 ...Wallace Denton, Ed.D.	M.S., M.A. or M.S.W.	Two semester group experience required	60 + semester hours	500	200	Ph.D.	1986
Syracuse University, Dept. of Child and Family Studies, 100 Walnut Place, Syracuse NY 13210 ...Charlotte Kahn, Ed.D.	B.A. + several yrs experience	Available; sometimes suggested	36 semester credit hours (45 semester credit hours beg. 5/82)	500	200	M.A.	1983
Texas Tech University, Marriage and Family Therapy Program, Dept. of Home and Family Life Lubbock TX 79409 ...Harvey Joanning, Ph.D.	M.A. or M.S. + counseling experience	Recommended & available	65 semester hours	600-700 5 semesters	100 indiv 200 group	Ph.D.	1986
University of Southern California, Dept. of Sociology, Los Angeles CA 90007 ...Carlfred Broderick, Ph.D.	B.A. or M.A.		64 units	1500 (4 semesters minimum, 15 hrs/wk total)	200 (1 hr. indiv/ 2 hrs grp per week)	Ph.D. + Cert.	1985
University of Wisconsin-Stout, Graduate Program in Marriage and Family Therapy, Menomonie WI 54751 ...Charles Barnard, Ed.D.	B.A. or equiv	Optional, but available	60 semester credits	500	Minimum 200 hrs	M.S. in MFT	*1982
Virginia Tech University, Marriage and Family Therapy Program, Dept. of Family and Child Development, Blacksburg VA 24061 ...James F. Keller, Ph.D.	B.A.; M.A. + counseling experience	Recommended	M.A.—70 quar hrs Ph.D.—80 quar hrs	M.A.—500 Ph.D.—960	Minimum 150 hrs	M.S.; Ph.D.	1986

APPENDIX A   Continued

Accredited Post-Degree Clinical Training Centers	Prerequisite	Personal Therapy	Didactic Hours	Practicum Minimum Hours	Supervision Minimum Hours	Leads To	Accreditation Expires
California Family Study Center, 4400 Riverside Dr., Burbank CA 91505 ...Edwin S. Cox, M.A.	M.A. in MFT or grad. degree approx Model Cur of AAMFT	Recommended	150	1500	100 indiv 200 group	Cert.	1983
Family Service of Milwaukee, Box 08434 Milwaukee WI 53208 ...David Hoffman, M.A.	M.A. or prof. grad. degree + 1500 hrs. supervised clinical experience	Recommended	2-4 hrs/wk	1500 (2 years)	200 (100 indiv/ 100 group)	Cert.	•1982
Institutes of Religion and Health (Blanton-Peale Graduate Institute), 3 W 29th Street, New York NY 10001 ...Thelma Dixon-Murphy, Ed.D.	M.A. or prof. grad. degree + 2 yrs experience	Required (From App. List)	80 credits coursework	Beginners 1350 650 (3 yrs, 8-15 hrs/wk)— Advanced (2 yrs, 8 hrs/wk)	350 (180 indiv/ 170 grp)	D. Min. +	1984
Marriage Council of Philadelphia, 4025 Chestnut Street, Philadelphia PA 19104 (Affiliated with University of Pennsylvania) ...Ellen M. Berman, M.D.	M.A. or prof. grad. degree & min. of 1 yr post-degree supervised cslg.	Recommended	10 courses 12 hrs/wk	500 (12 hrs/wk)	200 (2 indiv/ 2 grp per week)	Cert.	1985
CLSC-Metro (Peel Center), Marriage Counseling Service, 3647 Peel Street, Montreal PQ Canada H3A 1X1 ...Dorothy E. Barrier, P.S.W.	M.S.W. + 3 yrs supervised prof. practice	Recommended	4 full courses	560 (17½ hrs/wk)	200	Diploma	1984
	M.S.W. (in process)	Recommended	8 half courses	560 (17½ hrs/wk)	200	M.S.W.	
	M.Ed. (in process)	Recommended	6 full courses	1116 (31 hrs/wk)	210	M.Ed.	

* Renewal application in process.

Note: Reprinted by permission of the American Association for Marriage and Family Therapy, 1717 K Street Northwest, Suite 407, Washington, D.C. 20006, telephone (202) 429-1825.

American Association for Marriage and Family Therapy Membership Standards

Introduction

The AAMFT, founded in 1942, serves as the professional association for the field of marital and family therapy. AAMFT membership offers individuals the benefits of membership in a professional association, and serves the public interest through the advancement of the profession. This brochure describes the requirements and procedures for Clinical Members, Associates, and Students.

The following standards of academic preparation, clinical training, and supervision became effective for applications received after September 1, 1981. These standards are not retroactive and do not affect persons already admitted to any category of membership prior to the above date.

I. Clinical Member Requirements
A. Academic Requirements

The academic requirement for Clinical Membership is dependent upon the successful completion of a qualifying degree from a regionally accredited institution as defined below:

45 semester hours Master's degree in Marital and Family Therapy or a Doctoral degree in Marital and Family Therapy, or a graduate degree (45 semester hours) which meets the Course of Study as defined below. The following areas in the Course of Study below are basic to both Master's and Doctoral level programs. The Course of Study is based on the substantive content in degree programs, rather than specific course titles. The components of the graduate degree in Marital and Family Therapy are as follows:

1. **Marital and Family Systems** [2-4 courses]. This is a fundamental introduction to the systems approach to intervention. The student should learn to think in the systems terms on a number of levels across a wide variety of family structures, and regarding a diverse range of presenting problems. The following is a topical list of what is considered appropriate in this area of study:

   a. Nuclear family
   b. Marital, sibling, and individual sub-systems
   c. Family of origin
   d. External societal influences

2. **Marital and Family Therapy** [2-4 courses]. This area is intended to provide substantive understanding of the major theories of systems

change and the applied practices evolving from each orientation. Major theoretical approaches to be studied may include:

a. Strategic
b. Structural
c. Experimental
d. Neo-analytical—i.e. object relations
e. Communications
f. Behavioral

3. **Individual Development** [2-4 courses].* This area is intended to provide knowledge of individual personality development and its normal and abnormal manifestations. The student should engage in relevant courses in the following areas:

a. Human development across the life span
b. Personality theory
c. Psychopathology—behavioral pathology
d. Human sexuality

An attempt should be made to integrate this material with systems concepts.

*Several of the courses in this category may be required as prerequisites for some degree programs.

4. **Professional Studies** [1 course]. This area is intended to contribute to the development of a professional attitude and identity. Areas of study may include:

a. Professional socialization and the role of the professional organization
b. Licensure or certification legislation
c. Legal responsibilities and liabilities
d. Ethics and family law
e. Confidentiality
f. Independent practice and interprofessional cooperation

5. **Supervised Clinical Practice** [1 year]. This work should focus on the following:

a. Individual therapy
b. Marital therapy
c. Family therapy

This work should continue without interruption during the student's academic program or at least one calendar year. Students are expected to spend 8-10 hours in direct client contact per week.

6. **Research** [1 course]. This area is intended to provide assistance to students in becoming informed consumers of research in the marital and family field. The following content may be included:

a. Research design, methods and instruments
b. Statistics
c. Research in marital and family studies
d. Research in marital and family therapy

Familiarity with substantive findings, together with the ability to make critical judgments as to the adequacy of research reports, is encouraged.

Upon completion of the graduate professional degree plus the required supervised clinical experience, the candidate will be expected to have mastered the important theory in the field of Marital and Family Therapy as defined in the Course of Study.

Graduate and post-degree programs accredited by the Commission on Accreditation for Marriage and Family Therapy Education meet the requirements of the Course of Study.

B. Clinical Requirements

In addition to the clinical requirements in the above academic preparation, the applicant for AAMFT Clinical Membership shall have completed the following:

Two calendar years of work experience in marital and family therapy, following receipt of a qualifying degree, under supervision acceptable to the Membership Committee, such experience involving at least 1000 hours of direct clinical contact with couples and families and 200 hours of supervision of that work, at least 100 hours of which shall be in individual supervision. Students completing AAMFT accredited degree programs may identify up to 100 hours of supervision toward their required 200 hours for membership. Not more than 50 hours of this should be group supervision.

C. Personal Qualifications

Endorsement by two Clinical Members of the Association attesting to suitable qualities of personal maturity and integrity for the conduct of marital and family therapy.

II. Associate Member Requirements*

A. Academic Requirements

1. Completion of a qualifying degree from a regionally accredited educational institution, as defined under the section on Clinical Membership; or

2. Completion of a graduate degree which includes the Course of Study defined in Section I-A, 1 through 6. Applicants for Associate whose official transcripts reveal deficiencies in content will be required to submit to the Membership Committee a plan which documents how these deficiencies will be corrected.

B. Clinical Requirements

A plan for completion of the CLINICAL REQUIREMENTS as defined under the section on CLINICAL MEMBER REQUIREMENTS (Section I-B).

C. Personal Qualifications

Demonstration of PERSONAL QUALIFICATIONS as defined under the section on Clinical Membership.

*Associate membership shall be held for a maximum of five (5) years or until satisfactory completion of the requirements for admission as a Clinical Member, whichever comes first.

III. Student Member Requirements*

A. Academic Requirements

1. Current enrollment in a graduate program (master's or doctoral) in Marital and Family Therapy in a regionally accredited educational institution.

2. Current pursuit of a course of study substantially equivalent to the Course of Study described in the section on Clinical Membership.

B. Personal Qualifications

Demonstration of PERSONAL QUALIFICATIONS as defined under the section of Clinical Membership.

* Student membership shall be held for a maximum of five (5) years or until satisfactory completion and receipt of a qualifying degree.

IV. Admission Procedures for Membership in the AAMFT

Admission procedures for membership (Clinical, Associate, Student) are administered by the Association's professional staff under the direction of the AAMFT Membership Committee. In order to assess the qualifications of the applicants for all membership categories, applicants are required to submit the following:

A. Clinical Member

1. An official application for membership, including the names of at least two Clinical Members from whom the AAMFT can request official endorsements.

2. Official transcripts of graduate and professional education.

B. Associate Member

1. An official application for membership, including the names of at least two Clinical Members from whom the AAMFT can request official endorsements.

2. Official transcripts of graduate and professional education.

3. A plan for completion of the CLINICAL REQUIREMENTS as defined under the section on CLINICAL MEMBER REQUIREMENTS (Section I-B).

C. Student Member

1. An official application for membership, including the names of at least two Clinical Members from whom the AAMFT can request official endorsements.

2. A statement signed by the coordinator/director of a graduate (master's or doctoral) program in Marital and Family Therapy in a regionally accredited educational institution verifying the applicant's current enrollment in the program.

3. A description of the applicant's proposed graduate program, including the coursework to be taken. (This requirement is waived for students enrolled in programs accredited by the Commission on Accreditation for Marriage and Family Therapy Education.)

V. Procedures for Transfer of Category

A. Student to Associate

Members in the Student category, upon successful completion of their graduate education, are expected to request advancement to Associate membership. In order for this process to begin, Student members are required to submit:

1. An official application for membership, completing those portions of the application which are relevant to the request for Transfer of Category. This application form shall include the names of at least two Clinical Members from whom the AAMFT can request official endorsements.

2. Official transcripts of completed graduate and professional studies.

3. A plan for completion of requisite post-degree supervised clinical experience acceptable to the Membership Committee.

B. Associate to Clinical

Members in the Associate category, upon successful completion of all academic and clinical requirements, are required to submit:

1. An official application for membership, completing those portions of the application which are relevant to the request for Transfer of Category. This application form shall include the names of at least two Clinical Members from whom the AAMFT can request official endorsements.

2. Official transcripts of graduate and professional studies completed since entering the Associate category.

3. Reports of approved supervised clinical practice in Marital and Family Therapy must be submitted by the applicant's supervisor, according to the guidelines in the Approved Supervisor brochure.

DUES STRUCTURE
(Annual)

Clinical Member	$90-$160*
Associate	$50
Student	$25

*Depending on geographical division

Reprinted by permission of the American Association for Marriage and Family Therapy.

American Association for Marriage and Family Therapy Code of Ethical Principles

1. **Responsibilities to Clients.** Family therapists are dedicated to advancing the welfare of families and individuals, including respecting the rights of those persons seeking their assistance, and making reasonable efforts to insure that their services are used appropriately.

2. **Competence.** Family therapists are dedicated to maintaining high standards of competence, recognizing appropriate limitations to their competence and services and using consultation from other professionals.

3. **Integrity.** Family therapists are honest in dealing with clients, students, trainees, colleagues, and the public, seeking to eliminate incompetence or dishonesty from the work or representation of family therapist.

4. **Confidentiality.** Family therapists respect both the law and the rights of clients, and safeguard client confidences as permitted by law.

5. **Professional Responsibility.** Family therapists respect the rights and the responsibilities of professional colleagues and, as employees of organizations, remain accountable as individuals for the ethical principles of the profession.

6. **Professional Development.** Family therapists seek to continue their professional development, and strive to make pertinent knowledge available to clients, students, trainees, colleagues, and the public.

7. **Research Responsibility.** Family therapists recognize that while research is essential to the advancement of knowledge, all investigations must be conducted with full respect for the rights and dignity of participants and with full concern for their welfare.

8. **Social Responsibility.** Family therapists acknowledge a responsibility to participate in activities contributing to a better community in society, including devoting a portion of their professional activity to services for which there is little or no financial return.

Reprinted by permission of the American Association for Marriage and Family Therapy.

American Association for Marriage and Family Therapy Standards on Public Information and Advertising

Introduction

The practice of marital and family therapy as a mental health profession is in the public interest. Therefore, it is appropriate for the well-trained and qualified practioner to inform the public of the availability of his/her services. However, much needs to be done to educate the public to the services available from qualified marital and family therapists. Clinical Members of the American Association for Marriage and Family Therapy have a responsibility to the public to engage in appropriate informational activities; Clinical Members shall not engage in misrepresentation—that is, the use of false, fraudulent, misleading or deceptive statements in keeping with the following general principles.

Information for the Consumer

Selection of a marital and family therapist by a layperson should be made on an informed basis. Advice and recommendations of third parties—other professionals, relatives, friends, business acquaintances, and other associates—may be helpful. Advertisements and publications, whether in directories, announcement cards, newspapers, or on radio or television, should be formulated to convey information that is necessary to make an appropriate selection. Information that may be helpful would indicate:

- Office information, such as name, including a group name and names of professional associates, address, telephone number, credit card acceptability, languages spoken and written, and office hours;
- Earned degrees, state licensure and/or certification, and AAMFT Clinical Member status;
- Description of practice, including a statement that practice is limited to one or more fields of family therapy;
- Appropriate fee information.

Name and Affiliation

As the name under which a marital and family therapist conducts his/her practice may be a factor in the selection process, use of a name which could mislead the public concerning the identity, responsibility, source, and status of those practicing under that name would be improper. Likewise, one should not hold oneself out as being a partner or associate of a firm, if he/she is not one in fact. One should not use or participate in the use of a professional card, office sign, letterhead, telephone directory listing, association directory listing, or a similar professional notice or device if it includes a statement or claim that is false, fraudulent, misleading, or deceptive. Practicing under a name that is misleading as to the identity, responsibility, or status of those practicing thereunder is improper.

Areas of Specialization

A marital and family therapist should be accurate in the representation of his/her professional background, training, status, and areas of specialization in order to avoid the possibility of misleading the consumer. A member should not hold himself/herself out as a specialist without being able to provide evidence of training, education, and supervised experience in settings which meet recognized professional standards. Public announcements which accurately describe that one practices in limited areas of specialization in marital and family therapy for which he/she has been so trained are helpful to laypersons.

Fee Information

Marital and family therapists should exercise care to insure that fee information is complete and accurate. Because of the individuality of each problem, public statements regarding average, minimum, or estimated fees may be deceiving. Only factual assertions, and not opinions, should be made in public communications. Not only should commercial publicity be truthful, but its accurate meaning should be apparent to the average layperson.

Definition of False, Fraudulent, Misleading or Deceptive Statements

A statement is false, fraudulent, misleading, or deceptive when it includes a statement or claim which:

- Contains a material misrepresentation of fact;
- Fails to state any material fact necessary to make the statement, in light of all circumstances, not misleading;
- Is intended to or is likely to create an unjustified expectation; or
- Contains a representation or implication that is likely to cause an ordinary prudent person to misunderstand or be deceived or fails to contain reasonable warnings or disclaimers necessary to make a representation or implication not deceptive.

AAMFT Regulations

The American Association for Marriage and Family Therapy is the sole owner of its name, its logo and the abbreviated initials AAMFT. Use of the name, logo and initials is restricted to the following conditions:

- Only individual Clinical Members may identify their membership in AAMFT in public information or advertising materials, not Associates or Students or organizations.

- The initials AAMFT may not be used following one's name in the manner of an academic degree because this is misleading.
- Use of the logo is limited to the Association, its committees and regional divisions when they are engaged in bonafide activities as units or divisions of AAMFT.
- A regional division or chapter of AAMFT may use the AAMFT insignia to list its individual members as a group (e.g., in the Yellow Pages). When all Clinical Members practicing within a directory district have been invited to list, any one or more members may do so.

Reprinted by permission of the American Association for Marriage and Family Therapy.

American Psychological Association
Ethical Principles of Psychologists

Introduction

This version of the Ethical Principles of Psychologists (formerly entitled Ethical Standards of Psychologists) was adopted by the American
Psychological Association's Council of Representatives on January 24,
1981. The revised Ethical Principles contain both substantive and gram-
matical changes in each of the nine ethical principles constituting the
Ethical Standards of Psychologists previously adopted by the Council of
Representatives in 1979, plus a new tenth principle entitled Care and Use
of Animals. Inquiries concerning the Ethical Principles of Psychologists
should be addressed to the Administrative Officer for Ethics, American
Psychological Association, 1200 Seventeenth Street, N.W., Washington,
D.C. 20036.

These revised Ethical Principles apply to psychologists, to students of
psychology, and to others who do work of a psychological nature under
the supervision of a psychologist. They are also intended for the guidance
of nonmembers of the Association who are engaged in psychological research or practice.

Any complaints of unethical conduct filed after January 24, 1981, shall
be governed by this 1981 revision. However, conduct (a) complained
about after January 24, 1981, but which occurred prior to that date, and
(b) not considered unethical under prior versions of the principles but
considered unethical under the 1981 revision, shall not be deemed a violation of ethical principles. Any complaints pending as of January 24,
1981, shall be governed either by the 1979 or by the 1981 version of the
Ethical Principles, at the sound discretion of the Committee on Scientific
and Professional Ethics and Conduct.

Preamble

Psychologists respect the dignity and worth of the individual and strive for
the preservation and protection of fundamental human rights. They are committed
to increasing knowledge of human behavior and of people's understanding of
themselves and others and to the utilization of such knowledge for the promotion
of human welfare. While pursuing these objectives, they make every effort to
protect the welfare of those who seek their services and of the research participants that may be the object of study. They use their skills only for purposes
consistent with these values and do not knowingly permit their misuse by others.
While demanding for themselves freedom of inquiry and communication, psy-

chologists accept the responsibility this freedom requires: competence, objectivity in the application of skills, and concern for the best interests of clients, colleagues, students, research participants, and society. In the pursuit of these ideals, psychologists subscribe to principles in the following areas: 1. Responsibility, 2. Competence, 3. Moral and Legal Standards, 4. Public Statements, 5. Confidentiality, 6. Welfare of the Consumer, 7. Professional Relationships, 8. Assessment Techniques, 9. Research With Human Participants, and 10. Care and Use of Animals.

Acceptance of membership in the American Psychological Association commits the member to adherence to these principles.

Psychologists cooperate with duly constituted committees of the American Psychological Association, in particular, the Committee on Scientific and Professional Ethics and Conduct, by responding to inquiries promptly and completely. Members also respond promptly and completely to inquiries from duly constituted state association ethics committees and professional standards review committees.

Principle I
Responsibility

In providing services, psychologists maintain the highest standards of their profession. They accept responsibility for the consequences of their acts and make every effort to ensure that their services are used appropriately.

a. As scientists, psychologists accept responsibility for the selection of their research topics and the methods used in investigation, analysis, and reporting. They plan their research in ways to minimize the possibility that their findings will be misleading. They provide thorough discussion of the limitations of their data, especially where their work touches on social policy or might be construed to the detriment of persons in specific age, sex, ethnic, socioeconomic, or other social groups. In publishing reports of their work, they never suppress disconfirming data, and they acknowledge the existence of alternative hypotheses and explanations of their findings. Psychologists take credit only for work they have actually done.

b. Psychologists clarify in advance with all appropriate persons and agencies the expectations for sharing and utilizing research data. They avoid relationships that may limit their objectivity or create a conflict of interest. Interference with the milieu in which data are collected is kept to a minimum.

c. Psychologists have the responsibility to attempt to prevent distortion, misuse, or suppression of psychological findings by the institution or agency of which they are employees.

d. As members of governmental or other organizational bodies, psychologists remain accountable as individuals to the highest standards of their profession.

e. As teachers, psychologists recognize their primary obligation to help others acquire knowledge and skill. They maintain high standards of scholarship by presenting psychological information objectively, fully, and accurately.

f. As practitioners, psychologists know that they bear a heavy social responsibility because their recommendations and professional actions may alter the lives of others. They are alert to personal, social, organizational, financial, or political situations and pressures that might lead to misuse of their influence.

Principle 2
Competence

The maintenance of high standards of competence is a responsibility shared by all psychologists in the interest of the public and the profession as a whole. Psychologists recognize the boundaries of their competence and the limitations of their techniques. They only provide services and only use techniques for which they are qualified by training and experience. In those areas in which recognized standards do not yet exist, psychologists take whatever precautions are necessary to protect the welfare of their clients. They maintain knowledge of current scientific and professional information related to the services they render.

a. Psychologists accurately represent their competence, education, training, and experience. They claim as evidence of educational qualifications only those degrees obtained from institutions acceptable under the Bylaws and Rules of Council of the American Psychological Association.

b. As teachers, psychologists perform their duties on the basis of careful preparation so that their instruction is accurate, current, and scholarly.

c. Psychologists recognize the need for continuing education and are open to new procedures and changes in expectations and values over time.

d. Psychologists recognize differences among people, such as those that may be associated with age, sex, socioeconomic, and ethnic backgrounds. When necessary, they obtain training, experience, or counsel to assure competent service or research relating to such persons.

e. Psychologists responsible for decisions involving individuals or policies based on test results have an understanding of psychological or educational measurement, validation problems, and test research.

f. Psychologists recognize that personal problems and conflicts may interfere with professional effectiveness. Accordingly, they refrain from undertaking any activity in which their personal problems are likely to lead to inadequate performance or harm to a client, colleague, student, or research participant. If engaged in such activity when they become aware of their personal problems, they seek competent professional assistance to determine whether they should suspend, terminate, or limit the scope of their professional and/or scientific activities.

Principle 3
Moral and Legal Standards

Psychologists' moral and ethical standards of behavior are a personal matter to the same degree as they are for any other citizen, except as these may compromise the fulfillment of their professional responsibilities or reduce the public trust in psychology and psychologists. Regarding their own behavior, psychologists are sensitive to prevailing community standards and to the possible impact that conformity to or deviation from these standards may have upon the quality of their performance as psychologists. Psychologists are also aware of the possible impact of their public behavior upon the ability of colleagues to perform their professional duties.

a. As teachers, psychologists are aware of the fact that their personal values may affect the selection and presentation of instructional materials. When dealing with topics that may give offense, they recognize and respect the diverse attitudes that students may have toward such materials.

b. As employees or employers, psychologists do not engage in or condone practices that are inhumane or that result in illegal or unjustifiable actions. Such practices include, but are not limited to, those based on considerations of race, handicap, age, gender, sexual preference, religion, or national origin in hiring, promotion, or training.

c. In their professional roles, psychologists avoid any action that will violate or diminish the legal and civil rights of clients or of others who may be affected by their actions.

d. As practitioners and researchers, psychologists act in accord with Association standards and guidelines related to practice and to the conduct of research with human beings and animals. In the ordinary course of events, psychologists adhere to relevant governmental laws and institutional regulations. When federal, state, provincial, organizational, or institutional laws, regulations, or practices are in conflict with Association standards and guidelines, psychologists make known their commitment to Association standards and guidelines and, wherever possible, work toward a resolution of the conflict. Both practitioners and researchers are concerned with the development of such legal and quasi-legal regulations as best serve the public interest, and they work toward changing existing regulations that are not beneficial to the public interest.

Principle 4
Public Statements

Public statements, announcements of services, advertising, and promotional activities of psychologists serve the purpose of helping the public make informed judgments and choices. Psychologists represent accurately and objectively their professional qualifications, affiliations, and functions, as well as those of the institutions or organizations with which they or the statements may be associated. In public statements providing psychological information or professional opinions or providing information about the availability of psychological products, publications, and services, psychologists base their statements on scientifically acceptable psychological findings and techniques with full recognition of the limits and uncertainties of such evidence.

a. When announcing or advertising professional services, psychologists may list the following information to describe the provider and services provided: name, highest relevant academic degree earned from a regionally accredited institution, date, type, and level of certification or licensure, diplomate status, APA membership status, address, telephone number, office hours, a brief listing of the type of psychological services offered, an appropriate presentation of fee information, foreign languages spoken, and policy with regard to third-party payments. Additional relevant or important consumer information may be included if not prohibited by other sections of these Ethical Principles.

b. In announcing or advertising the availability of psychological products, publications, or services, psychologists do not present their affiliation with any organization in a manner that falsely implies sponsorship or certification by that organization. In particular and for example, psychologists do not state APA membership or fellow status in a way to suggest that such status implies specialized professional competence or qualifications. Public statements include, but are not limited to, communication by means of periodical, book, list, directory, television, radio, or motion picture. They do not contain (i) a false, fraudulent, misleading, deceptive, or unfair statement; (ii) a misinterpretation of fact or a statement likely to mislead or deceive because in context it makes only a partial disclosure of relevant facts; (iii) a testimonial from a patient regarding the quality of a psychologist's services or products; (iv) a statement intended or likely to create false or unjustified expectations of favorable results; (v) a statement implying unusual, unique, or one-of-a-kind abilities; (vi) a statement intended or likely to appeal to a client's fears, anxieties, or emotions concerning the possible results of failure to obtain the offered services; (vii) a statement concerning the comparative desirability of offered services; (viii) a statement of direct solicitation of individual clients.

c. Psychologists do not compensate or give anything of value to a representative of the press, radio, television, or other communication medium in anticipation of or in return for professional publicity in a news item. A paid advertisement must be identified as such, unless it is apparent from the context that it is a paid advertisement. If communicated to the public by use of radio or television, an advertisement is prerecorded and approved for broadcast by the psychologist, and a recording of the actual transmission is retained by the psychologist.

d. Announcements or advertisements of "personal growth groups," clinics, and agencies give a clear statement of purpose and a clear description of the experiences to be provided. The education, training, and experience of the staff members are appropriately specified.

e. Psychologists associated with the development or promotion of psychological devices, books, or other products offered for commercial sale make reasonable efforts to ensure that announcements and advertisements are presented in a professional, scientifically acceptable, and factually informative manner.

f. Psychologists do not participate for personal gain in commercial announcements or advertisements recommending to the public the purchase or use of proprietary or single-source products or services when that participation is based solely upon their identification as psychologists.

g. Psychologists present the science of psychology and offer their services, products, and publications fairly and accurately, avoiding misrepresentation through sensationalism, exaggeration, or superficiality. Psychologists are guided by the primary obligation to aid the public in developing informed judgments, opinions, and choices.

h. As teachers, psychologists ensure that statements in catalogs and course outlines are accurate and not misleading, particularly in terms of subject matter to be covered, bases for evaluating progress, and the nature of course experiences. Announcements, brochures, or advertisements describing workshops, seminars, or other educational programs accurately describe the audience for which the program is intended as well as eligibility requirements, educational objectives, and nature of the materials to be covered. These announcements also accurately represent the education, training, and experience of the psychologists presenting the programs and any fees involved.

i. Public announcements or advertisements soliciting research participants in which clinical services or other professional services are offered as an inducement make clear the nature of the services as well as the costs and other obligations to be accepted by participants in the research.

j. A psychologist accepts the obligation to correct others who represent the psychologist's professional qualifications, or associations with products or services, in a manner incompatible with these guidelines.

k. Individual diagnostic and therapeutic services are provided only in the context of a professional psychological relationship. When personal advice is given by means of public lectures or demonstrations, newspaper or magazine articles, radio or television programs, mail, or similar media, the psychologist utilizes the most current relevant data and exercises the highest level of professional judgment.

l. Products that are described or presented by means of public lectures or demonstrations, newspaper or magazine articles, radio or television programs, or similar media meet the same recognized standards as exist for products used in the context of a professional relationship.

Principle 5
Confidentiality

Psychologists have a primary obligation to respect the confidentiality of information obtained from persons in the course of their work as psychologists. They reveal such information to others only with the consent of the person or the person's legal representative, except in those unusual circumstances in which not to do so would result in clear danger to the person or to others. Where appropriate, psychologists inform their clients of the legal limits of confidentiality.

a. Information obtained in clinical or consulting relationships, or evaluative data concerning children, students, employees, and others, is discussed only for professional purposes and only with persons clearly concerned with the case. Written and oral reports present only data germane to the purposes of the evaluation, and every effort is made to avoid undue invasion of privacy.

b. Psychologists who present personal information obtained during the course of professional work in writings, lectures, or other public forums either obtain adequate prior consent to do so or adequately disguise all identifying information.

c. Psychologists make provisions for maintaining confidentiality in the storage and disposal of records.

d. When working with minors or other persons who are unable to give voluntary, informed consent, psychologists take special care to protect these persons' best interests.

Principle 6
Welfare of the Consumer

Psychologists respect the integrity and protect the welfare of the people and groups with whom they work. When conflicts of interest arise between clients and psychologists' employing institutions, psychologists clarify the nature and direction of their loyalties and responsibilities and keep all parties informed of their commitments. Psychologists fully inform consumers as to the purpose and nature of an evaluative, treatment, educational, or training procedure, and they freely acknowledge that clients, students, or participants in research have freedom of choice with regard to participation.

a. Psychologists are continually cognizant of their own needs and of their potentially influential position vis-à-vis persons such as clients, students, and subordinates. They avoid exploiting the trust and dependency of such persons. Psychologists make every effort to avoid dual relationships that could impair their professional judgment or increase the risk of exploitation. Examples of such dual relationships include, but are not limited to, research with and treatment of employees, students, supervisees, close friends, or relatives. Sexual intimacies with clients are unethical.

b. When a psychologist agrees to provide services to a client at the request of a third party, the psychologist assumes the responsibility of clarifying the nature of the relationships to all parties concerned.

c. Where the demands of an organization require psychologists to violate these Ethical Principles, psychologists clarify the nature of the conflict between the demands and these principles. They inform all parties of psychologists' ethical responsibilities and take appropriate action.

d. Psychologists make advance financial arrangements that safeguard the best interests of and are clearly understood by their clients. They neither give nor receive any remuneration for referring clients for professional services. They contribute a portion of their services to work for which they receive little or no financial return.

e. Psychologists terminate a clinical or consulting relationship when it is reasonably clear that the consumer is not benefiting from it. They offer to help the consumer locate alternative sources of assistance.

Principle 7
Professional Relationships

Psychologists act with due regard for the needs, special competencies, and obligations of their colleagues in psychology and other professions. They respect the prerogatives and obligations of the institutions or organizations with which these other colleagues are associated.

a. Psychologists understand the areas of competence of related professions. They make full use of all the professional, technical, and administrative resources that serve the best interests of consumers. The absence of formal relationships with other professional workers does not relieve psychologists of the responsibility of securing for their clients the best possible professional service, nor does it relieve them of the obligation to exercise foresight, diligence, and tact in obtaining the complementary or alternative assistance needed by clients.

b. Psychologists know and take into account the traditions and practices of other professional groups with whom they work and cooperate fully with such groups. If a person is receiving similar services from another professional, psychologists do not offer their own services directly to such a person. If a psychologist is contacted by a person who is already receiving similar services from another professional, the psychologist carefully considers that professional relationship and proceeds with caution and sensitivity to the therapeutic issues as well as the client's welfare. The psychologist discusses these issues with the client so as to minimize the risk of confusion and conflict.

c. Psychologists who employ or supervise other professionals or profession-

als in training accept the obligation to facilitate the further professional development of these individuals. They provide appropriate working conditions, timely
evaluations, constructive consultation, and experience opportunities.

d. Psychologists do not exploit their professional relationships with clients,
supervisees, students, employees, or research participants sexually or otherwise.
Psychologists do not condone or engage in sexual harassment. Sexual harassment
is defined as deliberate or repeated comments, gestures, or physical contacts of a
sexual nature that are unwanted by the recipient.

e. In conducting research in institutions or organizations, psychologists secure appropriate authorization to conduct such research. They are aware of their
obligations to future research workers and ensure that host institutions receive
adequate information about the research and proper acknowledgment of their
contributions.

f. Publication credit is assigned to those who have contributed to a publication in proportion to their professional contributions. Major contributions of a
professional character made by several persons to a common project are recognized by joint authorship, with the individual who made the principal contribution listed first. Minor contributions of a professional character and extensive cler-
ical or similar nonprofessional assistance may be acknowledged in footnotes or in
an introductory statement. Acknowledgment through specific citations is made for
unpublished as well as published material that has directly influenced the research or writing. Psychologists who compile and edit material of others for publication publish the material in the name of the originating group, if appropriate,
with their own name appearing as chairperson or editor. All contributions are to
be acknowledged and named.

g. When psychologists know of an ethical violation by another psychologist,
and it seems appropriate, they informally attempt to resolve the issue by bringing
the behavior to the attention of the psychologist. If the misconduct is of a minor
nature and/or appears to be due to lack of sensitivity, knowledge, or experience,
such an informal solution is usually appropriate. Such informal corrective efforts
are made with sensitivity to any rights to confidentiality involved. If the violation
does not seem amenable to an informal solution, or is of a more serious nature,
psychologists bring it to the attention of the appropriate local, state, and/or national committee on professional ethics and conduct.

Principle 8
Assessment Techniques

In the development, publication, and utilization of psychological assessment
techniques, psychologists make every effort to promote the welfare and best interests of the client. They guard against the misuse of assessment results. They respect the client's rights to know the results, the interpretations made, and the
bases for their conclusions and recommendations. Psychologists make every effort
to maintain the security of tests and other assessment techniques within limits of
legal mandates. They strive to ensure the appropriate use of assessment techniques by others.

a. In using assessment techniques, psychologists respect the right of clients
to have full explanations of the nature and purpose of the techniques in language

the clients can understand, unless an explicit exception to this right has been agreed upon in advance. When the explanations are to be provided by others, psychologists establish procedures for ensuring the adequacy of these explanations.

b. Psychologists responsible for the development and standardization of psychological tests and other assessment techniques utilize established scientific procedures and observe the relevant APA standards.

c. In reporting assessment results, psychologists indicate any reservations that exist regarding validity or reliability because of the circumstances of the assessment or the inappropriateness of the norms for the person tested. Psychologists strive to ensure that the results of assessments and their interpretations are not misused by others.

d. Psychologists recognize that assessment results may become obsolete. They make every effort to avoid and prevent the misuse of obsolete measures.

e. Psychologists offering scoring and interpretation services are able to produce appropriate evidence for the validity of the programs and procedures used in arriving at interpretations. The public offering of an automated interpretation service is considered a professional-to-professional consultation. Psychologists make every effort to avoid misuse of assessment reports.

f. Psychologists do not encourage or promote the use of psychological assessment techniques by inappropriately trained or otherwise unqualified persons through teaching, sponsorship, or supervision.

Principle 9
Research with Human Participants

The decision to undertake research rests upon a considered judgment by the individual psychologist about how best to contribute to psychological science and human welfare. Having made the decision to conduct research, the psychologist considers alternative directions in which research energies and resources might be invested. On the basis of this consideration, the psychologist carries out the investigation with respect and concern for the dignity and welfare of the people who participate and with cognizance of federal and state regulations and professional standards governing the conduct of research with human participants.

a. In planning a study, the investigator has the responsibility to make a careful evaluation of its ethical acceptability. To the extent that the weighing of scientific and human values suggests a compromise of any principle, the investigator incurs a correspondingly serious obligation to seek ethical advice and to observe stringent safeguards to protect the rights of human participants.

b. Considering whether a participant in a planned study will be a "subject at risk" or a "subject at minimal risk," according to recognized standards, is of primary ethical concern to the investigator.

c. The investigator always retains the responsibility for ensuring ethical practice in research. The investigator is also responsible for the ethical treatment of research participants by collaborators, assistants, students, and employees, all of whom, however, incur similar obligations.

d. Except in minimal-risk research, the investigator establishes a clear and fair agreement with research participants, prior to their participation, that clarifies the obligations and responsibilities of each. The investigator has the obligation to honor all promises and commitments included in that agreement. The investigator informs the participants of all aspects of the research that might reasonably be expected to influence willingness to participate and explains all other aspects of the research about which the participants inquire. Failure to make full disclosure prior to obtaining informed consent requires additional safeguards to protect the welfare and dignity of the research participants. Research with children or with participants who have impairments that would limit understanding and/or communication requires special safeguarding procedures.

e. Methodological requirements of a study may make the use of concealment or deception necessary. Before conducting such a study, the investigator has a special responsibility to (i) determine whether the use of such techniques is justified by the study's prospective scientific, educational, or applied value; (ii) determine whether alternative procedures are available that do not use concealment or deception; and (iii) ensure that the participants are provided with sufficient explanation as soon as possible.

f. The investigator respects the individual's freedom to decline to participate in or to withdraw from the research at any time. The obligation to protect this freedom requires careful thought and consideration when the investigator is in a position of authority or influence over the participant. Such positions of authority include, but are not limited to, situations in which research participation is required as part of employment or in which the participant is a student, client, or employee of the investigator.

g. The investigator protects the participant from physical and mental discomfort, harm, and danger that may arise from research procedures. If risks of such consequences exist, the investigator informs the participant of that fact. Research procedures likely to cause serious or lasting harm to a participant are not used unless the failure to use these procedures might expose the participant to risk of greater harm, or unless the research has great potential benefit and fully informed and voluntary consent is obtained from each participant. The participant should be informed of procedures for contacting the investigator within a reasonable time period following participation should stress, potential harm, or related questions or concerns arise.

h. After the data are collected, the investigator provides the participant with information about the nature of the study and attempts to remove any misconceptions that may have arisen. Where scientific or humane values justify delaying or withholding this information, the investigator incurs a special responsibility to monitor the research and to ensure that there are no damaging consequences for the participant.

i. Where research procedures result in undesirable consequences for the individual participant, the investigator has the responsibility to detect and remove or correct these consequences, including long-term effects.

j. Information obtained about a research participant during the course of an investigation is confidential unless otherwise agreed upon in advance. When the possibility exists that others may obtain access to such information, this possibility, together with the plans for protecting confidentiality, is explained to the participant as part of the procedure for obtaining informed consent.

Principle 10
Care and Use of Animals

An investigator of animal behavior strives to advance understanding of basic behavioral principles and/or to contribute to the improvement of human health and welfare. In seeking these ends, the investigator ensures the welfare of animals and treats them humanely. Laws and regulations notwithstanding, an animal's immediate protection depends upon the scientist's own conscience.

a. The acquisition, care, use, and disposal of all animals are in compliance with current federal, state or provincial, and local laws and regulations.

b. A psychologist trained in research methods and experienced in the care of laboratory animals closely supervises all procedures involving animals and is responsible for ensuring appropriate consideration of their comfort, health, and humane treatment.

c. Psychologists ensure that all individuals using animals under their supervision have received explicit instruction in experimental methods and in the care, maintenance, and handling of the species being used. Responsibilities and activities of individuals participating in a research project are consistent with their respective competencies.

d. Psychologists make every effort to minimize discomfort, illness, and pain of animals. A procedure subjecting animals to pain, stress, or privation is used only when an alternative procedure is unavailable and the goal is justified by its prospective scientific, educational, or applied value. Surgical procedures are performed under appropriate anesthesia; techniques to avoid infection and minimize pain are followed during and after surgery.

e. When it is appropriate that the animal's life be terminated, it is done rapidly and painlessly.

INDEX